# PARTS AND WHOLES
## FRAGMENTATION IN PREHISTORIC CONTEXT

# Parts and Wholes
## Fragmentation in Prehistoric Context

John Chapman and Bisserka Gaydarska

*with contributions from*
Ana Raduntcheva and Bistra Koleva

Oxbow Books

Published by
Oxbow Books, Park End Place, Oxford


© Oxbow Books, John Chapman and Bisserka Gaydarska, 2007

A CIP record of this book is available from the British Library


ISBN 978-1-84217-222-3      1-84217-222-0


*This book is available direct from*

Oxbow Books, Park End Place, Oxford OX1 1HN
(Phone: 01865-241249; Fax: 01865-794449)

and

The David Brown Book Company
PO Box 511, Oakville, CT 06779, USA
(Phone: 860-945-9329; Fax: 860-945-9468)

or from our website
www.oxbowbooks.com

*Front cover: The way we were – fragments from deep Balkan (and other) prehistories*

Printed in Great Britain by
Alden Press Ltd, Witney, Oxon

# Contents

List of figures ............................................................................................................................... vii

List of tables ................................................................................................................................. ix

List of plates ................................................................................................................................. x

Preface ........................................................................................................................................... xi

Acknowledgements ...................................................................................................................... xiii

1   Introduction to the life cycle of things – categorisation, fragmentation and enchainment ............................................. 1

2   What we can do with whole objects – the categorical analysis of pottery ...................................... 19

3   Parts and wholes – Hamangia figurines .......................................................................................... 53

4   Schiffer visits the Balkans ............................................................................................................... 71

5   Using objects after the break – beyond re-fitting studies .............................................................. 81

6   The biographical approach – fired clay figurines from the Late Eneolithic tell of Dolnoslav ...................................... 113

7   Personhood and the life cycle of *Spondylus* rings ......................................................................... 143

8   Re-fitting the narrative: beyond fragments .................................................................................... 173

9   Concluding pointers towards future research ................................................................................ 203

Appendix 1 ................................................................................................................................... 205

Appendix 2 ................................................................................................................................... 206

Appendix 3 ................................................................................................................................... 207

Appendix 4 ................................................................................................................................... 208

Appendix 5 ................................................................................................................................... 216

Bibliography ................................................................................................................................. 217

Indexes ......................................................................................................................................... 229

Colour plates

# List of Figures

1.1 A model for the transformation of material culture (source: Cziesla 1990, Fig. 7)

1.2 The identity triangle

2.1 Relationship between personhood, cognitive structures and social structures

2.2 Zonal structuring of pottery decoration

2.3 Common pottery forms and decoration from Rakitovo

2.4 Decorational reinforcement by context and form from Rakitovo

2.5 Common pottery forms and decoration from Hlebozavoda

2.6 Type of reinforcement by shape differentiation from Hlebozavoda II

2.7 Type of reinforcement by shape differentiation from Hlebozavoda II–I

2.8 Type of decorational reinforcement by vessel category from Hlebozavoda III

2.9 Type of decorational reinforcement by vessel category from Hlebozavoda II–I

2.10 Common pottery forms and decoration from Azmak

2.11 Profile differentiation by site

2.12 Decorational style by shape range from Azmak

2.13 Types of reinforcement by decorational style from Azmak

2.14 Common pottery forms and decoration from Dolnoslav

2.15 Decorational categories from Azmak and Dolnoslav

2.16 Decorational categories vs. shape ranges from Dolnoslav

2.17 Number of reinforcements by profile differentiation from Dolnoslav

2.18 Main forms of mortuary pottery from the Varna I cemetery, with a key to the shading used there

2.19 Vessel with multiple profile divisions, grave 5, Varna cemetery (source: Fol and Lichardus 1988, catalogue Abb. 117)

2.20 Presence/absence of decoration according to vessel profile breaks

2.21 Types of reinforcement by number of vessel profile breaks

3.1 Types of Hamangia figurines

3.2 Androgynous Hamangia figurines

3.3 The "Thinker", Cernavoda cemetery

3.4 Hamangia figurine from a hoard found in the cliffs above Balchik

3.5 Fragmentation chain for Hamangia figurines

3.6 Figurine completeness by context

3.7 Changing gender identities

3.8 Frequency of figurines in graves

3.9 Frequency of figurines in settlement contexts

4.1 Transformations of material culture (source: Deal 1985)

4.2 Six models of archaeological discard (source: Deal 1985)

5.1 Completeness index, Phylakopi anthropomorphic figurines

5.2 Completeness index, Phylakopi zoomorphic figurines

5.3 Horizontal sherd re-fits at Medieval Wyszogród (source: Kobyliński and Moszczyński 1992, Fig. 3)

5.4 Horizontal and vertical sherd re-fits, Early Neolithic Endrőd 119 (source: Makkay 1992, site plan)

5.5 Distribution of refitted fragments at Rocca di Rivoli (source: Dalla Riva 2003, figure, p. 98)

5.6 Completeness Index of Sedlare anthropomorphic figurines

5.7 Refitted Late Copper Age vessel from Durankulak

5.8 Completeness of pottery in Early Copper Age graves at Tiszapolgár-Basatanya

5.9 Completeness of pottery in Middle Copper Age graves at Tiszapolgár-Basatanya

5.10 Reconstruction of depositional processes at Runnymede Bridge (source: Needham 1996, Fig. 48)

5.11 Flow chart of depositional pathways, Runnymede Bridge (source: Needham 1996, Fig. 108)

5.12 Depositional sequence and horizontal sherd and lithic re-fits, Cluster B, Kilverstone, Area E (source: Garrow et al. 2005, Fig. 11)

5.13 Depositional sequence and horizontal sherd and lithic re-fits, Kilverstone, Area E (source: Garrow et al. 2005, Fig. 10)

5.14 Horizontal lithic re-fits between Lake Gyrinos sites (source: Schaller-Åhrberg 1990, Fig. 8)

5.15 Re-fitted fragments of an Ewart Park Late Bronze Age sword, found at Hanford and Trentham (source: Bradley and Ford 2004, Fig. 20.1)

6.1a  Site plan of the Late Copper Age features at tell Dolnoslav (source: Koleva 2002)

6.1b  Re-fitting of figurines at Dolnoslav: lines with arrows = re-fits between fragments from different contexts; filled pentagons = re-fits between fragments from the same context

6.2   Distribution of joins deriving from the middens

6.3   Figurines by gender from Dolnoslav

6.4   Distribution of left, right and neutral fragments

6.5   Distribution of left, right and neutral fragments, phase C

6.6   Distribution of left, right and neutral parts, middens

6.7   Distribution of left, right and neutral parts, open areas

6.8   Distribution of left, right and neutral parts, buildings

6.9   Distribution of left, right and neutral parts in each building

6.10  Example of category L (left torso, left leg and left arm)

6.11  Example of category R (right leg)

6.12  Example of category WL (whole upper torso and left arm)

6.13  Example of category WR (whole torso and right arm)

6.14  Distribution of lower and upper parts

6.15  Distribution of lower and upper parts, middens

6.16  Distribution of lower and upper parts, open areas

6.17  Distribution of lower and upper parts, buildings

6.18  Distribution of lower body parts

6.19  Distribution of upper body parts

6.20  Distribution of upper and lower body parts in each building

6.21  Figurine with hole in the stomach

6.22  Join 5

6.23  Decorational motif 167

6.24  Decorational motif 172

6.25  Join 11

6.26  Join 19

6.27  Join 14

6.28  Join 22

6.29  Join 10

7.1   Left-valve ring and right-valve ring, Durankulak cemetery

7.2   Type of rings by period, Durankulak cemetery

7.3   Natural features of Varna *Spondylus* ring

7.4   Natural features of Durankulak *Spondylus* ring

7.5   Natural features of Durankulak *Spondylus* ring

7.6   Natural features of Durankulak *Spondylus* ring

7.7   Natural features of Durankulak *Spondylus* ring

7.8   Natural features of Durankulak *Spondylus* ring

7.9   Rings with different natural pathways from Varna cemetery

7.10  Classes of natural shell features, Hamangia I–II

7.11  Classes of natural shell features, Hamangia, III–IV

7.12  Classes of natural shell features, Hamangia, Varna I–III

7.13  Classes of natural shell features, Varna cemetery

7.14  Complete rings in graves, Hamangia I–II

7.15  Fragmentary rings in graves, Hamangia I–II

7.16  Complete and fragmentary rings in graves, Hamangia I–II

7.17  Complete rings in graves, Hamangia III–IV

7.18  Fragmentary rings in graves, Hamangia III–IV

7.19  Complete and fragmentary rings in graves, Hamangia III–IV

7.20  Complete rings in graves, Varna I–III

7.21  Fragmentary rings in graves, Varna I–III

7.22  Complete and fragmentary rings in graves, Varna I–III

7.23  Complete rings in graves, Varna cemetery

7.24  Fragmentary rings in graves, Varna cemetery

7.25  Complete and fragmentary rings in graves, Varna cemetery

7.26  Completeness Indices of shell rings, Hamangia I–III

7.27  Completeness Indices of shell rings, Hamangia III–IV

7.28  Completeness Indices of shell rings, Varna I–III

7.29  Completeness Indices of shell rings, Varna cemetery

7.30  Rings with different life-histories from Varna

7.31  Rings with different life-histories from Durankulak

7.32  Rings with different life-histories from Durankulak

7.33  Rings with different life-histories from Durankulak

7.34  Rings with different life-histories from Varna

7.35  Rings with different life-histories from Varna

7.36  Completeness index for refitted shell ring fragments from Dimini

7.37  Size of rings from Dimini

7.38  Rings with burning by context from Dimini

7.39  Natural features on rings from Dimini

7.40  Representation of natural features on rings from Varna, Durankulak and Dimini

7.41  Rings with different natural pathways from Dimini

7.42  Rings with different natural pathways by context from Dimini

7.43  Phases in rings microstratigraphy

7.44  Microstratigraphic sequence groups by context groups from Dimini

8.1   Cultural complexity in all material media in the Climax Copper Age

# List of Tables

1.1 Social contexts for the study of fragmentation
1.2 Selected chronology of the Balkan Peninsula
2.1 Pottery assemblages investigated using categorical analysis
2.2 Summary of categorical analysis of Balkan Neolithic and Chalcolithic pottery
3.1 Two contrasting forms of personhood in Melanesia and Southern India
3.2 Categories of Hamangia figurines by gender and completeness
3.3 Combinations of female traits in Hamangia figurines
3.4 Distribution of Hamangia figurine gender traits by body parts
3.5 Hamangia figurines in Pit 1, Medgidia-Cocoaşe
3.6 Hamangia figurines in Pit 2, Durankulak-Nivata
3.7 Hamangia figurines in the Durankulak cemetery
5.1 Bollong's criteria for re-fitting sherds
6.1 Types of figurines according to their morphological characteristics
6.2 Frequency of figurine types in number of houses
6.3 Body parts according to number of gender representations
6.4 Joins between middens and buildings
6.5 Joins between middens
6.6 Joins between buildings

6.7 Joins between buildings and the open areas
6.8 Joins between middens and open areas
6.9 Joins between open areas
6.10 Fragments with secondary burning on axis break
6.11 Fragment with secondary burning on arm or neck break
6.12 Body parts with repetitive traces of wear
6.13 Fragments with secondary burning on torsos or legs
6.14 Number of figurines with combined treatment
7.1 Tsuneki's châine opératoire for *Spondylus* shell rings
7.2 Features of *Spondylus/Glycymeris* rings at Durankulak and Varna
7.3 *Spondylus* combinations of natural features from Varna cemetery
7.4 Differential life histories on re-fitted shell fragments
7.5 Physical and postulated re-fits between pairs of shell ring fragments, Late Neolithic Dimini
7.6 Differences between the Dimini settlement *Spondylus* ring assemblage and the Durankulak and Varna mortuary assemblages
8.1 Context classes for the assemblages under investigation
8.2 Inter-site re-fits
8.3 Intra-site re-fits from closed and semi-closed contexts
8.4 Orphan sherds from settlement contexts
8.5 Orphan fragments from closed contexts
8.6 Relations between key entities

# List of Plates

1   Map of sites mentioned in the text: South East and Central Europe
2   Map of sites mentioned in the text: Western Europe
3   Map of sites mentioned in the text: North and Meso-America
4   Grave 643 from the Durankulak cemetery
5   A rich set of grave goods, Varna cemetery, grave No. 43
6   Tell Karanovo, general view
7   Decorational reinforcement by context from Rakitovo
8   Black Burnished Ware vessel, Late Neolithic, tell Kaloyanovets (source: Kalchev 2005, 21, top left)
9   Place of decoration vs. vessel form by phase
10   Vessels with incised and white incrusted decoration
11   Type of reinforcement by profile differentiation from Azmak
12   Distribution of number of vessel profile breaks
13   Horned stand, Varna cemetery
14   Distribution of figurine parts in settlement
15   Distribution of figurine parts in graves
16   Distribution of simplified types of figurines in Dolnoslav
17   Figurine types by number of breaks
18   Site plan with refits between contexts, Dimini
19   Number of breaks, re-fitted fragments
20   Categories of sidedness and wholeness
21   Unified categories of sidedness and wholeness
22   Categories of sidedness and wholeness, phase C
23   Unified categories of sidedness and wholeness, phase C
24   Categories of sidedness and wholeness, middens
25   Unified categories of sidedness and wholeness, middens
26   Categories of sidedness and wholeness, open areas
27   Unified categories of sidedness and wholeness, open areas
28   Categories of sidedness and wholeness, buildings
29   Unified categories of sidedness and wholeness, buildings
30   Distribution of categories by building
31   Unmodified bivalves: upper and middle rows – *Spondylus gaederopus*; lower – *Glycymeris glycymeris*
32   Pair of re-fitted shell ring fragments, with lines and pitting, breaks, burning and light polish on 312 and lines, breaks, burning and light polish on 315 (Volos Museum Inv. Nos. 312 and 315)
33   Pair of re-fitted shell ring fragments, with garlands and notches, breaks, burnish and polish on 468 and sculpting and lines, a possible notch, breaks, burning and polish on 477 (Volos Museum Inv. Nos. 468 and 477)
34   Shell ring with complex linear pattern and chevrons, light polish, breaks and wear (Volos Museum Inv. No. 306)
35   Shell ring with lines and sculpting, one break, burning, polish and another break and flakes (Volos Museum Inv. No. 307)
36   Shell ring with notch, sculpting and lines, burning, polish, breraks, flakes, wear and stress marks (Volos Museum Inv. No. 318)
37   The only complete ring in the Dimini shell ring assemblage (Volos Museum Inv. No. 532)
38   Re-fitted pair of shell ring fragments, with lines and a notch, breaks, burning over part and all-over polish on 444 and lines and a groove, polish and breaks on 446.1 (Volos Museum Inv. Nos. 444 and 446.1)
39   Shell ring with sculpting, pitting and lines, breaks, heavy wear, flaking and stress marks (Volos Museum Inv. No. 561.002)
40   Shell ring with red lines, polish, one break, deposit and a second break (Volos Museum Inv. No. 488.2)
41   Shell ring with notches, sculpting, pitting and lines, polish, breaks and wear (Volos Museum Inv. No. 334)
42   Shell ring with sculpting and red lines, polish, breaks, deposit and flaking (Volos Museum Inv. No. 509.1)
43   Shell ring with sculpting and lines enhanced by burning, polish, breaks and flakes (Volos Museum Inv. No. 322)

# Preface

This book has grown out of our desire to write an integrated study of archaeology, social anthropology and material culture. Without any of these elements, the book would be much poorer and, indeed, fail to offer up its challenge to prehistorians. The challenge to which we refer is, in our view, fundamental to the further development of our discipline. It concerns the fragmentation premise – the idea that many objects in the past were deliberately broken and then re-used after that break. If archaeologists fail to take the fragmentation premise seriously, we believe that a great opportunity will be missed to travel down new roads of discovery in social archaeology.

We have approached the book from very different backgrounds, whether social, political or academic, and we consider these differences have been a strength of the volume. Bisserka would like to thank John for his inspiration and creative spirit, for the productive if not always peaceful discussions, as well as for the 10 o'clock tea during the last three months of intensive writing. While John would like to thank Bisserka for her patience in discussing fragments, her tact in urging me to deal with Balkan foibles in sensitive ways, her willingness to listen to new ideas, no matter how initially unformulated and disconnected, and, mostly, for being herself.

We both appreciate the contributions of Ana Raduntcheva and Bistra Koleva to the Dolnoslav figurine study in Chapter 6.

There have been many interesting by-products of our research. In the writing of this book, we have made a collection of the jokes about "fragments of knowledge", "fragmented world views", "the part is greater than the whole", etc., etc., that friends and colleagues have made at regular intervals. There has been at least one musical spin-off: the "Fragmentation blues" was written for the final dinner of the Prehistoric Society's Study Tour of Bulgaria (revising the words of the standard "All of me … baby, take all of me" to "Part of me… baby, take part of me …"). Inevitably, our social practices have changed, too. We are no longer afraid to drop plates at dinner parties or smash glasses against kitchen walls in moments of Balkan celebration. We no longer dread broken mirrors. We prefer not to examine complete museum objects.

We have become changed people. Like many in the art world, we respect the fragment and know how much we can learn from it. Fragments are, like the RAE, always with us – we cannot escape from them in our everyday lives. We are also aware of the deep psychological need of every fragmenterist – to find the missing part, that part that is always presenced by its matching part, that part that we desire more because it is absent. We hope that readers will (re-) discover the pleasures of the fragment and its significance.

JCC and BG
Meadowfield, Co. Durham, January 2006

# Acknowledgements

This book could not have been completed without research funding and research leave. We should like to thank the British Academy for their support to JCC through the Inter-Academy Exchange Visits scheme and their generous provision of a small research grant (SG-37513) to BG for her Dolnoslav research and JCC for his research on the Varna and Durankulak *Spondylus* shell ring collections. JCC would also like to thank the Bulgarian Academy of Sciences for their financial contributions and organizational support of his research visits to Bulgaria, as well as those who helped the research go smoothly – Dr. Vassil Nikolov, Professor Ivan Gatsov, Dr Boyan Dumanov and, not least, Tomina Lazova. Both of us are grateful to the British School in Athens, who supported our research visit to Volos with a grant from the Hector Catling Fund.

JCC wishes to pay tribute to Durham University for research leave during the academic year 2005–6 to enable completion of the writing-up and to his colleagues in the Department of Archaeology who have filled in on many occasions during his Balkan absences. We are both grateful to the staff of the University Library for patience and efficiency and to the Boston Spa ILL Service for magical skills in retrieving the unretrievable. Our three illustrators – Yvonne Beadnell, Vessela Yaneva and Elena Georgieva, have produced some of the highest-quality artifact illustrations yet to be published from the Balkans and we are both enormously grateful.

The writing of such a book requires a huge network of friends, colleagues and co-workers – collectively too numerous to thank individually. Nonetheless, we have tried to name the more important members of our network, listing their contributions by chapter.

Chapter 1: Richard Harrison (for details of the Grinsell funeral); Clive Gamble (for discussions on fragmentation in the Palaeolithic; Katerina Skoutopoulou (for discussing her works in press); Chris Fowler (for his lively contributions to personhood); Dragoş Gheorghiu, Ernest Budeş and Seth Priestman (for their collaboration in the Vădastra Project).

Chapter 2: Danny Miller and David Keightley (for inspiration on categorization); the Oxford Archaeological Unit (for references); Stratos Nanoglou (for discussing work in press and sharing information about Dikili Tash); Ana Raduntcheva (for her many kindnesses and open access to her Rakitovo and Chavdarova Cheshma materials); Tatjana Kuncheva (for open access to the Hlebozavoda collection); Petur Kalchev (for open access to the Azmashka mogila assemblage and for permission to reproduce a photograph as Plate 8); Ana Raduntcheva and Bistra Koleva (for open access to the Dolnoslav pottery); and the late Ivan Ivanov and Olga Pelevina (for access to the Varna cemetery pottery).

Chapter 3: Marga Diáz-Andreu (for friendship and discussions of sex and gender); Doug Bailey (for provocation); Todor Dimov and Sonja Dimitrova (for access to their Hamangia figurine collections); Puiu Haşotti (for access to his Hamangia figurine collection); and Marian Neagu (for discussions of Lower Danubian prehistory).

Chapter 5: Mark White (for corridor chats and information about Palaeolithic & Mesolithic re-fitting studies); Erich Claßen (for information about LBK re-fitting); Jacek Lech (for Polish references); Marie-Louise Stig Sørensen (for information about Scandinavian re-fits); Jim Skibo and Al Sullivan (for discussions on South West re-fits and their ceramic research); Martina Dalla Riva (for sending me her undergraduate dissertation and for many discussions about fragmentation); Robin Skeates (for many helpful discussions and information on Italian materials); Ana Raduntcheva, Pavel Petkov and Milen Kamarev (access to the Sedlare materials); Ilona Bausch (advice on and references for Japanese materials); Valentin Dergachev (information about Ukrainian burials); Bettina Arnold and Seth Schneider (information about the Heuneburg Landscape of Ancestors project, Seth for sending his unpublished M.A. dissertation); Imogen Wood (for sending her unpublished B.A. dissertation and many discussions on fragmentation); Duncan Garrow and the Cambrige Archaeological Unit (for access to the unpublished report on Kilverstone); Loïs Langouët and Chris Scarre (for advice and information about Breton megaliths); Stephen Aldhouse-Green (for advice on Palaeolithic re-fitting); Stephan Hartz and Maria-Julia Weber (for information on Hamburgian re-fitting); and Willem Willems and Arjen Bosman (information on the Velsen I re-fits).

Chapter 6: Ana Rauntcheva and Bistra Koleva (for hospitality, information and discussions of the Dolnoslav figurine collection); Ana Grebanarova and Elena Georgieva (for illustrations).

Chapter 7: Henrieta Todorova (for access to the Durankulak materials); Diana Borissova, Todor Dimov and Sonia Dimitrova (for helpful assistance and access to the Durankulak *Spondylus* shell rings); Valentin Pletnyov, Vladimir Slavchev and Olga Pelevina (access to and helpful discussions on the Varna cemetery *Spondylus* shell rings); Giorgios Hourmouziades and Mrs Adrymi-Sismani of the Volos Ephorate of Prehistoric Archaeology (for access to the Dimini *Spondylus* shell rings); Kostas Kotsakis, Evangelia Skafida, Stella Souvatzi, Paul Halstead, James Whitley and his staff at the BSA (for help with the Dimini *Spondylus* shell ring study); and Michel Séfériades and Johannes Müller (for information and offprints on *Spondylus*).

Research seminar visits, conferences and lunchtime papers have all been vital places for chewing the fat and ironing out problems in our research agenda. We should like to thank the following for invitations, hospitality and stimulation: Cambridge Research Seminar (Marie-Louise Stig Sørensen); the Cambridge "Image and Imagination" conference (Colin Renfrew); 2nd Chicago International Eurasian Archaeology conference (Adam Smith); Gothenburg Research Seminar (Jarl Nordbladh); Manchester TAG 24 (Chris Fowler); Rennes Research Seminar (Marie-Yvane Daire); Sheffield Research Seminar (John Barrett); Stara Zagora conference on "Prehistoric Thrace" (Vassil Nikolov); Thessaloniki Research Seminar (Kostas Kotsakis); Varna Round Table on Varna cemetery (Vladimir Slavchev) and Veliko Trnovo Worked Bone conference (Petur Zidarov).

Our greatest debts of gratitude are to our readers who have commented on all or parts of the book: most of all to Richard Bradley who has provided encouragement and inspiration throughout with the vitality of his approach to European prehistory; to Litsa Skafida for reading Chapter 7, and to Anthony Harding whose relaxed and always positive skepticism challenged us to find better ways of demonstrating the fragmentation premise.

# 1. Introduction to the life cycle of things – categorisation, fragmentation and enchainment

## The funeral of Leslie Grinsell

We can think of no better way of introducing the research topic of fragmentation than by recounting the story of Leslie Grinsell's funeral. Grinsell was one of the great British fieldwalkers of the AD 20th century, whose records of field monuments – especially long and round barrows of Southern Britain – were unsurpassed in his day. About 40 years before his death, Grinsell wrote a fascinating paper about the ceremonial 'killing' of objects at funerals – a magisterial survey of the ethnographic, folkloric and archaeological evidence for such practices (Grinsell 1960, for supplementary notes, see Grinsell 1973). So Grinsell understood very clearly the power of such ritual practices.

In his will, Grinsell had left detailed instructions as to the events of his funeral, their sequence and the participants – instructions that included the act about which he had written so informatively. After his body was cremated, the ashes were to be placed in a replica collared urn (a British Early Bronze Age mortuary vessel) and taken by a group of 12 close friends (he also helpfully provided a list of people excluded from this stage of the mortuary ritual!) first to a grand funeral lunch in a Cotswold hotel and then to the top of a hill overlooking one of Grinsell's favourite landscapes. The group was to stand on the summit of the round barrow on the top of the hill, while the collared urn was smashed, allowing the ashes to be blown off into the surrounding landscape. Then, each of the friends was to take a single large sherd of the broken urn as a token of their esteem, love and affection for Leslie. I am led to believe that each of the friends alive today still keeps their "Leslie sherd" as a treasured possession.

This touching narrative shows the close links between people, places and things that exist now and must have existed in the deep past. The supplementary "place-value" given to the hill by the presence on the summit of Grinsell's favourite monument class was increased further by the views to the surrounding landscape, which in turn would have contained further sites and monuments well known to Grinsell, each with their own biography of visitation by Grinsell and his friends. The final addition to the place-value of this hill would be the ceremony of the smashing of the urn, that took place relatively recently but is indelibly fixed in the minds of all those invited to participate (and in the minds of some "refused entry"). The sherd that each person treasures are also bound not only to the place of their fragmentation – the origin of the 12 parts constituting the whole – but also to the named, visited place of burial in the South-West where the specific collared urn used as the template for the replica urn was itself buried 3,500 years ago. But perhaps the closest links have been formed between the people and the things – obviously and primarily between Grinsell, his mortal remains and the replica urn. Here we see two examples of fractality – the concept that the same immanent relations are present at whatever the spatial scale of the phenomenon (Mandelbrot 2004; Prigogine 1987). The first is the dispersal of Leslie Grinsell's ashes over the landscape, just as Grinsell himself dispersed his enchained relationship formed during his life over the same, and many other, landscapes. The second example concerns the fragments of the replica urn in relation to the complete urn. While the latter embodied a close enchained relation with the newly-cremated person whose mortal remains it contained, as well as relations to other similar collared urns, each sherd from the urn that contained Grinsell's ashes maintained that same enchained relationship between vessel and ashes, as well as others based upon the shared partibility of each sherd that derived from the replica urn.

In addition, between Grinsell and all of his closest friends whose friendship was so valued by Grinsell that they were given "part" of Grinsell himself by which to remember him. This is what we mean by enchained relations of exchange – not only the material item but the personhood embodied in the thing are exchanged. The materiality of the broken collared urn sherds maintains this social memory of a great archaeologist in a way more specific and special than simply the memories of field trips in Grinsell's company. These sherds are tokens of a place, a group of related people and a very special person at the centre of the network. In effect, the sherds of Grinsell's replica urn have been dispersed across the modern landscape. And the Heraclitus-defying possibility that, in 10 years' time, the twelve friends could meet again at the "same" Cotswold hotel and walk to the "same" hilltop barrow to re-live that ceremony would be validated by the re-fitting of their sherds to form a complete replica urn.

Leslie Grinsell knew enough about the fragmentation of material culture to be sure that his own archaeological mortuary ritual would implicate the places, things and special friends in a material network symbolising collective memory and reinforcing social relations. Those twin points constitute the core of this book, whose principal aims are to demonstrate the premise of deliberate fragmentation of objects and to explore its consequences for the social practices of making, exchange and deposition. As we have written the book, we have found that three other themes have grown out of these two principal aims and developed in such a way as to become inseparable from fragmentation. These themes are artifact biographies, categorization and personhood. Fragmentation is, after all, but one stage in the complete biography of untold numbers of objects. With every consequent fracture, the object tells a different story, embodying different principles of categorization, many of which shed light on the creation of personhood. Moreover, the adoption of a fractal perspective on broken things reveals how fragmentation can provide another approach to personhood. The reader will understand that any such attempt to integrate such a wide variety of concepts and issues runs the risk of leading to a theoretically eclectic book, in which loose ends and culs-de-sacs vie for priority of place. Aware of these dangers, we have sought means of integrating our five issues in as many ways as possible.

In this chapter, the fragmentation premise is introduced and the new contributions which fragmentation studies can make to artifact biographies are outlined, especially the poorly documented middle stages of object life cycles. We introduce the research theme of fragmentation; summarise the debate since the publication of the first fragmentation book (Chapman 2000), examining both new developments and major criticisms; integrate archaeological fragmentation studies into wider perspectives; and proceed to a critical discussion of the key terms in the debate, which in turn leads to the definition of the research agenda of the book. The introductory chapter continues with an introduction to Balkan chronology, sites and material culture, before closing with a summary of the book's structure.

## Fragmentation studies: an introduction and brief history

There is an unavoidable tension between the whole object and the fragment that has been recognised since the Early Modern period in Western Europe – the time of the emergence of a new aesthetic of the part. It was realised that the isolated part could never be autonomous – that the part implied a relation, not a separate entity (Hillman and Mazzio 1997). It was then, too, that the separateness of the term 'individual' was emphasised for the first time, in terms of three entities – the individual person, the individual author and the individual word – a strong contrast to the large number of words for 'society' current in earlier centuries (Stallybrass 1992).

The 'isolated' part is one of the principal characteristics of the material culture that archaeologists discover. We have become so accustomed to this state of affairs – either as excavators or when studying museum collections – that broken things do not appear to be abnormal, interesting or curious. Any concept that disturbs an idea that is so deeply rooted in our *habitus* – our unspoken set of assumptions about how our archaeological world operates – will inevitably provoke resistance, scorn or even the closing of ranks and minds. One such deeply rooted idea is the notion that broken things are nothing but the result of accidental breakage or taphonomic processes – in other words, processes unrelated to human intentionality. This idea persists in many archaeologists' minds, despite the increasing acceptance of the active use of material culture – one of the main breakthroughs in post-processualism (Hodder 1982). When it comes to broken things, agency and social practices are rapidly forgotten, in favour of "the commonplace that archaeology is concerned with the rubbish of past generations" (Thomas 1999, 62). This assumption is used to construct approaches to material culture, such as Cziesla's model of dynamic artifact processes and lithic re-fitting (Cziesla 1990, Fig. 7 – here as Fig. 1.1), where there is no place for intentional breakage.

An earlier proposal was that, instead of this outdated foundation myth based upon 'rubbish', archaeology can be thought of as the "study of taphonomy and deposition" (Chapman 2000b). However, the weakness in this argument remained the discard from meals and production, which stubbornly retained its categorization as 'rubbish'. Sociologists such as Hetherington and Munro have developed new ideas about waste and its disposal, opening up a different but still contextually based approach to discard, where the struggle to maintain cultural order is played out through differential disposal of refuse in a variety of places. This approach implicitly accepts that fragments of different kinds can be used in wider cultural practices.

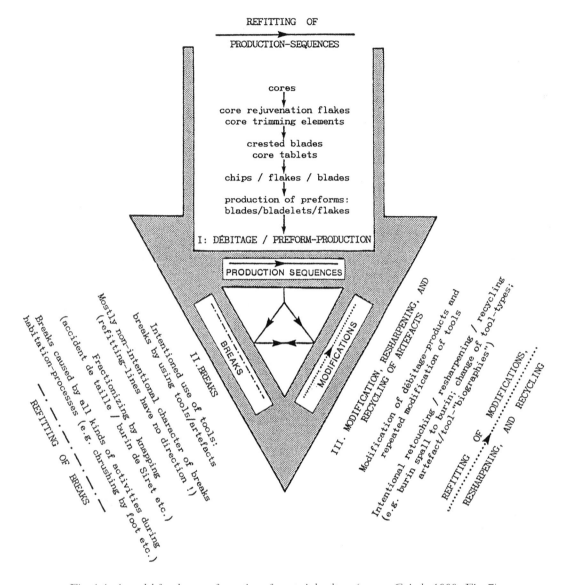

*Fig. 1.1 A model for the transformation of material culture (source: Cziesla 1990, Fig. 7)*

In the first fragmentation book, five possible causes of breakage were outlined and evaluated (Chapman 2000, 23–27):

- Accidental breakage
- Objects buried because they are broken (*e.g.* Garfinkel 1994)
- Ritual 'killing' of objects (*e.g.* Grinsell 1960; Hamilakis 1998)
- Dispersion to ensure fertility (*e.g.* Bausch 1994)
- Deliberate breakage for re-use in enchainment

In addition to the obvious taphonomic processes that can and do break things, all of these causes can be documented in the past. However, the key point that arises at a certain scale of spatial closure – a closed grave, a hoard, a burnt house assemblage, the lower levels of a pit, the delimited parts of an extensive midden, etc., – is that none of the first four processes or practices can explain the absence of parts of the broken thing. Hamilakis' (1998) study of ritual killings of swords and spears in Minoan Crete describes complete, if broken, objects in graves and pits; the same is true for Garfinkel's (1994) study of the breakage of worn figurines to remove their diminishing ritual power. For closed contexts, the phenomenon of the missing part is a good indication of deliberate object breakage. For more open settlement contexts, the complications are far greater and this is an important area of research discussed in this volume (see Chapters 4 and 5).

The archaeology of the Balkan Mesolithic, Neolithic

and Copper Age was used to explore the idea of deliberate fragmentation and the use of fragments in enchainment processes for the creation and maintenance of lasting bonds between persons or groups – bonds predicated on material culture (Chapman 2000, 226). Analogous relations of scale were found to exist between object fragments, complete things and sets of artifacts and fragments of bone, complete bodies and sets of bodies (*e.g.* cemeteries). One proposed explanation was that while persons embodied their social relations through fragment enchainment, households, lineages or communities encapsulated their identities with other corporate groups through set accumulation and deposition. Diachronic changes in the formation of personhood and in the predominant ways of symbolizing relationships came about particularly in the Climax Copper Age (5th millennium Cal BC), when the making of fine gold ornaments and heavy cast copper tools and weapons made fragmentation less effective. Nevertheless, many groups rejected set accumulation as the dominant social practice, maintaining the practice of body and fragment enchainment well into the post-climax period (2000, 230–231). It was therefore postulated that the tensions and contradictions between fragment enchainment and set

accumulation were one of the dynamic causes of social change and differentiation in later Balkan prehistory.

## Developments in fragmentation theory

A major development in fragmentation studies took place while the first fragmentation book was in press, with the presentation of a Session entitled "Fragmentation" held in Bournemouth under the auspices of the 1998 Annual Meeting of the European Association of Archaeologists (Chapman 1998a). The papers presented there significantly extended both the chronological and geographical scope of fragmentation studies beyond Balkan prehistory to include papers from the Neolithic to the ethnographic present and from Iberia to Japan via Greece, Central, Northern and Northwest Europe. These papers demonstrated that deliberate fragmentation of objects and re-use 'after the break' was a characteristic of many prehistoric and early historic societies in Eurasia, over a much longer timescale than had previously been anticipated. The range of social contexts where deliberate fragmentation has been proposed and confirmed is summarized below (Table 1.1).

In addition to times/places where fragmentation has

| PLACE | TIME | MATERIAL CULTURE | REFERENCE |
|---|---|---|---|
| Hungary | Neolithic | fired clay altar-lamps | Bánffy, n.d. |
| Bulgaria | Neolithic | fired clay figurines | Biehl, n.d. |
| Romania | Copper Age | fired clay figurines | Gheorghiu 2006 |
| Bulgaria/ Romania | Copper Age | Varna cemetery & burials | Catuna, n.d. |
| Oceania | ethnography | wooden sculptures | Küchler, n.d. |
| Greece/ Near East | Neolithic | severed heads | Talalay 2004 |
| Scandinavia | Neolithic | pottery near megaliths | Holten 2000 |
| N. Germany | Neolithic | megaliths | Holtorf 2003 |
| Britain | Bronze Age | domestic material culture | Brück (in press) |
| Greece | Bronze Age | mortuary domain | Hamilakis, n.d. |
| Slovenia | LBA – EIA | metalwork & hoards | Turk, n.d. |
| Spain | Iron Age | Iberian stone sculptures | Chapa Brunet, n.d. |
| France | Iron Age | mortuary domain | Olivier, n.d. |
| Britain | Iron Age | hillfort material culture | Hill, n.d. |
| Japan | Jomon | fired clay figurines | Bausch, n.d. |
| Poland | Medieval | settlement & mortuary pottery | Buko, n.d. |

*Table 1.1 Social contexts for the study of fragmentation*

been attested, fragmentation and its related concepts of enchainment and accumulation have made contributions to several major debates in world prehistory. In his re-assessment of the earliest hominids, the emergence of anatomically modern humans and the transition he terms the "sedentism revolution", Gamble (2004, 2005) has recognized the utility of concepts of fragmentation, enchainment and accumulation for the creation of a social framework for the Palaeolithic. For Gamble (2004, 23), "the practices of enchainment and accumulation reach down deep into our hominid ancestry", acting as a material demonstration of Palaeolithic social life and social networks from 2.5 million years BP. Practices such as butchery and stone tool making act as material demonstrations of Palaeolithic social life through the construction of social networks whose maintenance rests on the continual reproduction of dividuals and individuals.

Gamble (2004, 22–24) identifies the wider and denser networks of enchainment implicated in the more complex blade technology of the Cro-Magnons, in comparison with the flake and Levallois technologies of Neanderthal groups, as one of the neglected material aspects of the emergence of anatomically modern humans at the Middle – Upper Palaeolithic transition. The exchange of retouched tools made from exotic materials over large distances in the Middle and Upper Palaeolithic indicate enchained relations carrying personal and artifact biographies between locales and hunting groups. These locales became increasingly important as centres of social life and sites of accumulation for the increasing production of sets of things from 100,000 BP.

Gamble's criticism of the idea of the origins of accumulation in the Neolithic is well taken – the social life of sets clearly begins at an early point in the Palaeolithic! A good example of enchainment is the accumulation of fired clay figurines in the Gravettian sites of Moravia. Here, the high levels of figurine frag-mentation, as exemplified at Dolní Věstonice (Klíma 1963, 409, 422–427 and Tab. 106), are partly explained by the deliberate use of thermal shock to produce exploding bodies in the hearth (Vandiver et al. 1989) but the point overlooked by the interpretation of ritual explosions is that many of the figurines are left incomplete after the explosion, prompting the fragmenterist's question: "Where are the missing fragments?" The movement of figurine fragments out of the hearth-centred context of explosion was paralleled by the movement of body parts, especially skulls, into the burials of complete articulated persons (Svoboda et al. 1996, 170) – a sign of enchained relations based upon object and body fragments.

In his approach to the origins of Near Eastern sedentism, Gamble (2005) characterizes the materiality of the move towards sedentism in the Natufian and Pre-

Pottery Neolithic of the Levant in terms of a shift towards accumulation from enchainment through the increasing emphasis on containers rather than instruments. Here, the house is viewed as a container and villages as accumulations of houses, just as cemeteries are sets of Natufian bodies and PPN ossuaries are sets of fragments of the dead (2005, 91–92). Gamble interestingly extends the use of enchainment, accumulation and fragmentation to architecture, so houses are 'fragmented' into different rooms, 'enchained' by being juxtaposed in dense settlement and form the locales for often massive accumulations of artifacts. The social relations sustaining such practices are enchained relations that are extended by intensification not only of production but also of deposition – an early example of what has been termed the "Concentration Principle" (Chapman 2000b).

Another contribution by fragmentation theory to the debate over the origins of the Eurasian Neolithic is Jones and Richards' (2003) proposal that a critical gap in the model for social and symbolic domestication processes proposed by Cauvin (1972), Wilson (1988) and Hodder (1990) was the creative potential provided by social actions such as consumption and fragmentation. Rather than domestication arising out of a symbolic revolution represented by houses and villages, domestication was a set of novel relationships that occurred at different locales in the landscape – principally at villages composed of many houses. In another paper, Jones (2005, 216) recognises households as relational identities just as much as persons. The vital role of fragmentation in these new relationships was considered to be the way it enabled elements of the material world that were hitherto discrete to be brought into metaphorical relationship – elements such as butchered and divided animal bones, the osseous remains of human ancestors and fragments and complete objects. For Jones and Richards (2003, 46), each animal bone was enchained to all other bones of that animal and the anatomies of animals articulated with particular sets of human – animal relationships. While breaking and sharing established affiliations between actors, composite tools re-incorporated and re-articulated new sets of social relations (2003, 49). What Jones and Richards do not establish, however, is the ways in which fragmentation and enchainment are enacted in daily social practices.

This aspect of enchainment practices is discussed by Skourtopoulou (in press a and b) in her study of the lithic assemblage from the large open Late Neolithic settlement of Makriyalos, Northern Greece. Skourtopoulou (in press a) sees artifacts as "material metaphors of inter-personal relations" at various socio-spatial scales. Enchainment, then, uses this metaphorical value of artifacts in order to objectify social relations, with different aspects symbolised at these various scales – personal relations as things and people move within and between households, economic and symbolic values for exotic exchange surpassing the communal scale and embedded in inter-cultural contact (in press b). These insights are applied to intra-site lithic analysis in an attempt to extend social agency theory. They help us to see how enchainment works at the level of everyday practice by showing how an expedient quartzite flake is never only its material form but embodies production relations and personal skills that are rooted in settlement space. Although not explicitly mentioning enchainment, Hurcombe (2000) emphasises the gendered relations between persons involved in the different stages of any craft sequence – a position implying that often several people are enchained to any object at its birth, providing the basis for the metaphorical relations to which Skourtopoulou alludes.

## Criticisms of the fragmentation premise

This review of the ways in which other scholars have developed and extended different aspects of fragmentation theory indicates an awareness of its potential for a range of time/space problems. However, there are many archaeologists who, faced with strong evidence for deliberate fragmentation, ignore these approaches. In her review of Aegean fired clay figurines, Marangou (1996, 146) notes the widespread evidence for broken figurines but argues that most were broken at the vulnerable junctures, the joints between separately modeled parts. While admitting that "deliberate dismemberment … (of figurines) …cannot be ruled out in some cases" (1996, 146), Marangou misses the opportunity to ground figurine breakage in widespread social practices of enchainment and accumulation. Equally, Nanoglou (2005) emphasizes what he takes to be the circular argument that because figurines are broken along lines of weakness, the fragmentation was accidental – an argument countered by Gheorghiu (2006) for Cucuteni figurines, for whom the principle of breaking was built into making. For Nanoglou, the basic unit of analysis and conceptual entity of Greek Neolithic figurines was the complete figurine.

Yet other colleagues have raised objections to the fragmentation project. The most banal comment – but he surely has a point (!) – is Milisauskas' (2002, 859) observation that "testing the (fragmentation) hypothesis would involve an enormous amount of work and time and I doubt that any archaeologist would conduct such a study in the future". Fortunately, the work ethic outside New York State is stronger than Milisauskas would suspect! (see Chapters 4–7).

More serious criticisms are related to three main areas of fragmentation theory: (a) the relationship of fragmentation to fractality and the creation of personhood (principally Fowler 2004); (b) areas of additional concern to fragmentation theory (especially Gamble 2004, 2005;

Jones 2005); and (c) methodological issues (particularly Bailey 2001, 2005; Milisauskas 2002).

Fowler's (2004, 67–70) main criticism is that, just because enchainment has been documented in the Balkan Neolithic, it is not necessarily the same as enchainment as practiced in Melanesia. Whereas, in the latter, gift objects cannot be held by two persons at the same time, this is the defining trait of Balkan prehistoric partibility based upon fragments. This helpful observation leads us to the positive recognition of something different about the Balkan prehistoric past – not merely a similitude based on modern ethnography. As Gamble (2005, 89) has reminded us, fragmentation and enchainment are two different terms – the first relating to social action, the second to process. The Balkan prehistoric form of enchainment is based upon the fragmentation of the body and things, with each fragment standing for the whole (synecdoche), each whole potentially or actually part of a wider set of whole and partial objects and each set and each whole bearing the capacity for further sub-division. The overwhelming evidence that objects and bodies are treated in the same ways in respect of these three levels of completeness and in the course of their life histories (Chapman 2000) supports the notion that there is an interpenetration of persons and things that typifies fractal personhood. This reduces the contrastive force of Fowler's two kinds of fragments – those that are not wholes and are not used to make composite objects (*e.g.* figurine legs) and those fragments that Fowler describes as 'fractal' that are used to make composite things (*e.g.* beads in a necklace). Individual beads and shell fragments were not made originally as complete objects but from complete objects (shell ring fragments) or as parts of sets (beads). In our perspective, both types of object are fractal – indeed, we may think of object fragments as non-human dividuals. While Fowler is correct that fragmentation is not necessary for partible exchange relations, and vice versa, the Balkan prehistoric world provides good reasons for believing that both practices co-existed there.

Another concern over fractality has been expressed by A. Jones (2005) namely the inherent dangers of the reification of the dividual person rather than concentrating on ways of relating. We believe that this concern is misplaced if it is recognized that the dividual form of person is in tension with the individual – a fundamental point that LiPuma (1998) has demonstrated and which has won widespread acceptance in studies of personhood. However, Jones' (2002a, 170) identification of the space where personhood emerges as between the partible nature of artifacts and the bounded integrity of the human body misses the point about the metaphorical divisibility of the human body in life through fragment enchainment (the inalienable link between persons and exchanged objects) and its physical division after death (the movement of relics). The important aspect about prehistoric fractal persons and things is that both are implicated in each others' fractality and wholeness and that these relationships stands for other relationships in everyday life and in sacred space.

The principal emphasis on the relationships between persons and objects in the first Fragmentation book has attracted critical comment from several colleagues – comments that we accept in principle. Fowler (2004, 114) has objected that the exchange of substances was just as important as the exchange of objects in prehistory (cf. J. Thomas 1999). At the time, we felt that this was a step too far. Although Gamble (2005, 89 and Table 8.2) observes that the vital stage of consumption is missing from the first Fragmentation book, the practice is actually implicated in the process of accumulation that is a central feature of the book: it is worth re-emphasizing the distinction between consumption as a practice and accumulation as process. Recently, A. Jones (2005) has made a strong case for the importance of place and architecture in the creation of personhood. We can hardly disagree with Jones since the identity triangle on which much of our prehistoric research has been based (Fig. 1.2) includes the reflexive relationships between persons and things, things and places and persons and places. However, it is true that the impact on persons and personhood of living on the Vinča tell at various stages of its place–biography was not explored as fully as possible. Finally, Bailey (2001) asks the question of fragmentation studies: "Where is the mundane?", implying that if fragmentation, enchainment and accumulation did drive Balkan life, then such processes must be sought in the most mundane of activities and places. This seems at first sight a reasonable point but when Bailey criticizes the book's emphasis on special sites and classes of special artifacts rather than 'normal' sites

and things, we begin to see the emergence of a dangerous dichotomy between everyday and special (? 'ritual') that is unhelpful in studies of deposition. In point of fact, ritual things were just as important in everyday contexts as in special ceremonies, acting, for instance, as material citations (Jones A. 2005) in the domestic context for seasonal ceremonies. In any case, in his recent book, Bailey (2005, 198–199) undermines his own distinction in positing that "the importance of figurines lay in their frequency and continuous circulation and visibility in people's daily lives". This latter is a position that we accept and which forms the basis for a re-evaluation of the role of enchainment in everyday practices, as discussed above by Skourtopoulou (pp. 5–6). It is a position related to the point made by Fowler (2004, 67–70) about the social value of shell rings as compared to sherds – the former with an obvious and highly visible social value, the latter used in a different sort of enchainment, perhaps based upon the essential qualities of the clay or some historical or commemorative potential. One of the important research questions discussed in this book is the ways in which things made of different materials constructed different potentials for forming relationships.

The third focus of criticism questions the evidential basis for deliberate fragmentation. Both Milisauskas (2002) and Bailey (2001) complain that the first Fragmentation book did not provide a suitable method for distinguishing intentional breakage from discarded rubbish. Clearly, the discussion of the five principal ways of explaining broken artifacts did not satisfy these critics; neither did the identification of ways of breaking objects such as figurines that could never have been produced accidentally. At the time of publication, experimental fragmentation was in its infancy; now, we can provide a summary of the results of the Vădastra experiment (Chapman and Priestman, in press). A number of sets, with 10 examples in each set, of replica prehistoric objects was made by ceramics students from the University of Fine Arts, Bucureşti, under the supervision of Dragoş Gheorghiu and Ernest Budeş. Five of the objects in each set were broken accidentally by dropping them from a standard height of 1m onto five different kinds of 'prehistoric' surfaces – grass, a wooden floor, a stamped clay floor, a fired clay floor and a stone cobbled floor. Keeping one complete object as a reference collection, we tried to break the other four examples deliberately, with manual pressure and with a blow from a grindstone, a bovid mandible and a flint. Ceramics were more susceptible to accidental breakage than smaller, lighter objects such as fired clay figurines, pintaderas or altar-lamps. Nonetheless, even ceramics broke in fewer than 40% of cases on fired and stamped clay floors, with 80% breakage on stone cobbled floors. However, there are few examples of stone cobbled floors in Balkan prehistory!

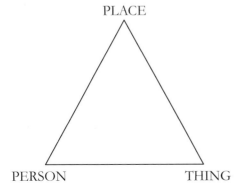

PLACE

PERSON          THING

*Fig. 1.2 The identity triangle*

There were very few vessels broken on grass or on the wooden floor. Deliberate fragmentation proved successful with all types of ceramics. In the case of the smaller objects, the only consistent accidental breakage occurred on stone cobbled floors, indicating the probable rarity of accidental breakage in prehistory. The study of the differences in the fractures produced by accidental and deliberate breakage is still continuing but, as yet, no fracture types unambiguously associated with either accidental or deliberate breakage have been identified – rather, combinations of fracture types showing higher or lower probabilities of being caused by one or the other action. This experiment goes some way to showing that accidental breakage of objects in the past was not as easy or as normal as is widely suspected. Further results of the Vădastra experiment will clarify the likelihood of identification of fracture types associated with any specific cause of breakage. This aspect of fragmentation research is clearly important, since a demonstration of deliberate breakage challenges the assumptions of prehistorians such as Bailey (2005, 179) who believe that rubbish is a primary category of material remains from prehistoric sites. The idea that figurines were made, used briefly (perhaps once?) and immediately discarded (Perlès 2001, 263; Marangou 1996, 146; Skafida in press; Bailey 2005) can readily be deconstructed through a study of object biographies (see below, Chapters 3, 6 and 7).

A second methodological criticism concerns the excavation strategies of the sites that had been selected to document deliberate fragmentation (Bailey 2001). This objection was anticipated and the three-part response is reiterated here. First, the mortuary and hoard evidence for missing parts of objects is extremely strong and, in our view, cannot be doubted. Secondly, precisely because rare classes of objects were selected for study, there was a higher probability that most, if not all, of their fragments would have been recovered in traditional settlement excavations, even those without dry-sieving, than for more mundane classes of things. Thirdly, the very breadth of the enquiry into ten or more classes of objects from a wide diversity of sites and monuments provide strength in breadth, if not in depth, to support the premise of deliberate fragmentation. However, the preference for breath over depth meant that detailed contextual studies were not provided in support of the premise. One of the major methodological objectives of this book is to provide such contextual studies, using sites where high standards of recovery can be demonstrated.

The same response can be made to the criticism that taphonomic assessments of the evidence from each relevant site were absent from the broad-brush approach of the first book (Milisauskas 2002; Bailey 2001). A second methodological objective of this research is the identification and assessment of taphonomic factors relevant to the spatial distribution of fragments as recovered by the excavators (see especially Chapters 4 and 5). While it is fully accepted that middle-range links should be made between the general premise of fragmentation and the detailed excavation data (cf. Whitelaw 1994), the repetition of a general pattern found in objects across a wide geographical area and through considerable time depth cannot be ignored in an assessment of the social practices and underlying principles of this part of Europe and indeed other parts of the world.

## The terms of the debate

After this review of both the positive uses and the criticisms of the fragmentation premise, let us re-state our understanding of the logic of deliberate fragmentation, using this to develop our view of the research agenda of this volume. The approach adopted is based on the fusion of the social approach to the biography of things (Appadurai 1986) and the '*chaîne opératoire*' approach to prehistoric technology. While Mauss (1936) defined the 'technical act' as consciously emerging from both individually and collectively constituted 'practical reason', Leroi-Gourhan (1964) formalized the approach and gave it practical coherence with respect to tool assemblages (cf. Schlanger 1996).

The study of the personal biographies of objects, people and places leads to a series of narratives about birth, life and death of each class of entity. We use the example of the biography of things, recognizing that the creation of personhood and the production of place are processes developing out things; indeed, Hoskins (1998) maintains that there is no such thing as the biography of Sumba persons, only the biography of the things that give them life. Each stage in an object's biography reveals transformations of the object's form and character or revelations of hidden essences that made the class of object distinctive. Each of these biographical stages was associated with one person or several, whose own biographies were thenceforward entwined in the story of the objects and who were encapsulated in the objects themselves. These relations between persons and things may be described as 'inalienable' – that is the relationship is inseparable from the act of transformation / revelation. At any part of the mid-life stage in an object biography, further transformations in the form of the thing may have occurred, such as breakage into fragments, wear, burning, further decoration, etc. We find objects with a very short life – made, used and discarded after a single act – and, equally, objects with a long and diversified biography. We are interested in understanding what brought about the differences in the length of an object's life.

Beginning with the birth of an object, the form and

decoration of the object were far from accidental creations but expressed principles of categorization that were fundamental to the society that produced the objects. One of the important tasks of the study of complete objects is the identification of such categorisational principles, which were related to the social structure out of which personhood would have emerged. The complexity of a vessel can be measured in terms of the number and type of divisions in its form – whether or not it has a foot, a neck or a handle – and the way(s) in which these divisions are reinforced by variations in colour, matt or gloss surface finish or decoration. These descriptive measures lead to the assessment of the importance of two major forms of categorization – the oppositional mode and the cross-cutting mode – both of which have analogies in the way that society itself was partitioned. Allied to an interest in categories is the study of the precision required for the performance of certain vessels. A vessel with a lid that is too small to fit is just as irritating to the user as a table with one short leg is to the patron of a restaurant. While open, globular forms required little precision for adequate performance, footed, lidded and handled vessels introduced to the makers ways of seeing the world that include symmetry, precision, compartmentalization (making things in parts) and standardisation. It will be informative to compare the ways in which different processes of making things – and eventually buildings – contributed to various aspects of personhood.

Another practice that was intimately bound up with the creation of personhood, and which could have occurred at any stage in the object's life, was the exchange of the object with other persons or groups. The exchange of such objects expressed a relationship of enchainment between the thing and the exchanger, such that part of the person metaphorically grew out of the exchange object passed on to the next exchange partner. However, in contradistinction to Melanesian enchainment, fragments as well as complete objects were exchanged in prehistory, creating a physical as well as an enchained link between exchange partners. Each fragment stood simultaneously as an object in its own right and a symbol of the once-complete object (synecdoche). Fragments of prehistoric objects can be described as 'fractal' because they interpenetrated other objects, humans and places, betokening relationships at all scales of their completeness – fragments, whole objects and sets of complete and/or broken objects. Fragments also evoke the missing parts of the object by presencing these desired things. Moreover, fragments could also evoke collective memories in the space left by the fragmentation of the original object, implying links that denoted a shared perspective. The fundamental point that we wish to emphasize here is that fragmentation signifies the attachment to one of the important forms of personhood

– fractal or dividual personhood, with all of its implications for the social structure of Balkan prehistory. This is not to say that the role of the individual in personhood is absent but that, following LiPuma (1998), the two forms of personhood were both present but in perpetual tension, as a potent source of social change.

The final stage in the biographies of fragmented or complete objects was their death – their consumption in closed contexts such as graves or burnt houses, semi-closed contexts such as pits or open contexts such as settlement layers. In such contexts of deposition, the process of accumulation has often been identified – a process held to be opposite to, and in tension with, that of enchainment. However, the sets that formed the products of accumulation themselves contained accumulations of personal biographies just as much as they held sets of objects – in relationships that were mutually constitutive. Their deposition formalized relations of enchainment tied to a particular place, in contrast to the fluid enchained relationships of exchange in the world of the living.

In terms of methodology, well-collected data from completely, or nearly completely, excavated sites allow the fragmentation analysis of different classes of objects to determine the completeness index of the objects, their biographical stages and the likelihood of re-fitting of fragments from the same object deposited in different contexts of the same site. The re-fitting studies developed here have been based upon previous re-fitting studies of, especially, lithics but using a more nuanced social approach in conjunction with the assessment of how the re-fitting fragments could have (been) moved to different places in the same site. Fragments of the same object in different houses on the same site could have stood for symbols of inter-household enchainment, as material markers of shared hospitality or feasting or some other common significant practice.

The absence of re-fits from a fragmentation analysis of well-excavated assemblages from totally excavated sites must indicate **either** that fragments of the incomplete objects were moved off the site for deposition elsewhere **or** that the orphan fragments found on the site were the only parts of the object moved on to the site. This situation would imply the existence of fragment dispersion across the landscape, over distances that are often difficult to define. In this case, enchainment can be given a landscape dimension that echoes the enchained exchange of exotics at the inter-regional level. The persons holding fragments of the same object while living on different sites have been enchained in relationships betokening at once a shared identity that was created out of the enchainment and commemorating participation in shared ceremonies and/or exchanges linking the two communities as well as the two persons.

Thus, the fragmentation premise – once defined in terms of the deliberate fragmentation and frequent re-use of a wide range of classes of objects – can be expanded to create a new premise about one of the principles on which personhood was created in later Balkan prehistory. We now turn to the Balkans and Greece in later prehistory to gain a sense of the archaeology that we find there and its relationship to fragmentation studies.

## *The Balkans and Greece in later prehistory*

The Balkan Peninsula is the gateway to Europe and it has been long believed that this is a secondary distribution area of the Neolithic lifestyles spreading from the Fertile Crescent toward Europe in the 8th – 7th millennia Cal BC (Gkiasta *et al.* 2003). The peninsula covers an area of 858,034 km², currently comprising 10 countries – Greece, Bulgaria, Romania, FYROM, Serbia and Montenegro, Albania, Croatia, Bosnia and Herzegovina, Slovenia and Hungary, with related prehistoric remains in a further three – Moldova, Trans-Dniestr and Ukraine. This brings the wider study area to over one million sq. km., or the combined size of the states of California and Texas. In the relevant archaeological traditions, the specific cultural and ecological characteristic of mainland Greece and the islands assigned to the Aegean a special role during prehistoric and early historic periods, thus separating studies of the prehistory of the Balkans from that of the present state of Greece. One of the disadvantages of such a division, which was further reinforced by the development of nationally based archaeologies at the Balkans in the 1950s, was the production of incommensurate chronological stages of the Neolithic phenomenon in Southeast Europe, each country wishing to date its key new stage earlier than the others. This complex picture is simplified and summarized below (Table 1.2).

Another major difficulty for anyone tempted to study prehistoric Southeast Europe is the variety of approaches and explanatory modes in different countries. A related issue – just as serious – concerns the imbalance of published data and the interpretations drawn from those data. An example is the continuing weakness of the case for local foragers at the onset of farming and the contingent difficulties of identifying relations between farmers and foragers, although this has rarely deterred researchers from drawing such inferences. For this reason, we have decided to begin our study some time after 7000 BC, when the Neolithic way of life is more or less well documented in the southern part of the Balkans. Ignoring present political boundaries, we shall focus on certain aspects of the material culture of prehistoric societies in Thessaly (Greece), Thrace, South Dobrogea and the Black Sea Coast (Bulgaria) and North Dobrogea (Romania)

(Plate 1). The end of our study coincides with a change in the "politics of being" (Bailey 2005), when a visible simplification of material culture is associated with drastic changes of lifeways characterizing the start of the Bronze Age. Other maps indicate locations of sites of importance to the fragmentation premise in Western Europe (Plate 2) and the Americas (Plate 3).

## The people

One of the most direct evidence for "seeing" the people of the past is the mortuary data. Human bones are a common, although not a frequent, component of the Balkan Neolithic. The detailed account of Southeast Europe burial evidence published by Băčvarov (2003) shows that separate bones and articulated bodies were found both inside settlements – under house floors, between houses and outside dwelling structures, in the settlement periphery. This was the most characteristic post-mortem treatment of human remains underlying the dominant social principle in the Neolithic Balkans – the link with the ancestors (Chapman 1994; Jones, A. 2005). Individuals of all gender/age groups were buried, thus extending any underlying concept of how and who to bury to include the whole society. A parallel practice of group and collective burials was also performed within the settlement. Group inhumations of bodies and separate bones seem to be related to inter-dwelling spaces, with single examples of burials under the houses and in the settlement periphery. Collective articulated inhumations are found only between houses, while separate bones of many individuals are found under and between dwelling structures. According to the Bulgarian evidence, during the late Neolithic, there is a tendency to concentrate human remains in the inter-dwelling spaces (Băčvarov 2003). Cremations were very rare in Balkan mortuary practices and the sites of Soufli Magoula and Platia Magoula Zarkou (Eastern Thessaly) with their many dozens of inurned cremations (Gallis 1996) stand as important exceptions to the Balkan Neolithic perception of death. The significance of fire during the rituals of transformation from living to dead may have been the key for understanding some of the burnt objects found at the Dimini settlement (Chapter 7). Objects taken from the cremation fire for circulation among the living or for secondary burning in commemoration practices would have maintained links with the ancestors.

The sites from Eastern Thessaly presented another important feature that is not common for contemporary mortuary practices – the burial of the dead in an extramural cemetery. Such a practice, however, is the major characteristic of the Late Neolithic Hamangia group in the Northeast Balkans (Southeast Romania and Northeast Bulgaria). In contrast to the light dwelling constructions

| Cal BC | Greece | Bulgaria | Romania | Serbia | Karanovo |
|---|---|---|---|---|---|
| 3000 | | | | | |
| 4000 | Final Neolithic or | Transitional Period | Copper Age | Copper Age | |
| | Chalcolithic | Late Copper Age | Late Neolithic | Late Neolithic | VI |
| | | Middle Copper Age | | | V |
| 5000 | Late Neolithic | Early Copper Age | Middle | Middle | |
| | | Late Neolithic | Neolithic | Neolithic | IV |
| 6000 | Middle Neolithic | Middle Neolithic | | | III |
| | | Early Neolithic | Early Neolithic | Early Neolithic | II |
| | | | | | I |
| 7000 | Early Neolithic | | | | |

*Table 1.2 Selected chronology of the Balkan Peninsula*

that may have been related to a less permanent lifestyle than on tells (Bailey 2005), the Hamangia graves revealed careful treatment of the dead body by inhumation, accompanied in most cases by a considerable variety of grave goods. With a few exceptions in the Boian and Vinča groups and in the Linearbandkeramik (Chapman 1983), this was the only Neolithic group in the Balkans with a predominantly extramural burial practice that became much more important in many regions in the Copper Age (for names and sequence of the Copper Age see Table 1.2). The biggest cemetery in Southeast Europe located on the Black Sea Coast at Durankulak (Plate 4) contained graves dated from the Late Neolithic to the Late Copper Age (Todorova *et al.* 2002, Higham *et al.* in press, Honch *et al.* 2006) and provides valuable information for continuity

and change in relations between the dead and the living operating at a time characterized by new materiality. The unique opportunity to explore the shift of how the person was perceived from the Late Neolithic to the Late Copper Age is exploited in Chapter 7 by examining one group of exotic grave goods. During the Copper Age, despite the continuation of intramural burials and the absence of cemeteries from some regions such as Thrace, extramural cemeteries became one standard way of burying the dead, well-grounded in the social development of different prehistoric communities (Chapman 1983). The number of dead, their age and sex, affiliated grave goods and spatial arrangements varied from place to place. What appears as a common pattern is individual inhumation of articulated bodies. The most spectacular emanation of the underlying social processes and categorisational principles of the Copper Age societies is the Varna cemetery (Plate 5) – an exuberant manifestation of wealth, prestige and status. The mammoth task of reading the meanings of the multi-dimensional messages deriving from the Varna data set is continued in this book by looking at some aspects of this unique concentration of material culture (Chapters 2, 6–7).

The earliest Balkan Neolithic evidence suggests that small numbers of people were chosen for symbolic retention among the living after their death. Whole bodies or parts of bodies would seem to be equally important for the purposes of creation and negotiation of social identity, firmly grounded in the permanent settlement area. The spatial variation in the deposition of bones or skeletons may have reflected some claims for differences in the process of social negotiation but the main principle of contribution to personhood creation remained the same – inhumations in intramural spaces. What may seem as an abrupt change in the perception of self and the dead, demonstrated by the development of extramural cemeteries, is not so radical if viewed alongside the settlement data. Just as in the Neolithic, a very small number of people was buried close to the same kind of permanent settlement areas in the Copper Age, whose major characteristic was the link with the ancestors. So, it was not that social negotiation in the settlement area was not any more valid but rather it was extended to external areas of formal deposition. If we accept the lack of Copper Age cemeteries in Thrace as genuine evidence of absence rather than the converse, then we are facing the possibility of two ways of defining Copper Age identity. The first built on and developed the earlier concept of self, while the other was more reductive in terms of the use of human remains, relying more on material symbolism to negotiate personhood. The internal dynamic of identity principles is further diversified by extramural cemeteries and cremation practices that are generally contemporary with intramural burials. It is possible that an individual extramural burial, often accepted as a token of increasing individualism, was actually used to reinforce the concept that the deceased's personhood was at the same time constituted by multiple material links. Another example is the cremated remains in vessels at Soufli Magoula, just as in the Leslie Grinsell story. Such links were visible in the variety of grave goods or in the dispersion of pots after cremation, as the embodiment of enchained relations between the living and the dead. We now turn to the places where such enchained relations were created.

## The places

Probably one of the strongest expressions of place-value (Chapman 1997) is people's choice to dwell in a particular area. Such a choice would have been multiply reinforced by any re-settling of the same place time and again. The self-perpetuating place-value, nourished and maintained by increasing ancestral power, was a fundamental principle for the formation of one of the main settlement elements in Balkan prehistory – settlement mounds. These mounds – termed tells – consisted mainly of the house rubble and the clay washed down from walls of each previous human occupation; in some cases, these processes eventually resulted in a massive silhouette 18 m in height, such as at Djadovo or Karanovo (Plate 6). These significant monuments varied in size and density of distribution but were surely landmarks and timemarks in the landscapes of Southeast European prehistory. The sites are usually enclosed by palisades or ditches or sometimes by both; discoveries of multiple enclosure have become more common with increasing use of remote sensing (Braasch 1995; Raczky et al. 2002). The enclosures reinforced the sense of bounded space and the concentration principle on the tells. On some of the few fully excavated tells, careful planning was implicated in the densely built area with its minimal unbuilt space (Chapman 1990). While most dwellings had one or two rooms, there were examples of multi-roomed houses reaching in one case the extreme number of 11 rooms (Chapman 1990). The vast majority of the dwellings comprised wattle-and-daub constructions. The rare cases of buildings with stone foundations are more common in Greece, exceptional in other parts of the Balkans. Furniture is one of the least explored issues in later Balkan prehistory but the use of clay, stone, wood and textiles would have created a variety of living environments at once intimate and personal, as well as creating forms of appropriate behaviour and everyday bodily positions.

The emergence of new flat sites with the potential to develop into tells was a more or less constant process that intensified especially during the Copper Age. Some of these sites did "grow" into mature tells, others developed into low "baby" mounds before abandonment, while yet others remained as flat sites with only one or two phases of occupation. While there were flat sites that reproduced the tight planning of the tell-to-be, there were also flat sites that were spread over a large area. Most of the flat sites excavated so far were located in upland basins – a distribution that has led to environmentally deterministic interpretations. It should be pointed out, however, that although rare, there are cases of upland baby tells (*e.g.* Rakitovo, Sedlare and Obre I) that question the equation upland zone/flat site. Moreover, some sites, such as Dimini, are located on hilltops, as if to imitate the silhouette of a tell. This is not to claim that every new site on the Balkan peninsula was meant to develop into a tell. Indeed, it was recently recognized that flat sites were an inseparable part of Neolithic landscapes but that the difficulties of incorporating them into existing interpretations of settlement patterns excluded short-live sites from the Balkan research agenda (Kotsakis 2005). Rather, we should think of Neolithic settlement patterns as a dynamic process of settling and re-settling areas, during which the main principle of creating and manipulating ancestral power through repeated occupation remained unchanged but at the same time was in constant tension with other social practices (such as budding off from traditional settlements) and environmental issues (*e.g.* the availability of resources). In this way, alternative practices diverging from tell lifeways led to the production and probable ultimate legitimization of the existence of other places of occupation, such as flat sites and formal deposition areas.

*Formal deposition areas*
While there has been an evolution of the concept of middening in British archeology from dumping rubbish for manure (Gaffney *et al.* 1985) to something much more structured (McOmish 1996), such a concept is basically unknown in the Balkans. There are two sites in the Balkan Peninsula where middening practices have been discovered. The first case concerns the soil micro-morphological studies at Hârşova (and also Borduşani) (Haită 1997), where secondary layers of ashes and charcoal, as well as waste zones have been identified. The second site is the Late Neolithic settlement at Makryalos (Papa *et al.* 2004), which demonstrated a practice opposite to those of Western European middens, which are associated mainly with off-site activities, and Hârşova, with its on-site layers of organic refuse. The Makryalos publication discussed the linkage of massive feasting to middening – an accurate characterization of the deposition of huge quantities of animal remains in pits. While consistent with the evidence, this interpretation reinforces a cluster of ideas well-known in the Balkans in which there is no distinction made between the three independent components – feasting, pits and settlement discard. Thus, the package of ideas could easily become a circular argument: if there were pits with some traces of feasting, this was a settlement, or, if a settlement had an accumulation of animal bones, this was evidence for feasting. Therefore, although certain elements of middening behavior can be recognized, selective publication of the vast majority of Balkan sites has prevented the identification of the type of activities leading to the accumulation of huge amount of material not only in pits within settlements but between buildings in settlements and in pits in the landscape.

One of most hotly debated issues in the prehistory of Southeast Europe is the straightforward association of pits with settlement activities (Bailey 2000, Chapman 2000c, Gaydarska 2004). Such settlements would have consisted of pits of various shapes and size that lacked any signs of planning. They were usually spread over areas larger than that of the average tell; some pit sites are enclosed, others are not. The main arguments in favour of the interpretation of pits as pit-dwellings are the presence of hearths and domestic material (Bailey 2000), which are contradicted by the difficulties of living in pits over a period longer than a week (*p.c.* D. Monah), by the irregular shape, construction and size of the negative features, and by the notion of structured deposition of objects in the pits (Chapman 2000c, Gaydarska 2004). The readily accepted ethno-historical parallels with pit-houses of the Medieval and Early Modern periods (Boyadžiev 2004) have prevented a careful examination of the constructional peculiarities and taphonomic processes that may have contributed to the present state of the features. Interestingly, they are characteristic only for a certain period (Early, Middle or Late Neolithic, depending on the sequences in different countries) in South East Europe and, after that, do not appear for several millennia. Related to the pit debate in Balkan prehistory is another current issue – the definition of rubbish (see above, p. 2). At present, there is evidence to suggest that far from all pits in Balkan Neolithic and Copper Age were used as rubbish dumps (Chapman 2000c). Their uses could have included raw material extraction, storage and short-term working places. However, the opposition between profane discard of refuse and structured deposition of meaningful objects is over-simplified and we should be aware of the multiple possibilities for the maintenance of cultural order through the disposal of refuse (see below, pp. 78–9).

At present, in the archaeology of Southeast Europe, there is no theoretical or methodological framework that defines and explains the differences between pits for living, pits for refuse, pits for storage, borrow pits and pits for rituals. Furthermore, pits appear within tell settlements, within flat sites and increasingly in areas of formal deposition dispersed over the landscape. Any re-evaluation of this huge data set requires a major collaborative research effort. However, there is no doubt that one of the important characteristics of the Balkan prehistory is pit-digging, which can be seen as a day-to-day social practice involving procurement, consumption, storage, celebration, and feasting but also as a more structured way of negotiating social reproduction and identity. Such practices take place in the domestic areas as well as in areas for formal deposition, where the pit-digging is more performative because people require a special visit, leading to the interrelation of the people and what they are doing with the places where they are doing it. Together with other places in the landscape, these places that are like the dots of Ingold's (1993) model of mobility which, although not necessarily visible now, were important contributors to social memory, myth creation and the negotiation of identity.

The dominant bulk of permanent tells, emphasized and celebrated by most archaeologists in South East Europe, casts a long shadow over the dynamic of settlement patterns in Balkan prehistory, making it hard to see other forms of settlement and, especially, smaller-scale practices such as daily acts, ritual performances, feasting, pit-digging and middening. A truly revealing account of personhood and fractality will require the integration of insights from both the large-scale and millennial and the small-scale and everyday.

## The things

One of the principal characteristics of the later prehistory of Southeast Europe is the abundance of objects and materials deriving from any form of human occupation – from small hamlet or pit-field in the landscape to monumental tells and cemeteries. The most numerous material was fired clay, in the form of highly or modestly decorated vessels, figurines, miniature house models and altars. The other product in the Balkans that involves a major technological transformation from its raw material to its final form is metal. While there were scattered examples of earlier metalwork, gold and copper became more common from the fifth millennium BC. The majority of the remaining artifacts utilized locally available or remote resources; their main characteristic is that they incorporated nature into day-to-day social practices. Some of the objects required relatively minor transformations from their initial appearance to the final product (*e.g.* antler tools), others need a longer process of acquisition (*e.g.* animal bones used for tool-making after culling and butchery) or processing (*e.g.* the transformation of matt, asymmetrical, coloured stone into highly polished symmetrical objects themselves representing cultural order). Each kind of raw material was used to produce a diverse repertoire of objects. The only exception is probably flint and other silica material that is found mainly as ready tools, blanks or debitage. Stone was utilized mainly for tools but also for figurines and ornaments. Worked bone and unworked animal bones were common finds on each later prehistoric site. The former consisted of ready tools or parts of composite tools, figurines and ornaments, while the latter were associated with contexts of meat consumption but also appear in more structured deposits. We can assume the use of other natural products, such as reeds and fibres, but their preservation was very poor.

Exotic objects constituted an important part of Neolithic and Copper Age lifeways, although a full list of such objects cannot yet be provided. Thus, for example what may have been considered exotica in Thrace or the Great Hungarian Plain was local in Thessaly (*e.g. Spondylus* and *Dentalium* shells) and vice versa: the honey-coloured flint local to Northeast Bulgaria was exotic for every Greek Neolithic site. However, the abundance of exotic objects on later prehistoric sites in Southeast Europe was beyond any doubt, grounding the existence of extended exchange networks that must have had a major impact on the perception of self in relation to Others (Chapman, in press c). Whether nephrite frogs or piece of volcanic rock (pumice), exotic objects were statements about the awareness of other worlds, whose "domestication" (Chapman 2003) was crucial for identity formation in prehistoric Balkans. Last but not least was the use of coloured substances, such as graphite or ochre, for decorative reinforcement or colour contrast.

Objects made of all of the above-mentioned materials were found in settlements in burnt and unburnt houses, pits or hoards. There were however, different local and regional scales of intensity in the use of materiality. Mainstream settlement finds would be considered to be pottery; stone, bone and flint tools, with ornaments made of bone, stone and shell rather more rare. Generally rare, if present at all, were the metal artifacts. Figurines, although not numerous, were common on most settlements, with exceptionally low frequencies in Hamangia domestic spaces. Exotic objects found on settlements were not equally and evenly distributed – *e.g.* nephrite objects were found at not more than a handful of sites, while *Spondylus* was found in small numbers on almost every excavated settlement. A very important feature of the exotic and rare artifacts in the domestic context is that they were usually deposited as hoards. It seems, therefore, that the everyday contacts within a settlement would not have involved a permanent demonstration of enchained relations with the Other. Rather, the objects embodied in day-to day prehistoric life were the main material media for the negotiation of personhood and relations, while the more rare objects were carefully curated for use in crucial moments of identity negotiation such as death, marriage or compensation to terminate unfriendly relations with neighbours.

Many hoards known so far, especially in the Copper Age, were deposited away from the settlement. Probably such places in the landscape were to commemorate events in which negotiations ended with a clear act confirming the relevant identity. The circumstances that have caused the deposition of hoards must have been of major importance for the prehistoric community since, once buried, the objects and what they represented were out of active circulation and negotiation processes, maintained only in social memory. Therefore, one may expect that specific persons, as well as certainly the community as a whole, would have maintained more or less constant inter-site and inter-regional contacts for the acquisition of new, more rare or exotic objects, leading to a flux of enchained relations supporting a varied range of types of personhood.

Materials sharing a distribution in both settlements and cemeteries comprised mostly pottery but also bone, flint and stone tools and personal ornaments. These were objects or raw materials that related the dead to everyday activities and encounters that were practiced in the settlement or while exploring and incorporating the surrounding landscape. These objects then became part of the everyday life of the deceased, therefore becoming part of the newly-dead. There were, however, some groups of objects that were predominantly related to mortuary deposition – *Spondylus* ornaments, other exotica like *Dentalium*, malachite and carnelian, as well as gold and copper. Importantly, the very same materials and objects were components of settlement hoards, thus reinforcing the principle of hoard deposition as being one way of creating and maintaining personhood. The Hamangia group presents another example of a very rare social practice – the incorporation of figurines in graves, which is in strong contrast to all contemporary Balkan communities that deposited figurines in the domestic domain. Such a practice was probably consequent upon the perception of self and what happened after death – a phenomenon that is explored in Chapter 3. In addition, Hamangia graves contained the skulls or parts of skulls of wild and domestic animals – a practice that is more readily associated with bull heads in the domestic arena (*e.g.* Çatal Höyük, Leibhammer 2000; Swogger 2000). Although hunted and herded animals were of major significance for prehistoric communities in southeast Europe, they appeared to be a particularly important component of identities in Hamangia societies.

In each extramural cemetery in the Balkan peninsula, there are graves with grave goods and graves without grave goods. Such differences were explicitly emphasised in cases of unprecedented material wealth such as the Varna cemetery. The lack of grave goods in some of the Varna graves and their abundance in other graves are the two ends of a scale of intensity of object deposition: both ends of this continuum held deep meaning for prehistoric communities and both aspects of these practices deserve our close attention. A similar pattern of different intensities in deposition is demonstrated by the discard of figurines on an average prehistoric settlement in comparison to their abundance on the Dolnoslav and Vinča tells. Such a pattern suggests that the total quantity of whole and fragmented objects may have been used to emphasize particular statements about the processes of creating personhood and the negotiation of enchained relations.

One could go into further details of the material evidence of the Balkans (Chapman 2000, Bailey 2000) or examine them on a more general level (cf. Jones, A. 2005):

both approaches can produce valuable insights into the formation of multi-faceted identities in the past. The more limited aim here was to present a balanced view of what people have used in their daily lives, when they were burying their dead or when celebrating a good crop. Through their quotidian practices and communal ceremonies, prehistoric people were constantly creating themselves in relation to others. Objects and places were inseparable from these processes of the constitution of identity, forming at the same time the results of, and constraints on, the changing perception of self.

Having set the research agenda in the time/place context of later Balkan prehistory, we can now turn to a summary of the book contents by chapters.

## The book contents

The book acknowledges the unpalatable truth that all objects were designed and created to be whole, even if the 'complete' object sometimes portrayed a part of a whole (*e.g.* a separately modelled foot). It is undeniable that the meanings represented by a whole object differed from those of a fragment and that it is important to understand both congeries of meanings. For this reason, the second chapter is devoted to a study of complete objects, in this case pottery, in order to elucidate the relationship between material culture, persons and society. A key social practice discussed in this chapter is categorisation.

In this chapter, we introduce the biographical approach to things as a way of transcending the style – function dichotomy that has derailed many material culture studies. The biographical approach rests, somewhat uneasily, on two root metaphors: first, a representational logic, whereby the way that societies make persons stands for the ways that people create things; and, secondly, a fractal logic, in which things, people and places extend out of other things, people and places. Societies often develop both ways of thinking about the world and the tension between them is itself comparable to the tension between the two co-existing forms of personhood – individuals, with their propensity for metaphorical representation and dividuals, with their inherently fractal nature.

An assessment is made of the various reflectionist relationships posited by archaeologists between material culture and society, including the weak version of reflectionism, whereby social relations are encoded in material culture, and the stronger version represented by symmetry analysis. It is suggested that one way of overcoming the problems of reflectionism is through a deeper understanding of processes of categorisation in the past, as a way of dealing with real-life complexities. There is an extended discussion of Danny Miller's study of pottery-making in the Indian village of Dangwara, in which Miller posits the embodiment of categorisation processes and cultural order in pottery. The social labour of division is discussed in terms of the boundaries people create between nature and culture and between people in society. The argument is advanced through a discussion of David Keightley's ground-breaking analysis of Chinese Neolithic ceramics, in which there are clear analogies between enhanced differentiation and cultural order in both material and cognitive realms. Keightley's consideration of variables such as symmetry, precision, standardisation and compartmentalisation provide a cross-cultural framework for individual context-based analyses. These approaches are integrated to provide a framework for the study of four closely related phenomena – material culture, social structure, cognitive complexity and personhood.

The method of categorical analysis of Balkan prehistoric pottery assemblages is based upon an integrated analysis of both shape and decoration. The analysis rests on the definition of six variables – shape categories, decorational categories, the zonality of decoration, zonal reinforcements, the measure of reinforcement and the measure of decorational intensity. These variables enable the characterization of a pottery assemblage in terms of the various categories that potters used to create the vessels, whether oppositional categories or cross-cutting dimensions. Six assemblages have been selected to provide snapshots from the Neolithic and Copper Age sequence – the Early Neolithic settlements of Rakitovo and Chavdarova Cheshma, the Late Neolithic settlement of Nova Zagora – Hlebozavoda, the Early Copper Age pottery from the Azmashka mogila, the Late Copper Age Varna cemetery and the Final Copper Age tell of Dolnoslav. The results of the categorical analyses are compared and contrasted to provide a long-term sequence of social and material change from the Early Neolithic to the Final Copper Age, in this way providing an overall social context for the study of practices dated to narrower time-spans in later chapters. However, chapter 2 comes with a health warning; those readers not minded to grapple with the necessary minutiae of ceramic analysis may prefer to jump straight to the interpretation section (p. 48).

In Chapter 3, the investigation of one such chronologically focussed body of evidence – a group of fired clay anthropomorphic figurines from the Late Neolithic and Early Copper Age period on the Black Sea coast – provides the opportunity for an extended discussion of the varied ways that societies have developed for the creation of personhood. In this chapter, we advance along the biographical pathway of things from their complete state to compare the use of complete figurines and what is done with fragments of these representations.

Our discussion of the culturally specific creation of personhood begins with a review and deconstruction of the two-sex, two-gender paradigm current in Western thinking for the last two centuries. The topical emphasis on the status and significance of the 'individual' in archaeological studies of personhood is questioned as a function of a remaining attachment to unrepresentative, Western forms of personhood. A consideration of alternative means of developing personhood in Melanesia, South India and Polynesia leads to an array of potentially useful scenarios for studying prehistoric societies and their forms of personhood, united by LiPuma's key insight that both individuals and dividuals are present in most societies, with the tensions between these kinds of person providing a framework for the study of personhood.

One criticism of recent approaches to personhood is that social agency is often omitted – a failing that finds its obverse in the lack of attention to personhood in recent discussions of agency. A productive integration of both of these approaches relies on the dynamic nominalist approach, in which categories and self-definitions of persons bring such persons into existence. This way of examining the formation of identities seeks to transcend the opposition between structure and agency that has been problematic since Giddens' early studies. Dynamic nominalist insights into the gendered basis of the creation of personhood show the frequency of androgyny as a bridge between different states of being, forming a key category in the alternating and cyclical transformations of gendered identities.

This approach is worked through using the Hamangia figurines from the Black Sea coastal zone, using categorisations of the figurines by material, gender and completeness. The re-interpretation of complete Hamangia figurines as androgynes leads to a dynamic reconstruction of their fragmentation pathways. A contextual study of these figurines in settlement contexts such as Medgidia and in both settlement and mortuary deposits at Durankulak leads to a refinement of the various, alternative and partly conflicting principles whereby different persons were created in Hamangia.

The focus in Chapter 4 shifts to a consideration of methodological issues of site formation, during which Michael Schiffer pays a metaphorical visit to the Balkan Peninsula in Chapter 4 to help colleagues working there avoid making unjustified assumptions about their rich and varied on-site evidence. The challenge in this chapter is to question the assumption that the excavated data is a more or less accurate reflection of the operation of past social practices. It is also a response to Whitelaw's claim that post-processual objectives require close attention to middle-range concerns. The particular focus for the general argument of the book is the extent to which the mobility of objects and their fragments has or has not been documented.

The challenge to reflectionist thinking came from two opposed directions – post-processualists who emphasised the active use of material culture and behavioural archaeologists who characterised a wide variety of formation processes which made reflectionism un-justifiable, even in so-called "Pompeii-type" situations. There follows a deconstruction of Schiffer's refuse typology, in which re-use processes are found to be of considerable significance and the archaeological methods used in the definition of activity areas are strongly criticised. The study of Tzeltal Mayan deposition by Michael Deal is used as an example of the creation of useful categories of depositional assemblage, such as pre-abandonment, abandonment and post-abandonment. The Tzeltal Maya and other case studies illustrate the diverse range of mobility for object fragments, in which multiple re-use of sherds is common.

The impact of these studies of site formation processes is summarised in the form of four challenges to any archaeologist seeking to understand site material assemblages:- object biographies and the mobility of fragments; the formation of each individual context; a more robust methodology for the definition of activity areas; and a definition of 'sites' that takes all disposal of material culture into account. The chapter concludes with a summary of the recent sociological work on rubbish and its disposal by Thompson, Munro and Hetherington. This approach starts from the importance of categoriza-tion and the work involved in keeping boundaries – Munro's 'labour of division' – and proceeds to discuss the 'resources' that refuse provides for the maintenance of cultural order.

In Chapter 5, we follow up the previous chapter's methodological insights into site formation processes with a more systematic survey of what happened to the missing pieces. Several well-documented scenarios can be introduced to explain object breakage when all of the re-fitting parts were discarded in the same place or context. However, it is now clear that the movement of fragments from the place of breakage can be explained in a number of ways – not only by deliberate artifact breakage. One response to this topic – ignoring it completely – has characterised much of past archaeology, which has treated the fragment as the basic unit of analysis and developed many methods for analysing the fragment. The main focus of this chapter is on re-fitting studies in the widest possible context – from intra-context to across the landscape.

A brief history of re-fitting provides an outline of the main methodological advances in the last century, including Schiffer's Completeness Index and his Fragmentation Index, as well as increasingly refined criteria for the acceptance/rejection of potential re-fits. The re-fitting studies are used to explore six classes of information. The first category of studies used re-fitting sherds and flakes to answer chronological and/or stratigraphic questions. The basic assumption of these experiments was challenged – viz. the contemporaneity of contexts from which re-fitting fragments derived. Another large group of studies concerns lithic re-fitting to gain technological and spatial information about the *châine opératoire* of stone tool production. Here, it was found that the most useful studies were those few that had moved beyond the technological and transcended the micro-scale of spatial analysis. The remaining four sets of studies may be regarded as some of the core data of the book in terms of a theory and practice of the re-fitting approach. Re-fitting experiments at the site level are divided into the contexts of the domestic domain and the mortuary arena. In both cases, attempts are made to explain fragment dispersion both within the site and off the site; special attention is paid to incomplete objects on totally excavated sites – and the implied fragment dispersion off the site. In the next suite of studies, the concept of 'orphan sherd' is fully discussed and a methodology proposed for its interpretation, based upon erosion and wear studies of the sherds linked to the analysis of formation processes. In the final section, those few examples of successful inter-site re-fitting are discussed and their significance considered for a dynamic landscape archaeology.

We return to Balkan later prehistory for the next two chapters, in which the biographical approach is combined with re-fitting studies to extend our understanding of two prominent yet poorly understood classes of material – fired clay anthropomorphic figurines (Chapter 6) and *Spondylus/Glycymeris* shell rings (Chapter 7).

One of the curious aspects about figurine studies in Eurasian prehistory is the paucity of studies of the figurines as fired clay objects whose bodies have received the imprint of many different treatments – or very few. The approach proposed here creates an alternative to the art history-dominated studies of complete individual figurines and the interpretation of broken figurine fragments as rubbish fit only for dumping. If the human body is now regarded as **the** 'site' of cultural creation and the importance given to materiality is to be merited, then surely it is worth investigating figurine bodies in terms of their own specific materiality through the traces left of its own individual biography.

This approach is utilised to gain a deeper understanding of figurines in general and the large (500 items) figurine assemblage from the Final Copper Age layers of the tell of Dolnoslav in particular. The combination of the biographical study and the intra-site re-fitting of almost 15% of all of the figurines produces a rich tapestry of variability at Dolnoslav, that should be contrasted to the principles of personhood defined for that site. The study of figurines from two different periods – the Late

Neolithic and Early Copper Age for the Hamangia group and the Final Copper Age for Dolnoslav – enables a comparison of the means by which personhood was constructed in the 5th millennium Cal BC. But the other significance of Dolnoslav is as a site of accumulation, where major middening of figurine fragments, sherds and animal bones outside the structures poses questions hardly ever framed, let alone answered, in Balkan later prehistory. The same health warning of a strong input of empirical detail applies to this chapter as to Chapter 2.

The contrasts between fired clay figurines and marine shell rings could hardly be greater in terms of the search for the raw materials, their *châine opératoire* and the symbolism of their form and decoration. In Chapter 7, the biographical pathways of shell rings are outlined from the three sites where intra-site re-fitting of the rings has been attempted – the Late Neolithic and Copper Age cemetery of Durankulak, the Late Copper Age Varna cemetery, both on the Black Sea coast, and the Late Neolithic settlement of Dimini near the Aegean coast in Thessaly. The results from the cemetery re-fittings proved so much at variance with those of the Dolnoslav figurine re-fitting that a further study was made at an almost totally excavated settlement

with a large assemblage of shell rings to ascertain whether the re-fitting results were related more to the material of the broken objects or to the kind of depositional context of the broken objects. The comparison of the biographical studies and the re-fitting experiments showed beyond reasonable doubt that shell rings were not only fine and precious ornaments but also had a life of their own which was extremely varied and yielded fascinating details of the practices in which the rings were involved.

The enquiry has led to a complex and highly fragmented picture of later prehistory in the Balkan peninsula. In Chapter 8, we summarise the evidence marshaled in support of the 'fragmentation premise' and examine its implications for Balkan later prehistory. We seek to put Balkan prehistory 'back together again' by looking at the variations in social practices and the construction of personhood at four different socio-spatial levels: the person, the household, the settlement-based corporate group and inter-settlement relations. We conclude the book with a short chapter setting the research agenda for future work linked to the fragmentation premise, both for Balkan later prehistory and, more generically, for archaeology as a whole.

# 2. What we can do with whole objects – the categorical analysis of pottery

One of the fundamental questions that archaeologists and ethnographers ask is what pottery can tell us about the societies that made the vessels. Surely, it is argued, a class of things so widespread and significant will hold important information about the people making, using, breaking and depositing ceramics. For the most part, this question has been examined through the prism of "style" – a term whose precise meaning has itself provoked lengthy debate (for a summary of the debate, see Conkey 1990) but which is generally held to promote the transfer of information by material means. However, Robin Boast (1997) has recently developed an incisive critique of "style", in which he grounds the term in the false dichotomy of function (doing a job) and signalling (bearing information). As he demonstrates, it is in fact impossible to prioritise the one over the other, whether chronologically or logically – there is an inescapable co-emergence of style and function. The alternative that Boast advances is that agency is not only human and that "once made, the object becomes an actor in its own right" (1997, 188); the object becomes meaningful because it is constitutive of active networks of social practices. Hence, for Boast (1997, 190), material culture is not the material objectification of the discussion over the relationship between people and things as much as a participant in the discussion; objects are made into discussants by the inscription of action. In seeking to undermine the concepts of style developed by Wobst, Wiessner and Sackett, Boast's perspective challenges us to think through the ways in which object agency really works (cf. the relationship of objects to place, Hetherington 1997).

The widespread acceptance of the active role of material culture in social life was an early success gained by the post-processualists (Hodder 1982). Such object agency challenged the traditional and processualist assumption of a "reflectionist" approach to material culture, viz., that pottery can reflect social, cultural and economic contexts, by proposing that human agents used material culture in pursuit of strategies of engagement, by which power relations could be masked (*e.g.* Shanks and Tilley 1982). An example comes from Neolithic Greece, where the predominance of decorated, open shapes (as well as open cooking facilities) in the Early and Middle Neolithic of Thessaly has recently been interpreted as 'probable indications of an idealised economic reality', in comparison to the unequal intra-site distribution of painted pottery, with its probable 'ideological' significance (Andreou *et al.* 1996, 559). But Andreou *et al.*'s interpretation of the decorated wares is based upon the assumption of a direct correlation between ceramic style and social reality. In any case, DeMarrais *et al.* (1996) have placed ideology in a broader context of material change through defining its use in materialising symbolic practices.

Boast would clearly have us go further, by developing a more "organic", personal approach to things, in which the biography of the object is intimately related to human life-histories. It is now widely recognised that creating things may involve not only processes of production but processes of reproduction, in which individuals "give birth" to things (Strathern 1988; Lemonnier 1993; Rowlands and Warnier 1993) In this sense, the creation of a decorated object at the time of its birth frames the trajectory of a historical past as well as a future biography. The birthing of a large Cucuteni-Tripolye cereal storage jar with elaborate painted decoration (Ellis 1984, 200–205, Figs. 73–76) would not only have strengthened the social and production relations between those collecting the clay, exchanging the pigments from far to the West, forming the vessel and painting the vessel – itself a complex inter-connected operation – but also recapitulated the history of tribal exchange, intensive cereal growing, ploughing and the taming of draught animals, cereal storage and the pottery birthing process itself. As DeBoer (1984, 530) says about Shipibo-Conibo ceramics, whose production depends upon remote raw materials, "an elaborately decorated beer-mug or water jug is, in itself, a geopolitical statement about a resource zone to which a potter has direct or indirect access". The creation of an object has already bequeathed to that object a complex biography, which can only be diversified in later life. That object also embodies what Andy Jones

(2005, 199–200) has termed 'material citation', whereby each material act refers to, and gains its meaning from, that which has gone before. The way in which this or that life develops, however, is related to a host of contingent factors, many of which beyond the control of the creator. But the complex biography created through the birth of an object always stands behind the trajectory of that thing, positioning it in the moral universe that gave it life.

There are, of course, limits to the biographical complexities of a single thing, especially one created through an expedient birthing process. Nonetheless, even a relatively simple thing such as a flint end-scraper can be deliberately fragmented and the two halves deposited in two different pits, as at the Earlier Neolithic site of Blewbury (Halpin 1984). It is when objects are combined in sets of two or many more that their potential for dramatic intervention in social life becomes far greater. Sets of different objects – whether hoards, grave groups, costume sets, ritual sets or burnt house assemblages (Chapman 2000) – can be conceptualised as "extended families" composed of local ancestral objects (heirlooms), younger local relatives formed from raw materials found within the settlement catchment, distant relatives marrying-in from another lineage and exotic family members, whose origin and social history is so remote that their biography is often less complex than those of local things. These extended families are not merely accumulations of valuable prestige goods but also form historical lineages of artifacts, each contributing their own cultural memories, sense of places experienced and links to a range of different individuals, whether creators, owners or traders.

Ellen (1988) reminds us that objects are frequently subject to the same rites of passage as humans. The related notion that objects can "die" at time of deposition is also widespread. Basden (1938, quoted in Barley 1994, 92) recounts how Igbo people are often grief-stricken with "violent distress" at the accidental breakage of a water jar. "Shrieks and wails rend the air and, for a time, the female owner is inconsolable." In the same way, the killing of pottery often accompanies the death of a person in African societies (Barley 1994, 92). In these ways, we can readily develop small-scale narratives of how objects perform a significant role in social life. One way to think this insight through is to use Kopytoff's (1986, 90–91) conclusion that the way society makes persons is analogous to the way persons create things.

However, we are also aware that, while the attribution of agency to objects repositions the debate, there are limits to the approach, as forcibly expressed by Douglas and Isherwood (1996). Nor does it necessarily answer the question of the relationship between material culture and society: making objects active participants in social life does not rule out debate over the form of their participation, nor the content of that form. We have alluded already to a common assumption about the relationship between material objects and their society – reflectionism. This approach can take a variety of forms. In the weak form, things have the *potential* to reflect socio-economic contexts. Thus the dense and highly structured ceramic decoration on the Late Neolithic pottery from Dimini is seen to mirror the compact and highly structured layout of the settlement and its spatial segments, while the homogenous distribution of even the finest painted wares in all houses and open spaces is interpreted as showing that fine wares are the mark of communal identity rather than household or individual status (Souvatzi and Skafida 2003; Souvatzi, in prep.). Similarly, the design fields on northern Greek prehistoric pottery from the Early Neolithic to the Early Bronze Age are seen as echoing the increasingly controlled use of settlement space (Halstead 1999). In the stronger form of reflectionism, well exemplified by symmetry studies, symmetry relations are one way that people used to describe their cosmological orientations and basic socio-cultural organisation (Washburn and Crowe 2004, xiii).

A second form of the relationship between material remains and societies is that there is a co-variation in the patterns found in both domains (David *et al.* 1988, 366). However, these authors (1988, 378) go further than mere co-variation when concluding that "decoration and the persistence of designs through social time and space are to be explained by their mnemonic visual expression of the underlying structures of belief and thought that most distinctively constitute the societies' unique identities." Mary Douglas (1973, 9, 42) also goes further than the co-variation approach in asserting that the pattern of material culture is symbolic in itself and serves to transmit culture by encoding, mediating and reinforcing patterns of social relations. In her later study with Baron Isherwood (1996, ix, 49), the authors emphasise the important potential of all goods to create meanings but not individually. This approach has been criticised by Lemonnier (1990, 30), who, in a plea to include techniques in the realm of socio-cultural practices, raises the related issue of how to equate a given meaning with a particular technical form. Moreover, Thomas (1999, 72) reminds us that even such a general structural attribute of ceramic design as bounded or unbounded patterns probably had different meanings in different contexts. It is not easy to answer this question but one way to approach it is the investigation of processes of categorisation.

## Categorisation processes and objects

There are few operations that cause such distress to students of archaeology as 'typology' – a term conjuring up a fatal combination of the worst excesses of traditional archaeology with mega-tedious descriptions of otherwise interesting material culture. However, Hodder has defended typology as "central to the development of contextual archaeology, along with the need to classify and categorise" (Hodder 1991, 136). Holten (2000, 287) expands this view by emphasising that human classification creates categories enabling us, through simplification, to 'think' the world and to engage with it. Such cultural categories define and divide the most important aspects of a society's daily life – persons, objects and places. While Morris (1994) has provided structural examples of the development of the cultural category of 'person' as reflexively related to the dominant cultural paradigm of the society in question, Nanoglou (2005) has theorised the everyday role of material culture as part of a reiterative discourse articulating social practices. In this perspective, material forms formed types because "the reproduction of the generic form … (in human representations) … made them intelligible through the re-articulation of elements of already known discourses. As with material citation, these repeated performances constituted the very field of intelligibility, framing the material forms so that they can act as an agent. These points ground Derrida's (1982, 315) observation that iterability lies at the heart of communication – not necessarily a mechanical repetition but the iterability of a viewpoint.

The embodiment of categorisation processes in objects is an important link between the world of objects and the relationships defining individuals and groups in fields of practice as objectified history. In his study of Dangwara pottery in an Indian village, Miller (1985, 11, 40–41) proposes that a study of how material forms embody categorisation processes can be used to study categorisation itself because potters created a particular cultural order embodied in the variability of the resultant ceramic forms. This means, for Miller, that material forms are part of the central order of cultural construction. However, the problem for archaeologists is that a pottery code can be articulated with almost any other aspect of conceptualisation. These open-ended possibilities can be limited, to some extent, by the identification of contextual differences in social practices of cooking and the purity of food, to water-carrying and caste, and to gendered parts of household space (Miller 1985, 151–156, 172). Material forms act as 'framing' devices – marking the appropriate and inappropriate settings for social practices.

Categorisation implies divisions, hierarchies and boundaries – a point not lost on Munro (1997) who reverses the familiar phrase 'division of labour' to discuss the labour of division – the work required by the divisions we make to see the world from a specific viewpoint, to hold to that position and to eliminate matter seen to be 'out of place' from that perspective. Munro stresses that divisions are just as much cultural artifacts as tables and chairs – and deserve to be analysed as well. Thus the labour of division produces a stable grid of representation within which we are made visible or not; as Cooper (1993) says, "there is no vision without division." This approach emphasises the key role of those who do the seeing and the categorising. An example of this appears in Welbourn's (1982, 24) study of Endo ceramics and society, where the power of conceptual division is the main **male** power – but this power requires frequent repetition and re-assertion because of the instability of the conceptual division and the visible reproduction of female power on an everyday basis.

One of the most basic boundaries drawn by social groups is between themselves and the natural world. While Lubar (1993) proposes that artifacts form boundaries between humans and the natural world, mediating our sense of the environment and stabilising our place in it in a physical sense, there is also a symbolic sense in which objects can emphasize the much-discussed division between nature and culture (*e.g.* the processing of millet, as represented in Mafa pot decoration: David *et al.* 1988; Joyce 1988). In this sense, artifacts are characterised as 'simultaneously a form of natural materials whose nature we experience through practice and the form through which we continually experience the particular nature of our cultural order (Miller 1987, 105). In addition, the divisions between people within society are another field of categorisation to which object design may be expected to relate (*e.g.* Hodder 1982, 169–171). However, there is a problem with the basic duality of human sociability, captured by Csikszentmihaly and Rochberg-Halton (1981) in their observation that things can serve as both a means of individual differentiation and as a means of collective integration or indeed both: all symbols of integration can act, at another level, as signs of collective difference or opposition (1981, 33, 36). This parallels the notion that each object is simultaneously an individual item in its own right and a member of a broader category of objects to which it is related.

Another relationship between artifacts and society has been proposed by Keightley (1987) in his illuminating discussion of the varying pottery traditions current in the Neolithic of the East Coast and the North West regions of China. Keightley attempts to infer from the contrasting ceramic assemblages a sense of the differing structure and content of the cognitive activities that underlay the behaviour of China's Neolithic inhabitants (1987, 93). He identifies a correlation between enhanced differentiation and increased order between material and cognitive realms in the East Coast region and an absence of such change in the North West. Expanding on the theme that 'people who make their pots differently live differently and … vice versa' (1987, 110), Keightley contrasts the sequential piece-making construction techniques of the East Coast, based upon specialised functions, formal differentiation, and greater co-ordination and standardisation, with the holistic coil-built techniques of the NorthWest, which produced a narrower range of general-purpose forms embellished with surface decoration. Specifically, two notions are introduced which would imply the emergence of new concepts of cultural order. First, the notion that the addition of lips, spouts, handles, lids and lugs to basic ceramic forms introduces constraints on pottery use, leading to choices between appropriate and incorrect behaviour. Secondly, the idea that the production of carefully fitting lids and legs of exactly the same dimensions leads to a more mathematical view of the world, in which specifications are followed more precisely than before. Keightley's case is strengthened by his references to similar trends not only in other crafts but also in the treatment of the human body in the mortuary domain. Rita Wright makes similar comparisons between pottery and other crafts in an application of Keightley's approach to Harappan India (Wright 1993); she emphasises the transformations central to the re-structuring of materials and the juxtapositions of shapes, textures and colours in finished artifacts. In both these cases, the relations between material order and cognitive processes are emphasised rather than the links between material categories and social categories. The development of novel conceptual frameworks for living in a material world formed another part of the creation of personhood for at least some individuals – and not only potters and metallurgists – living in prehistoric China and India. The embodiment of such perspectives in object design could have led to different attitudes to a wide range of practices, including food storage and preparation, hospitality and exchange, as well as to new approaches to the size and shape of things as varied as doors and windows, furniture, storage pits, altars and pig pens. The emergence of more subtle categories and finer gradations of behaviour could also have produced people more sensitive to such aspects of categorisation and other less aware of socially nuanced practice. The perhaps small changes in bodily self-discipline and personal hexis required for these developments would have influenced the practices by which persons were created, especially for younger people learning how to behave in appropriate ways but they were equally important for the creation of the material world that framed the developing persons.

There is widespread agreement amongst social scientists that one measure of social complexity is the number of sub-groups by which a community is differentiated and which are successfully integrated into that wider social grouping (Dürkheim 1933; Blau 1977; Turner 1984). Hence to Nandris' (1972) twin processes of cultural change – diffusion and differentiation – must

be added a third – the principle of integration. The social categories by which differentiation is characterised and integration maintained are not static but, rather, in constant negotiation by a multitude of different voices. Any changes in social differentiation had important consequences for each individual, for the way in which personhood was created and for the means by which their identities were defined, negotiated and maintained.

One of the most important strategies of negotiation of identities and categories is the use of material culture – in this case pottery – to stand for the social relations of production and production itself. The establishment not only of difference (individual objects versus other objects) but also of cross-cutting systems of difference (individual things as members of different groups) can be represented in many ways, including indirectly through the use of material analogies. But, in addition to this effect, material production is reflexively related to the cognitive categories necessary for production, especially notions of symmetry, precision, standardisation and compartmentalisation. These notions are related to human categorisation processes through the notion of articulation. The integration of the parts of a complex multi-part vessel into a pleasing and efficient total design is as powerful an analogy for social articulation as it is a representation of the cognitive processes underpinning manufacture. Therefore, in this discussion, we shall advance the case that not only were the social structures of Neolithic and Copper Age communities embodied in the material categories discernible in pottery and other material forms but that the cognitive structures that co-emerged with complex artifact designs formed an important enabling framework for the construction of persons out of things. This complex relationship can be depicted as follows (Fig. 2.1).

## Analytical techniques

It would appear *a priori* that the huge range of variability found in the ceramic assemblages of the Balkan Neolithic and Copper Age would be susceptible to a categorical analysis based upon the investigation of some of the principles of material and cultural order addressed by Keightley. The consequence of the excavation of many samples comprising tons of ceramics has been a strong interest in many aspects of ceramic production, especially the study of form and decoration. However, most ceramic studies have been restricted to monothetic typologies, often limited to a consideration of either form or decoration or each separately. A good example of the analysis of the structure of a decorational system is V. Nikolov's (2002) study of the Bulgarian Early Neolithic decoration on painted vessels, while Marinescu-Bîlcu (2000) studied both the form and the decoration on the

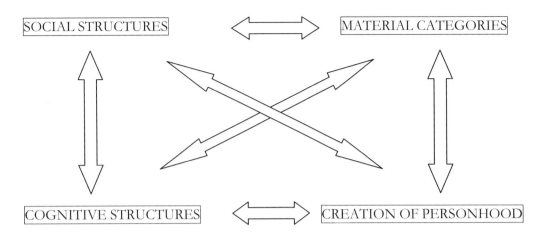

*Fig. 2.1 Relationship between personhood, cognitive structures and social structures*

Cucuteni pottery from Drăguşeni in great detail but not conjointly. Equally, few researchers have investigated the relationship between ceramics and society in the Balkan peninsula (for exceptions, see Kaiser 1990; Sherratt 1986; Perlès and Vitelli 1999). Here, we attempt a conjoint consideration of the structure of both the vessel form and its decoration in terms of the divisions, contrasts and oppositions that are inscribed on the surface of the pots.

In his discussion of pots as categories, Miller (1985, 10) makes a distinction between 'categorisation' and 'classification'. While the latter is considered as pertaining to the secondary level of evidence, for instance to a number of classes, as defined by producers, which are nonetheless derived from categories, the former concerns the order imposed on the world by the creation of cultural order, and hence is valuable in the study of social and material relations. The expectation is that the way in which artifacts are constructed will be related in some way to the perceptions of the external world in that community.

Miller (1985, 114–115, 147–149) has identified several dimensions of the Dangwara ceramic assemblage that are used to highlight contrasts useful for categorisation – colour, form and decoration. The most fundamental, and most visible, dimension is the difference in colour between black wares – sold on the market and identified with secular usage, food preparation, storage and presentation – and red wares, exchanged in a specialised system and associated with the transformation from secular to sacred. Each coloured ware has its appropriate uses in particular contexts and each colour symbolism is mediated by relations with other coloured media. Formal variability is concentrated on particular parts of the vessels – usually the neck and shoulder. Rim elaboration is used to differentiate vessels without a distinctive overall shape; the number of facets on the shoulder is used to differentiate containers, while the degree of mouth closure is related to the unity of form. Thirdly, analysis of the decorative system indicates the creation of a hierarchical gradation within and between pottery types, used by potters to mark distinctions in wealth and caste that were not necessarily exploited in everyday contexts. Such dimensions of variability enable the investigation of archaeological ceramic assemblages in order to understand the ways in which pottery aids an understanding of the world as well as a means of constituting it (Miller 1985, 205).

This approach underlies the present procedure of categorisation, which looks at a range of ways in which prehistoric potters created artifact differentiation. Given Keightley's identification of increased ceramic differentiation as a key criterion for changes in cultural order, it was important to define the widest range of those aspects of pottery in which differentiation could be identified and monitored in a series of samples that covered long-term developmental sequences. In view of the absence of large published samples of vessels with clay mineralogical identifications (cf. Jones, A. 2002), it was not possible to relate scientifically attributable variations in fabric to other dimensions based upon visual identification. Therefore, six principal dimensions of variability were considered (Chapman 2004):

– Shape categories (the major variants in shape, as defined by overall morphology; particular attention was paid to the number of vertical divisions per pot, as well as to the occurrence of vessels which were potentially manufactured in two or more parts)

– Decoration categories (single, or combinations of, decoration techniques, in relation to shape categories)

– Decorational structure (the frequency of zonally-structured decoration, whether vertical, horizontal or both)

– Zonal reinforcements (the reinforcement of shape division in one of the following ways: decorational reinforcement, matt-gloss contrast, colour contrast and decorational style contrast)
– Measures of reinforcement (the calculation of indices measuring the intensity of reinforcement of shape divisions by different kinds of zonal reinforcement)
– Decorational intensity (the variety of decorative motifs, zonal effects, and forms of zonal reinforcement)

A consideration of each dimension of variability, together with their inter-relationships, permits an assessment of the overall levels of ceramic differentiation in each sample, with the possibility of determining long-term trends and making structured comparisons with other cultural developments. Some key terms are defined at this juncture.

The categorisation of shape relies upon the definition of vertical divisions, in particular the presence of sharp divisions between vertical zones (or carinations). The presence of clearly defined necks, shoulders, carinated bellies and pedestals or feet is taken as a measure of the intensity of the division of vessel form. Formal divisions can be emphasised by techniques such as facetting (particularly common in the Varna cemetery assemblage) or by decorational means.

The definition of decorational techniques is generally unproblematic, since the main forms of operation upon the vessel surface can be clearly differentiated. Nonetheless, two kinds of surface treatment cause difficulties – burnishing and roughening. It is sometimes difficult to distinguish pattern burnish from the burnishing of a surface part of which is later modified in a contrasting way. In general, the resulting matt/gloss contrast is treated not as pattern burnish but as a distinct kind of zonal treatment. In the case of roughening, there is the problem of deciding the extent to which irregular surface roughening is extensive enough to be classed as pseudo-barbotine rather than simply surface irregularities. Pseudo-barbotine can, at least, be distinguished from true barbotine, in which an often linear motif is produced by working the still moist clay surface. The extent to which the surface is roughened is often the best way of deciding the issue. Deliberate and extensive roughening of the base of the vessel is a variant on other forms of pseudo-barbotine, used to increase the total area of the field available for decoration.

There are several ways of making a zonal structuring of pottery decoration (Fig. 2.2). Vertical zonation indicates the division of the decorative field into vertical bands of the same motif. Horizontal zonation indicates the division of the field into horizontal registers. Unreinforced zonation describes a vertical or horizontal zonation unrelated to any shape divisions, while reinforced zonation comprises decorative zones related to shape divisions. Vertical-and-horizontal zonation indicates the presence of vertical bands of different motifs or blanks areas reinforced by shape division, with at least one band divided into a minimum of two horizontally differentiated motifs. In contrast, vertical-horizontal zonation indicates the absence of shape-reinforced vertical zonation but the presence of horizontal registers within one or more vertical bands.

There are four main ways in which shape divisions can be reinforced. Decorational reinforcement has been discussed in the previous paragraph. Matt – gloss contrast indicates the juxtaposition of unburnished with burnished or, more rarely, polished surfaces. This can be combined with colour contrasts, as when white encrusted excision or incision is found alongside burnished undecorated bands, but colour contrasts are also found independently. Finally, the juxtaposition of two or more decorative techniques defines decorational style contrast. Notionally, any of these ways of shape division reinforcement can be combined with any other. However, as we shall see, there are period-specific clear choices over which method(s) of reinforcement to use, if any.

In view of the potential use of a wide range of zonal reinforcements, it was decided to attempt the calculation of a reinforcement index for each vessel profile category. Each vessel has a score based upon the number of reinforcements to the basic criterion of decorational zoning. Hence, a carinated bowl with unreinforced vertically-zoned decoration would score '0', while a dish with colour and matt/gloss contrasts and a combination of decorative techniques would score '3'. The calculation of an overall reinforcement measure for the whole assemblage is based upon the division of the sum of all vessel scores by the total number of vessels. An example of this calculation is provided in Appendix 2.

Finally, the index of decorational intensity measures the diversity of decoration on a class of vessels. For each decorated vessel, the number of vertical bands and horizontal registers are added to the techniques of zonal reinforcement to produce a vessel score; the mean of vessel scores for each shape class gives an index of decorational intensity for that class. The mean of the indices for all the shape classes at a single site produces an overall site decorational intensity index. Again, an example of this calculation is provided in Appendix 2.

It is believed that long-term variations in site ceramic assemblages will provide a valuable comparative picture of changing ceramic complexity and lead to important insights into related variations in human categorisation processes. The analysis required specific combinations of samples from two or more regions of South East Europe. A potential sample should optimally contain a large (n = minimum of 100) sample of complete vessels or

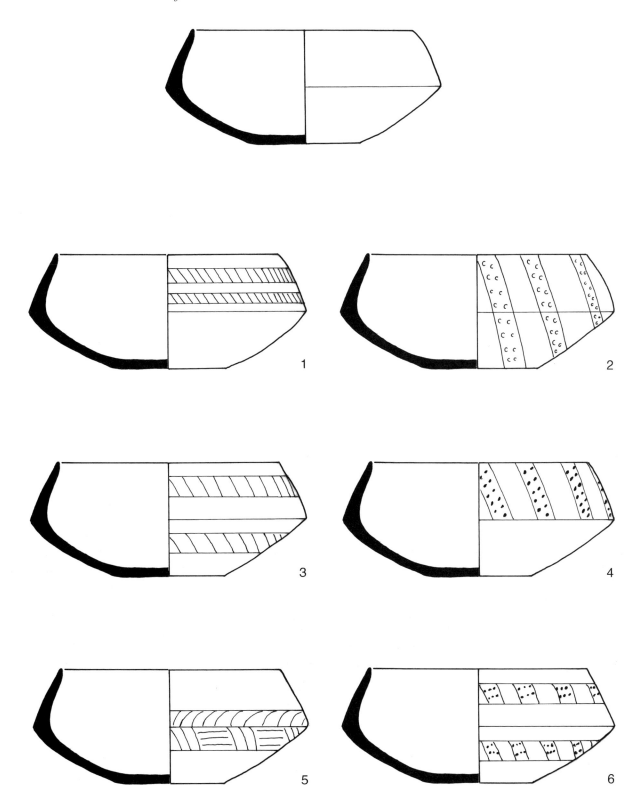

1. Vertical zonation    2. Horizontal zonation    3. Unreinforced zonation    4. Reinforced zonation
5. Vertical and horizontal zonation    6. Vertical and horizontal zonation

*Fig. 2.2 Zonal structuring of pottery decoration (drawn by Y. Beadnell)*

| SITE | PERIOD | CAL BC | REFERENCE(S) |
|---|---|---|---|
| Rakitovo | Early Neolithic | 6th millennium | Raduntcheva et al. 2002 |
| Chavdarova Cheshma | Early Neolithic | 6th millennium | unpublished |
| Nova Zagora-Hlebozavoda | Late Neolithic | start of 5th millennium | Kunchev & Kuncheva 1988 |
| Azmashka mogila | Early Chalcolithic | 4700–4500 | Georgiev 1965; |
| Varna cemetery | Late Chalcolithic | 4600–4400 | Ivanov 1988: 1991; Higham et al., submitted |
| Dolnoslav | Final Chalcolithic | end of 5th/start of 4th millennium | Raduntcheva 1996 |

*Table 2.1 Pottery assemblages investigated using categorical analysis*

restorable profiles from a single occupation horizon with contextual data. A potential study region should optimally comprise at least one satisfactory sample from each of the major chronological periods in the Neolithic and Copper Age sequence. In the first instance, Bulgaria was selected because of the reasonably large number of large samples available from tells and flat sites, as well as from the Varna cemetery. The available samples are listed below (Table 2.1).

The Early Neolithic (Karanovo I–II) samples are drawn from two differing parts of Bulgaria: Chavdarova Cheshma from the Thracian valley and Rakitovo from the lower slopes of the Rhodopes, in the South. Because of conditions of deposition in pits and unburnt houses, a very small proportion of complete vessels was found at any of these sites. Nevertheless, the sherd count represents some of the largest samples currently available for study. The Rakitovo sample was available only in the literature, while it was possible to study the painted ware component of the Chavdarova Cheshma assemblage in Sofia. All Rakitovo sherds were excavated from either house or pit contexts; in terms of Deal's typology (see below, pp. 73–75), both the pit finds and house groups derive from pre-abandonment contexts. Contextual information was not recorded for the Chavdarova Cheshma sherds. The same pattern of deposition in houses and working pits from pre-abandonment contexts was observed at Nova Zagora-Hlebozavoda; the sample studied comprised more than 90 % of the total of complete/restorable vessels in the Nova Zagora Museum.

By contrast, the Karanovo V and VI/IIIc samples from Azmashka mogila and Dolnoslav respectively comprise largely complete vessels or restorable profiles because of

the abandonment contexts of deposition in deliberately burnt houses and, in the case of Dolnoslav, also in midden deposits. The Azmashka mogila sample studied comprised cca. 50 % of the total of complete/restorable vessels in the outstation of the Stara Zagora Museum. A total of over 2,000 complete/restorable vessels was excavated from the final abandonment contexts of the Phase C of the Dolnoslav tell, predominantly from the burnt structures and the middens (for details of the site stratigraphy, see below, pp. 113–117). The 10% sample was selected in Plovdiv Museum, on the basis of recording the maximum variety of pottery forms and decorational techniques; therefore, common types are under-represented in comparison with rare amphora or storage-jar forms.

Finally, in view of the social complexity postulated on the basis of the mortuary goods at the richest cemetery yet found in Copper Age South East Europe, an analysis was made of a sample of vessels from graves of the Varna cemetery. These mortuary deposits fall outside Deal's typology but are most comparable to contexts of deliberate abandonment. A 15% sample was selected from the display and stores of the Archaeological Museum, Varna. Although the Varna assemblage is from another part of Bulgaria, it is valuable to make a comparison between a Late Copper Age mortuary group (Varna) and a somewhat later, Final Copper Age, settlement assemblage (Dolnoslav).

This study has retained the traditional phasing of the Bulgarian Neolithic (*viz.* the Karanovo I, II, III and IV phases of Georgiev (1961)), although the revisions proposed by V. Nikolov (1993) are undoubtedly more precise, if more complex to apply widely in Thrace.

## *The Early Neolithic assemblages from Chavdarova Cheshma and Rakitovo*

Because of the opportunity to study the Chavdarova Cheshma painted ware assemblage at first hand, it was decided to limit comparative analysis of the Rakitovo assemblage to the painted ware components. One common feature among the three assemblages was the absence of any painted ware sherd decorated in a second technique. Thus the decision to limit the study to the painted ware component prevented detailed consideration of decorative combinations; in any case, the site reports indicate that combinations are not a common feature of EN assemblages.

The shape repertoire at each of the three sites comprises a broadly similar number of vessel ranges – bowls, dishes, jars, amphorae and lids. With few exceptions (plates are found at Cheshma only; flasks at Rakitovo only), most ranges occur at both sites. The total number of vessel categories – the main vessel forms – is similar for each site, with an emphasis on bowl and dish categories. The vast majority of these categories emphasised rounded contours, the lack of vertical division and the potential for open, integrated fields for decoration (Fig. 2.3). Nonetheless, categories with a single break (a neck, a foot or a carination) occurred in fewer than 1 in ten cases and there is even a sprinkling of categories with two divisions. Such categories are more common at Chavdarova Cheshma than at Rakitovo and appear to have increased with time at Cheshma. Carinated forms were present at Chavdarova Cheshma but in very small numbers; the main divisions were formed by necks and feet. While necked categories are well represented at all sites, footed categories are far more prevalent at Rakitovo. Fracture patterns of footed vessels indicate manufacture in two parts, with subsequent joining of foot to vessel.

The painted decoration at these sites represents the most complex and most highly structured forms of decoration in the entire assemblages. The small size of the sherds available for study does not hide the complexity of painted decoration typifying these sites. One of the strongest trends in the organisation of painted decoration is the use of zonation, whether vertical and/or horizontal. There is considerable variety in the frequency of decorational zonation between the three sites. The percentage of vessels with decorational zonation is higher at Chavdarova Cheshma than at Rakitovo (73% cf. 65%); a similar finding pertains to the reinforcement of shape by decoration (37% cf. 14%).

The only zonational reinforcement utilised in the Early Neolithic is shape reinforcement. The decorative technique itself may be thought to obviate the need for other techniques of reinforcement, for two reasons: (a) the painting itself differentiates decoration from ground

by colour – usually white paint upon red ground; and (b) the whole surface of the fine painted wares is covered in a light burnished slip to which the paint is directly applied. Nonetheless, the exclusion of matt – gloss and additional colour contrasts are explicit choices which reinforce the distinctiveness of the painted technique.

There is considerable variation between the two sites in the frequencies of different styles of decorative zonation – both unreinforced and reinforced. With the former, vertical zonation is always the dominant category. With shape-reinforced zonation categories, vertical-and-horizontal zonation is least common at both sites, while vertical zonation is commoner than vertical-horizontal zonation at Rakitovo, with the converse at Cheshma. There is some variation in the importance of vessels with decoration on the interior as well as the exterior faces – very rare at Rakitovo (1%) and rare at Cheshma (9%).

In summary, the Early Neolithic painted wares of Chavdarova Cheshma and Rakitovo comprised a category of decorational style which was sharply differentiated from other styles on coarse and medium fine wares of a variety of darker colours and yet relatively homogenous internally. The use of a restricted number of generative principles with which to deploy a small number of key motifs produces a wide variety of decoration. Because the overall emphasis upon open forms and integrated design fields is in tension with the options of horizontal and vertical division, relatively little use is made of the reinforcement of shape zonation by decoration at Rakitovo. However, at Chavdarova Cheshma, over a third of the vessels have ornamentally-reinforced shape division. The differentiation of rounded forms favours necks over feet and both over carinations but this process is not far advanced: few vessels incorporate spouts, lugs, handles or high pedestals. Thus whereas the compartmentalisation and standardisation found by Keightley in the East Coast Chinese ceramics is poorly attested in these Early Neolithic assemblage, there is evidence for the symmetry of the painted motifs and the precision required for their execution. The painted lines were so fine (some were cca. 1mm) that the only possible paintbrushes were the bristles of *Sus scrofa*, the wild boar (p.c., A. Raduntcheva and P. Zidarov) – a neat conjunction of the wild and the domestic.

The contextual evidence from Rakitovo indicates that both painted and unpainted wares were deposited in every abandoned or destroyed household without distinction but in differing frequencies. While there was no general relationship between the frequency of painted sherds and the size of the houses, the complexity of their internal features and the diversity of their other finds, an exception was the largest house (house 9), with its range of complex internal features, a very diverse assemblage and the largest number of painted and unpainted sherds. However, a

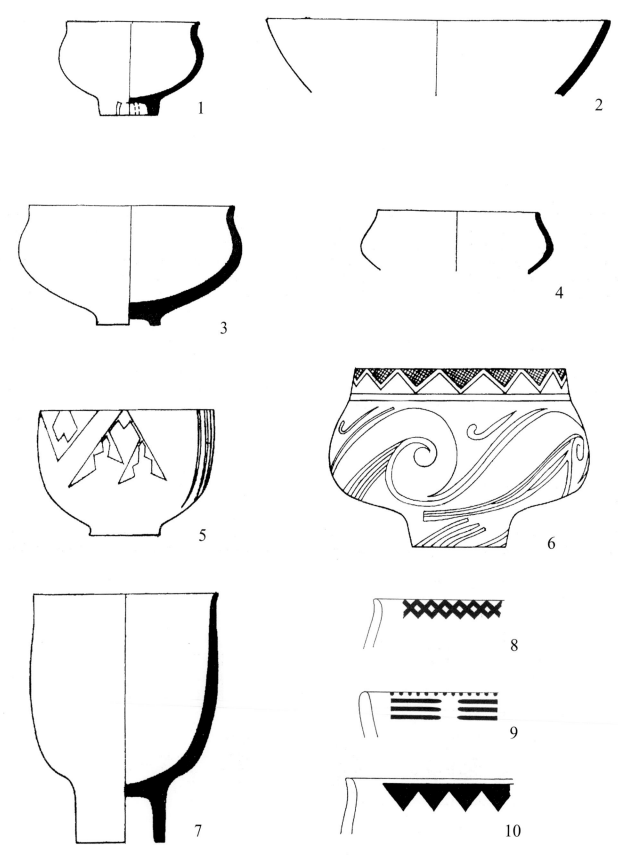

*Fig. 2.3 Common pottery forms and decoration from Rakitovo (source: Raduntcheva et al. 2002)*

comparison of decorational reinforcement by context indicates that House 9 had the highest percentage of painted wares without zonal decoration – while it was in House 1 that the highest percentage of complex (vertical + horizontal) zonation occurred (Plate 7). There was greater variation in decorational zonation between the houses than between the pit complexes (PC), where very few sherds with complex (vertical + horizontal) zonation were deposited. A calculation of the overall decorational intensity (Fig. 2.4) indicates the same level for both houses and pits and the same differentiation between bowls and dishes, with a higher value of between 4 and 5, and fruitstand forms, with a value of cca. 2.

The overall impression from these assemblages is that the potters have practised a limited range of mechanisms for the reinforcement of ceramic differentiation. The same mechanisms are available to the potters of both communities but different practices were applied at each site.

## The Late Neolithic assemblage of Nova Zagora – Hlebozavoda

The non-tell settlement of Nova Zagora – Hlebozavoda is one of the key sites for the so-called Karanovo IV, or Kalojanovec, phase of the Late Neolithic in the Thracian valley. Excavated periodically from 1968 to 1981, Hlebozavoda comprises a three-level site with a series of well-preserved houses in the later levels II and I and pits and houses in the earliest level (III). While there is overall stratigraphic continuity between the three levels at Hlebozavoda, there is no indication of the time differences between the levels. A large sample of complete or restorable vessels was recovered primarily from house

contexts although also from pits in level III. Because of the small number of vessels from level I (n = 13), the samples from levels II and I were combined, leaving two sub-samples of comparable size – Hlebozavoda III (n = 49) and II/I (n = 43).

A well-known feature of Balkan dark burnished wares is the strong emphasis upon carinated and sharply-profiled shapes. Hlebozavoda is no exception – the whole assemblage is dominated by necked and/or carinated vessels. In diffusionist arguments, this characteristic was held to indicate a 'Metallschock' – a form of ceramic skeuomorphism by which the sharp breaks in EBA metal vase profiles were imitated in Neolithic pottery (Schachermeyr 1955, cf. the Vinča-C 'Schock' of Lazarovici 1987). While the case for social, settlement and ceramic continuity between the Early and Middle Neolithic groups is now much stronger (Nikolov V. 1997; Chapman 1981), indigenists have rarely provided a satisfactory explanation for the trend towards a gradual adoption of either dark burnished surfaces or carinated profiles. The notion that the co-existence of both painted and dark burnished fine wares reflected the choice of different social groups, perhaps lineages, to use pottery to underline their corporate identities (Chapman 1981) fails to consider the structural implications of the pottery forms and decorational organisation for human categorisation processes.

Commentators have likewise overlooked the symbolic and metaphorical potential of the two most obvious characteristics of dark burnished ware assemblages all over the Balkans – namely their grey – black colour and their lustrous surface (Plate 8). The grey – black colour stands in strong contrast to the other wares, whether earth colours or light grey wares. Considerable firing skills were

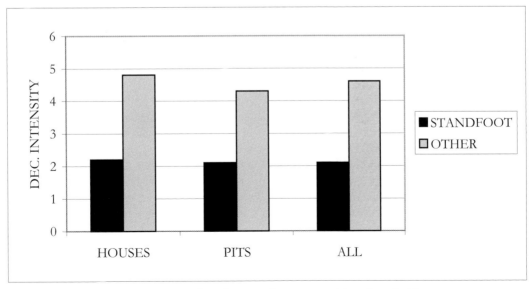

*Fig. 2.4 Decorational reinforcement by context and form from Rakitovo*

required to produce completely reducing firing conditions, which differentiated the resulting black wares from even medium and dark grey vessels. While true black burnished ware is common in metropolitan Vinča sites (Chapman 1981), it is virtually unknown from Middle and Late Neolithic Hungary, with its wide range of grey wares (*e.g.*, the Kökénydomb Late Neolithic assemblage: Archaeological Museum, Hódmezővásárhely). The most lustrous black burnished ware was produced by vitrification of the ceramic surface at temperatures of cca. 1200°C (Kaiser 1990). The aesthetic result of these two technical achievements was a startlingly attractive object that shone like an obsidian core, putting all other ceramics into the shadow. The combination of the new carinated shape with the new colour and the fabulous lustre provided a distinctive symbol of group identity and probably also ritual identity (for further discussion of lustre in shell rings, see below, Chapter 7).

The Hlebozavoda assemblages are typical of the dark burnished wares of the Balkan Late Neolithic. Their combination of forms shows a trend towards increased frequency of necks, carinations and feet from level III to levels II/I (Fig. 2.5). Fewer than a third of vessels in level III have rounded profiles, while this proportion falls to fewer than one in ten in levels II/I. However, the main component of this increase is the predominance of forms with a single break (a carination or a neck), which reaches over 80%. The proportion of vessels with two or more breaks actually declines as much as does the proportion of rounded vessels.

The changes in overall vessel form from the Early Neolithic to the Karanovo IV period masks the fact that there are only marginally more categories and sub-types at Hlebozavoda than in the Early Neolithic sites. Despite the changing emphases in carinated forms, a similar range of vessel forms is found in levels III and II/I. The overall similarities stand out more than minor variations in the frequency of sub-types – more necked carinated bowl and amphora sub-types in level III, more dish and cup sub-types in levels II/I.

The preference for dark surfaces at Hlebozavoda extends to almost all shape ranges, especially the commonest ranges of bowls and dishes. There are very few vessels or categories with a black burnished finish, and only slightly more with red or yellow surfaces. The vast majority of all categories has a brown, brown-grey, light grey or dark grey finish, usually burnished. But there is no evidence for a correlation between vessel form and surface colour in either level. The main innovation related to colour is the introduction of colour contrast as an additional form of zonal reinforcement (see below, pp. 32 and 34).

Another major change in the Karanovo IV period is the introduction of clear rules governing the choice of decorative techniques for particular vessel ranges. In level III, the principle of the decoration of bowls, amphorae and lids by channelling is strongly but not exclusively maintained (16/20 cases), while all decorated dishes, jars and cups are ornamented with incised, excised or impressed + relief styles (10/10 cases).

These specific and relatively rigid rules of linking decoration to shape are relaxed considerably in levels II/ I, when the variety of decorative techniques remains almost the same but their application to different vessel forms becomes much more varied. The range of dishes displays the closest adherence to the principles of level III: all examples but one employ incised or incised +excised decoration. By contrast, incised decoration becomes less common on cups, storage-jars, lids and pedestals. The level III rule of channelling on bowls breaks down, with more non-channelled than channelled decoration present, including the first example of the graphite painted decorative technique. The decline in the consistency with which this principle is applied in levels II/I should not obscure the fact that the differentiation of decorative technique by vessel form was formulated much more clearly than in the Early Neolithic painted ware assemblages, in which, with the exception of the largest storage vessels, painted decoration could be applied to almost all of the vessel shape ranges in use.

The contrast in decorative techniques and vessel forms can be made more specific in relation to the location of decorative fields (Fig. 2.5). As the excavators recognise, there are two main types of vessel form – relatively closed forms of bowl (to which may be added jars, beakers and amphorae) and relatively open forms of dish (to which may be added cups) (Kunchev and Kuncheva 1988, 82). The distinction between open and closed forms structures the location of the decorative field on the exterior or interior surfaces or both. This contrast becomes increasingly important at Hlebozavoda, where there are far more vessels with decoration on both surfaces than in the Early Neolithic sites. Almost two-thirds of decorated vessels in levels II/I have exterior/interior decoration, compared with one in five vessels in level III. This change marks the beginning of a trend towards the appreciation that it is possible to use the whole surface of the pot for decoration.

In level III, there is a categorical opposition between dishes and cups which can have decoration on the interior and/or the exterior surface and bowls, beakers, lids and amphorae, which are decorated on the exterior surface only (Plate 9). This same principle continues for dishes and cups in levels II/I but it begins to break down for bowls and lids which begin to carry decoration on the interior as well as the exterior (Plate 9). It is interesting to note that, as with principles governing decorative techniques and vessel forms, so the rules governing

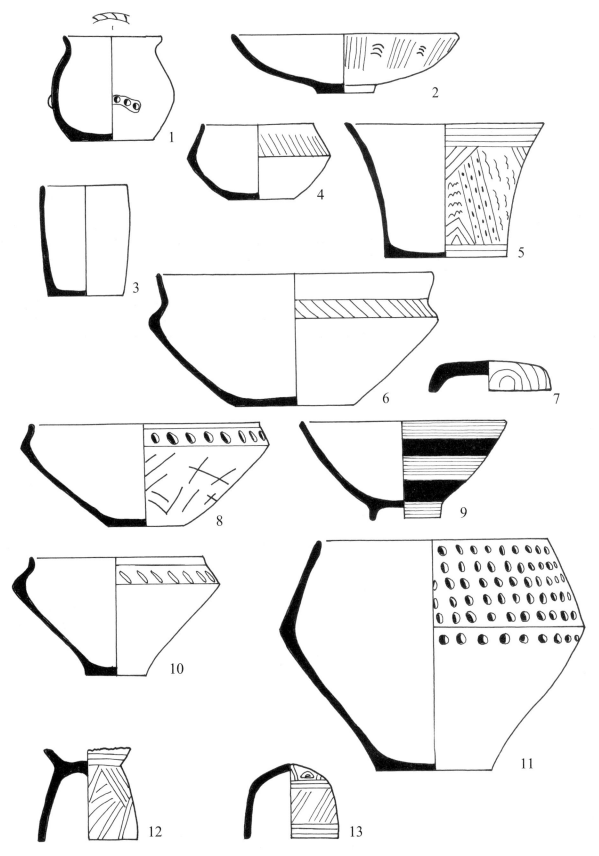

*Fig. 2.5 Common pottery forms and decoration from Hlebozavoda (source: Kunchev and Kuncheva 1988)*

location of decorative field are clearly defined and consistently expressed in level III but the rigour of their application declines in levels II/I.

In strong contrast to the Early Neolithic pottery groups, the Hlebozavoda assemblage makes use of all four types of decorative reinforcement known in the Bulgarian sequence – shape division, combination of decorative techniques, colour contrast and matt/gloss contrast. In level III, 92% of all decorated pots have zonal decoration, all with their decorational divisions reinforced in one or more ways. The figure rises to 100% in levels II/I. In level III, over a third of all decorated pots have their zonal decoration reinforced in more than one way; this figure rises to one-half in levels II/I.

By far the most important mutual reinforcement in both levels is that between shape divisions and zonal decoration. More than two-thirds of vessels with shape divisions have those divisions reinforced by decoration (Figs. 2.6–2.7). Another way of looking at this mutual reinforcement is to state that over 80% of all surfaces with zonal decoration have their zones reinforced by shape divisions. In either case, this is far higher than in the most developed instance of shape-decoration reinforcement in the Early Neolithic sites (Chavdarova Cheshma). By contrast, fewer than one in five vessels with rounded profiles have any zonal decoration that could reinforce the constituent parts of those profiles (*e.g.*, the neck zone

which is not separated from the shoulder by a sharp division). This suggests that there is a growing tendency to emphasize the differentiation of vessels with shape divisions from those with rounded profiles through the use of decorative zonation.

Another principle of decorative structure concerns the preferred types of decorative zonation by vessel shape range. The most clearly applied principle concerns level III bowls, beakers, lids and amphorae (closed forms), whose external decoration is organised almost entirely through vertical zonation (Fig. 2.8). In levels II/I, the principle is less consistently applied, with a combination of vertical + horizontal zonation as well as decoration on interior surfaces (Fig. 2.9). The principle of preferred zonation is less clear in the case of dishes and cups, where a combination of vertical +horizontal zonation is predominant in both periods.

The use of colour contrast on domestic vessels is adopted from the so-called 'altar-lamps', where such decoration was characteristic from the Early Neolithic onwards. Two forms of contrast are used: (a) the white encrustation of incised and/or excised lines against a dark surface background; and (b) the juxtaposition of dark burnished bands with zones of white encrusted excised and/or incised decoration (Plate 10). The latter is much less common than the former and relies on the combination of colour and matt/gloss contrasts. There is

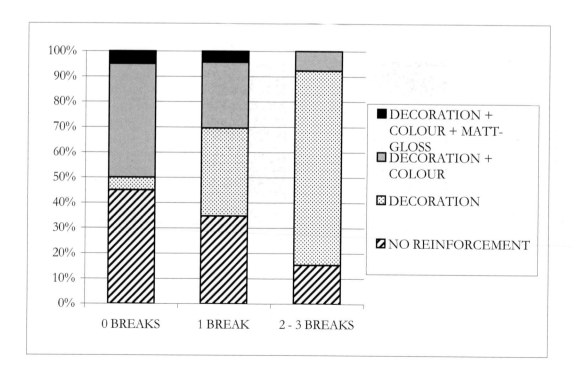

*Fig. 2.6 Type of reinforcement by shape differentiation from Hlebozavoda II*

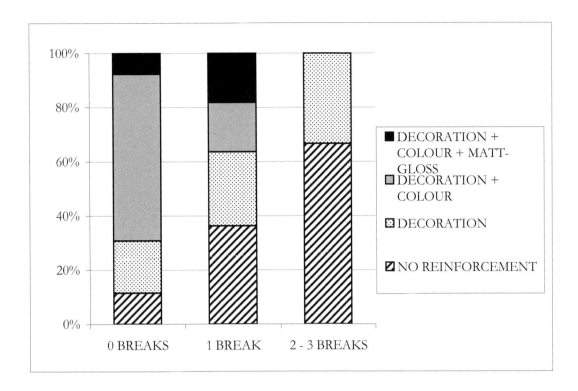

*Fig. 2.7 Type of reinforcement by shape differentiation from Hlebozavoda II–I*

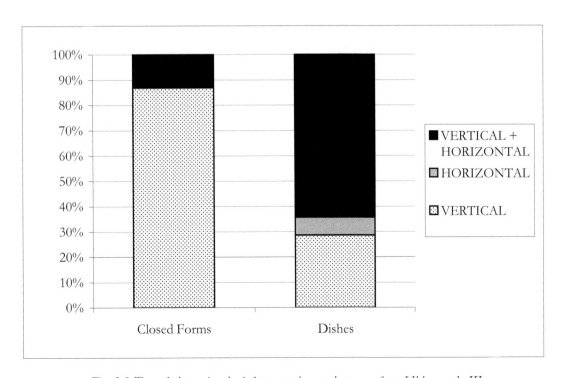

*Fig. 2.8 Type of decorational reinforcement by vessel category from Hlebozavoda III*

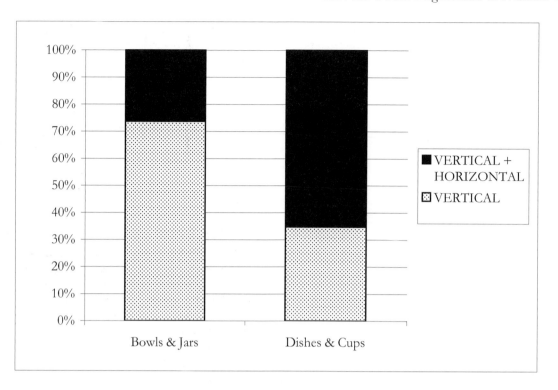

*Fig. 2.9 Type of decorational reinforcement by vessel category from Hlebozavoda II–I*

a change from the preference for colour contrasts on vessels with rounded profiles in level III to a far more widespread use (increasing by more than 60%) of colour contrast on vessels with shape divisions in levels II/I. The white / dark colour contrast is governed by two decorative principles – one for bowls, amphorae and lids, and another for dishes and cups. There is a general exclusion of colour contrast from bowls etc. in level III (19/22 cases: exceptions – one carinated bowl, one beaker and one lid). This principle weakens in levels II/I, with one-third of bowls, jars and lids using white encrusted decoration. By contrast, all the decorated dishes and cups in both levels exhibit colour contrast because of the incised and/or excised decoration both internally and externally.

There is a strong contrast between vessels with fine burnished surfaces and coarse ware vessels with unburnished surfaces at the level of individual pots. However, minimal use is made of matt/gloss contrasts within the same vessel at Hlebozavoda. Only one instance is known from each level: in both cases, a carinated bowl with burnishing above the carination and coarse surface texture, but without roughening, below the carination.

The juxtaposition of different decorative techniques on the same vessel surface (rather than on the interior vs. the exterior of the vessel) is moderately frequent in each

level of the site. Six distinct decorative techniques are known at Hlebozavoda. Of these, barbotine and graphite painting are not combined with other techniques; impression is known on its own and in combination with a seventh technique (relief), itself not known on its own; and incision, excision and channelling are combined to produce five further combination techniques. A broadly similar range of techniques is known from each level, with similar frequencies of combination techniques in comparison with single techniques. A comparison of the way in which decorative combinations are in turn combined with colour contrasts, matt/gloss contrasts and shape reinforcement indicates no significant difference from sherds decorated with a single technique.

The changes in the reinforcement indices for phases III and II/I reflect the shift from a single means of shape reinforcement predominant in phase III to the more frequent use of two means in II/I. It is striking that no vessels utilise the maximum of four contrastive techniques, while only one vessel in Phase II/I uses even three techniques. While Phase III has a reinforcement measure of 1.1, the measure for phase II/I rises to 1.5.

Finally, measures of decorational intensity were calculated for both levels at Hlebozavoda, using a points scoring system for each different decorational zone, whether vertical or horizontal, and with the addition of points for each different kind of zonational reinforcement (for an example of the calculation of this measure, see Appendix 2). The shape ranges were amalgamated to form groups of more open and more closed vessel forms for each level. The results are as follows:

| | LEVEL III | LEVEL II/I |
|---|---|---|
| BOWLS | 3.3 | 4.7 |
| DISHES | 8.3 | 11.6 |

Hence, two conclusions may be drawn: (a) decorational intensity is far greater in dishes than in bowls; and (b) the decorational intensity increases for both groups from level III to levels II/I. The higher measure for dishes is related to the propensity for interior as well as exterior decoration.

In summary, the Karanovo IV assemblage from Hlebozavoda comprises a much more differentiated series of whole or restorable vessels than was found in the Karanovo I–II sites. In almost every aspect of ceramic production, the Hlebozavoda assemblage displays a wider range of contrasts than is found earlier. All four of Keightley's principles can be found in abundance at Hlebozavoda. Precision and symmetry were evident in the interior and exterior decoration, as was the standardisation of several vessel shapes, especially open dishes. Compartmentalisation is attested in perhaps the most significant development – the strong emphasis on the vertical division of most vessels into separate zones – the neck, the shoulder, the belly and the foot. Whatever the specific explanation for the rise of vertically-divided vessels, such division makes a statement about the treatment of space on pottery: there exists the possibility that differentiation can be contained within an integrated vessel form. Such a principle is clearly applicable to social relations in general. The notion that the increasing differentiation of social groups may be portrayed metaphorically through ceramic differentiation is based upon the importance of categorisation of groups in society and the way in which artifacts are used in human categorisation processes. If one of the principal social contradictions in an increasingly differentiated society is the integration of these disparate and cross-cutting limited interest groups (to use Tim Taylor's useful term: Chapman and Dolukhanov 1993, 23), the problem has a ready formulation in the field of ceramic shape and decoration.

There are two aspects of the Hlebozavoda assemblage in which increased differentiation is not visible: shape variation at both the category and sub-type levels, and the potential reinforcement of shape variations through surface firing colour. In addition, differentiation through matt/gloss contrasts is still in its infancy and combinations in decorative techniques are also limited. These constraints on increasing diversification based upon vessel division, decorational zonation and zonal reinforcement limit the overall complexity of the assemblage.

Far from being a homogenous assemblage, the two ceramic groups from level III and levels II/I indicate considerable changes in the development of categories. In level III, there are several clearly defined principles governing the relationship of decorational technique to shape, the location of decoration and the relationship between decorational location and shape. While each principle emphasises exclusive contrasts, these principles lose clarity and focus in levels II/I, where overlapping sets become much more common. This trend is paralleled by the decline in 2-break profiles, indicating the loss of the clearest oppositional forms at the same time as the weakening of decorational exclusions. The changes in levels II/I also betoken increased decorational intensity, often achieved through greater reliance on colour contrasts, as well as single-division profiles that are always reinforced by another device. Such a congeries may be taken to indicate the difficulty with which oppositional structures are maintained in the face of increasing social diversification.

## The Karanovo V assemblage at Azmashka mogila

The rescue excavation of the whole of Azmashka mogila was completed over 4 years in 1960–1963. Partial and outline publication of the results provides us with the minimum information on the stratigraphic sequence. The main phases of occupation on the tell were a sequence of 3m of Karanovo I–II sediments and 4.5m of Copper Age sediments. The Karanovo V (or Maritsa) occupation is dated to the Early Copper Age in southern Bulgaria. Each of the major phases has produced a vast quantity of pottery, including several hundred complete and/or restorable vessels. The Karanovo V assemblage was selected for detailed analysis, since it is one of the largest Maritsa group samples in the Thracian valley. The majority of vessels (n = 97) came from burnt houses and pit fill. The vessels are treated as a single sample for the purposes of this analysis.

The major trend in the Azmashka mogila series is the differentiation of vessel forms (Fig. 2.10). In a larger sample than was available at Hlebozavoda, the Azmak pottery is divided into 18 categories (cf. 9 at Hlebozavoda II/I) and as many as 65 sub-types (cf. 26 at Hlebozavoda II/I or 40 sub-types in the whole of the Hlebozavoda sample). This diversification is found in all of the main ranges of pottery – bowls, dishes and plates, lids and other forms. The large number of new sub-types of lids is especially significant for an inference of behavioural

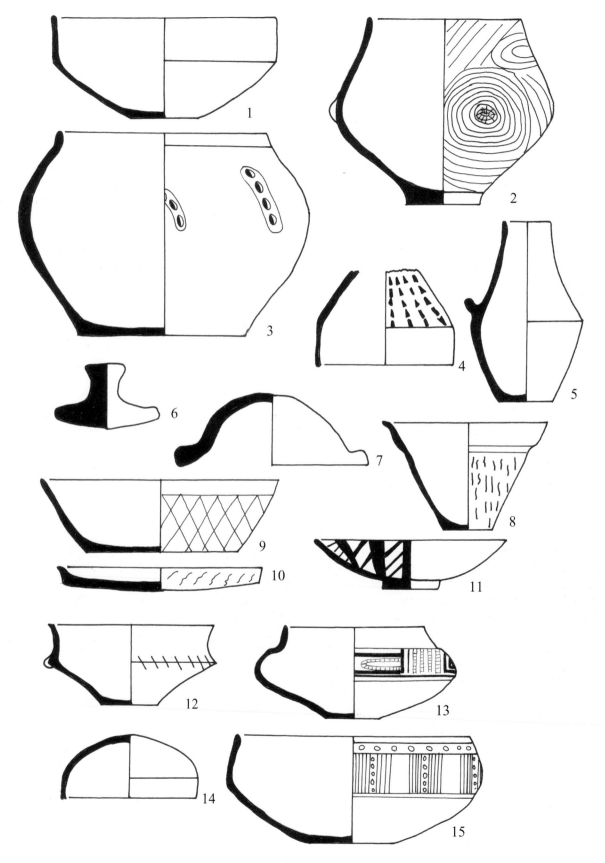

*Fig. 2.10 Common pottery forms and decoration from Azmak (drawn by Y. Beadnell)*

changes; Keightley (1987, 110) stresses that well-fitting lids imply not only careful storage and cleanliness but also an attention to precise specifications for both pot and lid. But the differentiation of all other shape ranges has important implications for functional specialisation and the related process of the increasingly subtle categorisation of activities and people. It is plausible that the two activities enhanced by the widening range of vessel shapes are secure storage and hospitality.

The opposite trend to the differentiation of vessel shape is found in the decline in shape divisions in comparison with the Hlebozavoda II/I sample, from nine out of ten to just over half (Fig. 2.11). This represents not only a major decrease in one-break profiles but also a relative decline in 2- and 3-break profiles. This would appear to be a major reversal of the trends in ceramic differentiation found in the Late Neolithic and requires an explanation. There would appear to be at least three possible reasons for this change: (a) an emphasis on a broader, less divided field provides the possibility for more representation of the totalities which are depicted in ceramic decoration; (b) more specifically, broad decorational fields provide greater scope for the main new decorative technique – graphite painting; and (c) the switching to representations of divisions by other means, such as colour or matt/gloss contrasts or contrasting decorative combinations. Such a major change is expected to affect all areas of ceramic production.

A third major development at Azmak is the extension of the potential field of surface treatment to the whole vessel. With rare exceptions, the interior, rim and the exterior of the vessel have constituted the field for surface treatment ever since the earliest use of pottery in the Early Neolithic. In the Maritsa phase, however, the field is regularly extended into two new vessel parts – well-fitting lids and the base of the pot. Akin to the contrast between an opposed stage/auditorium and theatre-in-the-round, these two extensions convert the potential decorative field into an all-over, multi-dimensional field-in-the-round. This shift heightens the sense that the unit of representation – the field of categorisation – is now the whole vessel. The increase in the significance of lids relates not only to questions of co-ordination in manufacture but also provides potential for new oppositions and symmetries: principally inside – outside, upper – lower and a combination of the two contrasts. The inclusion of pot bases into the total field enables two types of contrasts: contrasts between the base and the vessel wall, and contrasts between the base/lower wall and upper vessel wall. Surface treatment of the base often involves extreme surface roughening (*i.e.* a sub-type of the barbotine technique) which is different from the functional roughening of the base or the creation of textile impressions for added grip. In each case, the potential for

differentiation is increased at the same time as the representation of integration is emphasised.

Consideration of the firing colour of Azmak vessels indicates a more structured approach than at Hlebozavoda. The main addition to the range of surface colours at Azmak is the silver on light effect of graphite painting. The only vessel range for which lighter colours (yellow, red, or red-brown) are preferred is the lid. Dark colours, burnished or not, (brown-grey, grey, or grey-black) are strongly favoured for the bowl range, while graphitic silver on light colours are as common as dark colours for the dish, amphora and plate ranges. Bowls and plates with fully black surface colour are as rare at Azmak as in the Karanovo IV phase. There are no categorical oppositions at Azmak in the field of firing colours – rather preferences linked with other vessel characteristics.

It is well-known that the major change in decorative techniques in the Maritsa phase is the introduction on a far wider scale than before of graphite painting for both interior and exterior decoration (Leshtakov 2004; Kalchev 2004). Technological studies of graphite painting emphasise the careful surface preparation and the precise firing conditions and temperature required to produce the required finish – whether negative or positive motifs (Kingery and Frierman 1974). It has already been proposed that the introduction of graphite painting may have contributed to the choice of a wider range of rounded profiles in the Maritsa phase. What other decorative techniques were used to complement graphite painting?

Many of the non-graphite decorative techniques at Azmak were also found in the Karanovo IV assemblage at Hlebozavoda. Indeed, 7/11 types of technique at Hlebozavoda are still in use at Azmak, including four combination techniques. Hence the Azmak assemblage is characterised by a far greater differentiation of vessel shapes than of decorative techniques. The 16 decorative techniques at Azmak include 11 mixed techniques, a far higher proportion than at Hlebozavoda (5 out of 11); moreover, a higher proportion of vessels uses mixed decorative techniques at Azmak than at Hlebozavoda (one in four, compared to one in six). This, then, is an important development in zonal reinforcement which appears to replace the rules governing the relations between decorative technique and form found at Hlebozavoda.

We have seen how the principle of specific decorative techniques applied to particular vessel forms weakened from level III to levels II/I at Hlebozavoda; at Azmak, the trend continues, so that all major shape ranges are decorated with both graphite painting and non-graphite techniques (Fig. 2.12). The combination of non-graphite techniques found only on bowls at Hlebozavoda is now common on all vessel ranges at Azmak. However, there are clear principles that distinguish graphite painting from

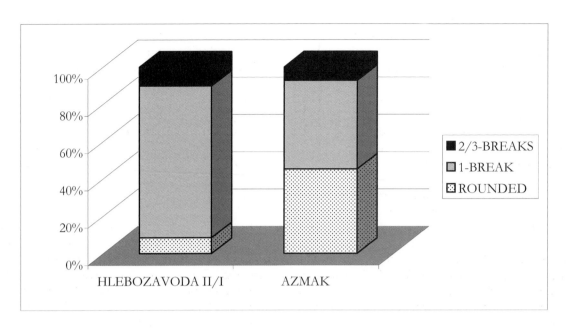

*Fig. 2.11 Profile differentiation by site*

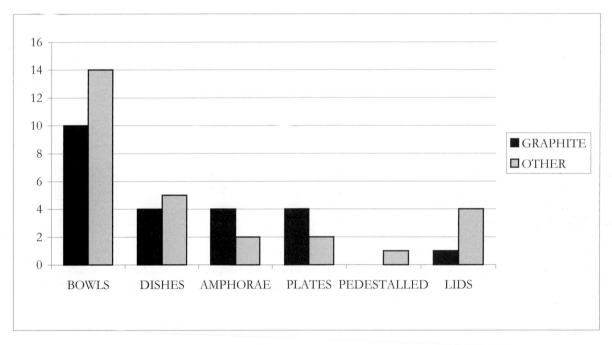

*Fig. 2.12 Decorational style by shape range from Azmak*

other techniques. The main rule is that, with few exceptions, graphite painting is not mixed with any other decorative technique on any vessel form. By contrast, the majority of non-graphite techniques are combinations used on a minority of surfaces. The other rule is that graphite painting can be applied to the interior as well as

the exterior of the vessel, whereas non-graphite techniques, with very few exceptions, avoid vessel interiors. Almost half of the vessels decorated with graphite have interior as well as exterior painting. However, despite the potential for interior decoration introduced by graphite painting, there is an abrupt fall in the proportion of vessels with interior decoration in comparison with the Hlebozavoda II/I group.

The categorical opposition between interior and exterior decoration on shape ranges of bowls and dishes, so important in the early level at Hlebozavoda, breaks down still further in the Azmak assemblage. Now, bowls can be decorated on the interior only, as well as on both interior and exterior; amphorae can have interior as well as exterior decoration; and dishes can have exterior only decoration as well as a combination of exterior and interior. At Azmak, there is a tendency for exterior decoration to be more common than interior on the ranges of bowls, dishes and amphorae. The only categorical oppositions that remain relate to the location of exterior decoration on lids and pedestals and the combination of exterior and interior decoration on plates.

The decline in vessel division at Azmak diminishes the contrast found at Hlebozavoda between vessels whose shape divisions are further reinforced, generally with decoration, and vessels without shape division and no reinforcement. At Azmak, there are fewer vessels with reinforced shape divisions than before but reinforcement occurs on the same proportion of vessels, whether with breaks or with rounded profiles (Plate 11). Moreover, there are minimal differences in means of reinforcement for the different profiles.

These variations point to an interesting development at Azmak – the re-emergence of the category of un-reinforced zonal decoration, a category which had virtually disappeared at Hlebozavoda; it is found on some 15% of all decorated surfaces (*e.g.* Fig. 2.10/9). This development is partly related to the frequency of graphite painting, with its penchant for broad, undivided fields; but fewer than half the instances involve graphite –painting. Unreinforced decoration also occurs in a variety of non-graphite techniques and, interestingly, on vessels with shape division more than on vessels with rounded profiles. Nonetheless, even with the re-emergence of this unreinforced category, zonal decoration is reinforced in some way or other on over 80% of decorated vessels.

The chief means of reinforcing zonal decoration remains shape reinforcement, although this proportion has declined a little in comparison with the Hlebozavoda group. In all categories of vessel profile, reinforced vertical zonation is the commonest type, with vertical-and-horizontal zonation declining in comparison with the earlier period.

The overall frequency of colour and matt/gloss contrasts shows a slight decline at Azmak in relation to the Hlebozavoda group. The decline in the use of colour contrasts is offset by the main development in zonal reinforcement – the sharp increase in the frequency of matt/gloss contrasts, on up to one-third of all decorated surfaces. Never used on its own at Hlebozavoda, matt/

gloss contrasts are found more on their own than in combination with other types of reinforcement at Azmak. Their distribution ranges across all types of vessel profile, with slightly more examples in rounded profiles than those with vertical divisions.

A comparison of how single and combination decorative techniques are related to other forms of zone reinforcement indicates that combination techniques are more likely to be found with vessels with other forms of reinforcement (colour, matt/gloss or shape) than are single decorative techniques (Fig. 2.13). In general, combination techniques are more important for reinforcing zonal contrasts at Azmak than at Hlebozavoda.

The results of the reinforcement index calculations indicate the prevalence of vessels with scores of 2 or 3, with very few pots with the maximum (*i.e.* 4) range of contrasts. Vessels with shape divisions scored '2' more often than vessels with rounded profiles, which tended to score the higher '3' more often. The overall Azmak reinforcement measure comes to 1.9, indicating the continuation of a trend to increased values from Hlebozavoda III (1.1) to II/I (1.5).

Finally, the measurement of decorational intensity is based on the same criteria as for Hlebozavoda. The decline in categorical oppositions based on the relationship between decorative techniques and location of decoration by vessel shape leads to a blurring of the contrast between decorational intensity on different shape ranges. The results are as follows:

CLOSED FORMS
(bowls, amphorae, lids, pedestals)                5

OPEN FORMS
(dishes and plates)                                        6.5

These results indicate that the peak in intensity for open forms was reached at Hlebozavoda levels II/I and they are now declining at Azmak, partly related to the decreased importance of interior decoration. By contrast, the intensity of decoration on more closed forms continues to increase.

In summary, two contradictory patterns can be identified in the Azmak pottery sample. On the one hand, the adoption of the whole pot as the potential decorative field, the significance of graphite painting in broad decorative fields and the decline in shape division, shape-reinforced zonal decoration and colour contrasts indicates a trend towards integration of decorative principles – in effect a denial of division. On the other hand, the major increase in vessel differentiation in both form and decorative techniques, together with increases in matt/gloss and combination decoration contrasts, underlines the diversity of ceramic categories and the divisions

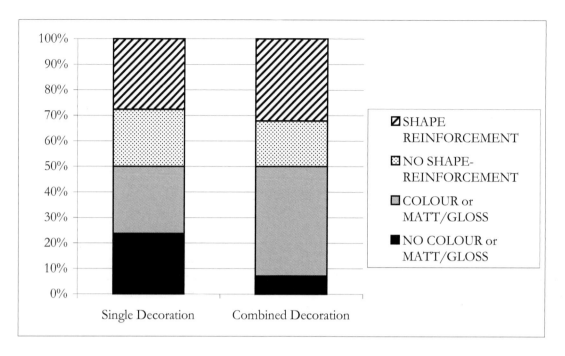

*2.13 Types of reinforcement by decorational style from Azmak.*

necessary to represent such diversity. There is little sign here of standardisation, although the symmetry and precision of decorative motifs is widespread. Even vessels with a rounded profile exhibit other types of contrast, which may well indicate the cross-cutting nature of social ties in long-term tell settlements. The widespread adoption of graphite painting itself stresses the same contradictory principles: the denial of difference leads to the decoration of the same shape ranges with both graphite painting and non-graphite decorative techniques. By contrast, a categorical opposition is largely if not totally maintained between graphite painting unmixed with other techniques and for use on both interiors and exteriors and the often mixed non-graphite techniques which typically decorate exterior surfaces only. The principles governing decorational organisation and shape differentiation are thus balanced between sub-division and integration; an increasing range of categories is linked by a more extensive set of principles of reinforcement. If the ceramic categorisation is directly related to processes of social categorisation, the message would be that the identity of the individual relative to an increasing range of social groups is being defined in ever more complex ways, some tending more to hierarchy, others to complementary, cross-cutting membership. The emphasis on integration, or its obverse, the denial of difference, is analogous to support for the importance of corporate bodies, perhaps lineages, over individual members. On the other hand, the differences between the Hlebozavoda

and Azmak assemblages introduce the likelihood that one of the mechanisms at work in producing ceramic change is the deliberate emphasis on difference – difference from the past structures embodied in the Hlebozavoda ceramics, while maintaining certain elements of continuity with the ceramic traditions of a recent past.

### The Karanovo VI/IIIc assemblage from the Dolnoslav tell

The Final Karanovo VI phase (now termed phase IIIc) is considered to represent the latest phase of the Late Copper Age (Petrova 2004), postdating by several centuries the Varna cemetery. Studies of Karanovo VI pottery indicate considerable morphological diversity allied to great decorational diversity (Todorova 1978; Le Premier Or 1989, 172–3). A large sample of complete and/or restorable vessels was thus required to capture as full a picture of this variability as was possible from a single site. The sample of 184 whole or restored vessels derives from the total excavation of the Karanovo VI occupation of the tell near Dolnoslav, in the Thracian valley (Raduntcheva 1996).

The trend towards increasing differentiation of vessel form found at Hlebozavoda and Azmashka mogila accelerates at Dolnoslav. Although a sample size approximately double that of Azmak undoubtedly contributed to this change, this trend remains the defining characteristic of the Dolnoslav assemblage. There is a dramatic increase in both shape categories and sub-types at Dolnoslav when compared to Azmak: 28 categories compared to 18 and 104 sub-types compared to 65 (Fig. 2.14). Substantial increases are found in most shape ranges, especially bowls (from 25 up to 50) and amphorae (from 6 up to 14). But there is a decrease in sub-types in two shape ranges – dishes / plates (from 14 to 8) and lids (from 15 to 11). This major change concerns both the functional differentiation of activities related to the new forms of pottery as much as the new systems of social categorisation which find their analogies in ceramic differentiation. One way of re-inforcing cross-cutting identities of individuals and limited interest groups is through the differentiation of activities whose performance is dialectically related to the emergence of those identities.

The second major trend in vessel shape at Dolnoslav is the substantial increase in the proportion of vessels with shape division when compared to Azmak. This change is focussed on vessels with 2- or 3-breaks, which increase fivefold at the expense of vessels with rounded profiles, rather than the 1-break vessels. This change means that there is a strong likelihood of increases in shape-reinforced decoration or other contrasts. Although the variety of lids found at Azmak declines in Dolnoslav, as does the frequency of the decorative treatment of pot bases, the total vessel nonetheless remains as the potential decorative field at Dolnoslav.

The range of decorative techniques at Dolnoslav mirrors that found at Azmak; there is evidence for strong continuity at the level of individual techniques between the two phases/sites. Eleven individual techniques are known at Dolnoslav, seven of which were common to both sites (Fig. 2.14). Of the shared techniques, three are found on the same shape ranges and a further two on closely related shape ranges. The three techniques no longer found at Dolnoslav comprise grooving, excision and barbed-wire impression. The new techniques found at Dolnoslav comprise barbotine, comb-impression, pattern burnishing and a non-graphitic form of black painting. Despite the similarity in the range of techniques at Azmak and Dolnoslav, the main difference is that the far wider range of combinations used at Dolnoslav. This leads to the recognition of 36 decorative techniques, which includes 25 categories of combined technique (Fig. 2.15). The Dolnoslav vessels include, for the first time in the Bulgarian prehistoric sequence, combinations of three spatially distinct decorative techniques (*i.e.*, graphite + impressed + channelling but **not** excised + white encrustation and another style). The proportion of vessels with combinations of decorative techniques rises at Dolnoslav. The extent of decorative combination varies by vessel shape range: single decorative techniques are predominant with dishes, amphorae and Other ranges,

while a two-combination decorative category is most frequent with the bowl range, which is also decorated most commonly with different 3-combination categories. All told, this development is responsible for as much of the total variability of the Dolnoslav sample as is the differentiation in vessel form. It makes decorative contrasts one of the most important types of zonal reinforcement.

Although regarded as one of the chief 'type-fossils' of the Karanovo VI phase (Georgiev 1961), graphite painting was by no means as common at Dolnoslav as at Azmak, where it accounted for half of all decorated surfaces. At Dolnoslav, graphite painting is just one of many decorative techniques, albeit with a wider range of motifs than most other techniques. The Azmak principle that graphite painting was not combined with any other technique is completely reversed at Dolnoslav, except for most of the few remaining dishes (Fig. 2.15). In the amphorae and Other ranges, single graphite painting is less common than combinations of graphite and other techniques, which are themselves far less common than combinations of non-graphite decoration. In the bowl range, half of the sides decorated by a single technique use graphite painting, with combined graphite painting also common. As at Azmak, all the Dolnoslav shape ranges are decorated with non-graphite decoration as well as with graphite painting. However, the importance of combined decorative techniques is far greater at Dolnoslav than at Azmak.

The decline in the use of open forms (dishes and plates) at Dolnoslav is, for the most part, responsible for the continued decline of combined interior-and-exterior decoration. This combined decorative location occurs in one in three vessels at Azmak but this had fallen to one in ten at Dolnoslav. Despite the rejection of this decorative option, the main decorative principle at Dolnoslav is the principle of maximum variability through re-combination. Combined decorative techniques are most common on bowls, with similar proportions on all other vessel ranges. (Fig. 2.16).

The reinforcement of shape divisions occurs far more often at Dolnoslav than at Azmak. Apart from vessels with rounded profiles, where over half were undecorated and a further quarter possessed unreinforced zonal decoration, a high proportion of vessels with shape divisions was reinforced by other means. There was a strong tendency to reinforce two-break vessels with two other contrasts, with the same less common for one-break vessels. The preferred zonal decoration in all profile types at Dolnoslav is vertically-zoned decoration, with vertical-and-horizontal decorational zoning also common. But there were more zonally-reinforced vessels with rounded profiles at Azmak than at Dolnoslav – the only shape cluster where this is true. Similarly, un-reinforced

*Fig. 2.14 Common pottery forms and decoration from Dolnoslav (drawn by Y. Beadnell)*

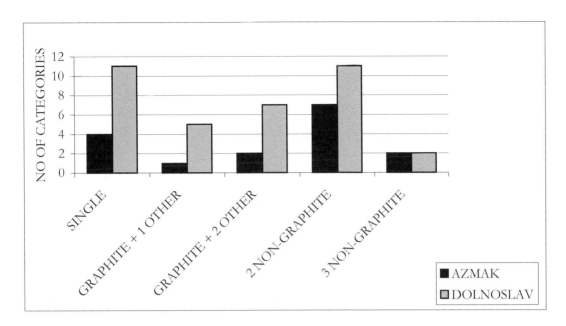

*Fig. 2.15 Decorational categories from Azmak and Dolnoslav*

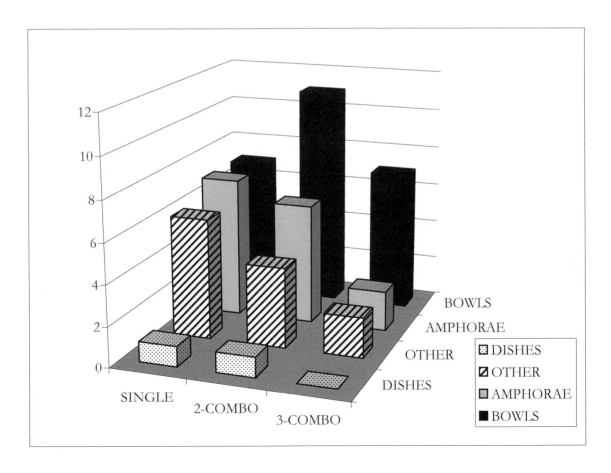

*Fig. 2.16 Decorational categories vs. shape ranges from Dolnoslav*

zonation, which enjoyed a resurgence at Azmak, is in decline at Dolnoslav. In general, this means that the vast majority of vessels with zonal decoration was reinforced by shape division and almost all vessels were reinforced by combinations of shape, colour and/or matt/gloss contrasts – higher than at Azmak and almost as high as in Hlebozavoda III and II/I.

An important characteristic of the Dolnoslav assemblage is the wide range of options for the reinforcement of zonation. Not only are the traditional four methods available – shape, colour, matt/gloss contrasts and decorative contrasts – but combinations of these means were more frequent (Fig. 2.17). If there is a hypothetical total of 15 ways in which the basic vertical and/or horizontal decorational zonation can be emphasised, 10 of them were in use at Dolnoslav. This means that a far more varied range of reinforcement options was in use at Dolnoslav compared to Azmak, especially on vessels with 2- and 3-break profiles.

There is a small increase in the frequency of colour and matt/gloss contrasts at Dolnoslav. As with decorative contrasts, the 2-break vessels are twice as likely to have colour and matt/gloss reinforcement as are 1-break vessels and vessels with rounded profiles. This finding underlines the importance of repeated zonal reinforcement at Dolnoslav. This is partly explained by the major increase in matt/gloss contrasts at Dolnoslav, where there is twice the likelihood that matt/gloss contrasts will be found as a single reinforcement than combined with colour contrasts. Single colour contrasts are more frequent

on rounded profiles than on 1-break profiles, but most common on 2-break vessels.

There is a strong tendency for decorative contrasts to reinforce both colour and matt/gloss contrasts as well as shape division – much more commonly than at Azmak. At Dolnoslav, there is not a single example of a vessel decorated with a combination of techniques that does not have reinforcement by shape division!

It is therefore hardly surprising that the reinforcement index for Dolnoslav is higher for vessels with shape division than at Azmak. Broadly speaking, higher proportions of Dolnoslav vessels with two or three shape divisions have high reinforcement indices (scores of 3 or 4), whereas higher proportions of Azmak vessels with rounded profiles or single breaks have lower reinforcement indices (scores of 0–2). The calculation of the overall reinforcement measure for Dolnoslav produces a value of 2.1 – somewhat higher than at Azmak (value of 1.9).

At the same time as all the main means of zonal reinforcement increase in frequency at Dolnoslav compared to Azmak, the decorative intensity index decreases. The indices for all the shape ranges fall within a narrow band of between 4 and 5.6, with the exception of the amphorae range (6.4). The major distinction between the indices of more closed and more open shape ranges, so prominent at Hlebozavoda and still important at Azmak, has now disappeared completely, to be replaced by other means of contrast. Thus the long-term trends for open forms indicate a decline from a peak in

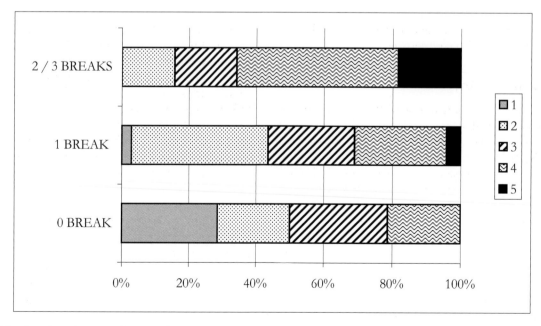

*Fig. 2.17 Number of reinforcements by profile differentiation from Dolnoslav. 1 – no reinforcement; 2 – 1 reinforcement; 3 – 2 reinforcements; 4 – 3 reinforcements; 5 – 4 reinforcements*

Hlebozavoda levels II/I, while similar indices have represented closed ranges since that same late Karanovo IV phase.

In summary, the almost complete absence of categorical oppositions used to structure the Final Karanovo VI assemblage at Dolnoslav is combined with the principle of total-vessel decorative fields to produce a wealth of cross-cutting contrasts. Not only is there a wider range of shape categories and sub-types than is seen at any other period in the Bulgarian prehistoric sequence but there is also a greater variety of combinations of zone reinforcement methods, not least decorative techniques. The range of combinations of decorative techniques reaches new peaks, including the first use of combinations of three techniques. Ten out of a theoretical maximum of 15 means of zone reinforcement were actually utilised at Dolnoslav. Compartmentalisation is widespread, not only in lids but also in the different elements integrated into the 360° design field, while symmetry and precision are major aspects of decoration at Dolnoslav. The huge diversity was, however, a denial of standardisation. Thus, the key principles in this assemblage are re-combination and differentiation. It is not difficult to see these techniques as analogies for human categorisation processes, in which the cross-cutting membership of increasing numbers of diverse social groups is what increasingly defines the social identity of Late Copper Age individuals. Indeed, it could be argued that, just as there are so many varied ceramic categorisations that identification with one set of contrasts is insufficient to define any single vessel, so it is the importance of cross-cutting membership of many limited interest groups, rather than membership of one group no matter how significant, which helps to define new ways of being a person in the Bulgarian Copper Age.

## The Varna cemetery

The Varna cemetery contains one of the richest and most diverse collection of grave goods in the Balkan Copper Age. In addition to the metal, stone, shell and bone finds, some 225 graves contain up to 608 vessels (Ivanov 1991, 130). Given the widespread interpretation of social complexity in the communities who buried their dead at Varna, a certain complexity may be expected in the categorisation of the mortuary pottery. Although dating earlier than Dolnoslav, the Varna assemblage is discussed after the Dolnoslav group because the site is a mortuary context, located far to the North East of all the other assemblages investigated.

The sample of 107 vessels studied in the Varna Archaeological Museum comprises a 18% sample, which covers a high proportion of the overall ceramic variability. An early finding was the strong difference between the

pottery assemblage from coeval settlements on the Varna Lakes and the ceramics from the mortuary domain (Margos 1978). This has led to the interpretation of the manufacture of the pottery specially for funerary deposition – a notion supported by the poorly fired pottery and claims for the absence of wear on these vessels (Ivanov 1975) and not challenged by the poor preservation of pottery in the stiff clay matrix. While there is no doubt of the poor firing of some vessels, the existence of some 25% of vessels with moderate to extreme wear on the base or feet in the sample investigated suggests that some of the Varna grave vessels were used before deposition. There are also several cases in which contrasts in colour or matt/gloss on the vessel surface were masked by the addition of a white slip, itself common in the mortuary assemblage. It would appear that the Varna pots may well have had a longer, more complex biography than has been previously recognised and this should be taken into account in the analysis of the cemetery.

The Varna assemblage studied here can be grouped into seven shape ranges (Figs. 2.18–2.19). The main variations come in the bowl range, with 13 categories and 38 sub-types – almost as many as in all the other vessel categories together. The diversity of bowl categories is far greater than at Dolnoslav, where there is greater variety at the sub-type level. Amphorae and storage jars are notable by their absence from the graves, while miniature vessels, lids and horned stands all show wide variability. The categorical variation in bowls is based upon the combination of elements such as feet, necks and shoulders with the basic carinated and rounded variants – a clear sign of compartmentalisation.

The defining characteristic of the Black Sea coastal assemblages in the Copper Age is the emphasis on multiple breaks in the vessel profile (Plate 12). At Varna, up to six profile breaks are found (Fig. 2.18/4), while profiles with four breaks are quite common. Even though vessels with a single or two profile breaks are commonest at Varna, the emphasis on vertical division of the vessel surface is a striking aspect of ceramic form. The emphasis on sharply profiled and facetted forms has a long history in the Black Sea coastal zone, as demonstrated by Haşotti's (1997, Fig. 106) *Typentafeln* of pottery shapes for each phase of the Black Sea sequence.

The decorative techniques used in the Varna cemetery are, for the most part, typical of the Black Sea variants of the Bulgarian Copper Age, with its preference for grooving, channelling and incision instead of graphite painting and barbotine. An unusually high proportion of vessels (for the Copper Age overall) remained undecorated or covered with a plain white slip. The majority of bowls have no decoration but a white slip is found on three bowls out of four. This suggests that the distinction between decorated and undecorated vessels was of greater

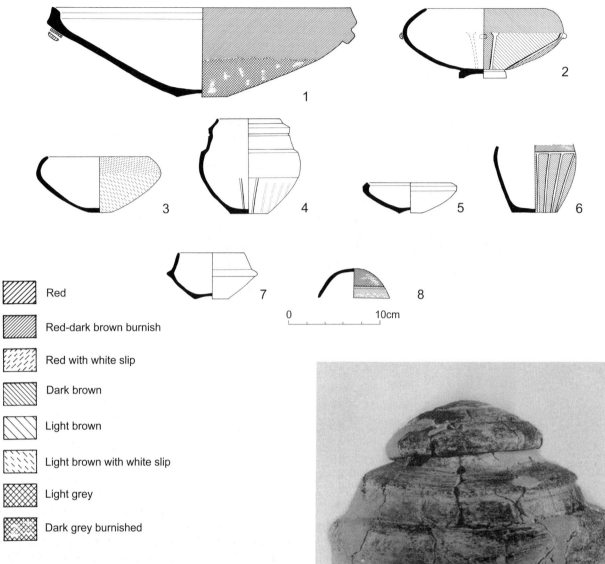

Red

Red-dark brown burnish

Red with white slip

Dark brown

Light brown

Light brown with white slip

Light grey

Dark grey burnished

*Fig. 2.18 Common pottery forms and decoration from Varna (drawn by Y. Beadnell)*

*Fig. 2.19 Vessel with multiple profile divisions, grave 5, Varna cemetery (source: Fol and Lichardus 1988, catalogue Abb. 117)*

than usual significance (Fig. 2.20). Eighteen decorative techniques are found on the 42 decorated vessels – a remarkably varied set of techniques for so few pots. The most unusual technique is the gold painting found on two special vessels (Éluère and Raub 1991). Half of the decorative techniques comprise combinations of two or three techniques, a lower proportion than at Dolnoslav but these combinations are more frequent on decorated sherds than at Dolnoslav. There are no clear rules of exclusion or inclusion in respect of the decorative techniques applied to different shape ranges at Varna. As at Dolnoslav, the emphasis is on combinations of different techniques on whatever vessels are deposited. There are very few examples of interior decoration – a decline

related to the decreasing importance of open forms such as dishes and plates. The practice of the deposition of vessels with their lids indicates the importance of surface decoration-in-the-round but, unlike at Dolnoslav, the inclusion of the base in the decorative field is very rare.

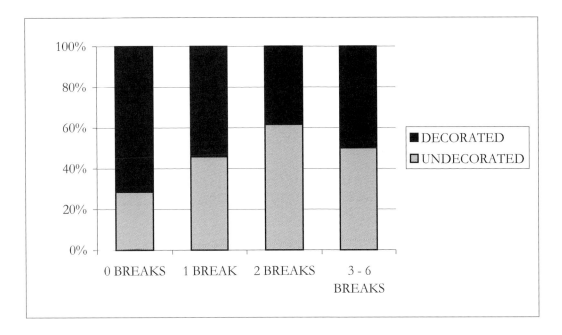

*Fig. 2.20 Presence/absence of decoration according to vessel profile breaks*

A surprisingly high proportion of vessels at Varna – over half – has no shape reinforcement at all, since they are undecorated. In the other half of the sample, the reinforcement of the many shape divisions found at Varna is accomplished mainly through decoration with other contrasts (Fig. 2.21). All decorated vessels with three or more profile breaks exhibit reinforcement of shape division by decorative means, with or without colour or matt/gloss contrasts. However, the commonest vessel profile with multiple reinforcement is that with one profile break. There is, nonetheless, a tendency for vessels with more profile breaks to have stronger, multiple reinforcement of their shape divisions. Conversely, as the number of profile breaks increases, there is an increasing proportion of vessels whose decorational zonation is reinforced by other means. Vertical zonation is more common on vessels with one or two profile breaks, while the vertical-and-horizontal zonation is preferred for vessels with three or more profile breaks. The Varna sample is the only assemblage examined so far where there are no examples of horizontal decorational zonation without vertical reinforcement.

The full range of four techniques of zonational reinforcement is available at Varna but the range of combinations of these techniques was far wider than at Dolnoslav. All combinations of reinforcement are found only on vessels with one profile break, with few examples of multiple reinforcement on vessels with two or more profile breaks. The calculation of the reinforcement index at Varna shows that the number of profile breaks makes

little difference – with only a marginally higher score for vessels with 3 or more breaks (2.2 compared to 2.0 for other profiles). The overall reinforcement measure for the Varna assemblage is 2.1, exactly the same as for Dolnoslav.

While the reinforcement measures of Dolnoslav and Varna are identical, there are signs that the index of decorational intensity is higher at Varna. The highest intensity is found in the shape range of horned stands, with bowls closely following and with particularly low measures for lids and dishes. The intensity index for the whole assemblage is 5.5, at the upper range of all the indices for Dolnoslav.

In summary, a comparison of the Dolnoslav and Varna assemblages indicates a wider range of cross-cutting contrasts at the former compared to the latter. Contrasts at Varna are based upon shape divisions, reinforced in less varied ways than at Dolnoslav and not so frequently – mostly by decorational zonation. The emphasis in vessel form and decoration at Varna has shifted from Dolnoslav's strong emphasis on decorational combinations and re-combinations to a narrower range of divisions, based upon shape combinations and oppositions between upper, middle and lower vessel parts. Symmetry and precision are notable aspects of decoration, while standardisation is more common than at Dolnoslav. The principle of vertical hierarchy of formal organisation gained ground at the expense of the principle of combination. The analogy in human categorisation processes is the tension between cross-cutting member-

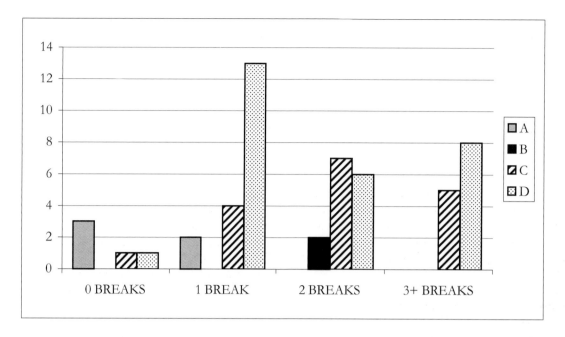

*Fig. 2.21 Types of reinforcement by number of vessel profile breaks: (a) no reinforcement; (b) no decoration but other reinforcement; (c) decoration reinforcement only; (d) decoration + other reinforcement*

ship of a diversity of limited interest groups and the principle of vertical differentiation through some kind of hierarchy. It is the co-existence of both principles in pottery decoration and form that provides an important clue to the workings of the communities who created the Varna cemetery.

## Discussion

The six ceramic assemblages under investigation provide no more and no less than snapshots – often blurred stills extracted from a moving picture of prehistoric life. Although every attempt has been made to ensure comparability of the ceramic samples, it remains the case that only partial assemblages were examined from the Karanovo I–II sites, even if the sample sizes of the four other sites were generally comparable. With the exception of the two Karanovo I–II sites under investigation, all other periods have been represented by a single site, sometimes chosen from different parts of Bulgaria. The main difference lies in the discovery contexts – unburnt houses and pits from pre-abandonment phases at Rakitovo, Chavdarova Cheshma and Hlebozavoda, burnt houses from an abandonment phase at Azmak, burnt houses and middens from the abandonment phase at Dolnoslav and graves with de facto materials at Varna (for an account of Michael Deal's typology of contexts, see below, pp. 43–75). Nevertheless, strong trends emerge from a comparison of the samples which appear to be a

product neither of the analytical framework nor of sampling inconsistencies but, rather, of prehistoric processes of change within varying contexts.

The decorated pottery of the first farmers (Karanovo I–II period) is dominated by a sharp differentiation between painted fine wares and non-painted medium or coarse wares as much as by the predominance of open forms and integrated design fields. This difference is partly related to statements about categorisation processes and partly to functional differences between cooking pots, storage vessels and fine wares for consumption and display. The categorical exclusion of mixed decorational styles at both sites implies a major social partition, mediated by contrasts in exterior surface colour and their enhancement, which may be related to gender or to different activity groups. Unlike at Franchthi Cave, where no evidence has been found for cooking-pots (Vitelli 1995), the heavy use-wear and burnt areas found on many medium and coarse ware pot bases indicates that ceramics were used for cooking and storage as well as for prestige objects in Early Neolithic villages in Bulgaria. The same findings have been made for the Early Neolithic pottery at Schela Cladovei (Chapman, in press). The importance of the earliest ceramics for cooking, food storage and food consumption has been discussed for Dalmatian and Italian Impressed Ware assemblages in an argument for the co-evolution of pottery and new social practices (Chapman 1988). Ceramics provide an efficient means of removing the toxins that are present in many common types of early domestic plants (Arnold 1985). Moreover, the association of a low percentage of animal bones with burnt marks at Early Neolithic sites such as Kovachevo (Ninov 1990) with the evidence for domesticated cereals at the same sites (Kreuz *et al.* 2005) suggests that boiling and stewing of meats and the cooking of cereal-based gruels were important activities to which ceramics were particularly well-suited. Finally, the importance of secure storage of foods and seed corn was another good reason for the use of clay containers. As discussed earlier (p. 5), Gamble (2005, 89–92) has argued that the key shift for sedentary life was the substitution of containers – usually fired clay – for instruments and the facility of containers for social practices of enchainment and fragmentation. The key point is the co-evolution of these important practices with the potential of ceramics for social signalling.

In parallel to the most important differentiating factor – the opposition of painted and unpainted wares – the categorical analysis of both Early Neolithic sites reveals the same pattern with minor variations – the predominance of open fields with a high degree of zonal decoration that was rarely reinforced by any other technique. The widespread deposition of both painted and unpainted wares in every house and pit suggests the use of these contrasting wares symbolised the integration of the maximal social group, while the differences between the wares embodied differences within the maximal group but also within the household. Functional differences are suggested in the use of the two major wares, mediated by gendered principles. This suggests both an acceptance of the importance of communal identity and the recognition of the realities of within-group, perhaps gender-based differentiation at both sites – but at Rakitovo more than at Chavdarova Cheshma. A low level of differentiation in cognitive structures is seen in the componential production of low footed vessels and the precision built into the small numbers of close-fitting lids.

In other Karanovo II assemblages not investigated in this study (*e.g.* Karanovo, Nikolov 1997; Central Bulgaria, Elenski 2004), the increasing frequency of dark burnished wares, sometimes with shape divisions, found in the same contexts as painted wares provides the possibility for the expression of the tensions between communal and individual categories in more oppositional ways. Hence the emergence of dark burnished wares indicates not only the potential of an alternative fine ware as metaphors for colour and sheen but also new ways of stressing difference from past traditions as well as the means to portray different kinds of human categorisation processes. This diachronic change differs from the two Chinese Neolithic assemblages compared by Keightley (1987) in which the different groups using respectively painted vessels with rounded profiles and unpainted vessels with angular, segmented or compartmentalised shapes were interpreted as having contrasting cognitive structures. In this period, we may have witnessed the emergence of some form of dual organisation, perhaps characterised by two lineages or two moieties, whose identities were rooted in the two contrasting categories of fine ware. Alternatively, as in the Dangwara case, there may well have been contrasting associations for each of the fine wares – one ritual, the other mundane. Further study is required using a large assemblage from the Karanovo II period.

The Karanovo III period marked the consolidation of the dark burnished ware tradition in the South Balkans. It was also a period of increased conceptual complexity in vessel production. A major similarity with the East Coast Chinese ceramics was the frequency of footed vessels, lugs and handles, indicating the regular production of multi-part vessels. Other componential production continued, with low-footed vessels now replaced by high footed vessels where the upper bowls or dishes would have been inverted for later addition of legs of equal length. There is a strong emphasis on handles of great size and diversity, also implying componential manufacture (Nikolov 1997). The footed bowls and the altar-lamps comprised a means of elevating material above the surface which relied upon componential production and the artificial inversion of vessels at some stage of production, held by Keightley to indicate a higher degree of abstract thinking because of the deviation from the 'natural' means of coil-building a vessel from the base up to the rim. In many cases, too, lids bore the inverted shape of rounded or carinated bowls and may even have been used in inverted ways (Fig. 2.14/2; Fig. 2.18/8). The virtual disappearance of painted wares from settlement deposits suggests the dominance of either one part of the dual structure – one lineage – or the merging of both ritual and quotidian practices in a single fine ware. Since dark burnished wares and unburnished, light-faced wares were found in every household, a similar set of intra-household identity differences was found to that prevalent in the Early Neolithic.

The overall message from the Karanovo IV ceramic assemblage remains clear – the continued emphasis on (a) dark burnished wares, (b) the proliferation of shape divisions and (c) a high degree of abstract thinking marks an identification with the preferred Karanovo III fine and medium wares in opposition to the abandoned painted ware tradition of Karanovo I–II. The similarity in the range of both shape categories and sub-types between Hlebozavoda and the Karanovo I–II assemblages reminds us of the constraints upon morphological differentiation in the Bulgarian Neolithic. It is also notable that simple shape divisions, such as one-break vessels, are far more common at Hlebozavoda than are complex forms. In contrast to the Karanovo I–II assemblages, there are few clear rules relating surface colour to either shape or decorational technique. Instead, the internal development between the early (Hlebozavoda III) level and the later (Hlebozavoda II–I) assemblages shows a shift from exclusive contrasts to overlapping sets of stylistic traits. This shift takes the form of the definition and later relaxation of relatively inflexible rules relating pottery form to decorational location, decorational technique, decorational zonation and colour contrasts. The increasing use of zonal reinforcement in all four major ways indicates the importance of overlapping sets to categorisation; the emphasis on increasing social differentiation at the expense of fairly simple oppositional modes of identity-formation. One interpretation of the changes at Hlebozavoda is that the shift in ceramic rules mirrors the tensions between a rigid dual model of community organisation and the increasing importance of flexibility of cross-cutting membership of several groups. The restricted nature of vessel shape divisions and the paucity of most kinds of zonal reinforcement set limits to the differentiation of categorisation expressed in the Karanovo IV pottery assemblage. If anything, the reduction in the cognitive complexity required for pottery forms, as in the decline in the use of high feet, lugs and handles, may well have been compensated for by the precision needed for many of the complex interior and exterior decorational designs.

The biggest change in all three Copper Age assemblages in comparison with the four Neolithic assemblages was the increased tension between the two fundamental principles of ceramic and social categorisation – integration in the face of division and diversity. The clearest example of this tension was found at Azmashka mogila, where the emphasis on the total, three-dimensional surface of the pot – lids and bases included – as the operative design field allowed the representation of increasing divisions and zonal reinforcements in the contents of that total field. This effect was managed through the use of cross-cutting differences rather than the imposition of rigid oppositional rules. In the Copper Age, in strong contrast to the Chinese Neolithic assemblages, painting and vessel divisions were found on the same vessels as often as not, representing two classes of inter-related variability. While most of the rules relating form and decorational technique and decorational location are more relaxed than in late Karanovo IV, the only rigid rules concern the newly introduced graphite painted technique, which remains uncombined with any other decorative technique, presumably because it is a prestigious innovation. However, the decline in the frequency of shape divisions at Azmak, as well as the emergence of unreinforced zonation after its disappearance in Karanovo IV, indicates that this Early

Copper Age assemblage is less concerned with categorical oppositions than in the previous period and consequently more attuned to cross-cutting differences and variable means of establishing identities.

Many Copper Age ceramic forms indicate componential production and the planning requisite for these linear steps. The key feature in Bulgarian Copper Age ceramics which is comparable to the East Coast Chinese assemblages is the diversity of lids, mostly well-fitting, with which to cover a great variety of vessel forms. The peak in lid production was identified in the Karanovo V period at Azmashka mogila, with sustained use in the Late Copper Age. The notion of manufacturing precision is demonstrated by several examples of lids at Dolnoslav which can be fitted neatly only onto the single vessel for which they were made.

The other major change from the Neolithic assemblages in the Copper Age is the dramatic differentiation of vessel form, which begins in the Karanovo V assemblage from Azmashka mogila and reaches an apogee with the Final Karanovo VI assemblage from Dolnoslav. The Dolnoslav ceramics combine design fields comprising the whole vessel with the maximum level of recombination and overlapping zonal reinforcements seen in the samples under investigation. This is seen in the combination of decorative techniques as much as in the juxtaposition of zonal reinforcement methods on as wide a range of vessel shapes as is seen anywhere in the Bulgarian prehistoric sequence. The rules concerning the location and the exclusivity of graphite painting that typified Azmashka mogila are no longer found at Dolnoslav, where all decorative combinations are possible on any shape category and on any surface colour. The added emphasis on shape divisions, often multiply reinforced, especially through decorational contrasts, indicates the importance of the categorisation of difference through oppositional means. But this aim pales into insignificance besides the emphasis on cross-cutting definitions through multiple recombination. There must be a strong presumption that Copper Age individuals established their identities not through exclusive association with one traditional communal group or another – households, lineages and moieties being the most obvious types of institution – but rather through multiple membership of a range of different groups, whether religious sodalities, women's clubs, warrior bands or exchange associations, in addition to consanguineous and residence groupings. The masking of the principle of hierarchical differentiation within such a tangled and complex pattern of ceramic production makes it hard to recognise its emergence in social categorisation, which is not to say that this did not occur in the Final Copper Age at Dolnoslav (see below, Chapter 6). Such a ceramic assemblage could hardly lack cognitive complexity, not least in the compositions of vessels with in-the-round design fields and in the complex and enormously varied forms.

The principle of hierarchical categorisation is represented more widely at the Varna cemetery than at any other site under investigation. The sharp structural difference between undecorated and decorated vessels, the strong emphasis on multiple shape divisions, supported by multiple zonal reinforcement, and the use of specifically prestigious decorative techniques such as gold vase-painting combine to suggest the greater significance of oppositional categorisations than was the case at Dolnoslav. A good example of componential production concerns the complex horned stands of the Varna cemetery (Plate 13), which suggest vertical differentiation in its elevation of the open vessel area above the surface. The artificial inversion of vessels at some stage of production is held by Keightley to indicate a higher degree of abstract thinking. Nonetheless, there remains much tension between exclusive categorisation and the use of recombination and cross-cutting categories of the kind best exemplified at Dolnoslav. The absence of rules governing the relationship of decorational technique to vessel form and the wide use of decorational combinations provide a very varied assemblage with a ready alternative to exclusive categorisation. It is the existence of both forms of categorisation that distinguishes the Varna cemetery from other Late Copper Age assemblages in the East Balkans. This interpretation cautions us against over-emphasising the hierarchical basis of the social organisation of those communities buried at Varna; rather, those multiple sources of individual identity found at Dolnoslav are still important enough at Varna to counterbalance any attempts by emergent elites to dominate processes of identity formation by categorisations narrowly focussed on exclusive, hierarchical roles. Despite the emphasis on multiple shape divisions, the cognitive complexity required by the Varna assemblage may be lower than at Dolnoslav, given the reduced usage of vessels with 360° design fields and the narrower range of vessel forms.

In summary, the comparison of trends in material categories, cognitive complexity and inferred social structures (Table 2.2) shows a complex picture that changes over two millennia. Many of the principles of categorisation can be grouped under the rubrics of opposed, or dichotomous, categories and cross-cutting categories. It is important to note that, in all cases, both dichotomous and cross-cutting categories are present and therefore in tension, with the predominance of opposed categories often related to the extent of hierarchical differentiation in the wider society (*e.g.* Karanovo IV and the Varna cemetery). Those periods where hierarchical principles came to the fore set apart the ways in which personhood was created, whether in the dominant corporate group or in a sub-dominant lineage. By contrast, increasing numbers of limited interest groups would have been embodied in assemblages with strongly cross-cutting categories (*e.g.* Karanovo V and VI). The Early Neolithic provides a hidden tension between the unified communal identities, underpinned by settlement-wide and regional similarities in fine wares, and the emergence of novel types of person in the new farming economy. Equally, periods such as the Late Copper Age, defined by high levels of social diversification and conceptualised in terms of complexity and cross-cutting membership of multiple limited interest groups, would have included even more new categories of people, few of whom sharing even a similar range of embodied skills, kinship relations and limited interest groups. What is less clear is the relationship between the cognitive complexity required by ceramic design and the inferred social structure. The greatest increases in cognitive complexity occurred at times of both increased hierarchisation (*e.g.* Karanovo III) **and** periods of maximum cross-cutting group membership (*e.g.* Karanovo VI).

In short, these changing forms of personhood suggest a dynamic sequence of social structures in the Neolithic and Copper Age periods in the South Balkans. It is clear from the above discussion that the categorical principles and practices exemplified in the pottery of the Balkan Neolithic and Copper Age do not highlight a message of increasing complexity from simple beginnings. Instead, a series of by turn complementary and contrastive messages were expressed about the persons, households and communities who used these things. We shall return to the tensions between the categorisational principles that characterise the different media of pottery, figurines, metals and lithics in Chapter 8. But it is now time to learn how the principles expressed in complete objects transmogrify into rather different statements once the objects have been broken.

| PERIOD | MATERIAL CATEGORIES | | COGNITIVE COMPLEXITY | SOCIAL STRUCTURE |
|---|---|---|---|---|
| Karanovo I | OPP: | Painted *vs.* unpainted wares | low level (low feet, lids) | unified communal identity vs. intra-household division (? Gender or task-related) |
| | X-CUT: | Open fields + zonal decoration Little re-inforcement | | |
| Karanovo II | OPP: | Painted *vs.* Dark burnished wares | low level (low feet, lids) | emergent dichotomous structure (? Dual) vs. intra-house division (cf. Kara. I) |
| | X-CUT: | Unburnished unpainted wares Open fields + zonal decoration Little re-inforcement | | |
| Karanovo III | OPP: | Dark burnished vs. unburnished light-faced wares | big increase in complexity (multi-part vessels, inversions, legs + precision, tight-fitting lids) | dominance of 1 of former units (lineage or clan or moiety) vs. intra-household divisions (cf. Kara. I-II) |
| | X-CUT: | | | |
| Karanovo IV | OPP: | Dark burnished vs. unburnished Light-faced wares (cf. Kara. III) Strict rules for form & decoration and form & colour contrasts | reduction in complexity of form (fewer lugs, handles & high feet) increased complexity for design of decoration | softening of dual organisation; increased complexity with multiple cross-cutting units & sub-units |
| | X-CUT: | More zonal re-inforcement Few rules on surface colour, form & decorational style | | |
| Karanovo V | OPP: | Tension between integration & diversity | major increase in complexity: peak in diversity of forms peak in production of varies lids 360° design fields | little evidence for hierarchical structures increased complexity with more cross-cutting units (unresolved tensions) |
| | X-CUT: | Less shape division; fewer rules for form & decorational style | | |
| Karanovo VI | OPP: | Increased shape divisions | maximum number of forms peak in 360° design field | little evidence of hierarchy increasing complexity, with greater diversity > integration |
| | X-CUT: | Maximum zonal re-inforcement Maximum decorational re-combination; no rules for form & decorational style | | |
| Varna cemy | OPP: | Hierarchical rules, with decorated vs. undecorated wares Special styles of decoration Emphasis on shape divisions | high level of complexity wide variety of shapes and decorational styles complex forms (horned stands & lids) | strong tensions between hierarchy, cross-cutting group membership & complexity |
| | X-CUT: | Few rules re form & decorative style; Wide range of decorational re-combinations Much zonal re-inforcement | | |

Key: OPP – ceramic practice based upon opposed categories; X-CUT – ceramic practice based upon cross-cutting categories

*Table 2.2 Summary of categorical analysis of Balkan Neolithic and Chalcolithic pottery*

# 3. Parts and wholes – Hamangia figurines

## Studying figurines

During the Neolithic and Copper Age, that area of Europe that Marija Gimbutas (1982) termed "Old Europe" (for the most part the Balkan Peninsula) had an overall cultural identity differentiating it from all other parts of Europe – in terms of the quantity and diversity of small-scale, material representations of deities, humans, birds, fish, animals, reptiles and combinations of these. If Gimbutas' interpretations of this material can be criticized for their universalizing palaeo-psychological assumptions and their emphasis on deities (cf. Meskell 1995; Conkey and Tringham 1995), she at least understood that small portable figurines were used in everyday life, for example during ceremonies and that they played an active role in the creation of an inhabited material world (Gimbutas 1982, 67–88).

Since the death of Marija Gimbutas, figurine research has opened up a maze of interpretative possibilities (*e.g.* Hamilton *et al.* 1996; Bailey 2005). These innovative approaches have been framed by three issues: the emergence of gender differentiation and multiple gender IDs, the creation of personhood and the tension between structure and agency. In this chapter, we discuss the gendering of human bodies and its relation to the creation of personhood through a case study of Late Neolithic and Early Copper Age figurines from the East Balkans.

## Sex and personhood

Laqueur (1990) dates the emergence of a two-sex model of humanity in Western Europe as recently as the late AD 18th century. Up to that period, there was a one-sex model of all humans, in which males and females were similar expressions grounded in a single archetypal body with 2 sets of sexual organs but with differences in temperament – females were more passionate and therefore more dangerous. However, the growing influence of the medical model of the late 18th century led to the sexing of matter into two divergent physiological and psycho-logical systems, each bound into the distinctive bodies of males and females. Broch-Due and Rudie (1993, 31–2)

attribute the change from a one-sex to a two-sex paradigm to the increasing influence of Cartesian duality and the scientific methodology wherein "analysis" breaks down entities into their constitutive elements in order to discover "difference". Once the two social genders had been (albeit incompletely) correlated with the two biological sexes, the sexed bodies were mediated and moulded by their own cultural values and discourses, leading to a further development of what it meant to be of male or female gender within the framework of the scientific biological discourse.

In general, the archaeological debate about sex and gender has followed the two-sex, two-gender paradigm, despite an early critique from Yates and Nordbladh (1990) that sex itself is a cultural construct chosen from a spectrum, rather than a duopoly, of sexual identities. Biehl (2003) seeks to exclude Balkan Copper Age figurines with no gender traits, insisting that they were abstractions of male or female figures. Sørensen (2000) identifies a concern with individual, sexual self-identity as a major cause for the study of sex as a cultural construction and cautions that most people construe sex in terms of "a few or only two sexes" (2000, 49). However, as Gilchrist (1999, 54–78) demonstrates, there is strong anthropological and historical evidence for the creation of alternative genders and third sexes and some relevant archaeological case studies (Marcus 1996; Yates 1993). The emphasis on individual self-identity among Western archaeologists is also flawed in that it posits a Western view of the centrality of the individual in prehistoric social relations.

The idea that personhood is a culturally created and negotiated concept is now a truism – one amply demonstrated by Mauss' summary of the historical development of the term 'person', from a socio-centric concept intrinsically linked to clan membership in prehistory, Vedanta and Samkhya notions of the person as a complete entity separate from society but not independent of God, a Stoic portrayal of the increasing awareness of 'self', the Christian conception of the individual as a 'moral' subject, the Enlightenment movement towards an 'autonomous human subject' and

Kant and Fichte's establishment of the psychological category of 'person' (Mauss 1985). This highly generalized and non-evolutionary sequence reminds us of the three concepts of 'person' in everyday usage: the person as a generic human, the person as a cultural category and the person as a psychological concept, *i.e.* a self.

A series of key anthropological studies in the 1980s and 1990s led to new notions of the relationships between individual persons, their societies and their artifacts (Strathern M. 1988; Weiner, A. 1992; Busby 1997). These studies questioned the application of a Western individualistic model of personhood to traditional societies in the present, not to mention to prehistoric communities. A recent and excellent study of these theoretical developments is Chris Fowler's (2004) book "The archaeology of personhood". Sub-titled "An anthropological approach", the study considers the importance of individual persons, as well as "dividual" persons (*i.e.* those whose inner identities are relational and inextricably linked to other persons), the extent to which persons are "self-contained" (*viz.* separated from the rest of the natural world) and the relative importance of such types of persons in comparison with wider social units such as families, exchange networks, lineages (2004, 14–21). Fowler emphasizes how personal identity can operate in a number of different ways, often interactive with other persons (2004, 20–21), with particular use made of two strongly contrasting ways of constructing personhood in

Melanesia and South India (summarized in 2004, Table 2.1; reproduced here as Table 3.1).

The central contrast is that, in Melanesia, gender is performative and produces partible people, while, in South India, gender is essential and produces permeable people. Both of these modes of creating personhood stand in strong contrast to the Western individualistic mode. One of the points which Fowler emphasizes is LiPuma's (1998, 57) insight that "persons emerge precisely from that tension between the dividual and individual aspects and relationships" – the terms and conditions of which tension vary historically. An example of this tension derives from the Vezo's refusal to collapse the category of sex into the category of gender since, for them, there is a creative tension between what is fixed in a person (their descent-based ancestral sexual essence) and what is transferable (their fluctuating performance-based gender identities). Thus Astuti (1998, 38) finds "a mosaic of male and female substance" with no sense of a cumulative sedimentation of gender through performance. Looking at gender and sex through the window of Melanesian or South Indian personhood may provide archaeologists with a wider range of possibilities than is currently available in Western gender studies.

To the extent to which the attributes of a person are concentrated more in the body than in the rest of the world – social or natural – increasing attention has been paid to human agency. However, if Western notions of

|  | Dividual and partible (Melanesia) | Dividual and permeable (southern India) |
|---|---|---|
| A person is | – collection of relations, any of which may be temporarily brought to the fore. Qualities can be added and extracted. | – fundamentally a collection of relations, and is a bounded being from whom qualities cannot be fully extracted though ratios may change. |
|  | Persons identify relations which are objectified as animals, objects, body parts, substances, etc. These can be externalized through separation or incorporated through encompassment. As well as being objectified they may be personified. | Substance-codes can permeate the "fluid boundaries" of the person. Flows of substance extend from persons, they are not objectified as a specific part of the person. |
|  | Thing fluctuate between being male and female, and singly and multiply gendered, depending on the context of their use. | Substance-codes have fixed properties (e.g. hot or cold). |
| Personhood is | – highly relational and identities are performed or presented. | – relational but is also strongly substantial. |

*Table 3.1 Two contrasting forms of personhood in Melanesia and Southern India (modified from Fowler 2004)*

personhood are found to be less appropriate for the study of past communities, the use of Western conceptions of agency may also be questioned. The relationship between structure and agency has been defined by Giddens (1984) as a reflexive relationship in which the existing social structure constrains individual action while individual action shapes and influences the long-term structure. Such an account can be criticized for failing to break down the very opposition between structure and agency that it seeks to understand. The use of a dynamic nominalist approach has been proposed to understanding the construction of identity through self-categorisation (Chapman 2000a, 34–37). In this approach, agency and structure come together in the formation of identities, which may be described as the process of self-description through categorisation. As Blake (1999) has argued, self-definition channels the process of knowledge acquisition, so important for people to negotiate a pathway through the habitus, providing actions with a description that is already part of the process of self-definition. The making of objects is one such action that needs a description, as we discussed in the previous chapter vis-à-vis the forms of categorisation embodied in vessels, which we sought to relate to categorization itself. The objectification of persons through their objects provides an important means of constructing cultural order, an order experienced each day through the objects that people saw and used and an order that framed the growth of personal identities. However, the constitution of aspects of identity such as age and sex is not merely a matter of categorization, through comparisons with the past and the Other, but is also a process, through which people grow in a historically contingent sequence of circumstances (*e.g.* for children, James *et al.* 1998; for identity more generally, see Jenkins 1997).

What neither Blake (1999) nor Chapman (2000a) included in their discussions of the dynamic nominalist approach was any reference to a relevant conception of personhood. The obverse is true of Fowler (2004), whose treatment of personhood excludes agency. This first oversight is, in fact, characteristic of archaeological discussions of agency, as can be seen from all of the chapters in Dobres and Robb's (2000) edited volume. The implicit view of these authors is that agency theory finds its roots in a Western capitalist notion of personhood based upon the homogenous, integral, individual actor. Such an assumption would find it hard to assimilate the indigenous perspectives summarized in, *e.g.* the Sabarl view that yams as much grow their subjects as the other way round (Battaglia 1995, 80). The existence of several routes to the construction of personhood implies the same for concepts of human, animal or even yam agency. LiPuma (1998, 60) puts this debate into a historical perspective by recognizing that it was the expansion of

colonialism and capitalism in Melanesia that led to the growth of the self-contained, self-shaping independent agent. Indeed, this is a classic example of dynamic nominalism, where a new kind of person develops at the same time as the description and category of such a person arises.

Three forms of agency can be traced as examples of a wide range of approaches to social action: the Melanesian, the Polynesian and the South Indian (see esp. Mosko 1992 for a comparison of Polynesian and Melanesian agency; Busby 1997). M. Strathern (1988) summarizes the Melanesian position by claiming that agency is more the pivot of relationships, acting with another's vantage-point in mind, than a locus for relationships. Insofar as each Melanesian person is a composite formed of relations with many other persons, each relation forms a capacity for action, which is externalized through that action. "By acting, … persons are *decomposed*. … Thus decomposing and externalizing their parts, relations or capacities, persons stimulate one another to action and reaction" (Mosko 1992, 702). In other words, people depend on others for their own self-definition; a Melanesian person's identity could be summarized by the network of transactions in which each person is engaged and can be expected to create in the future (Douglas and Ney 1998, 9).

Sahlins (1991, 63) has defined the significance of the Polynesian chief in terms of an epitome of the whole tribe – a divine personage whose capacities and actions summarize, unify, encompass and expansively internalize the relations of Polynesian society's members as a whole. In Mosko's (1992, 699) terms, the chief's centrality rests upon hierarchical *supercomposition*, with his personal boundaries expansively elastic to encompass the entire tribe. Persons of this magnitude portray their societies as "heroic societies", their personal histories becoming "heroic histories" (Sahlins 1985, 35).

The Mekeo are a group with Polynesian-style chiefdoms and Melanesian partibility, that nonetheless deviates from the classic Strathernian notion of the Melanesian person-actor (Mosko 1992). Mekeo agency relies upon gendered changes in life history, in which a androgynous baby is "decomposed" into a less complete but still androgynous adult, who only then is capable of effective social action. The creation of powerful persons such as chiefs and sorcerers depends on a further decomposition from androgynous adult to one-sex male. Thus, in Mekeo society, agency depends less of aggrandizement than on personal reduction and decomposition of gendered identities.

A quite different attitude to agency is found in South India, where essential, intrinsic gender differences are nonetheless performatively marked out in all areas of life (Busby 1997, 207). The strong connection between gender as a bodily attribute and the ability of persons to act in gendered ways is based upon a substantialization of the attributes of persons and things. However, this essential difference is dependent upon the co-operation and interactions of females and males in every area of life, including the vital transference of bodily fluids that carries the seeds of identity. A similar exchange of bodily substances based upon the principle of synecdoche is used to extend Navajo personhood far beyond individual bodies (Schwarz 1997, 239–241).

It can be demonstrated that each of these difference ways of characterizing agency can be characterized in terms of the dynamic nominalist approach, in which both the categories and the self-definition of persons bring such persons into existence. This works particularly clearly in the sequence of bodily development through a person's life history. Now that we have considered alternative ways of conceptualizing agency, we can return to the issue of personhood in greater depth.

## Creating personhood

Csordas (1994, 2–3) makes a key point in his assertion that the body can no longer be considered "a bounded entity", with a fixed life-course in prospect but rather an experiencing agent with a fluid life-course. This is seen particularly clearly in fluctuating gender identities in Melanesia, both on an everyday level and on a longer time-scale. On a quotidian time-scale, M. Strathern (1988) questions the differentiation of spheres of female and male activity, since females and males, and the tokens of themselves, are androgynously composed of both female and male parts and relationships. Thus the corporeal body is often presented as female or male for specific ritual effect but retains both gendered aspects internally. Mosko (1992, 705; 2000) takes this notion further in his discussion of Mekeo personhood: since the plural substances (blood and semen) composing each person are not only gendered but also androgynous, all persons are doubly androgynous. Enchained exchange permits the expression of gendered identities through the attachment or detachment of their respective gendered parts. Both A. Weiner (1992) and LiPuma (1998) make a similar comment for objects, which, as they see it, can switch from being seen as female or as male because almost all objects contain both female and male aspects. For these authors, the aim of social practice is to ensure smooth transitions between modalities.

By contrast, Busby (1997) shows that, in Southern India, men and women are seen as absolutely different in their capacities to engage with each other in a gendered way. This performative differentiation is found in all areas of life – in appearance, attributes and work. An important aspect of gender identification concerns the third sex –

*hijras* (viz., hemaphrodites) – who are defined through bodily difference and by negative comparisons with females and males – *i.e.* a person without a penis or without breasts or who cannot menstruate (Nanda 1990). We shall return to this example later (see below, pp. 58–62).

On the time-scale of a life-course, and in contrast to Western thought, many Melanesian societies construct personhood through a series of changing gendered identities. Astuti (1998) neatly demonstrates the active construction of the body in Vezo societies, where the body is acquired through practice and enactment but most of all through the embodiment of Vezo-ness. In this society, androgynous persons are a mosaic of female and male substances; single-sex is achieved through transacting in female or male things. Moore (1994) shows how the Hua of Papua New Guinea classify their children as male or female but believe that each contains both female and male bodily fluids, whose balance fluctuates through their lifetimes. Herdt (1982) demonstrates that rituals of nose-bleeding (to shed the female essence) and fellatio with tribal elders (to gain the male essence) are essential for the creation of manhood from boyhood. M. Strathern (1988) notes that Melanesian children are made incomplete (*i.e.*, one-sex) and it is only at marriage that the partner of the opposite gender makes a person "complete again" (viz., a new, androgynous person). Equally, Battaglia (1990) observes that while a pregnant Sabarl woman is androgynous, after birth, partibility leads to a new, categorically gendered condition. According to Clark (1991), Wiru children possess wholly female bodies, because they have been wholly created by women. However, they receive the impress of male **in**dividuality from men. Wiru persons born "male" become less female through time through gift exchange of red pearlshells, which creates the person by individualizing and masculinizing those receiving gifts (see below, chapter 7). Another relevant example is the Melpa (Strathern A. and Stewart 1998 and especially Fig. 11.1), in which the infant is born as androgynous, receiving female blood and male semen, continues as such through the consumption of female breast-milk and male-produced food and slowly develops into a predominantly (but never wholly) single-sex person based upon their bodily, sexual characteristics. Thus, life-course transformations in gender would appear to be typical for Melanesia but rather less common in South India. An exception to this is the Mekeo, whose de-conception of some persons into a state of pure masculinity from androgynous adulthood defines their hereditary status of sorcerers and chiefs (Mosko 1992, 706).

The nature and significance of androgynes, and their relationship to hermaphrodites, have been extensively discussed by Bleie (1993). Many societies regard androgynes as special, some in a positive light as embodying cosmological powers (*e.g.* the Navajo), others in a negative light, as divine errors (*e.g.* the Pokot)(1993, 263). M. Strathern emphasizes the role of Melanesian androgyny as a bridge between different states, plural and singular – between collective single-sexed, dividual persons and paired cross-sexed persons. Bleie (1993, 276) also notes the widespread occurrence, in Melanesia, Somalia, Kenya and Peru, of the transformation of the androgynous state into a single-sex state through ritual practices. However, another interpretation of androgyny emphasizes the importance of a union celebrating the complementarity of the two genders. M. Strathern has been criticized by Hoskins (1998, 187) for treating androgyny as "a confusion of male and female, an obscuring of gender or an absence of identifiably gendered objects." Instead, Hoskins' reading of androgyny in Sumba society identifies not so much a bridge between two states as a combination of both genders in a dualistic system. Hoskins' views are to a varying extent shared by other authors, such as Singer (1977), whose study of the wider nature of androgyny leads to a view of human nature as fundamentally androgynous, with androgyny as an inner totality, or Bem (1976), who argues that androgyny is a state of fusion and totality, akin to the merging/fusing of two persons in an ecstatic union (hierogamy). This latter state has been identified by Monah (1992, 1997) in his analyses of Balkan Copper Age (Cucuteni – Tripolye) figurines.

These examples from Southern India and Melanesia indicate the complexity of gendered identities and practices, which are fundamentally context-dependent. It is important to note the strong underlying contribution of androgyny to personhood as one of the instrumentalities that people use in the construction and reconstruction of their own worlds and the frequency with which alternating and cyclical transformations of gendered identities over the whole life-course includes the androgynous state at one or more stages. Is it possible to identify the state and significance of androgyny in the prehistoric past?

## *Hamangia figurine categorisation – gender and complementarity*

In their interpretations of Neolithic human representations, archaeologists have begun to recognize the existence of androgynous figurines in the corpus. Knapp and Meskell (1997) discuss the small number of androgynous figurines in Cyprus in the Late Neolithic (*e.g.* the ambiguously sexed limestone figure from Sotira Arkolies, Fig. 2), the Copper Age (the limestone "Lemba Lady", with phallic neck and pubic triangle, Fig. 5) and

several Bronze Age androgynes (195 and Fig. 6). The previous year, the Greek archaeologists Kokkinidou and Nikolaidou (1996) had proposed that the elongated "necks" of the so-called rod head figurine class, so typical of the Early Neolithic in Thessaly, could also be regarded as phallic members, sometimes in combination with other female traits; shortly afterwards, Whittle (1997) proposed a similar interpretation for the Körös rod head figurines of Eastern Hungary. One of the authors has noted a similar characteristic – an elongated phallic neck – on the commonest form of Late Neolithic and Early Copper Age Hamangia figurines (Chapman 1999, 2000). Similarities between Hamangia figurines and other images with phallic necks are noted by Bailey (2005, 155) but he makes no further use of this insight in his study of Hamangia (2005, Chapter 3). Trogmayer (1990) also recognised androgyny in the famous class of throned figurines, some with sickles, in the Late Neolithic Tisza group of Eastern Hungary. However, none of these commentators has sought to locate androgynes in any kind of theoretical framework of personhood. I should like to consider the Hamangia figurines in greater depth here, because of the distinctive social practices with which they are associated.

Hamangia figurines differ strongly in form from most other figurines made in the Balkan Neolithic and Copper Age but the most striking difference is that, in contrast to the typically domestic context of deposition of other representations, the vast majority of Hamangia figurines were deposited in the mortuary arena. One reason for this is the emphasis on large cemeteries that stand out as the major features of the Hamangia landscapes (Berciu 1966; Todorova 2002) – far more dramatic than most small-scale dwelling deposits, found at Late Neolithic sites such as Medgidia and Tîrgşoru Veche (Haşotti 1997). However, the settlement form changes in the Early Copper Age, with the occurrence of what appears to be permanent settlements at sites such as the Big Island at Durankulak (Todorova 2002b). There two contrasts are seen, first between the active use of figurines in different forms of Hamangia settlement (a diachronic contrast) and secondly between daily practices involving figurines in Hamangia settlements and permanent disposal in large, formal cemeteries (a synchronic contrast).

The contrast in figurine use between domestic and mortuary domains is recognised by Bailey in his recent consideration of Hamangia figurines (2005, Chapter 3) but Bailey makes little of the contextual difference. Indeed, elsewhere in the book, he downplays the potential of contextual studies for understanding figurines (2005, 179), since very few were found in "primary contexts" (*i.e.* contexts of use); therefore, figurine fragments are described as "merely the detritus of life, kicked into the corners of the room, tossed out into the yard, thrown into rubbish pits" (2005, 179). These are serious errors of perception that can be readily refuted (see below, Chapters 5 and 6, as well as in the following pages). While Bailey is full of questions about Hamangia figurines, he unfortunately provides no answers and few insights. Where Bailey's work chimes better with our discussion of personhood is his idea that Neolithic communities took the human body to be the primary site of the individual and the self (2005, 201), building up understandings of persons over time through the incorporation of multiple images (2005, 79). What Bailey ignores, and what fragmentation studies can illuminate, is their contribution to the construction and deconstruction of personhood, as we now seek to illustrate with Hamangia figurines. As Lévi-Strauss might have said, figurines were indeed good for thinking.

A reasonably large group of Hamangia figurines (n = 58) was published over a decade ago by I. Vajsov (1992), who emphasized the conservatism in the design of the group. Together with additions from museum collections, this group forms the basis of the current study. A closer look at the figurines suggests rather more variability than noted by Vajsov and others. Five basic categories are found in the figurine group – standing fired clay, seated fired clay, shell miniature, marble miniature and schematic astragalus figurines (Fig. 3.1). These categories are based upon oppositions in form, size or both. While the miniature figurines share some of the traits of the larger fired clay examples, they are uniformly small (< 4 cm in height) and made, using reductive technologies, of materials that are closer to nature. The seated and standing fired clay figurines form Vajsov's (1992) two basic types. In contrast to most of the standing examples, the seated examples are, for the most part, self-supporting. This group includes the most famous pair of Hamangia

figurines – the so-called "Thinker" and his consort – found without secure stratigraphic context in the Cernavoda cemetery (Berciu 1960). This "couple" has been glorified as works of high prehistoric art (Dumitrescu 1968) but are not even typical of the group, insofar as they were provided with heads as well as necks. The standing types are distinguished by their elongated necks and lack of head. The schematic astragali are not so much altered as those in the K-G-K VI network (Comşa 1995, 61–66 and Fig. 63) or in the Cucuteni group (Marinescu-Bîlcu 1981), exhibiting minimal traces of forming, which underlines the ambiguity of the claim for the anthropomorphic nature of this type.

These categories can be further sub-divided on the basis of two variables – gender and completeness (Table 3.2). Any categorisation by gender is predicated upon the sexual traits by which the person can be identified. In Vajsov's (1992) study and other past studies of Hamangia figurines (*e.g.* Berciu 1966; Dumitrescu 1968), the female characteristics have been noted as distinctive and predominant. However, the recognition that long necks could have possessed phallic properties conferring maleness on these objects adjusts our perspectives on the gender of these figurines. This insight means that complete Hamangia figurines were normally androgynous (Fig. 3.2). Significantly, the androgynous figurine was found from the beginning of the Hamangia group in the Late Neolithic until the Middle Copper Age. While maleness was identified only through the phallic neck, a rich array of traits characterised femaleness, including up to four traits on a single figurine.

Can we be sure that the cylindrical neck symbolised maleness? Two points support this interpretation: first, the form was deliberately chosen from a wide array of possible head/neck forms and often bears a close

| Category | Complete | | | Fragmentary | | | |
|---|---|---|---|---|---|---|---|
| Standing Fired clay | F | H | | F | H | G-N | NO |
| Seated Fired clay | | M | H | G-N | F | H | |
| Miniature Shell | | | G-N | | | | |
| Miniature Marble | | | | F | | G-N | |
| Schematic Astragalus | | | | | | G-N | |
| Key: F – female; M – male; H – hermaphrodite; G-N – gender-neutral; NO – no evidence | | | | | | | |

*Table 3.2 Categories of Hamangia figurines by gender and completeness*

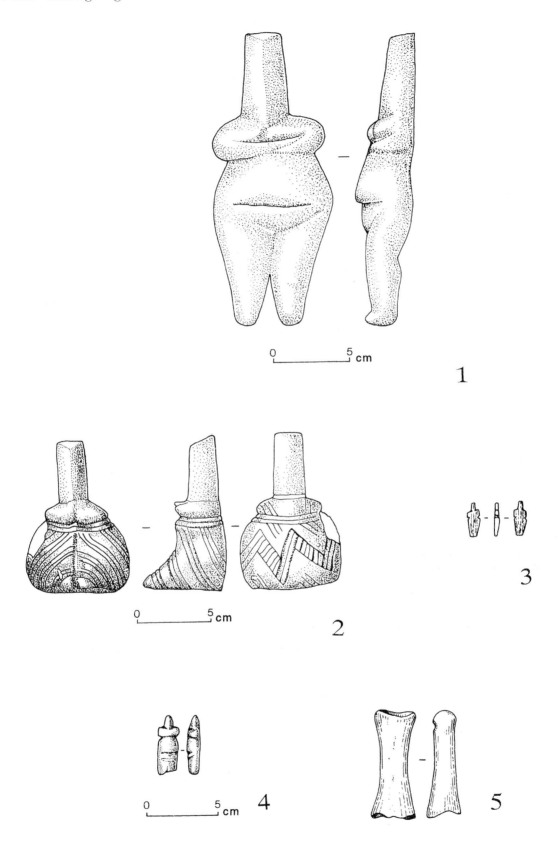

*Fig. 3.1 Types of Hamangia figurines*

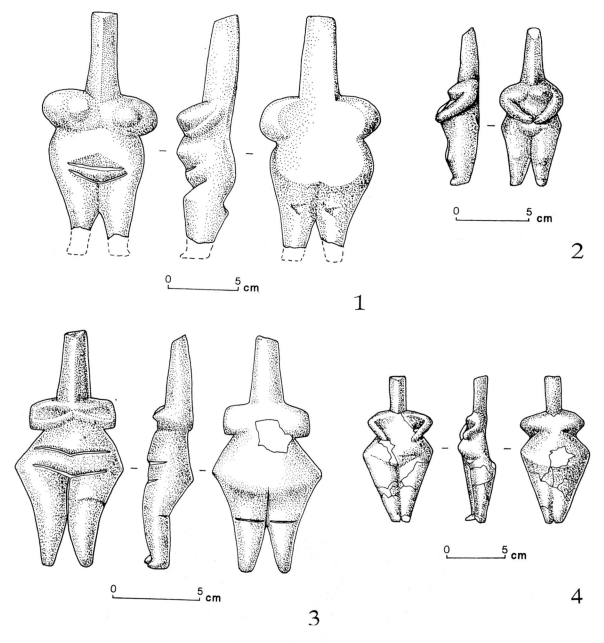

*Fig. 3.2 Androgynous Hamangia figurines*

resemblance to the male organ (cylindrical form, broader at base, narrowing to a point at the top). Secondly, the swelling of the "breasts" at the base of the "neck" on some figurines resembles the male gonads, especially from the front (Fig. 3.2).

However, if androgyny is typical for many of the complete Hamangia figurines, there are four categorical exceptions to this rule:

– The complete miniature shell figurines, all of which are gender-neutral (Fig. 3.1, 3–4)

– The "Thinker" and his consort from Cernavoda (Berciu 1960; here, Fig. 3.3), which is gender-neutral insofar as the presence of the face prevents the cylindrical neck from being phallic

– The elaborately decorated female figurine from Balchik (Vajsov 1992, Tabl. XX, here, Fig. 3.4), with two female traits

– The male figurine from Cernavoda (Vajsov 1992, Fig. VIII:1), lacking the long, cylindrical neck and with no female traits

*Fig. 3.3 The "Thinker", Cernavoda cemetery*

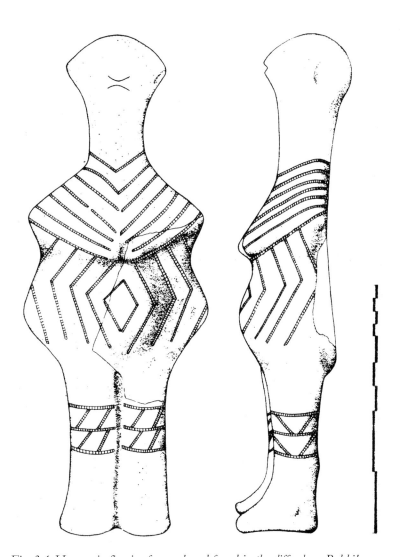

*Fig. 3.4 Hamangia figurine from a hoard found in the cliffs above Balchik*

If it is this wide range of gendered forms which is so characteristic of Hamangia communities, then the choice depends crucially on the completeness of the representation. If the assumption is made that Hamangia figurines were complete when made, and, for the most part, androgynous, then figurine fragmentation alters the gendered identity. In the absence of penises on Hamangia figurines, the removal of the head means that the maleness is lost or, more accurately, divided from the female part. According to Vajsov (1992, 61), the majority of figurines have been found as fragments and, of all the body parts, what he terms the "head" (here = the "neck") is the most commonly found part. However, the significance of the fragmented penis has escaped Vajsov, who does not illustrate a single broken member in his otherwise well-illustrated article.

We have already alluded to the wide array of female sexual traits found on Hamangia figurines. The basic traits are the following: breasts (varying in size from delicate to buxom), pregnant stomach (also varying in size), pubic triangle and wide, exaggerated hips, as if prepared for childbirth. The representation of both breasts and stomach provides the opportunity for the portrayal of individual characteristics. With breasts, age and/or physique can be reflected in the small or pointed, large and pendulous or sagging form, while the stomach can indicate differing stages of pregnancy. Ten out of the total of 15 possible combinations of these four traits are represented (Table 3.3). This allows for the representation of a spectrum of gendered identities, not merely a polarised male – female but a range from gender-neutral to strongly androgynous and strongly female.

A very low proportion of complete Hamangia figurines revealed no sexual traits at all; it is possible that such figurines represent *hijras* – the South Indian third-sex person defined by their lack of breasts and a penis (see above, p. 56). The important role played by gendered bodily parts in Hamangia imagery suggests that the decision to *omit* such parts is culturally significant in that it portrays a third-sex type such as a *hijra*. What this range of diverse gender identities shows is that gender categorisation must have been of major significance to Hamangia society.

The second axis of categorisation is fragmentation. While Vajsov (1992) following Todorova (1980), divides Hamangia figurines into "complete" and "fragmentary", neither researcher takes the distinction further. This is interesting, since one of the most important general characteristics of those graves often containing Hamangia figurines is the frequent association of complete objects with complete bodies (Chapman 2000, 75–79). There is a strong difference in the proportion of figurines of differing completeness according to context.

The figurines deposited in Hamangia settlements (n = 42) had passed through a much more varied life-history than those in graves (Figs. 3.5–3.6 and Plate 14). Wear traces are common on the Durankulak settlement fragments, often heavy and repeated and indicating repeated use in social practices as well as an element of post-depositional plough damage. All forms of broken figurines were found in settlement deposits, with a strong emphasis of 2/3rds on single parts (necks, torsos or legs). The least common figurine part was the neck/torso combination (5%). Only 12% of the Hamangia figurines found in settlement contexts were complete.

The figurines found in graves were far less heavily fragmented than those in settlement contexts. Over 40% of figurines in graves consisted of the torso/legs combination, while 35% of figurines found in graves were complete (Figs. 3.5, 3.6 and Plate 15). It is interesting to note that, although gender integration in graves was symbolised by complete figurines, there appear to be examples of separate phallic necks that re-fitted to female torsos in some of the Durankulak graves. The problem with this interpretation is that it is hard to exclude the possibility that a complete androgyne was broken by the pressure of soil in the grave. While soil pressure may have caused the separation of the phallic necks from their

| Breasts | Pregnant stomach | Pubic triangle | Exaggerated hips | Frequency |
|---|---|---|---|---|
| * | | | | 16 |
| | * | | | 1 |
| * | * | | | 5 |
| * | | | * | 2 |
| | * | * | | 2 |
| * | * | * | | 1 |
| * | * | | * | 3 |
| * | | * | * | 3 |
| * | * | * | * | 10 |

*Table 3.3 Combinations of female traits in Hamangia figurines*

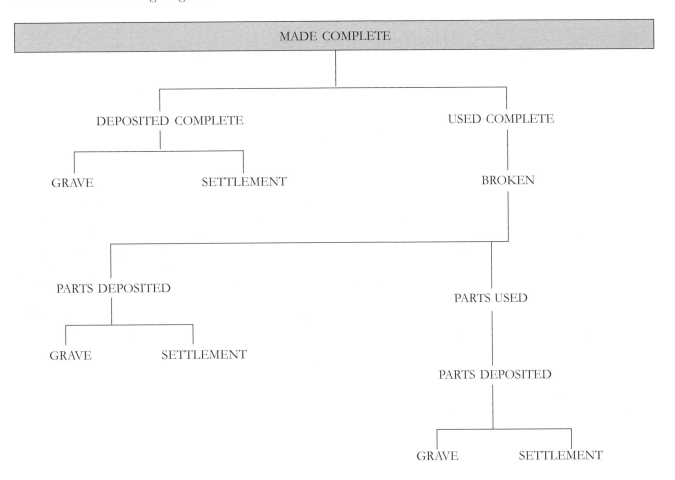

*Fig. 3.5 Fragmentation chain for Hamangia figurines*

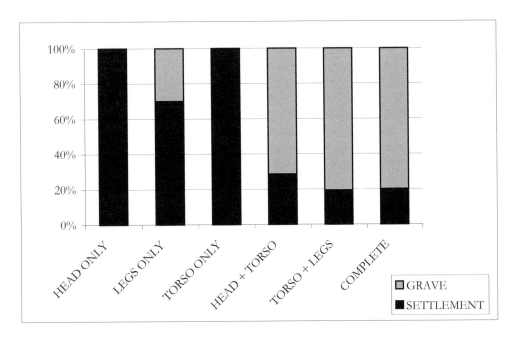

*Fig. 3.6 Figurine completeness by context*

| Body part | F/1-2 | F/1-3 | M | H(F1-2) | H(F3-4) | G-N | NO | Total |
|---|---|---|---|---|---|---|---|---|
| Neck/torso | - | - | - | 4(1) | - | 1 | - | 5(1) |
| Torso | (1) | - | - | - | - | (3) | - | (4) |
| Neck/torso/body | - | - | - | - | 1 | - | - | 1 |
| Torso/body/legs | 12 | 6 | - | - | 1 | 1(1) | - | 20(1) |
| Legs | 1 | - | - | - | - | - | 2(1) | 3(1) |
| Vertically split | - | 1 | - | - | 2 | - | - | 3 |
| Fragments of H/T/L | - | - | - | 1 | - | - | - | 1 |
| Complete | 1 | - | 1 | 5 | 6 | 5 | - | 18 |

Key: F/1-2 – female with 1 or 2 female traits; F/1–3 – female with 1, 2 or 3 female traits; M – male; H(F1-2) – hermaphrodite with 1 or 2 female traits; H(F3-4) – hermaphrodite with 3 or 4 female traits; G-N – gender neutral; NO – no evidence. Numbers in brackets – Durankulak settlement finds.

*Table 3.4 Distribution of Hamangia figurine gender traits by body parts*

torsos in graves 601A, 626 and 642, it appears that the phallic neck and torso with one breast in grave 609A were deposited separately, indicating the re-integration of the two genders into an androgynous whole in at least one case. Two-thirds of the figurines in the mortuary context were incomplete, indicating a high incidence of orphan figurine fragments. One may assume that the missing parts were placed somewhere in the land of the living.

While there is clearly a greater probability of random breakage or loss in settlement contexts, there can be little doubt that the placing of only parts of figurines in the often undisturbed and closed contexts of Hamangia graves, as well as in certain settlement pits, was a deliberate and frequent social practice. How does this practice relate to gender identities?

The relationship between fragmentation and gender identity on Hamangia figurines is complex (Table 3.4 and Fig. 3.7). In view of Vajsov's (1992) failure to illustrate separate phallic necks despite being the commonest class of fragment, it is useful to record the sample by body part and gender characteristic. There is thus a trend from complete figurines in which, for the most part, androgyny is built into the form of the object, to small body parts such as legs, which effectively lack gender traits. However, an important group of small fragments – phallic necks and some torsos – continues to exhibit their gender identities, despite their small size, multiple fragmentation and incompleteness. Two aspects of these small but gendered fragments are important – the resistance to the

dissolution of gender, which is part of the materiality of the fired clay figurines, and the continued enchainment between even small fragments and the remaining parts of the figurine, wherever its/their place of deposition.

**The depositional context of Hamangia figurines**

There are several published examples of the context of Hamangia figurines, whether from settlements, from graves or from the wider landscape, which permit the development of a narrative about their significance. The exception to all other known Hamangia figurines, which are found in either graves or settlements, is the restored female figurine (approximately 70% complete) from Balchik (Fig. 3.4), which had been inserted into the limestone cleft near the top of a cliff overlooking a salty liman by the shore of the Black Sea (Todorova 1972). The figurine is unusual in two respects other than its context of discovery: it has a unique form in the Hamangia corpus and is one of the rare figurines more than 50% complete yet lacking an androgynous gender identity. The find is reminiscent of later, Copper Age metal hoards all over the Balkans, deposited in the landscape far from settlements (Chapman 2000, 112–121).

Deposition of a single figurine – generally a fragment – characterised the vast majority of settlement contexts (12 out of 15: Fig. 3.9). A good example is the settlement of Tîrgşoru-Urs, where three figurines were found – one in each of three pits: a Legs/Feet combination with no

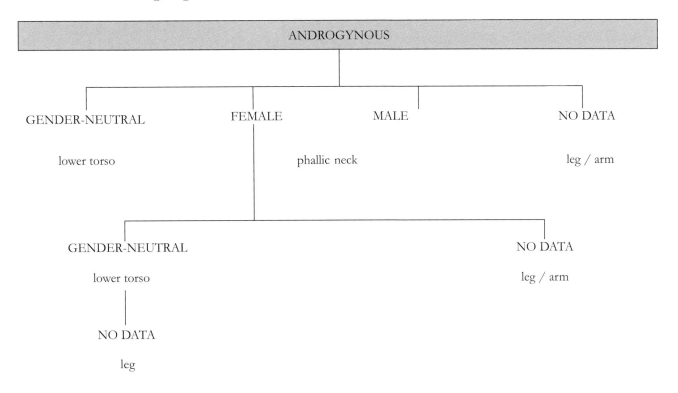

Fig. 3.7 *Changing gender identities*

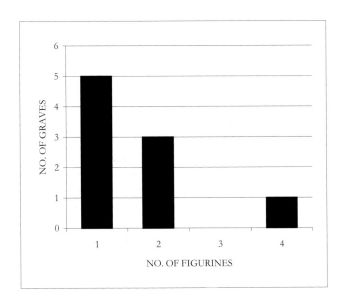

Fig. 3.8 *Frequency of figurines in graves*

one concentration and two fragments each found in a separate pit (Berciu 1966). The four figurines were found in Trench 1960/I, in the South West part of a spread of heavily burnt daub, which also included re-fired sherds and a polished stone axe; this area, which lacked walls, has been interpreted as a ritual construction (1966, 235–239). The figurines consisted of three fragmentary standing female torsos and one standing androgyne, with part of a phallic neck attached to a Torso/Legs combination. Each female figurine displayed different female traits – breasts and swollen stomach, breast and wide hips and breast, pubic triangle and wide hips – as if to emphasise the variety of female forms or, conceivably, the (in)dividuality of different persons (1966, Fig. 42–43). The other figurines were of quite different form – one a small seated fragment with part of a non-phallic neck and the left arm missing, the other a fragmentary right leg with no gender identity (1966, Fig. 44). The contrasts between the group of figurines in the burnt building and the individual fragments in their separate pits suggest two ways of using figurines. The first represents an accumulation of parts reinforcing the variety of female identity, which sometimes included an element of maleness, each with a break to the phallic neck. The others consist of a statement about the difference of individual identities in specific social contexts.

One of the best-known examples of structured pit

gender identity in Pit 3, an almost complete androgyne missing the top of the cylindrical neck in Dwelling-Pit 3 and a fragment of a phallic neck in Pit 1 (Haşotti 1986).

At the settlement of Baia-Goloviţa, figurines were deposited in three different contexts: a group of four in

deposition in the Balkan Neolithic concerns Pit 1 at the Early Hamangia settlement of Medgidia-Cocoaşe (Haşotti 1985, 1997; Chapman 2000c). The contents of the pit can be divided into two zones – a Northern zone devoid of figurines and containing a largely complete range of raw materials in daily use, and a Southern zone, with animal bones – mostly cattle – freshwater shells and a group of eight figurines (Table 3.5).

This is the most varied assemblage of figurines yet known from the entire Hamangia society, with stone as well as fired clay materials, a wide range of body parts and gender identities and a contrast between burnt and unburnt figurines. The burning of two figurines – one stone and one fired clay – is reminiscent of the burnt daub from Tirgşoru-Urs and links the figurines to the theme of transformation by fire – evoking both their initial creation from mud and their final deposition in a heavily cultured place. What is striking about the Medgidia figurine group is the incorporation of every human category known to Hamangia society, with a strong emphasis on all of the positively gendered identities (5/8 or 63%: here, gender-neutrality is considered as a gendered identity but not as a positive one). The figurines in the Medgidia pit represent all the gendered life-stages through which Hamangia individuals and their figurines pass – an

accumulation of social identities that may well mark a significant rite of passage for those dwelling at Medgidia.

The second context with a large group of Hamangia figurines derives from Pit 2 in the Early Hamangia settlement at Durankulak-Nivata (Vajsov 1992). This is a rectangular pit with several internal spaces, measuring 14.5m × 7.6m and up to 1.4m in depth. Burnt daub is concentrated in the middle of the pit (Todorova and Dimov 1989). Here, seven figurines were found in a state of considerable wear and tear, some heavily fragmented (Table 3.6).

This group is by no means as varied as the Medgidia group, in terms of the absence of burnt and stone figurines, as well as a narrower range of gendered identities. In this pit, the absence of separate or broken phallic necks means that males are not represented as a separate category, only as part of an androgynous identity. To anticipate a later discussion, separate phallic necks are also absent from graves in the Durankulak cemetery, so this is an important negative aspect of the distribution of figurines in the entire Durankulak complex. Nonetheless, apart from the male identity, all of the other four Hamangia gendered categories are present in this Pit, suggesting another accumulation of social identities but not as broadly based as at Medgidia; after all, the

---

| 1 | almost complete standing fired clay androgyne, with top of neck missing and no breasts; burnt |
| 2 | a fragmentary standing fired clay androgyne, with part of the right side missing, with phallic neck and swollen stomach; unburnt |
| 3 | fragmentary female fired clay Torso/Legs combination, with swollen stomach; unburnt |
| 4 | fragmentary stone standing figurine, comprising a Torso/Legs combination; gender-neutral; burnt |
| 5 | complete standing gritstone figurine, gender-neutral; unburnt |
| 6 | a fragmentary fired clay female Upper Torso with breasts; unburnt |
| 7 | a fragmentary male fired clay phallic neck; unburnt |
| 8 | fragmentary fired clay Legs, with no gender identity; unburnt. |

*Table 3.5 Hamangia figurines in Pit 1, Medgidia-Cocoaşe*

---

| 1 | a fragmentary female torso |
| 2 | a fragmentary gender-neutral torso |
| 3 | a fragmentary androgyne, with a Neck/Torso combination |
| 4 | a fragmentary gender-neutral lower torso |
| 5 | a fragmentary gender-neutral lower torso |
| 6 | a fragmentary gender-neutral Lower Torso/Legs combination |
| 7 | a fragmentary base of a standing figurine, with no gender identity |

*Table 3.6 Hamangia figurines in Pit 2, Durankulak-Nivata*

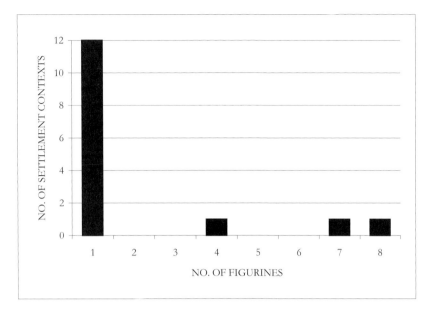

*Fig. 3.9 Frequency of figurines in settlement contexts*

Durankulak group contains a far lower proportion of figurines with positive gender identities (2/7 or 30%).

In the Durankulak cemetery, all of the nine graves where figurines have been placed are dated to the Late Hamangia phase III, or Early Copper Age (Todorova *et al.* 2002= Catalogue). The figurines are placed in two grave classes – cenotaphs (Graves 601A and 609A) and inhumations (*e.g.* Graves. 13 and 1036). The age/sex categories of the deceased and their grave goods show a complex relationship with the figurines (Table 3.7 and Fig. 3.8).

These data indicate that 2/3rds of the figurines placed in the Durankulak graves are androgynous, with three shell figurines with no gender identity and two female figurines. A high percentage of figurines reveal positive gendered identity (80%) – higher than in any settlement context. While three out of the nine graves are cenotaphs or have only traces of bones surviving, the other six graves contain skeletons with age-sex categories as follows – four adult female, one adult male and one infant skeleton. There is no straightforward correlation between skeletal categories and figurine gender categories. Androgynes are placed with cenotaphs, females and the only male, though the figurine with the male burial is unusual in three respects – it is seated, stylised and unburnt. Miniature shell figurines occur with both the infant and a young female. However, the only three fragmentary female figurines are found exclusively with young female skeletons (NB, other female skeletons are associated with androgynes). In terms of completeness, the complete figurines were placed with all of the four skeletal categories, whereas broken figurines were, interestingly,

associated with only female skeletons. There is uncertainty over the timing of the breakage of the phallic necks from the female torsos – prior to deposition or post-depositionally.

The vast majority of grave goods in graves with figurines consists of personal jewellery, often of exotic raw materials – none more so than the carnelian, which may derive from Armenia (Kostov *et al.* 2004). In Grave 626, miniature malachite beads were made specially for the figurines. Only four personal tools were found – a polished stone axe and a flint blade with the male in Grave 1036, a bone awl with the female in Grave 609 and a flint blade with the female in Grave 13. This grave also contains one of the rare animal remains – an animal tooth, while a shed roe deer antler (quite natural and not a sceptre, as claimed by Todorova *et al.* 2002, 80) was placed in Grave 1036. This range of grave goods is typical for the Hamangia III graves in the Durankulak cemetery as a whole. The grave goods presence a wide range of local environments, from the sea to local woodlands and steppe, to distant areas known by most of the deceased only through myth and legend. Their inclusion in graves extends the range of gendered associations, since each object would have a personal biography linked to both people and places. While there is no definite provenance for the copper, malachite and flint objects, metal sources are not known locally, the closest being the Burgas area, while many lithics derive from inland North East Bulgaria. *Dentalium*, *Glycymeris* and *Spondylus* shells all derive from the Aegean, at least 200 km from Durankulak. *Spondylus* ornaments were clearly an important means by which local personhood was constructed through the appropriation

| GRAVE NO. | FIGURINE | AGE/SEX OF SKELETON | GRAVE GOODS |
|---|---|---|---|
| 13 | frag. female with LT/L | female of ? age, with figurine near scapula | flint blade; bracelet of *Spondylus* beads/ animal tooth |
| 88 | 2 frag. androgynes, 1 missing neck, 1 missing parts of LT/UL | traces of bones, with figurine near skull | malachite/*Spondylus* necklace; 2 rings of *Glycymeris* |
| 601A | complete androgyne | cenotaph | *Spondylus* bead |
| 609 | complete miniature shell figurine; frag. female with T/L and left part missing | 20-year old female, with figurines near legs | very rich (*) |
| 609A | 2 frags, refitting to an androgyne + 1 breast | cenotaph | fragment *Spondylus* ring |
| 621 | 2 complete miniature shell figurines | 8–12 year infant | figurines form part of copper bead/ *Dentalium* necklace; sherds from 3 vessels |
| 626 | 2 complete androgynes; 1 frag. androgyne, with N/UT/LL; 1 frag. female with LT/L. | 20–25-year female, with figurines under skull | figurines wear malachite beads; (**) |
| 642 | frag. androgyne, with N/UT | 25-year female, with figurine fragments near left hand/legs | sherds from 2 vessels; steppe ass phalange |
| 1036 | unfired, stylised, seated, complete androgyne | 30-year male, with (***) figurine near head | |

Key:  frag. – fragmentary; N – Neck; T – Torso; UT – Upper Torso; LT – Lower Torso; L – Legs; LL – lower leg;

(*) The grave goods from Grave 609 consist of:- *Dentalium* pendants; small cup and 2 fragmentary vessels; necklace of carnelian, and *Spondylus* beads and *Dentalium* pendants; necklace of malachite and lignite beads and *Dentalium* pendants; bone ring; steppe ass phalange; fragmentary bone awl.

(**) The grave goods from Grave 626 consist of:- miniature malachite beads and a fragmentary vessel under the skull, near the figurines; *Spondylus* ring; a necklace of copper, malachite and *Spondylus* beads; bone ring; *Dentalium* pendants.

(***)The grave goods from Grave 1036 consist of:- a complete steppe ass phalange and a *Spondylus* ring near the figurine; a fragmentary vessel; 1 roe deer shed antler; a flint blade and a polished stone axe.

*Table 3.7 Hamangia figurines in the Durankulak cemetery (source: Todorova* et al. *2002)*

of the exotic. Their incorporation as both complete and fragmentary objects resembles the performances involving figurines, emphasising both integration and enchained relations with the land of the living.

One important class of local grave goods merits special attention – steppe ass phalanges. These distinctive bones consist of largely unmodified parts of the lower legs of *Equus asinus hydruntinus*, whose survival in the Black Sea zone is the latest anywhere in Europe (Spassov and Iliev 2002). The phalanges presenced an important part of the local natural world, whose crania were often placed, as hunting trophies, in Hamangia graves, while post-cranial elements were deposited in the Hamangia settlement at Nivata (Spassov and Iliev 2002). Moreover, in their close resemblance to the male member, especially at the proximal end (Todorova *et al.* 2002, Tabl. 103/11), phalanges contributed to the gendered identity of the deceased. Phalanges were placed in three graves containing figurines:

– Grave 609: young female skeleton + miniature shell figurine (no gender information) + fragmentary female figurine + male phalange

– Grave 642: young female skeleton + androgynous figurine + male phalange

– Grave 1036: young male skeleton + androgynous figurine + male phalange

M. Strathern (1988, 325–339) has remarked that every thing has both a male and a female aspect and it is the selection of the gendered identity in context that is important. While there were probably other artifact classes with distinctive gendered identities that contribute to the narrative of the grave, such as the cranial elements of the wild cattle *Bos primigenius*, steppe ass phalanges make an obvious physical reference to maleness, supporting the agrios-based ideology of hunting prowess (Hodder 1990). Their association with female graves may be taken as a sign of either female hunting skills or some aspect of a relationship with a mighty hunter.

The final comment on the Durankulak cemetery figurines is concerned with enchainment. Just as fragmentary objects in graves are related to their missing parts – presumably located somewhere in the domain of the living – so almost half of the figurines – all in graves with female skeletons – are missing a substantial part, enough to be removed by deliberate means and taken elsewhere. Since the Hamangia III levels on the Big Island tell remain to be excavated, no re-fitting of these figurine fragments is yet possible. But the implication of the orphan figurine fragments in the graves at Durankulak is that material links existed between the living and the dead but not between different graves. This theme is explored further in Chapters 5, 6 and 7.

## The significance of Hamangia figurines: gender, fragmentation and personhood

Hamangia figurines depict as wide a variety of gender identities, in fragmented or complete form, as any comparable figurine corpus in the Balkan Neolithic and Copper Age. Two competing principles may be proposed to account for this variability. The first principle, exhibited

by the majority of figurines, is that complete figurines are androgynous and that changes in gendered identity – to male or female, later to gender-neutral and finally to "no gendered information" – follow the cumulatively fragmented life-history of each figurine. However, the deposition of either complete figurines, or fragments that re-fit to complete images, in graves characterises a return to androgynous whole at death. The second principle is that single-sex, gender-neutral or third-sex identities can occasionally be exhibited by complete figurines. At the very least, this suggests that gender categorisation was of considerable importance to Hamangia communities and that material culture was a vital means of negotiating gender issues amongst the living and the dead ancestors.

It also seems highly probable that the cumulative fragmentation of once-androgynous figurines into other gendered identities betokens at least some of the Hamangia concepts of personhood. While there are many societies whose notions of personhood relies upon androgyny, the Hamangia concepts resemble those of Melanesian societies such as the Melpa most closely, with an androgynous person at birth, who gradually takes on the aspects of single-sex, only to revert in later life to a more complete two-sex identity. The wider significance of the first Hamangia principle is that there may well have been no clearly distinguishable sphere of male or female influence in a community, since all persons were androgynously composed of both female and male parts and relationships. This interpretation is in tension with the second Hamangia principle of non-androgynous complete personhood, as represented by a minority of figurines. Such gendered tensions over authority and social power may be expected in small-scale communities where particular individuals are seeking to expand their reputations through strategies such as control over imagery, gift exchange and/or the mortuary domain.

If Hamangia persons were created, at least partly, on the basis of the physical principle of partibility – *viz.*, removal of bodily parts from a complete or partial representation – we should expect other supporting data in material culture such as enchained forms of gift exchange. This is well documented in the Hamangia group, not least in the peculiarly Balkan form of fragment enchainment (Chapman 2000). This specific form of enchainment differentiates Balkan prehistoric partibility from the Melanesian form, since, in the former, people share part of the same thing at the same time, whereas, in the latter, gift exchange objects cannot be held by two persons at once (Fowler 2004, 67–70). Support for fragment dispersion and enchainment is found in those Hamangia graves with fragmentary grave goods – including figurines – the missing parts of which were deposited outside the cemetery, presumably in the domain of the living (see below, pp. 95–96).

The deposition of Hamangia figurines in three different types of context – landscape, settlements and graves – illustrates a further differentiation of the Hamangia group from most other Balkan Neolithic and Copper Age groups, where figurine deposition is overwhelmingly concentrated in settlement contexts (for exceptions, see Bánffy 1990/1). The single female of unusual form placed in the cleft of a rock at Balchik could indicate the special association between females and rocky environments or, indeed, the marginalisation of women from the probable salt source of Balchiska tuzla (Gaydarska 2004a). The placing of often fragmented figurines in settlement contexts suggests that this deposition is part of a rite of passage, marking either a return to the site or its abandonment. Two patterns can be identified in settlement deposits. The first pattern is found in the burnt house at Baia-Goloviţa, with a concentration of female figurine fragments and one androgyne suggesting an emphasis on femaleness in this special structure – perhaps a birthing hut (cf. Beausang 2005)? The second is found in pits at both Durankulak – Nivata and Medgidia and concerns the deposition of the full range of life-stages of the Hamangia person, as represented by all of the gendered identities known to the community. These deposits are summary statements linking the transformation of the Hamangia person through the gendered life-history to transformations of nature into culture, as betokened in the other finds deposited in the pits.

The most complex depositions are represented by the figurines in graves, since both competing Hamangia principles of personhood are represented here. The first principle is found in the complete androgynous figurines, which would indicate the return to the fusion and totality of a dual-sex identity at the end of a person's life. Vajsov (2002, 260) observed the low firing temperature of the Hamangia figurines in graves at Durankulak, perhaps a sign of making these images specially for the mortuary domain. There is some evidence that figurine fragments were re-fitted for burial as a mark of the re-integration of the female and male genders into an androgynous whole. Fragmentary female figurine parts in graves emphasise both the links to the domain of the living presenced by the missing male figurine part and the identity of the dead female. The second principle is represented in the miniature shell *astragalus* figures, found only in graves, in association with young adults, both female and male. This is a sign of the renewed emphasis on the identity of the newly-dead, who had barely reached the one-sex stage of adulthood yet who were associated with hunting prowess and the *agrios*. Rare representations such as the non-androgynous complete "Thinkers" from Cernavoda make a statement about the alternative approaches to personhood which do not subscribe to an androgynous concept of the dividual person, underlining the existence of social tensions about identity and gender in Hamangia society. In the following chapters, we shall investigate other ways of creating personhood through the use of Late Copper Age figurines and both Neolithic and Copper Age personal body ornaments made of exotic marine shell. For now, it is important to underline the definition of a specifically Hamangia way in which persons were created – based upon the coeval possessions of object fragments characterising an enchained relationship between dividual persons.

# 4. Schiffer visits the Balkans

In an earlier study of intra-site re-fitting, the assumption was made that this practice denoted deliberate fragmentation followed by re-use of the fragments and ultimate deliberate fragment deposition (Chapman 2000, 60–64). In fact, this assumption was part of a wider underlying belief that the excavated data represented, more or less directly, the operation of past social practices. Bailey (2001, 1182) has sensibly questioned this assumption, which forms part of a much wider debate over site formation processes. It is the purpose of this chapter to summarise the salient points in this debate, sifting the valuable results of this often painstaking research from unsustainable commitment to law-like generalisations – Flannery's "Mickey Mouse laws" – and other 60s/70s trivia. This chapter is thus a response to Whitelaw's (1994, 237) stricture that "post-processual objectives cannot be effectively pursued without adequate attention to the middle-range concerns." It also considers the question of 'rubbish' and its disposal. Since Michael Schiffer has been so closely involved in the search for significant site formation processes, this chapter envisages a metaphorical Schifferian visit to Balkan prehistory, which has hitherto been relatively unencumbered with the formation processes debate.

## Fossilised behaviour and reflectionism

One of the few developments in the archaeology of the late 20th century to which V. Gordon Childe did **not** contribute was the debate on site formation processes. According to Childe (1956, 1), human behaviour was "fossilized" in the archaeological record – a direct precursor of Binford's famous claim (1964, 425) that: "The loss, breakage and abandonment of implements and facilities at different locations … leaves a "fossil" record of the actual operation of an extinct society." This assumption was generalised in the widespread "reflectionist" approach to archaeology, in which material remains were viewed as a direct reflection of past social conditions (Peebles 1979; Sherratt 1982; Smith, C. A. 1992, 40–46). Moreover, this aspect of the continuity

between traditional and processual archaeologists was inherited by the spatial analysts – those seeking activity areas through the discovery of patterning in the archaeological record (see below, 72–73).

There have been two distinctive challenges to the reflectionist view of past material remains – made by groups with utterly opposed research agendas – behavioural archaeologists and post-processualists. It is interesting to note the range of theoretical positions that are incompatible with a reflectionist viewpoint. We shall treat the two objections in reverse chronological order.

The later challenge derived from post-processualists, who recognised that the active use of material culture in the negotiation of daily social practices meant that meanings radically different from those found to exist in social life could be generated by material discard strategies, just as could partial distortions of social life and genuine reflections thereof (Hodder 1982; Shanks and Tilley 1982; Johnson 1989). An example of the first process is the standard Christian burial without grave goods, as if to deny the social reality of hierarchy and material differentiation but promote the equality of the deceased before God. This tenet of early post-processualism – the absence of universal isomorphic relationships between material culture and social life – is now widely accepted and hardly needs further debate here.

The earlier challenge to "reflectionism" arose from behavioural archaeologists, led by M. B. Schiffer (1976, 1987), who were concerned not so much with ideological issues as with the interpretation of patterning in excavated material culture. Schiffer (1976, 10–11) argued that, between the systemic context of past use ('living assemblages') and the archaeological context of current excavation, there was a series of cultural and natural processes which caused spatial, quantitative, formal and relational transformations of the systemic context, which went well beyond Ascher's (1968) entropy processes and the degradation of artifacts in introducing patterning of their own.

Schiffer defined three main refuse types in his search for processes of cultural transformation:

- primary discard – refuse discarded at the place of use (1976, 30);

- secondary discard – refuse discarded away from the place of use (1976, 30); the main characteristics of secondary refuse areas were predominantly worn out, broken or unusable artifacts, a high diversity of materials and a high relative density of finds (1976, 129).

- *de facto* refuse – discarded but still usable refuse; *e.g.* if a household anticipates leaving the house, they collect *de facto* refuse from inside the house (1976, 33).

This typology of refuse, which applies also to refuse deposits and refuse areas, is a challenge to the assumption that the distribution of objects replicates the places of their manufacture or use; it has engendered a heated and ongoing debate. Here, it is important to note that all the main alternative typologists (Sullivan 1978; Hayden and Cannon 1983; Hill, J. D. 1995; Needham and Spence 1997) explicitly argue against the reflectionist view, especially Sullivan, who maintains that similar depositional histories are **not** entailed by the sum of observable properties (site size, site type, etc.) (1978, 190–191).

Critics of the Schifferian approach to refuse types include DeBoer, who doubted that "… any archaeological record can be … made isomorphic with its systemic context" because there are too many variables affecting things (1983, 27), and Sullivan, who maintains that Schiffer's (1976) waste types obscure the diversity of site-building processes (1978, 201). Moreover, DeBoer felt unsure that the proveniences conventionally discriminated in archaeological excavations were sensitive enough to distinguish Schiffer's refuse categories (1985, 348). It should be noted that even Schiffer (1987, 266) has rejected the assumption that a "deposit" is produced by a single, discrete, clearly defined process but is, rather, formed by a mixed bag of processes. This represents a distancing from claims for universal laws of refuse disposal (*e.g.* Schiffer 1976; cf. Gould's claim that "residue behaviour, like language, is universal to man"; Gould 1978, 7) and has prompted the use of scientific studies of deposits using soil micromorphology. This technique can be used specifically to investigate Schifferian site formation processes and to provide insights into "the genesis of complex deposits formed by many processes" (Matthews *et al.* 1997, 281).

One diversion from the main debate about reflectionism, which nonetheless has important implications for the Balkan Neolithic, concerns Binford's (1981) strong attack on Schiffer's behavioural approach. Binford identified the main failings as twofold: (a) the assumption that site interpretation requires Pompeii-like *de facto* refuse inventories; and (b) the disregard of the importance of the cultural-transforms that actually make up the basis of

site studies. This critique was the origin of the infamous "Pompeii Premise" – still the unstated lodestone of many archaeologists, as in the echo in Parker Pearson and Richards' (1994, 41) comment on a Scottish Pompeii – "hence the almost perfect survival of the most famous Neolithic settlement in Britain, Skara Brae". However, it turns out that Binford's attack was misdirected, since Schiffer (1985, 18) denied he ever argued that inferences are only possible with inventories of Pompeii-like *de facto* refuse! Schiffer claimed, first, that his 1976 book was written largely about secondary refuse but that, more importantly, the real Pompeii premise in question was to treat house-floor assemblages **as if** they were Pompeii-like systemic inventories (1985, 18). It is worth noting Schiffer's later position that it is primarily **re-use processes** that created the historical record (1987, 28–32).

In turn, Hayden & Cannon (1983, 118) have criticised Binford's Pompeii Premise approach, noting that his main emphasis on the structure of the "distorted stuff" (*i.e.* culturally transformed material culture) results in interpretative sterility and a loss of meaning. Instead, they recommend that we follow the material system through its several transformational phases, from Pompeii-like contexts to utter destruction, referring back to the origins of the materials as a meaningful point of departure. Their case study of refuse disposal in the Maya Highlands (1983) is an excellent example of this approach, with many useful lessons (see below, pp. 75–76).

A more recent contribution to the Pompeii Premise sideline comes, appropriately enough, from Pompeii itself. Recent fieldwork at Pompeii indicated that Pompeii-like systemic inventories rarely occur even at Pompeii (Allison 1992, 49)! Bon (1997, 9–10) further demonstrated that there is no basis for the assumption that no re-use, scavenging and movement/export of objects occurred, since, prior to the final eruption, a series of small earthquakes caused the abandonment of some buildings, with the re-occupation of others and therefore likely looting of materials. Even greater transformations probably occurred through pre-scientific excavation and the removal and looting of artifacts!

One of the classic areas of archaeological research that relies upon Pompeii-like assemblages is activity area research. The spatial analysis of house floors and the search for 'primary refuse' has occupied many archaeologists, few more than Susan Kent (1984, 1987, 1991; but see also Carr 1984). In her doctoral thesis on ethnoarchaeological study of activity areas, Kent tested three hypotheses: (1) activity areas could be recognised from the distinctive content and patterning of artifactual and faunal remains; (2) activities were sex-specific; and (3) activities were mono-functional. Kent's results showed a validation of the first hypothesis but that neither of the other societies (Navajo, Spanish-American) had the typical Euro-American pattern of sex-specific, mono-functional activity areas. However, in later studies, not only Kent (1991) but also Sanders (1990) in his analysis of EM Myrtos, Grøn (1991) writing about Early Mesolithic hut floors and Malmer (1991) on Alvastra pile-dwellings, treat activity areas and room functions as givens, without any reference to disposal transformations or formation processes. This is unfortunate in the light of Hayden & Cannon's (1983) observation that "Artifact distributions in sedentary contexts provide the least reliable, most ambiguous indicators of specific activity areas, but are nevertheless the indicators most widely used." Or, as Hally (1983, 179) summarises the implications of Murray's (1980) research on discard, "These findings imply that the distribution of trash on a site may bear little relationship to the distribution of activities that produced it". In a postscript to a volume on the interpretation of archaeological spatial patterning for hunter-gatherers, Price (1991) admits "a failure of spatial models to identify activity areas". This lesson has not been heeded in settlement archaeology in the Balkan Neolithic and Copper Age, where reflectionist thinking continues more or less unchecked.

To summarise the debate so far, the notion that the archaeological record was a "fossilized" record of human behaviour has been so strongly attacked that it is no longer tenable. The ultimate statement of this reflectionist view – the Pompeii Premise – has been shown to be deficient even at Pompeii! The means of investigating the transformations from living assemblage to archaeological assemblage have been the object of long-term and ongoing debate – but it appears that most individual excavation contexts (a) have complex origins involving several processes and (b) fit uneasily into most of the typologies of discard advanced so far. To that extent, it is difficult to support the interpretation of activity areas without careful site formation research.

## Towards an archaeology of deposition

The investigation of deposition in hunter-gatherer communities has a long and interesting history (*e.g.* Kroll and Price 1991). While some fundamental regularities arise from this research, in this section particular attention is paid to the not so frequent but often detailed studies of the depositional practices of sedentary communities. Once the Schifferian search for general behavioural laws is abandoned, we can begin to utilise general principles that characterise such practices. In this respect, and given the high concentrations of artifacts on Balkan prehistoric sites, two principles are of particular significance: (a) the "Clarke Effect" – the variety of discarded artifacts tends to increase in line with the length of the occupation (Schiffer 1975);

and (b) the notion that the more intensive the activity, the more useful it is to have structured activity places, including provisional disposal places (Hayden and Cannon 1983, 156). Counterbalancing these principles at the empirical level, however, there are often very complex depositional patterns that vary across cultural groups and through time, while being defined by the spatial context as well as the completeness and/or fragmentation of the pottery. This is well exemplified by Kobayashi's excellent early (1974) study of Jomon pottery deposition, as well as by the study of the Bronze Age deposition at Runnymede Bridge Area 16 East (Needham *et al.* 1996) (for further discussion of these studies, see below, pp. 93–94, 101–103).

Perhaps the most useful overall framework for the study of deposition is Deal's (1985) division of finds from modern Tzeltal Mayan villages in Highland Mexico into four assemblages – use and re-use; disposal; abandonment; and archaeological – characterising three stages – the pre-abandonment stage; the abandonment stage; and the post-abandonment stage. Three types of transformations are recognised in the growth of one assemblage from another: disposal modes, abandonment modes and post-abandonment modes. In turn, each of these modes is defined by several characteristic decisions and practices (1985, Fig. 4: here as Fig. 4.1). This scheme maps onto Sullivan's (1978, 195–8) definition of three types of contexts:- interactive (objects during use: *i.e.* pre-abandonment); depositional (objects between use events: *i.e.* disposal); and discard (objects during disuse: *i.e.* abandonment). In the following survey of the four stages of use, disposal, abandonment and post-abandonment, we choose to use Deal's terminology, since Sullivan gives an over-specific meaning to the term "deposition".

Beginning with use and re-use, Deal notes in the Mayan case that most items spend most of their time between use-events (viz. in contexts of "disposal"), since not all materials or activity areas are or can be in use all of the time (Deal 1985, 248–9). If such assemblages were to be excavated, they would form in-use assemblages. However, such objects are rarely static, which is why Schiffer (1987, 28–32) claimed that it is primarily re-use processes that have created the archaeological record. It also underpins Schiffer's (1987, 59) opposition to the assumption that living floors represent "primary refuse"; large quantities of primary refuse were rare because of interference with daily activities.

Moving on to disposal, it is Stevenson's (1991, 275–276) claim that, while systematic refuse cleaning tends to be typify sedentary sites, expedient, unscheduled disposal typified **most** sites. Such unscheduled disposal could include dumping, for as Deal (1985, 258) observes, the greatest part of the refuse in Highland Mayan villages was processed through "dumped disposal" – whether

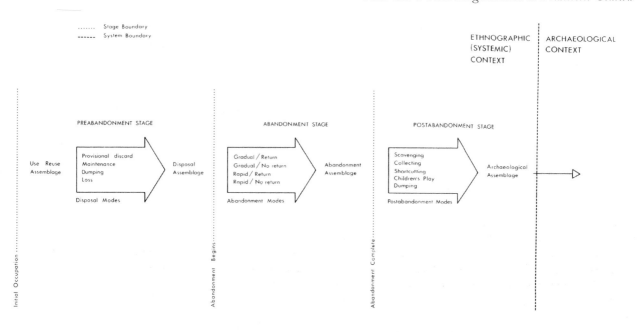

*Fig. 4.1 Transformations of material culture (source: Deal 1985)*

discrete or dispersed (cf. Schiffer 1976, 30). Schiffer would term this the "concentration effect" – that trash attracts trash (Schiffer 1987, 62). The two key factors identified by Hayden and Cannon (1983, 147) in refuse disposal practices were potential hindrance and convenience of disposal: *viz.*, large objects should be removed from activity areas, to be placed in nearby rather than remote discard locales (often dumps). In Mayan villages, three common disposal areas were found: house compounds, ravines and streets. Refuse was rarely found in gardens, because it interfered with cultivation (Hayden and Cannon 1983, 148). Another important factor was the pattern of intra-site nucleation/dispersion of houses: if the houses were strongly nucleated, more refuse was thrown off-site (*e.g.* into ravines).

One mode of disposal not discussed at all by Deal (1985) is the deliberate deposition of material culture as part of structured practices. Ritual abandonment produces considerable quantities of what Schiffer (1976) termed *de facto* refuse, whether after the burning of the house following the death of an adult occupant, as in burnt Navajo hogans (Kent 1984, 140) or amongst the Ainu of Hokkaido (Kobayashi 1974, 168; cf. Schiffer 1987, 65–66). Kent's (1984, 140) claim that assemblages in burnt hogans are "systemic" (*i.e.* living) assemblages, however, ignores the possibility of adding material culture from other structures. In this case, the concentration of pottery offerings in an abandoned and/or soon-to-be-burned house means the impoverishment of another domestic context (Seymour and Schiffer 1987, 552, 571). In their study of the Hokoham site of Snaketown,

Seymour and Schiffer (1987, 571–572) identify the consistent association of ritual breakage and artifact deposition with household abandonment following the death of the household head. Such practices are of obvious significance for Balkan Neolithic and Copper Age burnt house assemblages, even though it would appear that the significance of *de facto* refuse has been consistently downplayed ever since Schiffer's own (1985) attack on activity areas.

Another important aspect of disposal assemblages that Deal (1985, Fig. 4) mistakenly ascribes to only post-abandonment practices concerns the effects of children's activities (play). Hayden and Cannon (1983, 132–133) underlined the importance of children moving and dispersing refuse from structures, temporary storage areas and provisional discard areas (*e.g.* into the house compound or the toft) – all long before abandonment of houses. Stevenson (1991, 273) emphasised that children tend to play away from the main activity areas, usually with larger/salient objects in provisional or final stages of discard (*i.e.* the more interesting things).

Turning to the third stage – site abandonment, the clearest summary of the motives for household and village abandonment has been provided by Cameron (1991), who identifies the main reasons for abandonment of a structure as: social (death/illness, divorce, new family arrangements, population changes, warfare) or environmental (structural decay, natural catastrophe) (1991, 157–172). In partial contrast, the reasons for the abandonment of a village are specified as: environmental degradation, changing location of services; external colonisation/

attacks; natural catastrophes and disease (1991, 173–183).

The most quoted study of the effects of different modes of abandonment upon the remaining assemblages has been written by Stevenson (1982), who examined contrasting abandonment behaviour at two Yukon gold rush sites. All of the four proposed expectations were confirmed: (1) more secondary refuse was deposited in special locations at the site with a planned abandonment; (2) more clustered refuse was found at the site with a planned abandonment; (3) more *de facto* refuse was found at the site which was rapidly abandoned with little or no planning; and (4) more *de facto* refuse was placed in use areas when return is likely to a site after a planned abandonment. Unfortunately, there can be a danger of circular argumentation in the application of these conclusions to archaeological assemblages.

Deal (1985) has identified five post-abandonment modes: scavenging, collecting, shortcutting, children's play and dumping. In the present context, there is little to add to these practices, which can be widespread and lead not only to reduced but also to biased samples. An interesting possibility raised by DeBoer and Lathrap (1979) is that the presence of existing archaeological sites as middens for resources is a neglected factor influencing settlement location. A good example is the collection of chipped stone tools discarded on a Late Neolithic tell by the Bronze Age community living on a nearby tell for re-use using their own specific *chaîne opératoire* (Late Neolithic Polgár-Csöszhalom and Bronze Age Polgár-Kenderföld, Chapman *et al.* 2003).

The study of deposition is therefore a complex procedure, with the large number of significant factors making it difficult to demonstrate widely shared general practices. Whatever the precise content of defined refuse types, it remains fundamental that what is discarded rarely remains in the same place or state, unless it is a case of structured deposition, and that there are many and varied transformations from initial discard to final deposition. This conclusion is important for fragmentation studies and, in particular, the specialised study of artifact re-fitting. We now turn to the discussion of the extent of temporal and spatial dispersal of object fragments.

## Object fragments – a question of mobility

There is considerable variation in the form in which objects are discovered in excavation, from whole items to large fragments and many small fragments. Concerning pottery, Schiffer (1987, 338) asserted that the formation processes affecting restored pots, orphan sherds and pot fragments are generally quite different. However, it is more straightforward to discuss issues of object transformation by taking an integrated perspective that pays due attention to all sizes of artifact remains.

One of the basic conclusions arising from studies of the transformations of material culture after breakage and initial discard is that many objects are not immediately disposed of when broken. At the time of Deal's (1985) survey in the two Highland Mayan communities, 21% of the household inventories was in re-use – almost all consisting of broken vessels and sherds. Broken vessels were thus treated as a form of temporary storage (1985, 258 and Fig. 17 = here Fig. 4.2). The question of the length of time elapsed since discard and final deposition could be investigated archaeologically through the study of wear traces on vessels and sherds.

One of the most insightful studies of the purposes of ceramic re-use is Stanislawski's (1978) study of Hopi pottery. He found that many Hopi potters collect, stockpile and re-use in their homes both prehistoric and modern Hopi potsherds, with the following multiple re-uses recorded for the sherds (1978, 221–4):

– incorporated as part of door- or window frame of house

– used as chinking material in walls or bread ovens

– used to scrape and finish pottery during shaping

– protection of other pots during firing (wasters)

– placed in shrines for use as divining the future

– placed in shrines to avert the bad luck of a pot breaking during firing

– "templates" from which designs are copied in pottery making (helps continuity of tradition)

– sherds traded between Hopi potters, building up a collection of each other's pottery

– grinding down of sherds for temper

– whole vessels taken from deceased's funerary assemblage (chip rim to placate deceased's spirit)

Hayden and Cannon's (1983) study of the same Highland Mayan communities as Deal (1985) showed that fragments of most things were kept for some time, in case they turned out to be useful for something (1983, 131). Subsequent re-use and recycling resulted in substantial displacements, scatterings and breakage of many large sherds. The children's play factor was emphasised, leading to the dispersion of fragments of an artifact, the enlargement of scatters and the transportation of artifacts from one refuse area to another (1983, 132). Similarly, DeBoer and Lathrap (1979) found that re-use and recycling of pottery in many activities typify the Shipibo-Conibo, who keep pottery until it is damaged beyond repair (1979, 126–127). Weigand (1969, 23–24) also reported as many re-used potsherds as new vessels in an average *rancho* under study. Their uses included a cracked water jar for food storage and large basal sherds for scoops, water bowls for animals, wax melting and

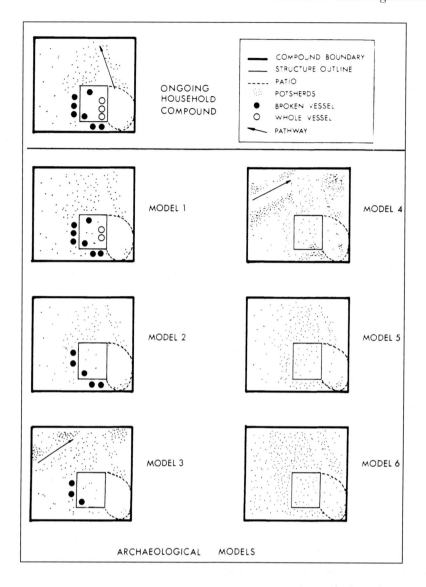

*Fig. 4.2 Six models of archaeological discard (source: Deal 1985)*

candle dipping, food ladles, spindle whorl weights and lids on other jars.

It is therefore far from a safe assumption that, once an object is broken, its use-life is finished. The parts of objects can be displaced both temporally and spatially from the time/place of initial breakage. A fascinating example of time/place transformations of two objects comes from the work of Weigand (1969), who traced the history of each sherd from two individually broken pots. While Pot 1 had only two phases of spatially stable re-use (first as a comal, later as a table top), Pot 2 went through a much more varied series of transformations, as follows:

– part of the vessel was soon re-used as a water jar;

– other parts were taken to the kitchen wall and kept (as de facto refuse);

– children collected some of these sherds and threw them on an outside refuse dump; some sherds ended up 100m away from the house;

– some rim sherds remained on the outside wall of the house for 5 months;

– 1 of these sherds were re-used as an artifact;

– 38 small sherds were left outside the wall;

– after 3 more days, all 38 sherds were thrown onto a dump.

There is no evidence either way to suggest that the life-history of Pot 2 was more or less varied than that of most other vessels; we can merely bear in mind the variation in life-histories between Pots 1 and 2. The general lesson is clear, however: we cannot afford to ignore the potentially high mobility of sherds in both time and in place.

In summary, while some objects are deposited soon after initial damage or breakage, many artifacts are retained, often in a rather fragmentary condition, for future re-use. In the case of Hopi ceramics, as many as 10 different re-use functions have been identified (Stanislawski 1978), while similar, if not so diversified, cases are known. Often ceramics continue in reuse until the fragments are damaged beyond repair. It is therefore not surprising that a lengthy and varied biography of an increasingly fragmented object leads to a high degree of dispersal both in time and in place.

## Overall perspectives

It is a common rhetorical strategy for proponents of new advances in archaeological theory-building first to attack existing theories and approaches, later studiously to ignore them as if they had never existed. With few exceptions (*e.g.* Whitelaw 1994), such has been the fate of Schiffer's behavioural archaeology at the hands of the post-processualists, who consciously developed a rhetoric and technical vocabulary that excluded terms such as "site formation processes", "middle range theory" and "*de facto* refuse", even though these were precisely the issues under discussion (Barrett 1994; Hodder 2001; Renfrew 2001; Thomas 2001; Chapman 2000b). We are confident that this chapter has resurrected some principles and approaches developed in the 1970s and 1980s by behavioural archaeologists that are still valuable in the interpretation of archaeological sites and their material culture remains. The fatally compromised state of the overall reflectionist model means that we have to select pertinent principles from among the surviving elements of the behaviourist programme while resolutely rejecting the other ideas. We suggest that there are four challenges to archaeological interpretation that cannot readily be overlooked in any attempt at site interpretation.

## The challenge for object biographies

The range of object mobility after initial damage or breakage is greater than has often been assumed (*e.g.* Chapman 2000), with implications both for the distance between fragments from the same object and the time over which fragments are re-used. While neither deliberate nor ritual deposition of fragments, nor indeed fragment enchainment, can be ruled out as significant practices, there are many alternative reasons for extending the use-life of a fragment beyond the initial break – reasons that

can in principle be investigated through use-wear studies of vessels and sherds, as well as controlled comparisons with sensitive ethno-archaeological studies. The main point is that transformational research raises the possibility of a greatly extended biography for some objects, which can differentiate the value of things within their extended depositional contexts. Although the extension of the biography of an object deliberately deposited in a special place would normally include a wider range of persons in the associations of such a thing, the specific re-use would determine whether or not that was the case for such fragments (for children's play, this is far less likely than for re-use of painted vessel fragment as a scoop used daily in the kitchen).

## The challenge for individual contexts

It is much more challenging to account for the origins, formation and content of excavation contexts than earlier. While the continued identification of the single-origin unit (*e.g.* an aeolian sediment covering an eroded drystone wall foundation) is not in doubt, many "cultural" units may have been of multiple origins, incorporating the remains of different and varied practices. In addition, the objects associated with an individual context can present different types of biographies, which need to be harmonised in an overall interpretation. Soil micro-morphology has become one medium-cost response to such an issue. Another high-cost strategy is practised at Çatalhöyük, involving detailed daily feedback between specialists and excavators on the nature of objects, faunal and botanical remains and soil micromorphology, so as to provide the excavators more information on which to base their context interpretations (Hodder 1999).

## The challenge for activity areas

There is a tension between, on the one hand, claims that the longer and more intensive the occupation, the more valuable become specialised spaces (Hayden and Cannon 1983) and, on the other, the difficulty of demonstrating the existence of activity areas through spatial analysis of assemblages patently not *in situ*. As usual, it is important not to throw the baby out with the bathwater. Our impression of the activity area debate is that it resembles the study of migrations and invasions in traditional archaeology and as criticised by processualists and post-processualists: it would be unwise to deny the existence of migrations and invasions in prehistory – but traditional methodologies were insufficiently rigorous to allow the drawing of such inferences (Anthony 1997; Chapman and Hamerow 1997). Thus, the challenge is to integrate the structural remains (ovens, hearths, etc.) characterising a certain place with assemblages consistent with specific stages in the *chaîne opératoire* of a certain production practice deposited nearby. An important source of information for stages in the production process is those small discarded objects that were not cleaned up during maintenance activities in the place suspected of being an activity area.

## *The challenge for the notion of "site"*

The broadening of the spatial contexts for material discard implies a wider consideration of the characterisation of a site. We are not necessarily referring to 'off-site' archaeology here – rather, the interstitial or outer **margins** of sites defined by the discard of artefact concentrations. Those topographic areas between residential zones that may have been overlooked before or simply treated as liminal areas may well offer important information about depositional practices (*e.g.* the deeply incised stream beds lying within some Tripolye mega-sites (Gaydarska 2003)). The edges of islands may well be rich areas of object discard, especially with closely packed settlement features on the island (*e.g.* the lakeshore of the Big Island at Durankulak: Todorova 2002). There are also zones within sites not necessarily defined by topography but that are preferentially selected for the final deposition place of the majority of objects – Needham and Spence's (1997) refuse-rich contexts and areas. Transformational research challenges us to refine our overall characterisation of sites and their immediate surrounds.

This group of four challenges poses a more general challenge to fragmentation theory – the development of a methodology for discriminating between deliberate fragment enchainment, fragment dispersal and deposition and the wide variety of other practices, often involving children's play, whose intended or unintended consequences include the temporal and spatial dispersal of object fragments. Meeting this challenge could potentially lead to a strengthening of the theory through the development of a more comprehensive methodology. However, we suggest that one reason for the limited success of the trans-formational programme is their insistence on the salience of a narrow and functionalist view of "refuse" for their studies. Gould (1978, 2) may have claimed that "The garbage heap is where archaeology and ethnology meet …" but he failed to draw out the implications of cultural variations in the perception of "rubbish". The view that "archaeology is concerned with the rubbish of past generations" (Thomas 1999, 62) permeates the discipline yet is potentially very misleading. In a previous critique of this view, Chapman (2000b) identified two principal characteristics of the modern Euro-American view of rubbish: rubbish designates something once active, once in use but which now is passive, no longer in use – which should therefore be segregated from the processes of the

living, whether for health or for ideological reasons. The dangers in transferring these assumptions to past practices were twofold: they increased the distance between "dead rubbish" and once-living people, making it harder to make and interpret the connections between them; and they drastically narrowed the range of interpretative possibilities for understanding deposition, since refuse disposal can hardly be anything but unproblematic and unsophisticated (Chapman 2000b, 349). The alternatives to "straight-forward" refuse disposal that Chapman posited involved more structured practices as well as discard and disposal. However, the issue of the utility of differentiating everyday from structured practices of disposal remained. Indeed, one of the originators of the term "structured deposition" has abandoned its use in view of the much greater complexities of discard and deposition (*p.c.,* Colin Richards). It has to be recognised that the avoidance of the term 'rubbish' does not remove the problem!

A more nuanced approach to 'rubbish' takes a fresh look at Mary Douglas' (1966) notions of purity and pollution and the many ways in which societies maintained cultural order by categorisation and disposal of waste. Recently, Fowler (2004, 59) has reminded us that even waste products may have been involved in sacred cycles of fertility and reproduction. Clearly Fowler is not thinking only of manuring spreads but a wider range of objects deposited in particular, often liminal places to convey specific messages. A parallel debate amongst sociologists has been occurring in recent years – one that echoes discussions in prehistory but in which there appears to have been no mutual feedback. Hetherington (2004) observes that, if disposal of waste is about 'absence' and more about placing than about waste, then disposal is concerned with placing absences and the consequences for social relations (2004, 159). This idea means that a contextual approach is vital in characterising which classes of places are associated which categories of rubbish. Generalising these insights, Hetherington (2004, 168) has made the key point in this approach: "disposal is about the mobilisation, ordering and arrangement of the agency of the absent." If the key aim of disposal is to remove dirt, or what Lord Chesterfield termed 'matter out of place' (Thompson 1979, 116; cf. Douglas 1966), it is essential that things are disposed of in a proper manner. This link with Douglas reminds us that waste disposal is an important practice in maintaining cultural order and that its treatment of waste helps a society to make sense of itself. Whether differentiated through the kind of material itself, the place where it is disposed or the associations between different types of waste disposed of in the same act or place, the categorisation of refuse is an important way for societies to establish their cultural order. Just as the birth of things in specific forms with particular decoration was a potent source of cultural order (see above, Chapter 2), so their death produces further opportunities for cultural work. Hetherington (2004, 167) emphasises that the work that people do through what they dispose of and how it is disposed is indeed constitutive of group identity and membership.

Far from being homogenous, these sociological approaches to rubbish have established contrasting positions on the nature of refuse. While Munro (1997) sees refuse as a 'problem', Thompson (1979) and Hetherington consider it a 'resource'.

Munro (1997) has developed the concept of 'conduits of disposal' as the repeated, standardised ways that a society has selected for the disposal of waste, unwanted images and unwanted meanings. However, waste is a 'problem' for Munro because the conduits do not work particularly well because it is hard to get rid of the consequences of one's actions. Archaeologists are familiar with the idea that the absent never fully disappears – presencing has been with us since the 1980s (Ray 1987). Munro, however, develops the notion, suggesting that this means that the work of producing cultural order is unceasing and that there is no closure of cultural work, as Mary Douglas tried to argue. Hetherington (2004) sought to extend the notion of 'conduits of disposal' to storage – a view that the transformational research of Schiffer and Deal does not fully support because of the potential for re-use of stored objects. Archaeologists have in fact developed their own versions of conduits of disposal much more systematically than Hetherington or Munro (see above, pp. 73–77) – it is the continuing work needed to keep conduits open and functioning to which archaeologists have paid less attention.

In his model of rubbish that emphasises its potential as a resource, Thompson (1979) defined three categories of things – durable (*e.g.* a Queen Anne chair), transient (a Trabant) and rubbish (a pizza box). He identified the recursive way in which rubbish was implicated in relationships between objects, their relative status and their value. Thompson (1979, Fig. 5) became very interested in those categorical transformations that could happen (*e.g.*, from transient to rubbish or from rubbish to durable) and those that could not without warning of the collapse of the category system (*e.g.*, from durable to transient and vice versa). This was because, for Thompson, social mobility itself and the continual re-alignment of social power and status depended upon permissible transfers between categories. Indeed, Thompson's big claim was that the three categories of the transient, the durable and rubbish permitted the uneven distribution of social power and status in our society, forming the basis for cultural differences between classes (1979, 198).

However, it should be noted that three variants on one

of Thompson's impermissible categorical transformations (1979, 103–105) – the shift from durable to rubbish – are not only permissible but commonplace in archaeology. The first is the total removal of durables from circulation (as in grave goods), the second the occasional destruction of a durable (as in deliberate fragmentation, the killing of an object or, in more extreme form – a potlatch) and the third the slow deterioration of the physical condition of a durable to the point of becoming rubbish (the oxidisation of the brown, shiny surface of a copper shaft-hole axe to a rough, matt green colour). At this juncture, it begins to appear that Thompson's model is culture-bound and of narrow applicability.

What archaeologists can take from Thompson's approach is that the boundaries between rubbish and non-rubbish are socially defined and that objects can change categories, often to devastating effect. The effect of increasing social differentiation is to create not one but a whole internally varied series of category systems, providing each limited interest group with different rules and practices in relation to the creation of value. Our category systems impose certain important properties on physical objects; Thompson believes that if such properties were not conferred on objects, then human social life would not be possible (1979, 77). It is worth emphasising the central role of material culture in Thompson's scheme.

Rather than reifying modern concepts such as 'refuse' and 'disposal', this approach to rubbish applies anthropological notions of purity and pollution and broadens their relevance to studies of modern rubbish. It would seem useful to consider four implications of the approach for prehistory: it prompts us to consider the placing of rubbish, rather than simply the matter that requires disposal, in all the contexts in which disposal takes place; it avoids the divisions between structured and other forms of deposition, that have become increasingly difficult to maintain; it emphasises the way that disposal of refuse establishes and maintains principles of cultural order; and it enables the extension of a categorical approach to objects into the study of rubbish. What the sociological approach to rubbish lacks is an appreciation of the diversity of conduits of disposal already defined, and hotly debated, in archaeology over the last three decades.

In this chapter, we have outlined the ways that refuse can be used in the continual struggle to maintain cultural order. We have also demonstrated from ethno-archaeological research the perhaps surprising extent of fragment mobility 'after the break', with a correspondingly wide range of practices and persons involved in such dispersion. In Chapter 5, we turn to the archaeological evidence for the other side of the coin – the re-fitting of fragments from different contexts and even sites.

# 5. Using objects after the break – beyond re-fitting studies

## Introduction

What happens when a complete object breaks into fragments? In many cases, the fragments are permanently discarded and a replacement is made or acquired. But the last two chapters indicate that this was not always the case. It turns out that there are many reasons for the extension of a fragment's biography well after the break, whether for further use in another capacity, for *ad hoc* building material, as a container or for children's play. In some societies, such as the Hamangia communities of the Black Sea zone, fragments were gendered differently from complete figurines and these fragments were used in negotiations of issues of gender, categorization and personhood.

Thus, when a complete object breaks, the fragments may have remained in one place or they may have been dispersed. There have been two parallel responses to these distributions. In the first response, visible from an early stage of the discipline (Petrie 1899), the distribution has been ignored and the single fragment (often the sherd) treated as the basic unit of analysis, for the extraction of information about chrono-types, patterning and meaning from sites (see Orton *et al.* 1993 for a history of ceramic studies). A wide variety of statistical treatments has been used on ceramic data and evaluated (Millett 1979). A particularly relevant feature of these investigations is the multiplicity of methods for inferring the characteristics of whole vessels from fragments (Chase 1985; Orton 1993; Schiffer 1987, 282–287), in the realization that very different approaches are relevant for complete vessels, as is usually studied in ethno-archaeology, and fragments – the hallmark of archaeology (Skibo *et al.* 1989).

The second approach typifies Palaeolithic and Mesolithic lithic assemblages and ceramic assemblages from excavations in the Near East, Anatolia, Greece and the Balkans and many parts of America. In major lithic or pottery re-fitting operations, the analyst seeks to process large quantities of objects per season in order to maximize the joins between fragments in different contexts (*e.g.* the 40,000 lithics from the Lousberg flint workshop, Germany: Weiner, J. 1990; the 80,000 sherds of Late Neolithic Dikili Tash, Northern Greece: Tsirtoni 2000,

9). While both methods have a long history, the two have developed in radically different directions. For lithics analysis, the identification of the *châine opératoire* has been used since the 1970s to answer technological and functional questions (Cziesla 1990 = his chapter 1; many chapters in Hofman and Enloe 1992), including the production of vital spatial information. By contrast, given the paucity of careful contextual data from the majority of ceramic re-fitting operations, it would appear that the overall priorities remain the re-creation of whole vessels for study and display rather than understanding fragment dispersion.

It is to the credit of Michael Schiffer that he developed methods of investigation not only for the location of the fragments but also for the extent to which the fragments found on-site comprise a complete vessel. As part of his site formation research, Schiffer (1987, 282–287) defined two indices – the completeness index (or CI) and the fragmentation index (or FI). The CI measures how much of a vessel is present and is determined by determining the fraction of each pot represented by the sherds, usually by weight. The FI measures the number of fragments into which the whole vessel has been broken and is calculated by the formula

$$FI = \frac{1}{1 + \log_{10}(P)}$$

where P is the number of pieces of the object. These indices are best suited to ceramics and glass, where a relative small sample size from any particular context is adequate. Although Schiffer used these indices to develop hypotheses about site formation processes (Schiffer 1987), these measures form a fundamental part of research into fragment biographies and contribute important concepts and measures to re-fitting studies. These indices are complemented by a term that, as we shall see, has many uses in re-fitting studies: the "orphan sherd" – a fragment without 'local' re-fits.

In this chapter, we discuss the attempts of archaeologists to reverse the irreversible 2nd Law of

Thermodynamics in their search to re-fit dispersed fragments and to make inferences from the re-fitted material and the contexts 'joined' by the re-fits. Before we proceed to examine previous re-fitting studies, we should ask what information on past social practices re-fitting studies can actually provide? Hofman (1992, 2) has argued that re-fitting studies have moved on from maps with lines to contributions to occupation type, duration, redundancy and use of space. But is this so? Do such time-consuming studies simply provide an estimate of low-level taphonomic processes concerned with object breakage and dispersion? Or is there more to re-fitting than meets the eye?

There are six general classes of information that have been inferred from re-fitting studies on both an intra-site and an inter-site level: (1) chronological – stratigraphic (taphonomic) information; (2) information on the sequence, and the spatial distribution of by-products, of the *châine opératoire*; (3) interpretations of re-fitting experiments in the settlement domain; (4) interpretations of re-fitting studies in mortuary and settlement domains; (5) interpretations of the material objects themselves; and (6) interpretation of the movement of fragments over the landscape. Before a discussion of examples of each class of information, we turn to the important issue of defining what is or may be a re-fit.

## The criteria for re-fitting

Many early re-fitting studies shared the same lack of criteria for recognition of re-fits and the same direct, case-specific explanation for the occurrence of the re-fit (*e.g.* Hall 1914; Hatt 1957). It would be a further three decades before explicit criteria for re-fitting studies appeared in print. Three studies from the American Southwest reached broadly similar conclusions. For Sullivan (1989, 104), sherds were considered to be from the same vessel if they matched for ceramic type, vessel form, decoration style, temper type, density and distribution of temper, wall thickness, core colour and finishing techniques. In her re-fitting study at Broken K Pueblo, Kowalski judged painted motifs to be most important, followed by thickness, colour and temper (Skibo *et al.* 1989). Thirdly, at Site 205, Southern Arizona, sherd similarities were assessed with respect to paste characteristics, surface finish, core colour and wall thickness, with the first two considered to be most reliable because they showed little post-depositional change (Sullivan *et al.* 1991). In her re-fitting study of Italian Neolithic pottery, the criteria that Fontana (1998) used for re-fitting included fabric, surface treatment, wall curvature and thickness and colour.

Bollong (1994, 17) refined the notion that not only were direct re-fits present but also sherds from the same vessel but with no physical re-fit. He went on to list six re-fit codes used in his own re-fitting experiments to distinguish between varying probabilities that two or more sherds have derived from a common vessel (1994, Table 1; here Table 5.1).

To our knowledge, Bollong's criteria are the most detailed that have so far been published and will be utilized in this review of other re-fitting studies, as well as in our own re-fitting studies (see below, Chapters 6 and 7).

| | |
|---|---|
| Code 1 | physical re-fit between sherds. Association certain. |
| Code 2 | no physical re-fit but similarity of morphological characteristics indicate sherds from the same area of a common vessel |
| Code 3 | no physical re-fit but similarity of morphological characteristics indicate sherds from one common vessel |
| Code 4 | no re-fit but >50% chance of sherds coming from one common vessel |
| Code 5 | "orphan sherd" (pace Schiffer 1987, 298–302). Unlike any other sherd in the assemblage. Probably represents one vessel. |
| Code 6 | Not determinable. No vessel designation is possible. |

*Table 5.1 Bollong's criteria for re-fitting sherds (source: Bollong 1994: Table 1)*

## Re-fitting studies and chronological – stratigraphic assumptions

One way to relate re-fitting studies to broader archaeological questions was to make the chronological supposition that re-fitting fragments from the same object that were deposited in different contexts dated the contexts to the same time or stratigraphic phase. This assumption – soon to become a principle! – could be applied to both horizontal re-fits, within the same horizon, or to vertical re-fits, linking different strata and became a basic tool for taphonomic investigation (Larson and Ingbar 1992).

One of the American pioneers of re-fitting studies – Robert Burgh (1959) – introduced the concept of the "time level" – *i.e.* proveniences with sherds from the same vessel should be coeval – in his study of the painted wares from the partial excavation of the Western Mound of the Western Pueblo site of Awatovi, Arizona. Burgh made whole or partial restorations of 38 vessels from sherds in 13 different rooms, interpreting this result as the dumping of debris/trash in rooms abandoned at similar times (1959, 189–191). Our analysis of the distances between re-fitting sherds indicates that most were found within the same context, with the furthest pair separated by three rooms and 8m. Burgh (1959, 189) further noted that even the largest vessels were seldom more than two thirds complete – perhaps an effect of the incomplete excavation (131/250 rooms). Thus, there may well have been the deposition of orphan sherds at Awatovi but dispersion of their linked sherds beyond the site cannot be stated with confidence.

An extreme re-statement of the concept of the 'time level' was formulated by the American historical archaeologist Stanley South (1977, 291), who argued that "the gluing of (pottery) fragments together joins the features as well". Examples of horizontal re-fitting are rarer than those with vertical re-fits and include Machnik's (1961) study of Early Medieval Igołomia, near Kraków, Southern Poland, where he inferred the same date for two pits that contained sherds from the same vessel, and W. Smith's work (quoted by Stanislawski 1978) on a Western Pueblo (Hopi) site, where sherds from the same vessel were found at vertical spacings of between 1m and 12 rooms apart (W. Smith 1971). In her review article of ceramic ethno-archaeology, Kramer (1985, 91–92) discusses the rare studies of the re-use of broken sherds and their re-fitting. Although her main thrust is concerned with chronological and/or stratigraphic matching of re-fitted sherds, Kramer does recognize that sherds of different dates may end up in the same depositional context, without noting the converse (sherds from the same vessel may end up in contexts of differing dates!).

Vertical re-fitting of fragments has been documented in many cases. Myers (1958, 138–9) observed that, at 'Abka, Sudan, the vertical distribution of broken sherds from the same pot formed a distribution curve, even though the strata were well-defined. Villa (1982) reports the results of four re-fitting studies in which post-depositional bioturbation is claimed:

– Terra Amata, a Lower Palaeolithic cave site near Nice, where flints could be re-fitted over a vertical span of 0.20–0.30m. In total, 5% of the whole assemblage could be re-fitted and 40% of the re-fitted pieces joined to flints several levels apart;

– Meer II, an Epipalaeolithic site in Holland, where 18% of an assemblage of over 3,000 flints could be re-fitted across a vertical span of 0.40m;

– Grotte de Hortus, a French Palaeolithic cave, were fragments of the same wolf bone could be conjoined across a vertical span of over 1m and Neanderthal tooth remains from supposedly the same individual were discovered across 4 or 5 levels; and

– Gombe Point, a multi-period site in Zaire, where hundreds of re-fitted artifacts were found to conjoin across layers built up over millennia, mainly through alternate sequences of wetting and drying.

In Villa and Courtin's (1983) study of sherd re-fitting in the French prehistoric cave of Fontbrégoua, near Marseilles, vertical displacement of up to 0.25–0.30m was observed for sherds from the same vessel. Five reasons were proposed – the soil fauna, tree roots, alternate wetting and drying, the digging and leveling activities of the prehistoric occupants and trampling. Greenfield and Drașovean (1994) examined sherds from above and below what they took to be a single occupation horizon at the Early Neolithic Criș site of Foeni, Western Romania, finding that the sherds had been post-depositionally moved both up or down from the occupation floor to give the impression of a "deeper" stratigraphy. In his analysis of the Early Neolithic (LBK) single farmstead at Frimmersdorf 122, Claßen (1998, 1999, in press, Abb. 2) traced re-fits between the pottery found on the NE side of the long-house and one of its SW postholes and five adjacent pits, as well as between two different pits in the household cluster. The most complex re-fit was a group of three sherds from the same vessel derived from one house posthole and two pits. The re-fittings were used to demonstrate the contemporaneity of the long-house and the adjacent pits. Similar studies have been completed on the larger-scale excavations of Langweiler 8 and Bruchenbrücken with broadly comparable results (Drew 1988, Stäuble 1997, Kloos 1997).

A more sophisticated re-fitting study forms part of the report on Renfrew's (1985) excavations at the palace sanctuary at Phylakopi on Melos, Greece, where many ritual finds were discovered in the complex sequence of Late Cycladic III shrines. The aim of Callum Macfarlane's detailed re-fitting study of the sherds and figurines from these contexts (Macfarlane 1985) was the stratigraphic correlation of unrelated sequences in different parts of the sanctuary. The recognition of differential wear on fragments from the same figurine and the occasional re-use of figurine fragments after breakage (!) disqualified any simple equation of levels between which there were joins in favour of a more detailed method based upon the primary context of each figurine and pot (1985, 453). The discovery of many figurine fragments in each of the shrines and each level of the shrines led to the inference that the shrines were the primary context of the figurines. The discovery of many re-fits provided the necessary stratigraphic linkages (1985, Fig. 12.1), although the explanation of how the fragments reached different discard locations related to room or corridor clearance or their incorporation in fill. However, Macfarlane does not comment on the Completeness Indices of the figurines, saying little also on the vertical or horizontal distances between re-fitting fragments. Completeness Indices for the zoomorphs and anthropomorphs (Figs. 5.1–5.2) shows a low index of completeness even after re-fitting: over 40% of the anthropomorphs are less than 60% complete, while the percentage rises to 60% for the zoomorphs. Again, the question of the location of the missing fragments is not raised, although the majority of the palace has been excavated (Renfrew 1985, Fig. 2.1). In terms of vertical displacement, parts of almost half of the figurines were separated by at least one shrine floor,

while fragments from a further 30% were separated by two shrine floors. Horizontal displacement over more than two spaces (viz., a room or a corridor) was rare but four-space displacements is known for one pair of re-fitted fragments. Thus, the re-fitting pattern at Phylakopi is much more complex than was recognized by Macfarlane, who avoided any social questions in his explanation of fragment dispersion in his attention to stratigraphic linkages.

One of the few collections of essays concerned with object re-fitting is Hofman and Enloe's (1992) edited volume "Piecing together the past: applications of re-fitting studies in archaeology". Although the range of raw materials involved in the re-fitting is impressively wide (pottery, lithics, shell and bone), most of the authors continue to utilize re-fitted objects as chronological and/or stratigraphic markers, despite Larson & Ingbar's (1992) critique of the assumptions underlying this approach. However, since there are many ways in which sherds from the same vessel can be recycled in their own future life histories, the assumption about the role of re-fitting sherds as chrono-stratigraphical markers can no longer be supported.

Re-fitting studies on a far larger scale than anything attempted either before or since were made possible by state funding in the previous, Socialist era in Poland (Kobyliński and Moszczyński 1992). The excavations in the Early Medieval Site 2A at Wyszogród, Płock Province, Eastern Poland, produced over 14,000 sherds from mainly domestic contexts outside the hillfort (Site 2). A long-term re-fitting study of the entire assemblage identified

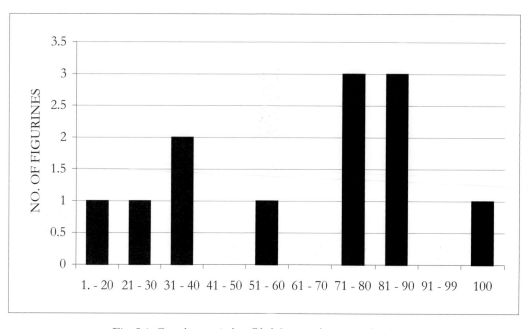

*Fig. 5.1 Completeness index, Phylakopi anthropomorphic figurines*

two kinds of re-fits: 132 re-fitted sherds linking different layers in the same context; and re-fits from 14 vessels from different contexts (1992, Fig. 3 = here as Fig. 5.3). For the former, local stratigraphic processes may be the explanation (1992, 118–9). For the latter, re-fits usually consisted of two re-fitting sherds but, in one case, as many as 17 sherds were re-fitted from five different contexts, some up to 40m apart (1992, Figs. 3 and 8). In this last case, the authors (1992, 121) state, without supporting argument, that "We can probably disregard the hypothesis of the deliberate deposition of the sherds of this vessel in so many different deposits", subsequently seeking to prove the contemporaneity of the five contexts. However, this attempt founders on the previously-determined stratigraphic relations and the authors need special pleading to revise their stratigraphic matrix (1992, Fig. 9). Another case, where sherds from the same vessel are stratified on the lowest deposit in two pit-houses (1992, Fig. 6), could hardly have arisen without deliberate deposition in the two places. This study is an extremely important piece of research, since it is by far the largest re-fitting study ever completed. The results indicate a combination of local depositional processes and deliberate deposition of fragments in different contexts.

All of these case-studies that seek to use re-fitting fragments for chronological or stratigraphic purposes leave something to be desired. This observation is not meant to downplay the importance of taphonomic processes, which clearly are significant in the four cases presented by Villa (1982), or accurate stratigraphic sequences, which are the basis of excavation records. The

assumption can be challenged on two fronts. Lindauer (1992) and von Gernet (1982) have observed that the deposits with a vessel's fragments could be mixed with later or earlier materials and re-deposited "in association" (Schiffer 1987, 285–6). In addition, social practices such as keeping heirlooms or relics and the creation of middens of material for future use are well documented in prehistory and falsify with minimal effort the underlying chrono-stratigraphic assumption of this research.

## The chaîne opératoire and its significance

André Leroi-Gourhan (1964) introduced the term *"chaîne opératoire"* to lithic studies in the 1960 – at the time the field was dominated by typological studies but with new approaches competing for attention. After numerous developments, not least by Geneste (1985), Pigeot (1987) and Schlanger (1996), the approach is now the mainstream way of developing rigorous interpretations of Palaeolithic lithic assemblages. In its essence, the *chaîne opératoire* seeks to define stages in the fabrication of a product, each of which can be recognised by diagnostic débitage. The re-fitting of lithic pieces is a fundamental part of this research. Cziesla (1990, 9–10 & Fig. 7, here = Fig. 1.1, p. 3) has distinguished three kinds of lithic re-fits: (1) re-fitting artifacts in a production sequence, i.e. the reconstruction of core reduction sequences; (2) re-fitting broken artifacts, possibly including non-intentional breakages; and (3) re-fitting the products of artifact modifications such as axe re-sharpening. However, there is no mention of deliberate fragmentation in this

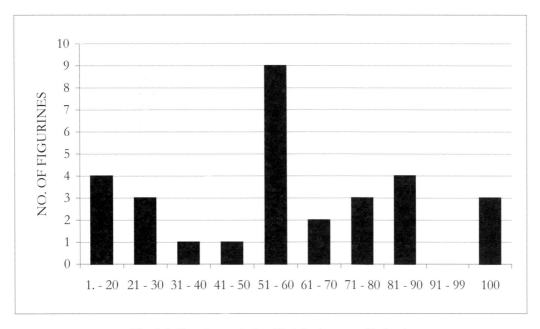

*Fig. 5.2 Completeness index, Phylakopi zoomorphic figurines*

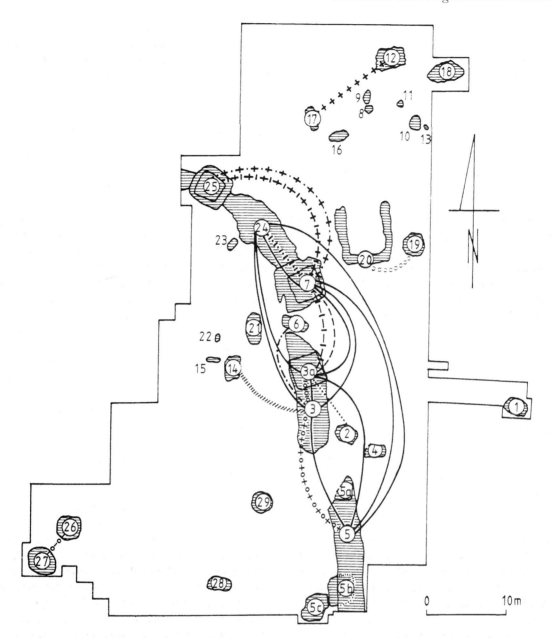

*Fig. 5.3 Horizontal sherd re-fits at Medieval Wyszogród (source: Kobyliński and Moszczyński 1992, Fig. 3)*

categorisation of breakage. Nonetheless, the breadth of insights offered by this approach is amply demonstrated in the massive corpus of studies edited by Cziesla *et al.* (1990): only a few examples from this volume will suffice.

Some of the best technical studies derive from the long-term study of the Upper Palaeolithic, Magdalenian campsites at Pincevent, near Paris (Bodu *et al.* 1990). The team explain that, through re-fitting, they are looking for group behaviour but behind the analysis is the individual knapper (1990, 146). Three kinds of knapper are identified – the best technician, less talented technicians and apprentice – débutants (1990, 148). Re-fitting of flint

fragments has been demonstrated up to a distance of 100m (1990, 160 and Fig. 12) – a spatial scale termed "long-distance refits between sites" (1990, 159) (!!). This admission indicates both the strength and the weakness of many re-fitting studies – the very limited spatial scale of the analysis, which rarely approaches the possibility of inter-site refitting.

The same small spatial scale is implicated in J. Weiner's (1990) intensive re-fitting study of the material objects from the flint workshop at the Lousberg mine, Germany. Two person-years were needed for the re-fitting of 40,000 waste pieces and tools, which yielded re-fits of 2% of the objects, including non-flint and antler pieces as well as mined flint (1990, 180–1). This study enabled the reconstruct the detailed sequence of knapping for the main workshop products.

In a study of Bandkeramik re-fitting, De Grooth (1990) developed the *chaîne opératoire* approach further in deriving predictions for the types of re-fits found under the operation of four kinds of mode of production: domestic, lineage, loose and supralocal. At Langweiler 8 (the pottery re-fits were discussed above: see p. 83), all re-fit sets were discarded within the same farmyard, suggesting the domestic mode of production. The supralocal mode of production was indicated by artefacts made from "light grey Belgian flint", one blade of which had a high probability of deriving from the same core as a blade from the nearby site of Langweiler 9 – *i.e.* a probable inter-site re-fit or Bollong code 3 (1990, 204). However, the method has its limitations, as found in the study of the flint assemblage from Elsloo, where overlapping criteria occurred for the three local production modes (1990, 205).

There are relatively few examples of lithic re-fitting between different parts of settlement complexes. One such is Verhart's (1990) investigation of the flint assemblages from a series of small Late Neolithic (Vlaardingen group) artifact scatters along a palaeo-levee at Hekelingen, Holland. Distributed over an area of 120 × 50m (1990, Figs. 6–9), Sites D, E and F were 'linked' by re-fitting lithics made of high-quality imported flint in two re-working stages of the operational chain. Interpreting these findings as indicating coeval occupation by three single households, Verhart rejects the possibility of functionally distinct 'sites' in favour of the re-fittings indicating "a reflection of the behaviour of the inhabitants". Although the social practices are not specified, we take to mean this as a form of enchainment linking two of the pairs of households more closely than the third pair.

While it is evident that the *chaîne opératoire* approach has produced some technical research of the highest standards, there are two problems for embedding these studies into broader fragmentation perspectives. First, the research is often focused on a minute spatial scale, rarely transcending the site level and, secondly, there are still few practitioners who ask basic questions of the material, such as "where are the missing pieces?" A major exception to this damaging absence is the Maastricht-Belvédère project, Holland, in which Roebroeks and colleagues set lithic production, use and discard in a broader landscape setting of some 3 km² (Roebroeks and Hennekens 1990; Roebroeks *et al.* 1992). Nonetheless, since there are signs that the social is beginning to make a tentative appearance in lithic re-fitting studies (*e.g.* De Grooth 1990), we can expect future efforts to exploit the enormous social

potential of these detailed investigations. The enchainment of person to person through intra-household and inter-household exchange can probably best be studied by the *chaîne opératoire* approach to lithics (*e.g.* Skourtopoulou, in press a and b) and other materials.

## Re-fitting studies on settlements

By far the greatest number of re-fitting studies have been attempted on ceramic assemblages from settlements, both in the Old and the New World. Most of these studies focus on the principal methodological characteristic of settlements as being *in statu nascendi* – a perpetually changing and modifying set of dwelling practices that blur the distinctions between the once-clear results or by-products of individual practices.

Given Michael Schiffer's strong influence on fragmentation studies and related research into site formation processes (especially Schiffer 1987), it would be surprising if many re-fitting studies were not focused on the elucidation of on-site taphonomic processes. In fact, the link between re-fitting and taphonomy goes back to the early AD 20th century – to E. A. Hall's (1914, 108) excavation at the Late Minoan IIIB site of Vrokastro, Eastern Crete, where fragments of the same fired clay horse figurine were found in Rooms 7 and 11 (1914, Plate XVIII) – separated from each other by a natural rock outcrop and a minimum of one room (either 7, 12 or 13) – a minimum distance of 5m. These rooms may have been different rooms of the same house or possibly rooms in different houses. The excavator interpreted this fragmentation as the clearing out of a shrine (Room 17), its offerings thrown out into neighbouring areas. Similar findings were made by Jażdżewski (1955, 209) in his re-fitting study of sherds in Early Medieval Gdańsk, NW Poland, where sherds from the same vessel were deposited in different contexts – inside buildings, in front of buildings, in the small yards between streets and in the lanes between buildings. However, the notion that a vessel can be broken and its constituent sherds deposited deliberately in different contexts is by no means a recent idea. A good example of this thinking concerns Hatt's (1957, 173, 264, 362 and Fig. 200a–b) excavations at the Early Iron Age settlement of Nørre Fjand, where two large sherds from the same one-handled, decorated vessel were found in two different burnt houses – House VII and House IX. The sherds from House IX were burnt more heavily than the sherds from House VII. Hatt interpreted this as the fragmentation of the vessel, with part of it carried from one house across the street to the other house prior to the deliberate burning of the two houses.

Most of the larger re-fitting studies have been conducted at the site level, often in complete or nearly complete excavations. Studies such as that of Cressey *et al.* (1982)'s re-fitting of sherds in privy – well deposits at the AD 20th century site of Alexandria, Virginia are less common but nevertheless valuable. The finding that 85% of the sherds could be re-fitted to make complete vessels indicated the direct disposal of the majority of vessels into these deposits. However, some otherwise promising re-fitting studies have examined data from contexts in isolation, rather than searching for re-fits between structures. Two examples of this come from both the Old World and the New.

Skibo *et al.* (1989) re-examined the ceramics deposited at the Broken K Pueblo, excavated by Hill (1970) and used to derive social reconstructions from ceramic data. Their aim was to identify the site formation processes in the light of new ceramic re-fitting data. Despite curation problems (25% of the sherds could not be located in store), Kowalski successfully focused on intra-room re-fitting of sherds from 16 rooms – those rooms pinpointed by Schiffer (1989) as having a high probability of containing "missed pots" (*i.e.* sherds that could have been re-fitted to form complete pots but were not). The re-fitting resulted in the discovery of seven complete painted vessels additional to the 12 whole pots recorded earlier (Martin *et al.* 1967) and 12 more plainware or corrugated ware vessels; both of these totals represent minimum numbers since other potentially re-fitting painted sherds were excluded from the analysis since they lacked provenance and plainware sherds were often discarded on site (Skibo *et al.* 1989, 391–2). This analysis has shown that Hill's (1970) reconstruction of kinship residence patterns on the basis of painted motif distributions is flawed since the decorated sherds often derived from the same vessel! What is unfortunately lacking in this analysis, in view of the results of Burgh (1959) and W. Smith (1971) for inter-room sherd re-fits, is a re-fitting study of all of the extant sherds for all of the rooms – viz. a complete inter-room re-fitting study.

Similarly, at the Copper Age enclosed site of Boussargues, in the Hérault, SW France, Jallot's (1990) re-fitting study of the pottery indicated that almost all of the sets of conjoined sherds were re-fitted within a single structure – usually within a 2-m diameter (1990, Figs. 115–117). Although data is presented on the Completeness Index of the 34 vessels from cabane 1 (8 complete vessels, 7 at 41–60%, 6 at 61–80%, etc.; 1990, 175 and Fig. 113), it appears that no attempt has been made to re-fit sherds between structures or between buildings and outside space and no attempt made to answer the question "where are the missing sherds?".

A more wide-ranging study at the site level was conducted by Hally (1983) for the pottery from the AD 16th–17th century site of Little Egypt, NW Georgia. Here, Hally targeted the excavation of three main structures, yielding over 4,500 sherds. Pottery restoration produced 10 whole vessels and 37 partial vessels. As only a few of the 4,500 sherds could be assigned to these vessels, the majority could be described as "orphan sherds". A search for sherd cross-mends was restricted to rim sherds and sherds with distinctive incised decoration (n = 675) (1983, 166).

The re-fitting produced 25 cross-mends – all restricted to their own structure. Most cross-mends were recovered from single or adjacent squares on the edge of the structure, beyond the central use sector, with **no** evidence for intentional discard of sherds in abandoned structures (1983, 169). Probably this sherd refuse was left to accumulate after discard, with little subsequent movement (1983, 170) – an indication of the remains of a living assemblage deposited in structures that had rarely had a thorough cleaning.

Of the three classes of pottery, the whole vessels were found to be 75–95% complete, with Hally claiming that missing sherds were lost because only half of the house floor deposits were subject to flotation – therefore, it was assumed that all of these vessels were deposited whole. The partial vessels were found to be 5–60% complete; the extant fragments were selected as having high potential, both in size and shape, for re-use as pot lids, serving bowls, water dishes, griddles or scoops. The three vessels with traces of re-firing were probably used as griddles (1983, 171, 176). Of the orphan sherds found in the structures, "hundreds of vessels are represented by one or a few sherds that presumably were not picked up when vessels broke" (1983, 180). On this basis, Hally claimed that the assemblages from the three structures represent systemic inventories with minimal disturbance. However, the notion that 25% of an otherwise whole vessel could be missing because of a lack of flotation seems a trifle exaggerated. If sherds could be detached from broken pots that are removed from a house, it seems at least possible that sherds could be removed from vessels remaining in the house. Hally does not formulate the question "where are the missing parts?" for his structural assemblages – just as pertinent for the partial vessels, with up to 90% missing. It is possible that the vast majority of the missing vessel parts were transformed into an abandonment assemblage through processes of re-use and recycling. But it does appear as if 70–80% of the total ceramic assemblage is missing from the parts that represent it. It is worth underlining the occurrence of such a pattern in AD 16th–17th century Georgia, in view of the occurrence of similar patterns in prehistoric Europe (see below, pp. 100–103).

A promising approach to site formation processes has been developed by researchers working in the American South West, who have developed innovative ways of approaching the use of fragments of vessels. Three examples of their work are presented here. First, re-fitting was made on a complete ceramic assemblage from the total excavation of AZ I:1:17 [ASM], a small Kayenta Anasazi settlement near the Grand Canyon, that was burnt down after a 15-year occupation (AD 1049–1064) (Sullivan 1989, 102–3). Out of a grand total of 2,067 sherds, 615 sherds were found in the burnt architectural debris of the four structures. Five hypotheses were investigated to account for the presence of these sherds:

1. Discarded artifacts that had been dumped in the houses
2. Vessels stored on the rooves that then broke when the houses burnt down
3. Scavenged refuse incorporated into the houses when built
4. Vessel fragments that had been stored on the rooves as "provisional discard"
5. Sherds as construction materials used to repair the houses.

The re-fitting study produced 84 separate vessels, while only 14 orphan sherds did not match these sherd groups. One intact vessel was found, and the number of sherds comprising a vessel ranged from two to 103 (1989, 105). Fourteen vessels were definitely found on the floors of the houses at the time of the fire. There was no support for Hypotheses 1, 2 and 3, while Hypothesis 4 could explain 1/3 of the data. The most probable hypothesis was that the sherds were used in repairing structures on site, since differences in the size and weight of the sherds in the house assemblages could in each case be related to the specific form of house building. However, no social factors were introduced into the interpretation of this site, such as the enchained relationship between the persons who made and used the ceramics whose fragments were incorporated into repaired structures.

The same absence of the social is evident in the second study, in which Sullivan *et al.* (1991) tested the re-fitting of all sherds at the completely excavated Hokoham agave-processing Site 205, in the Sonoran Desert of Southern Arizona. Three rockpiles and an agave-roasting pit defined the site features, which included an assemblage of 946 sherds, mostly plainware (1991, 244), 176 of which were too burnt for further study. A suite of 82 batches of matching or re-fitting sherds was identified from this assemblage. Not one single complete vessel was found in the re-fitting; in fact, the sherd batches never amounted to more than 25% of any vessel, while many represented as little as 5% (the single-sherd batches) (*p.c.* J. Skibo and A. Sullivan). Conjoinable sherds comprised only 7% of the assemblage, while the batches ranged from one sherd to 88 (1991, 248 and Table 2). These facts point to the absence of complete vessels on site, indicating that

previously broken sherds were transported to the site for agave processing. Use-wear analysis of many sherds is consistent with their use in constructing or emptying roasting pits. This is one of the few re-fitting studies in which the possibility is entertained that vessel fragments did not derive from whole vessels used on site but, rather, derived from other incomplete vessels at other locations in the landscape.

Another such study is Lindauer's (1992) re-fitting study of the partly excavated AD 12th–13th site of Shoofly Village (AZ), where black wares and white wares appeared as intrusive to the local red and brown ware assemblage. Lindauer claimed that only one of the eight ancient re-fits resulted from the introduction of a complete vessel onto the site, while the remaining re-fits were made between worn and eroded sherds introduced as sherds collected from nearby abandoned sites. Of the 1,000 intrusive sherds, some 40 were re-used on site as sherd scrapers. However, no inter-room fits were attempted because of the partial excavation of the site.

Two Hungarian Neolithic re-fitting studies on assemblages from total excavations provide interesting *comparanda* for the New World cases – the Early Neolithic site of Endrőd 119 (Makkay 1992; Bökönyi 1992) and the Middle Neolithic site of Füzesabony-Gubakút (Domboróczky 2003).

Endrőd 119, in South East Hungary, is the only Early Neolithic Körös settlement that has been totally excavated (Makkay 1992; Bökönyi 1992). The site measures 75 × 50m, with a 0.50–0.60cm thick cultural layer badly damaged by ploughing. According to Makkay's preliminary report on the stratigraphy, there are at least two phases:

– an earlier phase with all of the eight sacrificial pits, the large Pits 4, 5, 12 and 13, Oven 8, Fireplace 2, and Graves 1 – 4, 9–11 & 13
– a later Phase, with two surface houses, large pits 9 & 10 and Fireplace 9.

A re-fitting study of all sherds produced three kinds of re-fits: (a) vertical re-fits in one and the same pit; (b) sherds deriving from a common vessel re-fitted from two or more different contexts; and (c) sherds with the same distinctive decoration (white on red painted ware) probably deriving from the same vessel and deposited in different contexts (Fig. 5.4).

Vertical re-fits were found within four Pits – 4, 10, 12 and 13 – *i.e.* in both Phases. The mean distance between the re-fitted sherds varies from pit to pit: 0.60m for Pit 10, 0.80m for Pit 12, 0.90m for Pit 4 and 1.20m for Pit 13. These data suggest that vessels were being broken and some fragments conserved (perhaps for children's play, perhaps for re-cycling) while other parts were immediately deposited.

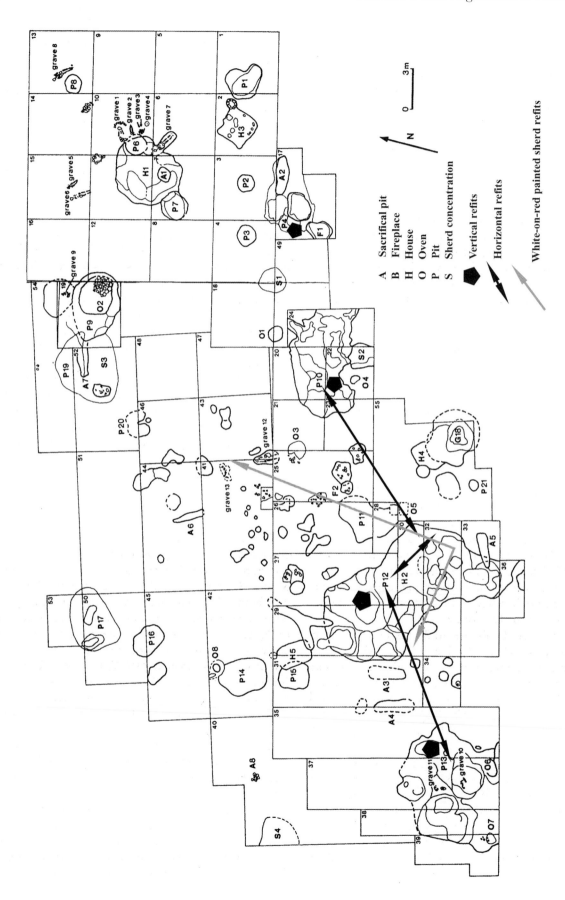

*Fig. 5.4 Horizontal and vertical sherd re-fits, Early Neolithic Endröd 119 (source: Makkay 1992, site plan)*

The re-fits between sherds from different contexts indicate weak links within the earlier Phase (pits 12 and 13: 5m apart), strong links between Pit 12 (the earlier Phase) and House 2 (the later Phase), as well as weak links within the later Phase (House 2 and Pit 10: over 10m apart). Even taking into account the short time that elapsed between the earlier and the later Phases at Endrőd 119, there is clear evidence from the strongest links – Pit 12 and House 2, linked between Phases – for conservation of sherd material prior to potential enchainment and later deposition. A similar practice is probably responsible for the re-fittings between contexts in the same Phase. Likewise, it is highly probable that the same vessel was broken to yield the only three white-on-red painted ware sherds on the entire site, which were deposited in the earlier Phase at distances of between 5 and 12m.

It is notable that all of the re-fits link contexts in the Western part of the site, without a single sherd match in the Eastern part. Since the site has been totally excavated, and the vast majority of the vessels, even the restored pottery, is missing major parts, it seems highly probable that sherds have been both brought onto the site and taken off the site.

Re-fitting on all excavated pottery was attempted at a slightly later site on the Northern edge of the Great Hungarian Plain – the Alföld Linear Pottery settlement of Füzesabony-Gubakút (Domboróczky 2003). A recent revision of the sequencing of the site houses and pits on the basis of 16 [14]C dates proposes three phases – an Early phase (with 3 houses, 4 pits and 4 burials), a Middle phase (with 3 or 4 houses, 5 pits and 4 burials) and a Late phase (with no obvious houses) (Chapman *et al.*, in press). The transition from the Early to Middle phase falls around 5400–5370 Cal BC, the Middle to Late transition at 5250–5200 Cal BC. This variation on the excavator's sequence suggests a hamlet in the Early phase, an expansion to a village in the Middle phase and a contraction to a single-household site in the Late phase.

The re-fitting study discovered 33 vessel re-fits from different contexts (2003, 16–17 and Figs. 5–6). Almost half of the re-fits derive from pits in both the Early and Middle phases (n = 16/33), with eight re-fits between different Middle-phase contexts and 9 re-fits between dated phases and contexts of uncertain date. Domboróczky's explanation is that various parts of whole vessels were discarded in different areas of the site and became worn through trampling prior to eventual incorporation into different pits; no reference was made to the enchainment of sherds in different houses, where the fragments continued their lives, eventually becoming worn through use before their deliberate discard in pits. There are also no details on the Completion Index of the assemblage or the frequency and distribution of orphan sherds.

Two independent re-fitting studies on Neolithic lakeside villages produce interesting comparisons for the Hungarian examples. The first is Pétrequin *et al.*'s (1994) excavation of half of the burnt-down lakeside Final Neolithic village of Chalain 2C, with its seven timber-framed houses. The study of the ceramic assemblage included a spatial analysis of the pottery, its temper, its decorative motifs and forms and its fragmentation characteristics. The strong impression of household choice over all ceramic variables within a homogeneous potting tradition stands, to some extent, in contrast to the fragmentation of the vessels, that can be divided into three classes: 10 complete pots, 20 pots with a Completeness Index exceeding 50% and the remainder of the vessels (76) represented by only a few sherds. The excavators propose that most vessels were deposited because they were broken and afterwards discarded on the periphery of the village rather than near the houses. However, the spatial plan of re-fitted sherds (1994, 410 and Fig. 3) indicates considerable variation in the patterning of the 18 re-fitted vessels (13 with two sherds, 3 with 3 sherds and 1 each with 5 and 6 sherds). The majority of vessels (n = 8) have one sherd in a house and one outside that house, five vessels with both/all sherds outside any house, two vessels with re-fitted sherds within the same house and three vessels with sherds in two houses, twice with additional sherds outside the houses. If they are not caused by adult re-use of fragments or children playing with sherds (see above, pp. 73–75: Deal 1985), the cases with sherds from the same vessel in different houses are more likely to represent some form of enchainment between houses.

The other re-fitting study at a lakeside settlement was conducted by Fontana (1998) on the pottery in and around Structure 3 at the Square Mouth Pottery settlement of Molino Casarotto, on the shore of Lake Fimon, in Northern Italy, where three timber structures were found. An estimated total of 108 vessels, from an original sample of 1,180 sherds, was used as the basis for six further analyses of the pottery associated with timber platform no. 3: (1) the estimated MINV; (2a) Schiffer's (1987) fragmentation index; (2b) the index of conservation (an estimate of the amount of a vessel surviving); (3) an evaluation of the horizontal and vertical dispersion of fragments belonging to one common vessel; (4) graphical representation of (3); (5) functional analysis of vessels and sherds; and (6) distributional analysis of sherds in relation to structures. Not a single vessel on the site was found to be complete. The majority of vessels are represented by only a 25% Completeness Index, while one-sixth had a 50% Completeness Index, nine had 75% and two had 90%. The sherd disposal is used to identify five patterns of maintenance activities and refuse disposal: (1) large sherds were discarded away from the platform to keep the living areas "clean"; (2) small re-fitting sherds were abandoned near the hearth; (3) vessels with highest Completeness Index were left near the hearth at its final use; (4) fragments from necked water-jars were broken on the path to the lake; and (5) a residential area was completely lacking in sherds. However, this otherwise interesting study omits any discussion of the distances over which sherds from the same vessel were found, as well as what happened to the missing sherds.

These omissions are largely rectified in an unpublished B. A. (Hons.) dissertation by Martina Dalla Riva (2003), in a comparison of the Fimon data with the re-fitting data from another North Italian Neolithic site – the Rocca di Rivoli (Barfield and Bagolini 1976). The main features of Site L at the latter was a series of Neolithic pits of varying shapes and sizes, all with secondary deposition of sherds (1976, 7–13). Dalla Riva's study confirms that the vast majority of re-fitting sherds at Fimon were discarded in the same house or house area, with five exceptions (linking Houses 1 to 2, 1 to 3 and, in one case all three Houses) (2003, 92–94). According to her calculations, the orphan sherds would have represented between 16 and 22% of all vessels in the three Houses (2003, 30–31). A quite diffcrent pattern pertains at Rivoli, where each decorated sherd in a pit is itself an orphan sherd – *i.e.* it **represents** an absent whole vessel. Two of the orphan sherds derived from long-distance exchange – one from Chassey communities and one from Aichbühl groups (Barfield and Bagolini 1976). Thirteen re-fits were found at Rivoli – three of which were from different contexts up to a distance of 2.5m (2003, 95–97 and Figure, p. 98; here = Fig. 5.5). While this spatial information suggests localized disturbance rather than deliberate deposition of enchained fragments, there are two instances of re-fitting sherds from different levels of the same pit – perhaps a sign of curation of material culture.

Dalla Riva (2003, 36–43) interprets the differences between the two sites in terms of variant uses of material culture. The intensive use of enchainment tokens at Rivoli enchained the site with other settlements, often quite remote. The pattern of one decorated sherd representing each vessel has also been found on the Parța tell, western Romania (Chapman 2000, 50). Several different practices could be identified at Fimon, including early post-abandonment scavenging, re-use of some sherds and the sharing of food between households as symbolized in sherd enchainment. Dalla Riva emphasizes that not every transaction may have required a material expression of its validity, which was often implicit – especially those transactions between people in everyday face-to-face contact. This could explain the many missing sherds, which were carried to other sites. On the methodological level, Dalla Riva (2003, 43) found it difficult to distinguish between enchainment and other processes on a site such

as Fimon, where pottery is ubiquitous. This valuable study indicates both the strengths and weaknesses of the umbrella term "enchainment", while suggesting a reason for the absence of sherds from site assemblages.

Very few formal re-fitting studies have examined material culture other than sherds. However, in the earlier fragmentation book, Chapman (2000, 55–57, 62 and Table 3.4) summarized the results of four studies of the fragmentation of fired clay anthropomorphic figurines and/or altar tables from completely excavated sites in Bulgaria – Neolithic Ovcharovo-Gorata and the three Copper Age tells of Ovcharovo, Goljamo Delchevo and Vinitsa. To this list, we may now add the completely excavated Late Copper Age layers from the tell of Sedlare (*p.c.*, A. Raduntcheva). At Ovcharovo-Gorata, six re-fits – three between pairs of figurine fragments, three between altar table fragments – were found out of a total of over 100 figurines and over 50 altar tables, with each re-fitted fragment deposited in a different pit (*p.c.* I. Angelova, 1996). The Copper Age tells indicate a different pattern, with no re-fits obvious between the 137 figurines (77% fragments) from Goljamo Delchevo (Todorova *et al.* 1975), between the 41 figurines (68% fragments) at Ovcharovo (Todorova *et al.* 1983) or between the 37 figurines (95% broken) at Vinitsa (Raduntcheva 1976). This pattern strongly indicates the removal of parts of figurines from the tells, for fragment dispersion elsewhere – perhaps for use and deposition off the tell (as at the Omurtag tell), perhaps to other sites.

Our recent re-fitting study of the fired clay anthropomorphic and zoomorphic figurines from the Late Copper Age tell of Sedlare, in the Eastern Rhodopes, Bulgaria indicates a similar pattern. An assemblage of 80 figurines (94% in fragments) showed a high degree of fragmentation (Fig. 5.6), with no physical re-fits and no signs even of fragments from the same figurine – *i.e.* conforming to Bollong codes 2, 3 and 4. This finding supports the interpretation of either the removal of figurine fragments from the tell or the transport onto the tell of fragments of figurines whose larger parts were kept elsewhere. These figurine studies show great consistency and form the backdrop to the detailed re-fitting of the Dolnoslav figurines (see below, Chapter 6).

Figurine re-fitting has a long tradition in Japanese archaeology. While there are many studies of successful re-fits within the same context, the re-fitting of two anthropomorphic figurine fragments from two different settlement foci was reported for the Shakadô complex in Japan, dating to the Middle Jomon phase (Bausch 1994, 92, 108; Chapman 2000, 26–7). Whether these foci, 230m apart, are two separate "sites" or different parts of the same "complex" is a matter for local definition. Fifteen other cases of re-fitting figurine fragments have been found at Shakadô, but the spatial dispersion is less than

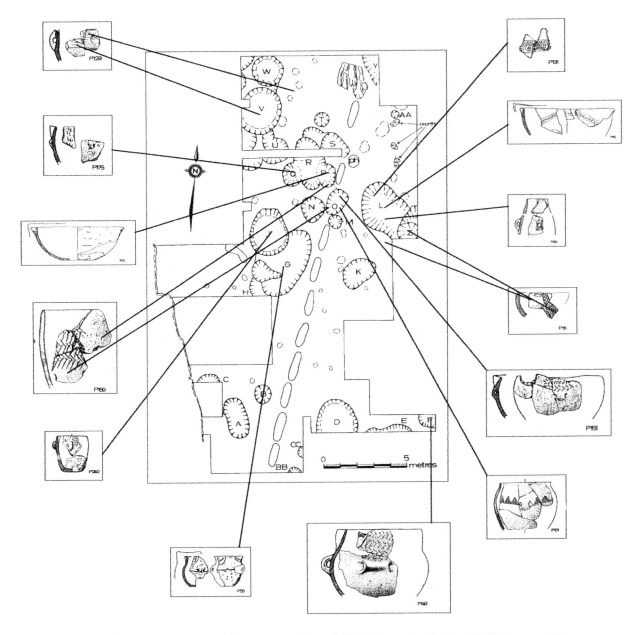

*Fig. 5.5 Distribution of refitted fragments at Rocca di Rivoli (source: Dalla Riva 2003, figure, p. 98)*

230m. But, at 3500–2500 Cal BC, this remains one of the earliest examples in Japan in which the human form is deliberately broken and the fragments used in different parts of the same complex. It seems improbable that we are dealing with accidental refuse or the result of children's playing, since the conjoining fragments were carefully placed, together with other unusual things, in different special disposal areas, termed "dokisuteba" (Bausch 1994). The Shakadô pattern resembles that found at Neolithic Ovcharovo-Gorata rather than the other pattern pertaining to Bulgarian Copper Age tells.

Remaining in Japan, we now turn to a single synthetic article presenting the results of re-fitting analyses on the level of an entire cultural phase – in this case, the Early Jomon. Kobayashi (1974, 167) has defined six main patterns of ceramic deposition for this phase; sherds formed an important part of four of his six Patterns. In Pattern C1 (sherds in fill deposits), sherds were found in the fill of pit-dwellings and the remainder of the vessel was discarded elsewhere, although no explanation for this was offered. In Pattern C2 (random discard on house floors), broken pots were dropped and left on the floor

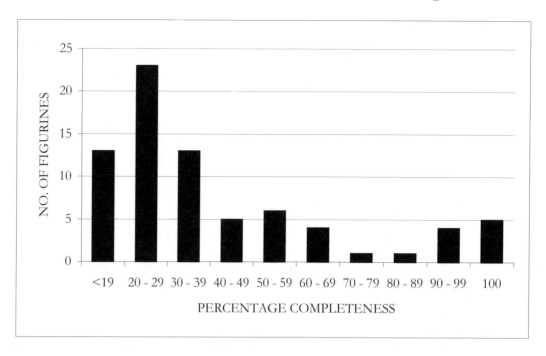

*Fig. 5.6 Completeness Index of Sedlare anthropomorphic figurines*

while the building was occupied. But it is curious that the larger sherds were not sufficient of a hindrance to movement to provoke disposal outside the house. In Pattern D (pottery mounds), large numbers of sherds were found with whole vessels in pot concentrations, again with no explanation of where the missing sherds had gone. Finally, in Pattern E (random dispersion) as exemplified at the Earliest Jomon site of Tama New Town 99, potsherds were scattered over the 1,000 m² area and sherds of the same vessel were found at considerable distances from one another.

Several factors can help to interpret the Jomon study. The first point is technological, viz., because Early Jomon pottery was fired simply at low temperatures, it was easily fragmented by light shocks. Vessels could be broken into as many as 200 small fragments (Kobayashi 1974, 168). Thus, the ceramic assemblage had a high potential for fragmentation – perhaps higher than in the Middle and Late Jomon phases, which showed an improvement in ceramic technology. Secondly, one can identify several different depositional practices at these sites: in parallel with the discard of the larger part of a broken pot where it was broken and the movement elsewhere of the other fragments (1974, 169), there was the inverse practice of placing sherds in the fill of a pit and removing the remainder of the vessel elsewhere (1974, 170). The dispersal of sherds from the same vessel in the random Pattern E may well be explained by adults moving sherds for re-use, by children's play or the accidental consequences of some other practice. But the main weakness

in the research, however, concerns the lack of explanation for moving parts of the same vessel elsewhere – especially if in one case it is the larger semi-intact part and, in the other case, it is the sherds that are deposited. It would seem that the perennial question of the fragmenterist – where are the missing parts? – has not been formulated, let alone answered.

In summary, the study of site formation processes through fragment re-fitting has produced a mix of significant results and predictable findings. Several trends can be discerned in studies spanning the Old and New Worlds. First, at most of the sites, all, or the vast majority of, re-fitted sherds were discarded within the same structure (Pattern C1 in Early Jomon, Neolithic Fimon and Rivoli, Copper Age Boussargues, Broken K Pueblo, Little Egypt, Alexandria, AZ I:1:17 and Sonoran Desert Site 205), although in the Boussargues and Broken K Pueblo studies, no attempt was made to check for inter-structure re-fits! However, the obverse of this pattern is that a few re-fitted sherds were found in different contexts, though sometimes as a result of secondary movement and accidental burial. This pattern has been interpreted as a sign of a living (*pace* Schiffer, "systemic") assemblage (Little Egypt), direct dumping in wells or privies (Alexandria) and refuse disposal with maintenance activities, sherd re-use and post-abandonment scavenging (Fimon). The second pattern, which is much rarer, is the predominant disposal of re-fitting fragments in different contexts (Endröd 119, Gubakut and Chalain 2C) – perhaps because of adult sherd re-use, children's play or other secondary uses but also perhaps related to food exchange symbolized by sherd enchainment. This pattern is repeated at Middle Jomon Shakadô and at Balkan Neolithic Ovcharovo-Gorata using the medium of anthropomorphic figurines.

The third pattern, equally widespread as the first, is the occurrence of varying proportions of orphan fragments in all assemblages. The lowest proportion of orphan sherds was found at AZ I:1:17 (2.3%), where the fragmentation pattern was explained by sherd use in structural repairs, and the highest at Rocca di Rivoli (100%), with the postulated use of sherds as tokens of enchainment between sites. The finding of 100% orphan fragments typifying the figurine assemblages of four Copper Age tells in Bulgaria indicates that this pattern is not restricted to potsherds. The tendency is for the absence of high proportions of ceramics by weight, volume or surface area – 75–80% at Little Egypt and perhaps more at Fimon, where a fifth of the vessels in each house were represented by orphan sherds. Even when sherds can be re-fitted, the combined sherds rarely comprise a complete vessel, indicating a complex sequence of fragment dispersion. This pattern has been found at the few other completely excavated sites with re-fitting, use-wear and erosion studies (see below, pp. 100–105). While fundamental for assessing the likelihood of explanations other than enchainment of sherds for orphan sherds and partial pots, these re-fitting studies have rarely posed the question: "where are the missing fragments?" An exception to this research gap is the Sonoran Desert Site 205 study, where it is argued that large sherds, from vessels previously broken elsewhere, were brought to the site for agave processing. Another question, also relevant to *chaîne opératoire* studies, concerns the later life of an enchained fragment: once a person has been given a fragment enchaining them to another person, what is she to do with that piece? Three possibilities emerge: fragment the fragment further, curate it or use it as an active part of domestic material culture.

In general, a methodological difficulty with settlements is the lack of closed contexts and the complementary probability of fragment re-use and recycling. Careful single-context excavation with the 3-D recording of every fragment may well be the only way forward for fragmentation studies on settlements. We now turn to re-fitting studies on sites with fragmentation of finds in the mortuary domain, where the significantly greater closure of contexts helps us to provide some details on the later biographies of enchained fragments.

### Re-fitting studies involving the mortuary domain

The lower frequency of sites that combine both the domestic and the mortuary domains (as compared to one or the other arena: cf. Chapman 1991) means that relatively few studies have focussed on possible re-fits between these two domains. I shall present just two examples – one from the Balkan Copper Age, the other from the British Bronze Age.

The Durankulak complex, on the Northern part of the Bulgarian Black Sea coast, comprises a long-lived cemetery with both Neolithic (Early Hamangia) and Copper Age (Middle – Late Hamangia and Varna groups) burials in the largest-known cemetery in the Balkans, lying on the shores of a lagoon (Todorova 2002). The Neolithic settlement lies near the cemetery on the lagoon shore (Todorova and Dimov 1989), while the Copper Age settlement was moved onto an island in the lagoon in the early 5th millennium Cal BC (Todorova 1997; for new AMS dates for Durankulak, see Higham *et al.*, submitted; Honch *et al.* 2006).

A single example of conjoined pottery has been published, concerning half of a decorated vessel from the Varna group Grave 584, that re-fits to a large decorated sherd deposited in a house in horizon VII of the tell on the island (Todorova *et al.* 2002, 59–60 and Tabl. 99/11: here = Fig. 5.7). The use of an elaborately decorated necked carinated bowl whose two parts were recognised by the principal excavator across different excavation seasons underlines the visual importance of fragmentation practices – that those insiders who know the story (a category obviously including Professor Todorova!) will recognise the whole from which the part has been separated and reconstruct it in their mind's eye as the part symbolising the whole. The re-fitting of vessel fragments from both the mortuary and the domestic domains underlines the importance of maintaining enchained links between the dead and the living, even though the spatial scale is no more than 200m. Once again, it should be emphasised that the Durankulak example is an unequivocal case of deliberate fragmentation followed by fragment dispersion. The restoration of the sherds to form a largely complete vessel (the illustration suggests a Completeness Index of 60–70%) has prevented study of the condition of the sherd fractures; the exterior surface of the vessel suggests a similar life history for each fragment. The conjoined vessel is still missing a substantial fragment – possibly deposited on the tell in an as yet unexcavated area or, yet again, on another settlement or cemetery. A final question concerns the relative and absolute dating of the house in Level VII in comparison with the date of the burial in Grave 584. While both Grave 584 and the tell's VIIth Horizon have been dated to the Hamangia IV phase (Middle Copper Age), it would be valuable to have AMS dates for the two contexts in question, to estimate the gap in social time, if any, between the two acts of deposition. A final contrast

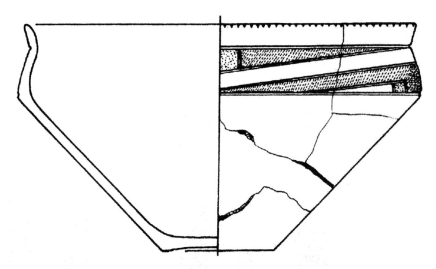

*Fig. 5.7 Refitted Late Copper Age vessel from Durankulak (source: Todorova et al. 2002)*

within the Durankulak complex is the lack of re-fits of figurine fragments, whether between different graves of the cemetery or between the cemetery and the tell examples.

A comparable case of conjoined vessel parts – one in a grave, the other in a house – is documented for the Middle Bronze Age of Southern Britain at the Itford Hill complex. One primary and 16 secondary cremation burials were buried under a barrow (Holden 1972), located 90m North of the supposedly coeval settlement excavated 18 years earlier (Burstow and Holleyman 1957). In Cremation 10, the partial remains of a cremated body had been placed inside a handled globular vessel that was only 75% complete (Holden 1972, 79; Ellison 1972, 110 and Fig. 8, 7). The vessel was packed with flint in a small pit, which was then sealed with a layer of flint (Holden 1972, 79, 88). One rim sherd and possibly the missing handle from this vessel was found on the settlement (Ellison 1972, 110; Burstow and Holleyman 1957, Fig. 24A and B). Although there was no physical re-fit, the sherds in the settlement matched the vessel in Cremation 10 in fabric, filler, colour, form, decoration and sooting marks; in terms of the Bollong criteria, this was a code 3. While Holden (1972, 88) interprets this re-fitting in terms of expedient behaviour, the selection of only parts of vessels and parts of cremated bones for burials shows that this is a recurrent practice related to enchainment. The material emphasis on enchained links between the recent dead and the domain of the living is just one example of the objectification of people in objects that has recently been well documented for this period (Brück 1999). It is interesting that Ellison (1972) emphasized the chronological aspect of this re-fit to indicate contemporaneity of cemetery barrow and settlement.

The frequently closed nature of individual burial contexts provides fragmenterists with an opportunity to identify object fragments whose missing parts have not been placed in the grave and which can therefore establish enchained relations between different domains. Nevertheless, care must be taken to document the closed nature of the context, especially since the work of Buko has demonstrated the ease with which more recent deposits can be trapped in middle and upper grave fills (Buko 1998).

A good example of a collection of published graves whose material has not yet been studied at first hand, but which shows a clear pattern of deliberate fragmentation, is the ceramic grave goods from the Copper Age cemetery of Tiszapolgár – Basatanya, in Eastern Hungary (Bognár-Kutzián 1963, 1972). Individual inhumation burials of men, women and children were dated to the Early and Middle phases of the Copper Age, cca. 4500–3600 Cal BC) (Chapman 2000a). In both phases, ceramic grave goods were common, varying with the life-stage of both sexes (Sofaer Derevenski 1997). The vessels could be classified in three groups according to their Completeness Index: (1) fully complete vessels (termed "C"); (2) vessels that had been restored to a complete profile but with minor or substantial parts missing (termed "R"); and (3) orphan sherds (termed "S").

In the Early Copper Age graves, only 6% of the graves with ceramic grave goods contained complete vessels without any Restored pots or orphan Sherds (Fig. 5.8). The remaining graves showed a complex patterning of vessels, dominated by graves with complete and restored vessels. Most of the pots had missing fragments that must have been deposited elsewhere – most probably in the domain of the living. It is possible that the missing sherds were deposited in other graves in the same phase, or even as heirlooms in Middle Copper Age graves – but this

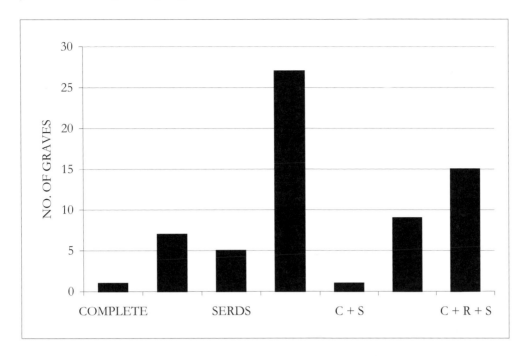

*Fig. 5.8 Completeness of pottery in Early Copper Age graves at Tiszapolgar-Basatanya*

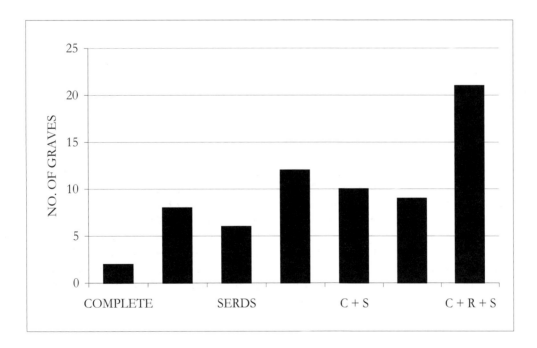

*Fig. 5.9 Completeness of pottery in Middle Copper Age graves at Tiszapolgar-Basatanya*

possibility remains for future research. In the Middle Copper Age, the percentage of graves with no restored vessels or orphan sherds had dropped to 4% (Fig. 5.9), with the graves dominated by assemblages with all ceramic classes – Complete, Restored and orphan Sherds. In both phases, there was a complex relationship between the completeness of the vessels deposited as grave goods and the age/sex category of the person buried (Chapman 2000, 51–53 and Table 3.2).

Although incomplete, the fragmentation study of the Tiszapolgár-Basatanya cemetery provides an example of the intensity of enchained relations connecting those buried in a single cemetery and settlements dispersed across the landscape. Only four graves in the entire cemetery did not rely on enchained relations to those outside the graves for this potent material statement of their identities and social relations. In these phases of the Copper Age in Eastern Hungary, the dominant settlement form is the dispersed farm or homestead (Bognár-Kutzian 1972; Chapman 1994, 1995). In intensive systematic fieldwalking of the Basatanya area in 1991, the Upper Tisza Project defined a number of surface scatters that probably constituted the material remains discarded from such homesteads (Chapman *et al.* 2003). The homesteads radiated out as far as 5 km from the central cemetery – at that time the dominant landscape feature in that part of the Hungarian Plain. If, as seems probable, the enchained relations partially documented at Basatanya linked the cemetery to those homesteads, the landscape implications are clear and, in fact, reminiscent of the Leslie Grinsell story (see above pp. 1–2). The family of the deceased would have carried the newly-dead from the homestead across the Plain to Basatanya, placing complete vessels in the grave to symbolise the integration of the lineage group, the completeness of the deceased's life journey or her/his integrated identities finally achieved in death, or a combination of these ideas. More distant kin members could have broken a vessel by the graveside, leaving the greater part of the vessel in the grave and carrying off the remaining fragment as a memento of the dead. Those with still less intimate links to the deceased may have broken a vessel at home and carried only an "orphan sherd" to Basatanya, to be thrown into the grave as a token of respect. In this way, the Completeness Index of the vessels in the Basatanya graves may have stood metaphorically for the closeness of the social relations of the mourner to the deceased. If found, conjoint fragments between two or more different graves could indicate the enchained relations between mourners and two or more newly-dead and between the dead themselves. It was not only by the people buried there but also by the material left in memory of the dead that the Basatanya cemetery enchained a group of homesteads dispersed across the landscape at a local spatial scale of the order of 5 km.

The barrow burials found a millennium later in the Alföld Plain and in many regions to the East also provide an opportunity for the assessment of inter-burial re-fits. One rare example of such research concerns a barrow related to the Varna supra-regional exchange network (Chapman 2003) – the Khvalynsk-group barrow of Shlyakovsky, in the Volgograd region (Klepikov 1994). Three burials were made in pits dug into the ancient ground surface prior to the heaping of the barrow. In burials 3 and 4 were found two fragments of the same flint macroblade – the proximal part in grave 3, the medial – distal part in grave 4 – conjoining to produce a complete object (Klepikov 1994, Ris. 3/3a + b). Here we have an example of fragmentation in the mortuary domain where different parts of the same object sustained enchained links between the dead in two different graves. Although the landscape links in such intra-barrow re-fitting are not so strong as in the case of the Varna cemetery (see chapter 7), the important point to underline is the close kinship connections between the two graves – links manifested and materialised by the conjoint lithics. It would be an interesting study to check for the existence of inter-grave re-fitting in other Eurasian barrows and barrow clusters.

The principle of studying (relatively) closed grave contexts can be extended to special spaces in and around monuments such as the Neolithic megaliths investigated by Lars Holten (2000). In the TRB period, many megaliths had courtyards that provided a spatial focus for the ritual smashing of often hundreds of vessels (Midgely 1992). Larsen's re-fitting studies at the Nissehøj megalith showed that 80% by weight of all of the smashed pottery was missing from the courtyard (and none of the "missing" sherds was placed in the tomb!) but that the re-fitted sherds present were widely dispersed over the entire courtyard. Holten suggests that the ritual sequence of destruction of vessels was related to the desirability of controlling Neolithic death. Where the remaining (missing) 80% of the vessels had gone is not a question that Holten poses.

Many Bronze Age scholars would consider hoards as a form of closed find (Hänsel, A. and B.1997; Harding, A. 2000). Thus, in a period such as the Late Bronze Age, characterized as it is by the frequency of "founders' hoards" – viz., hoards of heavily fragmented bronzes, it may be expected that the general principles of fragmentation analysis may be useful. Peter Turk (1997) has conducted a re-fitting exercise of an extraordinary hoarded deposit in a karstic sink-hole at Mušja Jama, Slovenia, into which thousands of bronze fragments, burnt animal bones and charcoal had been thrown over the entire 600-year period of the Late Bronze Age. Over 80% of all bronzes were fragments, including almost all of the swords and spearheads. The most convincing case of deliberate fragmentation concerned two fragments of the same spearhead, with a pin placed in one of the fragment's broken socket. Yet there were very few re-fits at Mušja Jama, indicating a very high proportion of orphan bronze fragments. The search for re-fits between this site and other coeval bronze hoards within Slovenia, such as Dragomelj, has so far yielded no result (*p.c.* Peter Turk).

Returning to mortuary contexts, important new interpretations have arisen from two studies of British Late Neolithic/Early Bronze Age grave goods – Beaker pottery and amber and jet necklaces (Jones, A. 2002a; Woodward 2002). These periods were marked by the expansion and consolidation of the single-grave tradition into Britain, through which the sense of an "individual's" identity and her/his kinship relations were conveyed through variations in grave goods.

Woodward noted that many of the eponymous vessels in "Beaker" graves were in fact incomplete, although there was a widespread museological tradition of restoring the pots to whole for purposes of exhibition. Thus, in the recently discovered Lockington gold hoard, the Completeness Indices of the two Beakers were only 50% each (Woodward 2000). Although Woodward did not explicitly use an interpretation related to enchained kin relations (though she mentions enchainment), she observed that the missing part was probably used as a "carefully curated family or ancestral property, with the missing portions continuing circulation as heirlooms" (2002, 1041) – an interpretation following Parker Pearson (1999, 85–86). She terms other non-specific fragments 'relics' – "an object invested with interest by reason of its antiquity or associations with the past" (2002, 1041).

Woodward developed the latter idea of heirlooms to explain the almost invariably incomplete necklaces comprising a handful of amber or jet beads placed in these same graves. While the very few purportedly complete necklaces contained sufficient beads to be deemed "complete" (*e.g.* the Upton Lovell amber necklace, with over 1,500 beads), the vast majority of graves contained fewer than 100 beads (2002, Fig. 1). Similarly, Andy Jones has noted that one Beaker necklace was composed of parts of two other distinct necklaces (Jones, A. 2002a, 167–8). Both Jones and Woodward interpreted this type of fragmentation in terms of families depositing parts of amber or jet necklaces with the newly-dead, while keeping the rest of the necklaces for further circulation. These increasingly mature bead segments slowly took on the mantle of ancestral objects, becoming heirlooms after many years of use in the same family or remaining as commemorative items in the absence of any close family links. It will be seen that this interpretation is closely related to the notion of enchained relations between the newly-dead and the land of the living. It is also closely related to the concept of the object biography, narrating the extent of the use-life and its wear patterns, its burning or secondary decoration. Implied, too, is the movement of necklace parts across the landscape, both locally, between barrow cemetery and dispersed settlement focus, and at an inter-regional landscape level across Europe, whereby amber necklaces from Northern Europe reached the Myceneans in the Aegean as very worn relics (Woodward 2002).

A final instance of re-fitting in the mortuary domain concerns the recent "Heuneburg landscape of ancestors" project (Arnold and Murray 2002), in which new excavations at the Hohmichele monumental mortuary barrow and two of the nearby barrows (T17 and T18) in

the Hohmichele barrow cemetery (the so-called "Speckhau group") have been integrated with the results of the long-running programme of excavations at the Early Iron Age hillfort of the Heuneburg, in South West Germany. At the Hohmichele and barrows T17 and T18, sherd re-fitting was carried out for all of the Early Iron Age pottery (the T18 results have not yet been processed).

The contexts in which the sherds were deposited were primarily threefold: (a) individual graves; (b) barrow fill; and (c) charcoal deposits. In their analysis of the Hohmichele, Kurz (2001) and Kurz and Schiek (2002) report multiple re-fits between sherds of vessels deposited in both cremation and inhumation graves and sherds from the same vessels in the mound fill and, less frequently, in the charcoal deposits. In barrow Speckhau 17, Schneider (2003) found sherd re-fits for almost 400 of the vessel fragments out a total of over 1,000 sherds. While most of the re-fits occurred within the same mound context, two were between features and four linked the mound core (the central grave chamber) and the mound mantle (2003, 80–83 and Figs. 55–56). Laurent Olivier's (1999) study of the timescale of barrow construction in the Early Iron Age monumental barrow tradition indicates the passing of variable but not inconsequential social time between the construction of the central burial chamber and the burial itself, as well as between the burial and the construction, often in several stages, of the barrow itself. At the very least, the Speckhau barrow sherd re-fits indicate the deliberate fragmentation of vessels during the overall mortuary rites, as well as the storage of sherds conjoining with buried sherds for later deposition. The deposition of sherds in the upper barrow fill was not apparently linked to the deposition of human remains. However, the pottery deposited in Grave 5 indicated curation of material from older settlements, as early as the Middle Bronze Age, for burial in the Early Iron Age. Noting that the use of the concept 'curation' has been unnecessarily restricted to studies of settlement materials, Schneider (2003) proposes that this term should be extended to the mortuary domain (cf. Woodward, above, pp. 98–9).

Throwing some of the fragments onto the upper barrow mound did not, however, complete the deposition of the sherds, since the re-fitting did not yield a single complete Early Iron Age vessel. After the completion of the Speckhau 18 sherd re-fitting study, it is the project's aim to seek re-fits between the three barrows. While the other barrows remain a probable destination for the missing 70–80% of the vessels whose fragments were deposited in the Hohmichele and Speckhau 17, it is also possible that the missing sherds travelled further across the landscape, one obvious place being the Heuneburg hillfort. The complex narratives made possible by re-fitting studies in barrow cemeteries raise intriguing possibilities for the abundant

Bronze Age and Iron Age barrow cemeteries of Eurasia, provided that re-fitting studies are taken seriously and built into future research strategies.

There are several important implications of intra-site re-fitting studies that includes the mortuary arena. Each of them depends upon a good to excellent recovery rate and a good understanding of different taphonomic processes from those affecting settlements. First, it has been possible to isolate practices of deliberate fragmentation through the demonstration of missing parts of objects. The missing parts indicate enchained relations between persons on the site and persons off the site, in other parts of the landscape. Secondly, enchainment is practised with many types of material culture – pottery, lithics, shell, amber and jet ornaments, etc. Initial results indicate the likelihood of different types of enchainment practices with each kind of raw material. Thirdly, one of the hardest things to tell is whether a fragment has been broken away from the site and then brought onto the site **or** a whole object on the site was broken and parts of that object removed off the site. This question is just as problematic in the mortuary as in the domestic context. Fourthly, the spatial scale of enchained fragment dispersion is variable: there does seem to be some support for networks of enchainment at the local scale (up to 5 km), while, at supra-local centres such as Varna and Mycenae, the spatial scale of enchainment was much greater. Hence the exchange of sherds over long distances should not be ruled out at this stage of research and understanding. Fifthly, the concepts of heirlooms and commemorative pieces – both with ancestral significance – could with advantage be integrated into the interpretative framework of fragmentation studies as sub-sets of enchained relations.

## What happened to the things?

In many ways, the most important concept that Schiffer introduced into fragmentation studies was that of the "orphan sherd" – even though he baulked at full research into the implications of orphan sherds. Schiffer (1987, 299–302 and Table 10.1) identified multiple sources for the origins of orphan sherds, without often tying down the specific source of any single sherd. In a re-evaluation of the Broken K pueblo excavations, Schiffer found that he could not determine the origins of orphan sherds without examining each sherd for traces of its life-history (1987, 335–6); regrettably, his solution was to remove them from future analysis (!), as he also did in the re-fitting analysis of the Hokoham site of Snaketown (Seymour and Schiffer 1987). This points the way to an alternative methodology, involving intensive studies of each sherd for size, weight, abrasion and other traces of the sherd's life-history – studies that have been taken

seriously in five recent British studies of prehistoric pottery and/or lithics.

The first two studies provide a comparison between two Late Neolithic assemblages at opposite ends of the country – Barnhouse on Orkney and Tremough in Cornwall. Andy Jones' (2002, 117–144) multi-facetted investigation of the Late Neolithic ceramics from Barnhouse, on Orkney, used data on morphological attributes, performance characteristics (including volume, fabric, use-wear, soothing and organic residues) and depositional information to develop a biographical approach to the domestic assemblage. Three size ranges for the vessels were identified, each with different wall thickness, decoration and fabric. While each household tended to use one large vessel, 12–15 medium-sized vessels and 2 small vessels, keeping them in similar places, the "recipes" for vessel production (tempers + clay) were different for each group of houses but all houses used identical decorations. The food contents varied with size of vessel, as did preferences for cooking; pottery proved vital in separating out different kinds of foods for consumption.

Jones (2002, 141 and Fig. 6.21) presented selected results of a fragmentation analysis of Grooved Ware sherds at Barnhouse: a sherd from House 9 was found in the House 2 dump, two sherds from House 3 were deposited in the House 9 dump and sherds from Houses 2 and 5 in the House 3 dump. By contrast, large vessels from all of the earlier houses on the site were deposited in the large pottery dump near House 3. Jones proposed a degree of circulation of vessels between House 2 and the other houses – *i.e.* a sherd in a house dump means that the sherd was moved into the house related to that dump (2002, 135–6). What is interesting about these data is that, as in Endröd 119 (see above, pp. 89–91), the re-fit links are limited to one part of the settlement – here the Western part (2002, Fig. 6.21) and that they are confined to the early phase of the settlement. He did not comment further on why re-fitting sherds passed from house to house and there is no commentary on the Completeness Index of the Barnhouse pottery. The question of the mechanism by which the re-fitted sherds were moved to different houses was hardly discussed. If children's play is involved, there was no need for the sherds to be moved first to the house instead of directly to the dump. If a more deliberate approach to fragmentation is assumed, house-to-house movement indicating enchained relationships is more probable.

The multi-period settlement of Tremough was investigated by the Cornwall Archaeological Unit over five years (1999–2003). In her undergraduate dissertation, Imogen Wood (2004) made a re-fitting, completeness and erosion analysis of two of the main, and totally excavated, phases of the site occupation – the Late Neolithic – Early

Bronze Age (henceforth "LANEBA") (n = 332 sherds) and the Romano-Cornish (n = 545 sherds). Since Wood's dissertation, new 14-C determinations have dated the five post-hole structures to the Middle Bronze Age (*p.c.*, R. Bradley), leaving the LANEBA features as a set of eight shallow pits, while enclosure ditches and a single house contained the majority of the Romano-Cornish assemblage. No complete vessels were found in any of the three assemblages and not a single re-fit could be found between sherds unless deposited together within 1m². All assemblages were dominated by sherds representing <2% of the vessel, with no or very little abrasion on the Romano-Cornish sherds and contrasting abrasion on the Late Neolithic and Bronze Age sherds. These last two assemblages consisted of 48 fabric types, supporting the idea that each sherd represented a different vessel. One large Romano-Cornish storage vessel (pot no. 1063) stood 1 metre high when it was deliberately placed in the enclosure ditch. Another vessel (no. 1027) had a completeness index of 89% and its sherds were placed in the upper level of a pit, well outside the enclosure. Wood (2004, Chapter 5) suggests that the remaining sherds were removed for deposition elsewhere, in this case probably off the site. The overall conclusion is that a very high proportion of most vessels at Tremough are now missing – either destroyed by post-depositional processes or moved off the site for deposition or enchainment.

The third example concerns Jo Brück's (1999, 375–380) study of the re-fits, wear and abrasions on Early Bronze Age pottery deposited in the upper levels of the Neolithic causewayed ditches at Windmill Hill, Wiltshire (Whittle *et al.* 1999). Brück identified re-fits between sherds from the same vessel at different depths of up to 0.50m in the ditch fills (1999, 376). Moreover, there was a strong tendency for different wear traces on the re-fitting sherds (1999, 376–378), suggesting different biographies since the breaking of the vessel as well as differing episodes of deposition for different sherds from the same vessel. Brück (1999, 377) also proposes that finds from contexts with very varied pottery styles and different wear traces may well have been kept on a midden for later deposition together in the ditch fill (cf. the curation of sherds at Speckhau T 17: see above, pp. 99–100). After these interesting points, the overall conclusion-that "the finds assemblage from Trench B can best be described as the product of refuse disposal activities" is rather disappointing. At the very least, we have cases of sherds being treated as relics or heirlooms, with separate episodes of deposition – each of which celebrated the biographies not only of the sherds and whole vessels but also of their makers and breakers.

The fourth example from Britain concerns a study of the Later Bronze Age ceramics from Runnymede Area 16 East, where the team excavated an assemblage of 9,505 sherds, deriving from an estimated total of 470 vessels (Needham 1996; Sørensen 1996). Completeness, re-fitting and erosion studies were performed on this material. A total of 204 vessels had a complete or nearly complete profile or important decoration or forms, while many of these vessels were represented by a single sherd. Pot groups formed a distinctive part of the Runnymede site – areas where a large part of a pot had been deposited in a single act (Sørensen 1996, 62–4 and Figs. 37–38). Occasionally, re-fitting sherds were found several metres from the main constituents of the pot group but the distance was rarely more than this. Sørensen interprets the pot groups as rejected domestic ware rather than ritually deposited vessels (1996, 65). Only 340 conjoining fragments were found outside the pot groups, probably deposited into small dumps with much secondary deposition (1996, 66). Using a wider data set, Needham (1996, 76 and Table 3) arrived at a total of 112 vessel equivalents whose parts were divided up between either different stratigraphic units (73 vessels) or different contexts within the same unit (39 vessels).

Needham sought an explanation of these re-fits in terms of on-site stratigraphic processes (both social practices and post-depositional events) (1996, 77). To this purpose, he presented a useful reconstruction of possible pathways of sherd mobility (1996, 75 and Fig. 48 = here as Fig. 5.10). These hypothetical pathways are important and should be considered carefully in any evaluation of sherd mobility identified through sherd re-fitting (cf. also Fig. 108 = here as Fig. 5.11). However, there was no attempt to take into account the deliberate fragmentation of objects and the subsequent social practices affecting their deposition, although the authors subsequently raise the possibility of visitors to the site bringing in material that is ultimately deposited on site (Needham and Spence 1997, 246–247).

The fifth study – in many ways the most remarkable – is Garrow *et al.*'s (2005) analysis of sherds from the complete excavation of 226 Earlier Neolithic pits from Areas A and E at the site of Kilverstone, Norfolk. Re-fitting analysis of the pottery and flints indicated a striking pattern of deposition at three spatial levels – within pits, between pits and between pit clusters. The ceramic and flint assemblages were both incomplete – not a single complete vessel was deposited on site and in only one case was there deposition of a nearly complete vessel: many vessels were represented by one or two sherds. Moreover, the deposited flintwork showed no sign of a single complete operational chain for a worked lithic, even though, overall, the complete operation was represented.

The explanation of post-depositional truncation of the pits was rejected for the incompleteness of the assemblage in favour of deliberate selection of re-fitted sherds and flints that had experienced different life histories. This

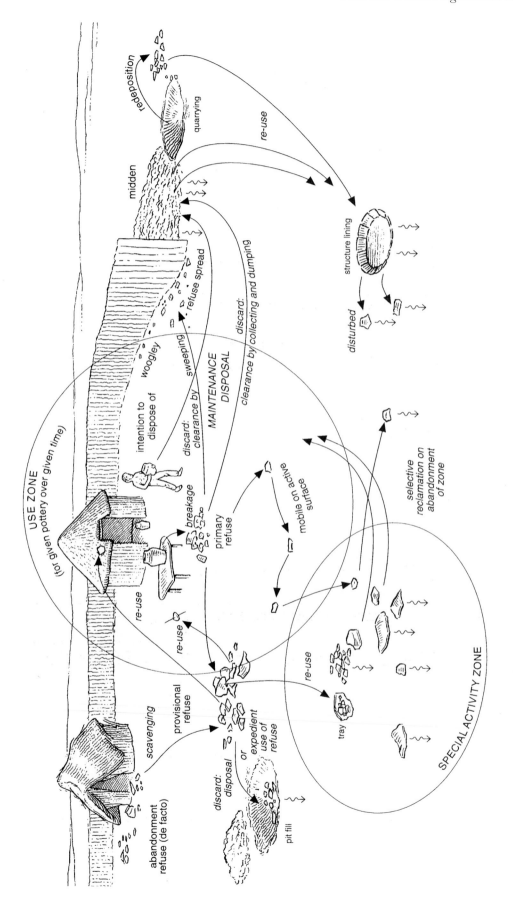

*Fig. 5.10 Reconstruction of depositional processes at Runnymede Bridge (source: Needham 1996, Fig. 48)*

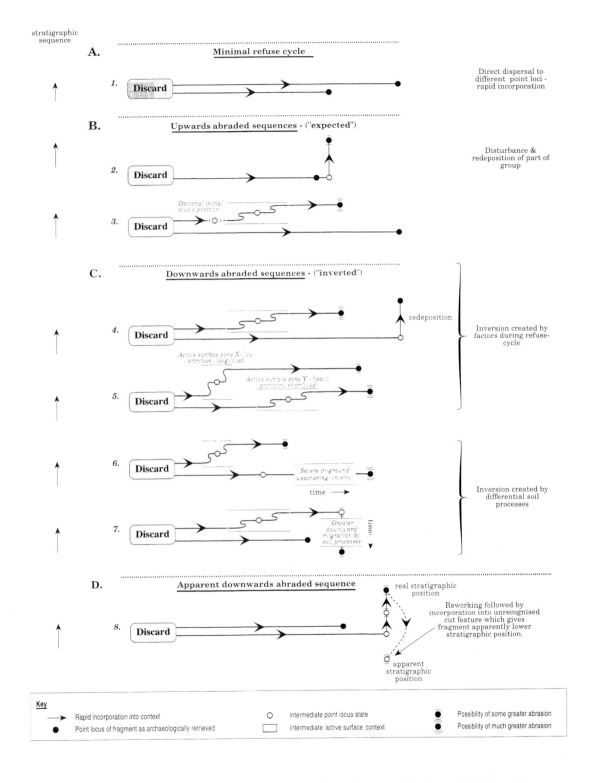

*Fig. 5.11 Flow chart of depositional pathways, Runnymede Bridge (source: Needham 1996, Fig. 108)*

occurred especially between burnt and unburnt fragments of the same object, as well as between weathered and unweathered parts. Deposition fitted a sequential filling of the pits within a single cluster, with sherds from a common vessel found in up to five pits (*e.g.* Fig. 11 = here as Fig. 5.12). The overall pattern of re-fitting showed re-fits overwhelmingly more frequent within pit clusters than between pit clusters (Fig. 10 = here as Fig. 5.13)

Four points from the Kilverstone study are of wider significance. First, Garrow *et al.*'s interpretation of a sequence of visits and return visits to Kilverstone – each visit marked by the digging of pits and the deposition of broken things – would indicate repeated movements across the landscape, linking, as well as structuring the lives of, people, places and objects. Secondly, the pits at Kilverstone constitute relatively, if not completely, closed depositional contexts, rendering the interpretation of the conjoined fragments more straightforward than at Runnymede Bridge. Thirdly, the fact that the conjoining pattern found in the ceramics at two of the three different on-site spatial levels (within pits and between pits in the same cluster but **not** between clusters!), is matched by the lithics indicates that we are not simply dealing with differential preservation of a fragile material in an inclement climate but with deliberate selection of different stages of the *châine opératoire* for deposition in specific places and segments of places. Fourthly, even after re-fitting, there are many incomplete objects whose missing parts were deposited elsewhere, in a reciprocal presencing of absent fragments.

These detailed studies of individual sherds point to several important aspects of the biography of fragments and complete vessels. Orphan sherds and lithic fragments are very common at all of the sites, with most vessels at the completely excavated sites of Tremough and Runnymede Bridge now missing 80% or more of their constituent parts. Even given the North West European climate and its destructive potential, it is hard to imagine that such a high proportion of vessels would have disappeared from the site through post-depositional climatic effects alone. We are forced to consider the social practices that could account for such fragment dispersion. One answer comes from the Windmill Hill study, with Brück's evidence for middening of sherds. The removal of material for storage until the next phase of deposition could explain the selective absence of 80% of most vessels. Another key point arising from these studies is the presence of re-fitting fragments that have gone through different life histories since fragmentation. This is found with the Kilverstone flints and sherds, as well as with sherds from Windmill Hill. This strongly suggests deliberate fragmentation with the intention to re-use the parts in different ways "after the break".

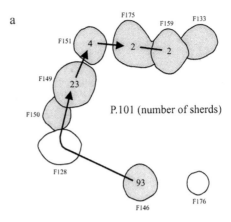

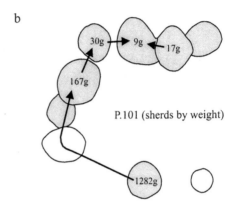

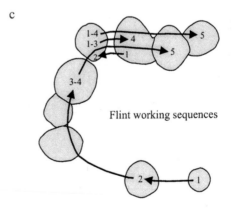

*Fig. 5.12 Depositional sequence and horizontal sherd and lithic re-fits, Cluster B, Kilverstone, Area E (source: Garrow et al. 2005, Fig. 11)*

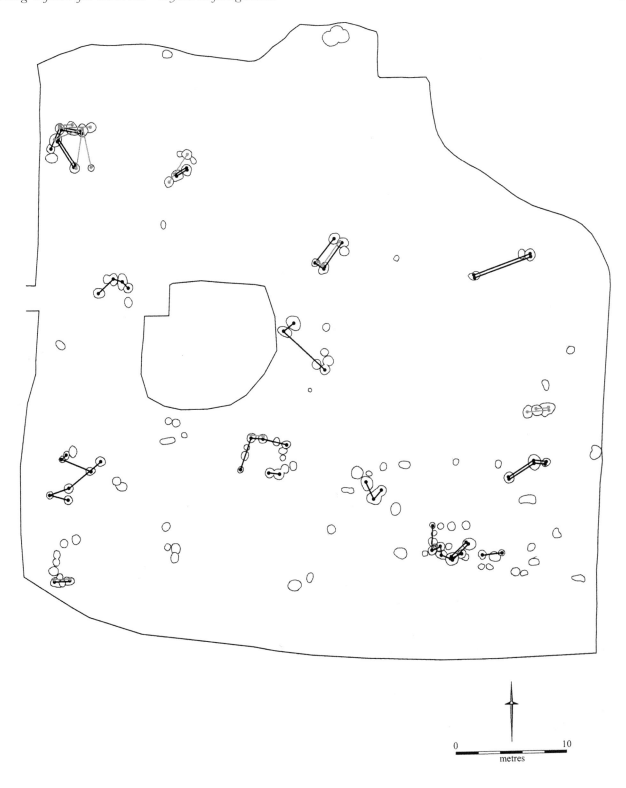

*Fig. 5.13 Depositional sequence and horizontal sherd and lithic re-fits, Kilverstone, Area E (source: Garrow et al. 2005, Fig. 10)*

## Fragmentation in the landscape

How do the concept and social practice of deliberate object (and body) fragmentation map onto landscape archaeology – onto landscapes? Landscapes consist of a network of places – some natural, some culturally constituted, some created by human manipulation of the landscape. It is this network of places that gives human lives their meaning, through an identification of past activities and present embodiment. The key element of landscape archaeology is, thus, the relationships between different places. Whenever fragment dispersion is mapped onto places, the practice of fragmentation can be linked to landscape archaeology. This practice is but one of a series of practices constituting "inhabitation". According to John Barrett, inhabitation is not merely "occupying" a place BUT understanding the relevance of actions executed at that place by reference to other frames of reference/other time/places (Barrett 1999, 258–260). Enchained social relations provide one such key frame of reference because, following Mauss, each gift carries within it the history of all previous gift exchanges. If enchainment presences absent people, fragments of things and places, it is fundamental to the process of inhabitation as described by Barrett. But how can this notion be demonstrated?

At the methodological level, the key linking concept between fragmentation and landscape studies is that of fragment dispersion. While the previous claim that we should at least consider the possibility of trade and exchange based upon fragmentary objects (*e.g.* exotic sherds rather than complete exotic vessels) (Chapman 2000, 63–65) is still valid, if difficult to prove (see above, p. 92, the Rocca di Rivoli study), there are two methods that implicate movement of fragments across the landscape – at spatial scales that are becoming increasingly possible to define. We have already examined intra-site re-fitting studies, often at completely excavated sites or phases with good to excellent recovery, where the Completeness Index of the objects suggests that the missing fragments were taken off the site and dispersed across the landscape or, in the case of the Sonoran Desert Site 205, fragments were brought onto a site for special purposes. If there are no other practices that would destroy ceramics (*e.g.* the use of chamotte) or remove them from the site (*e.g.*, manuring scatters), fragment dispersion over the landscape is highly probable.

The first method is the physical re-fitting of fragments from the same object found deposited at two or more different sites, not only at two locales within the same complex as at Durankulak, Itford Hill and Shakadô (see above, p. 92). Here, two places in the landscape are linked by the parts of a broken object in an enchained, dispersed relationship. It has also been found that, even after re-

fitting, the object is still missing some parts, so that enchained dispersion can be assumed to go still further, linking a third or more places. The second method relies on good to excellent recovery at completely excavated sites and the presence there of orphan fragments to infer movement of potentially conjoining fragments across the landscape. The first method is, of course, much more revealing than the second. In practice, inter-site re-fitting depends initially on chance and a very good visual sense of pattern recognition.

A welcome exception to the exclusive use of re-fitted fragments for chrono-stratigraphic markers, as pursued by most authors in Hofman and Enloe (1992), is the study of conjoint sherds from the intensive survey of over 80 km² in the Rio Grande valley, New Mexico (Mills *et al.* 1992). Three distinctive wares (n = 778 sherds) were used in the study and the re-fitting sherds were grouped into Sample 1 (131 vessels with 2+ joins) and Sample 2 (60 vessels with 3+ joins) (1992, 219). While almost all re-fittings occurred within the same spatial area, some were found in different clusters up to 150m apart and one re-fit was made between survey areas (1992, 219–221). The authors argue that areas with archaeological features were more likely to contain conjoint sherds, perhaps because of sherd re-use (1992, 222). Proclaiming that there is no evidence that pottery joins provide evidence of contemporaneity, they propose instead that re-fits are evidence for "systematic linkages within a long-term land use system" (1992, 223). In offering an invaluable antidote to the "chronological marker" view of re-fitted objects, Mills *et al.* help to take re-fitting beyond the single event, even if they hardly include the social in their discussion of the landscape context for fragment dispersion.

The largest example of inter-site re-fitting relates structural members of a famous class of monuments – the geometrically decorated stone slabs forming the most elaborately decorated parts of megalithic monuments in Brittany – some of the earliest monumental remains in western Europe (Scarre 2002). There are now several examples of decorated menhirs whose engraved patterns were broken across the image, with one part built into one monument and the other half used to construct a second tomb. The best-studied is the menhir decorated with what Whittle interprets as a whale, fragmented into three pieces, one of which was built into each of the megaliths of Gavrinis, Er-Grah and La Table des Marchand, 5 km apart (L'Helgouach and Le Roux 1986; Whittle 2000); other pairs of megaliths linked through fragments of engraved stones have been found (Calado 2002, 26, 30). A recent discovery next to La Table des Marchand is a menhir-breaking site, where débitage from the chipping away of menhirs has been excavated in Neolithic contexts (*p.c.*, Loïc Langouët). On this basis, the four great fragments of Le Grand Menhir Brisé may have been broken deliberately, ready for onward transport to four different megaliths – except for a change of plan. However, Hornsey (1987) maintains that the great menhir fell because of a weakness in the granite and the next largest stone was erected as second-best.

What are the implications of these material links? – the most monumental examples of enchainment yet discovered in Europe. Le Roux' (1992) identification of "the iconoclastic rage of the new generation of builders" mistakenly transplants Medieval religious fervour back into deep prehistory. Instead, we can integrate the three elements of people, places and things that were helpful in drawing out the implications of the Grinsell narrative by emphasising the embodied nature of these practices. The first implication concerns the design of the paired megaliths. Since it is clear that not every stone block would have fitted into a place in the passage of these megaliths, an agreed design was required in advance for the part of the tombs incorporating the broken fragments of the impressive menhirs. This meant several meetings and several trips between the pairs of megaliths for several builders to ensure the design would produce the desired effect and that the stones were broken to approximately the correct dimensions. Secondly, the transport of the stone blocks – perhaps from a third site, certainly from one megalith to the other and presumably to one more hitherto undiscovered megalithic monument (the missing third piece of the menhir!). In the case of Gavrinis – Er-Grah – La Table des Marchand, the blocks of stone each weighed several tons and required land and river transport over 3 km, marginally easier since, at the time, Gavrinis was not an island. In a recent conference paper, Colin Richards (n.d.) characterized the labour of moving huge stones as a ritual practice, more concerned with social processes than engineering. He emphasized the long prior planning for making things needed to move the stone (rope, timber), for finding the right size and shape of stone and for negotiating with local people to take the stone. In other words, social relations were created by the massive stones before they had even moved! What Richards omitted was the ceremonial passage of the stone, the sounds of the workers and the accompanying musicians ensuring that the processional movement of the stone through the landscape always made an acoustic impact. The labour of movement would have brought together numerous individuals – perhaps 20–30 people, (?) mostly males – from several dispersed communities, with the task bringing all team-members together in the coordinated display of embodied skills. The enchained relations developed through these tasks were surely not a one-off practice but led to longer-term social relations cemented by the paired stones. The places with enchained links included not only the settlements of the team members but the source of the rock – the menhir – the

places visited *en route* and the final burial-places of the decorated stones. The processions across the landscape, embodying the formal movement of the stones, linked other megaliths with their own ancestral place-values, as well as integrating stretches of other paths perhaps not related before in a single route. The people whose bones were later stored in the paired megaliths were also enchained to those who made the link between the megaliths material in the first place. What is implied, therefore, by megalithic-scale enchainment is a complex network of social relations, practices, people, places and things, which had temporal and spatial scale and limits, while at the same time emphasising specific ancestral and lineage connections. They are the largest-known example yet known of fragment dispersion across the landscape.

How widespread is this practice? It is not yet possible to give an adequate answer to this question because no systematic investigations into fragmentation of stones have been made in Val Camonica, Monte Bego or other major rock art sites. But the incorporation of decorated, cup-and/or-ring-marked stones into Late Neolithic pits in henges and into Early Bronze Age cist graves in Britain has revealed a number of fragmented stones broken across the motif(s) (Bradley 1997, 136–150; Waddington 1998, 43–45; Bueno Ramírez and Behrmann 2000), indicating that the practice of megalithic fragmentation is by no means limited to Neolithic Brittany (Cassen 2000, with references back to 1828!). Eogan (1998) has documented the presence of a now-vanished mound with a major concentration of decorated stones in the Brugh na Bóinne area, which was destroyed in the Neolithic prior to the construction of Knowth Site 1 and Newgrange Large, since both megaliths contained stones re-used from the earlier monument.

Turning to smaller objects, I shall discuss five cases of artifact dispersion across landscapes – four prehistoric and one from the early historic period. These examples indicate a mixture of chance discoveries and carefully planned research programmes.

The earliest case of inter-site re-fitting is reported from the Gravettian of the Achtal, in Germany, where re-fitting studies of the cave stratigraphies at the Geissenklösterle and the Brillenhöhle showed much stratigraphic mixing (Scheer 1990, 627–636). The extension of the re-fitting programme to the inter-site level showed fragments of the same lithics re-fitted from four different cave sites, two of which – the Geissenklösterle and the Brillenhöhle are 3 km apart and had nine re-fits (1990, 639–646 and Abb. 7–9). Scheer infers an indirect connection between pairs of caves from the use of the same raw materials in the same *châine opératoire* – an approach that allow the drawing of directional lines between fragments, since the re-fits can be placed in a micro-sequence of tool manufacture (1990, 645 and Abb. 9). The excavators interpreted this practice as a way of characterising the spatial dispersion of the *chaîne opératoire* of Gravettian core reduction by mobile groups moving from cave to cave. What it also shows is the enchained identity of these groups was materialised by discard in several linked places across the landscape.

An as yet unsuccessful inter-site re-fitting concerned two of the Hamburgian (Final Palaeolithic) sites located in the Ahrensburg tunnel valley in Schleswig, North Germany. The lithic collections from Hasewisch were studied for the frequent intra-site flake re-fits (Hartz 1990) and the intra-site re-fitting programme was extended to Teltwisch 1 and Poggenwisch. At the former, 551 flint objects have been re-fitted, mostly preparation flakes but also some long blades broken into two shorter ones. The re-fitting at the latter site is still in progress but showed the same pattern as at Teltwisch 1 – re-fitting of fragments of scrapers, long blades but mostly preparation flakes. However, the inter-site re-fitting between these two sites, which are less than 500m apart, did not yield any conjoint flakes (*p.c.* M.-J. Weber).

A later lithic re-fitting study showed similar re-fits between sites occupied for short periods at the Mesolithic

– Neolithic transition in the South Norwegian Highlands (Schaller-Åhrberg 1990). Total or almost complete excavation of six small sites located around the shore of Lake Gyrinos (lake dimensions: 5 × 2 km) produced radiocarbon dates spanning the 7th–5th millennia Cal BC. An overall 35% of the flint material could be sorted into 12 different groups – each deriving from a single core. Apart from the off-white flint for axe making, each of the other 11 groups had at least 2 and up to 48 conjoining flakes (1990, 617–620 and Figs. 4–7). Lithics from ten of the groups were found at two or more sites, with stronger links between several pairs of sites (1990, Fig. 8 = here Fig. 5.14). The excavator interprets these re-fits as indicating coeval occupations of sites rather than the use of earlier sites as raw material sources (1990, 620–621). No social interpretations were proposed, although the materialization of enchained relations between groups not necessarily in daily contact would be a valuable social practice.

We turn to a different material – bronze – for a startling example of inter-site re-fitting at the landscape scale – the Trent Valley Ewart Park bronze sword fragments from Hanford and Trentham (Bradley and Ford 2004). The

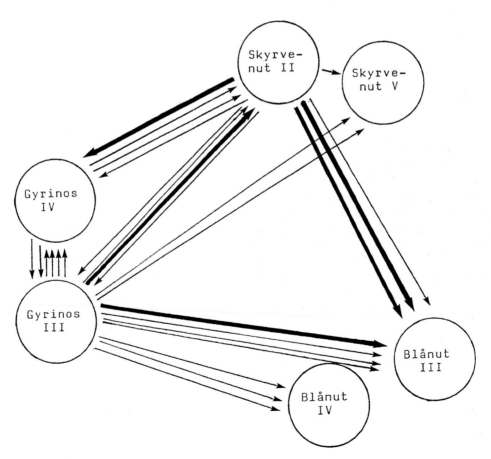

*Fig. 5.14 Horizontal lithic re-fits between Lake Gyrinos sites (source: Schaller-Åhrberg 1990, Fig. 8)*

lower part of a bronze sword was found at Trentham in the early 1990s by a metal-detectorist, who passed the find to Stoke-on-Trent Museum. Thirteen years later, a different metal-detectorist, working on a hilltop on the other side of the Trent valley at Hanford, found part of a bronze sword and also brought it into the museum. The two fragments fitted to make an almost complete bronze sword (the hilt is still missing!) (2004, Fig. 20.1 = here Fig. 5.15). The two hilltops were 5 km apart and inter-visible across the valley. The deposition of bronze swords is characteristic of the British Late Bronze Age but this is the first time that anyone has tried re-fitting sword fragments together from different "sites". The inter-visibility of the places makes it possible to conceive of a simultaneous deposition of the sword fragments, constituting a landscape link between two ritual foci in the Trent valley. But such coeval practices are not necessary to support the enchained links between people, places and objects. There were significant differences in the life histories of the two fragments – the sword-point was worn and the fracture was more rounded in the lower part than in the upper. This suggests that breakage had preceded deposition by not a short period of time – perhaps years – suggesting that sword fragments had an independent life of their own in the routine practices of the valley. M. Williams (2001) has made the interesting suggestion that Late Bronze Age swords may have been seen as persons in view of the ritual killings they have suffered, the burial of swords with people and the similar treatment of dead bodies and swords. The dismember-ment of the Trent valley sword bears a striking resemblance to the deliberate fragmentation of human bodies in Late Bronze Age Europe and the movement of body parts across the landscape.

In our fifth example, the elaboration of pottery decoration offers the potential for different persons to recognise that "their" fragment, if broken across the motif, is linked to another piece of the same vessel. The re-fitting process has been used extensively in intra-site ceramic studies, most frequently for purposes of stratigraphic linkage (see above, pp. 83–85). But inter-site re-fitting of decorated sherds is a rare discovery, requiring too much time and effort for researchers, such as Milisauskas (2002), needing quick results. The only instance yet known to this author is the example of re-fitted Roman-period Samian bowls in Holland (Brandt 1983; Vons and Bosman 1988). The two Early Roman forts established at Velsen were occupied for only a short time (Velsen I between AD 15–28, Velsen II between AD 40 and 50) before changes to the defence of the *limes* elsewhere (Brandt 1983, 132). Refits have been made at 80% probability, consistent with Bollong code 3, between (1) decorated fragments of a rare Samian bowl type (Dragendorff 27) found respectively at Velsen I and

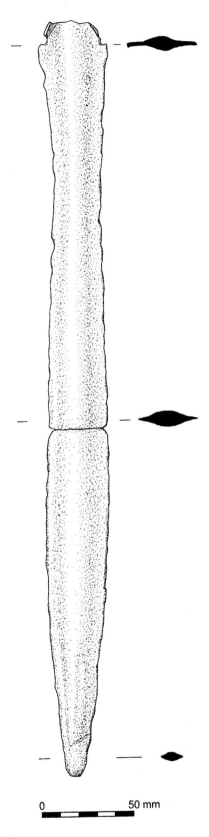

*Fig. 5.15 Re-fitted fragments of an Ewart Park Late Bronze Age sword, found at Hanford and Trentham (source: Bradley and Ford 2004, Fig. 20.1)*

Hoogovens site 21 (Vons and Bosman 1988, Figs. 2–4); (2) decorated fragments of another rare Samian bowl type (Dragendorff 29) also found at two sites – Velsen I and 't Hain site 39 (Vons and Bosman 1988, Figs. 5–8); and (3) decorated body sherds of another example of the Dragendorff 29 type found at Velsen I and on the Roman site beneath the Medieval castle of Brederode, on a sand ridge 4.5 km South West of Velsen (Bosman 1994). The refits between Velsen I and the three local sites indicates movement of some 3–8 kms.

The initial interpretation has been that the local population raided the abandoned fort for valuable materials and, in the process, also removed small pottery fragments to take back to their settlements as trophies – the "pick-up" explanation (Bogaers 1968). This notion would indicate the value placed on incomplete objects, perhaps for re-use. Research on ethnographic discard among the Maya has shown that large sherds were often re-used as scoops or spoons (cf. Hayden and Cannon 1983). But these highly decorated, distinctively coloured Samian sherds were so different from the local potting tradition that a symbolic element in the appropriation of the material culture of the "Other" is surely present. They were also too small for re-use as scoops!

A second explanation is that soldiers at the Velsen fort entered into enchained relations with local populations through exchange of things complete **and** incomplete (Brandt 1983). Brandt (1983, 137) lists the classes of Roman objects found on "local" sites: glass, fibulae, "scrap" metalwork and pottery, including 350 decorated Samian sherds – all small and many eroded. Interestingly, each small Samian sherd came from a different vessel, as did the glass fragments. These observations prompted Brandt to discuss the possibility of deliberate frag-mentation of Samian vessels, perhaps for use as primitive money (their wear suggests frequent use), as ritual objects (their red colour and sheen) or for re-distribution as fragments by local elites (1983, 140–2). The re-fitting demonstrates that at least some Samian vessels were broken at Velsen II but this does not rule out further redistribution of fragments in local communities. Bosman (1997) and Vons and Bosman (1998) returned to the issue, criticising Brandt's explanations of primitive money and exchange by arguing that the dating evidence does not place the sherds on local sites at the same date as the occupation of the Velsen forts. The latter prefer a "pick-up" explanation for all of the Roman finds found on what they claim to be *later* (*i.e.* post-Velsen I and II) local sites, things that now also include amphora, mortaria and grinding stone fragments. The chronological issue can only be settled by multiple AMS dating of the local sites.

In one sense, it does not matter whether the refitting Samian sherds were traded or picked-up – here is a well-documented case of inter-site re-fitting across an "ethnic" division, by which the material identity of an invading population is valued sufficiently by the local indigenous groups to promote the further use of *fragments* as trinkets or heirlooms after breakage. These re-fittings document links across this low-lying landscape that enable the closer identification of the mechanism of dispersal.

In summary, there are several important implications of inter-site re-fitting over the landscape. The first is that, because of the distance between sites, we can exclude accidental discard, the movement of objects through cleaning of structures, dumping and children's play. If we can exclude the use of abandoned sites for raw material sources, this means that we have a number of documented cases of deliberate fragmentation with subsequent discard in different places. Secondly, although the rationale behind the movement of fragments between sites is different (contrast Velsen I and the Achtal caves), there remains an important commonality of links between people, places and broken things, by which the identity of each of the three elements is mutually constituted in relation to the other two elements. Thirdly, in several cases (the Achtal caves, Lake Gyrinos, Trent valley), the notion of enchainment applies to the fragmentation practices, suggesting a certain kind of relationship between people and things that involves the objectification and fractality of personhood. This has major consequences for the way we view past material and social worlds. Fourthly, and of particular relevance to this volume, inter-site re-fitting means that fragmentation has a landscape dimension – a result leading to the theorisation of materiality and movement *across* the landscape, not only at specific places *in* the landscape. Issues include the extent to which broken objects are enchained to places along the routes between starting-point and destination (*e.g.* of a decorated megalithic panel). Finally, the broad time/place span of these practices suggests that, even if the examples are as yet few in number, this could be a significant practice over a much wider range of European prehistory and early history than we currently have evidence for. Naturally, this cannot be documented at the present time but the questions raised set an archaeological agenda for future investigations.

It would be disingenuous to deny the problems any researcher faces in seeking inter-site re-fitting: (a) a large, if not huge, labour input – with the potential for no results; (b) few examples of previous good practice; and (c) the potential obstacles placed in the way of the research by museum directors not permitting collections to be moved to nearby museums for re-fitting tests. Nonetheless, none of these problems is insuperable. Of particular value for re-fitting studies are national museums in smaller nation-states (*e.g.*, Slovenia, Eire and Latvia), whose collections include the majority of archaeological finds from most of the key sites. There is a temptation to quote from a late

Newcastle colleague, who observed: "If you don't buy a ticket, you surely won't win a prize!"

The evidence for inter-site re-fitting currently derives from a restricted number of cases – primarily because few archaeologists have looked for the material evidence indicating the practice of deliberate fragment dispersion. Currently, there are more examples of intra-site investigations into object fragmentation than of inter-site studies, since the complexities of research are somewhat reduced. If high levels of object recovery can be demonstrated, and this is not always the case, a case can be made for the development of social practices centred on the differential use of fragments and, indeed, fragment dispersion across the landscape.

## Discussion and conclusions

While all parts of the landscape can, and often do, take on cultural significance (Bradley 2000), the places of inhabitation known as settlements and cemeteries can often express a socio-cultural identity through what Richard Bradley has called "special attention markers" – elaborately decorated structures or naturally distinctive features – or through what has been termed "timemarks" – the association of a place with a significant historical event that took place there at a specific time (Chapman 1997). Often in a more concentrated way than natural places, inhabited places are sites of accumulation, with the accumulated things bringing with them associations, experiences and histories – creating memory and place-value. We can now recognize that enchained identities were regularly materialized through discard of fragments, while accepting that not every social practice would have required such materialisation.

The three patterns discernable from the intra-site re-fitting studies guide us to some important implications. First, the finding that conjoining fragments have been discarded within the same structure at most sites provides the norm for re-fitting studies. However, it may not always be assumed that such a minimal level of dispersion within a structure as this was caused by random behaviour, since the vertical separation of sherds between pit levels in the same pit may indicate deliberate curation of material rather than kicking or throwing unwanted finds into a convenient receptacle at different times. If such discard of fragments is the norm, then, any deviation from that norm should be considered as a potential case for enchainment. Thus, the second finding – a small group of sites where discard of conjoining fragments was more often in different contexts than in the same structure – prompt careful investigations of taphonomic issues and related social practices.

Perhaps the principal issue raised by many of the intra-site re-fitting studies concerns the often high incidence of orphan sherds. There is now a significant number of re-fitting studies completed on completely excavated sites where the vast majority of the vessel parts on the vast majority of vessels can no longer be found on site. It is obviously important to assess the impact of taphonomic issues, including post-depositional degradation and erosion, the use of chamotte and the practice of manuring. But after full consideration of each of these factors, if there remains a high proportion of pottery missing from the sites, an explanation more related to deliberate social practice should at least be entertained. There are three possible practices – (1) fragment curation in an off-site location; (2) enchained relations between sites, with fragments taken off the site; and (3) the introduction of sherds onto the site from another site where the greater part of the vessel has been deposited. While each of these notions is relatively problematic, we should take them seriously unless we are able to explain, in taphonomic terms, the absence of 80–90% of the site's vessel population. These thoughts invariably return us to the issue of fragmentation in the landscape.

Some of the things that are particularly effective in the creation and maintenance of cultural memory and place-value are those objects embodying enchained relations between kinsfolk or non-kin across the landscape. Of the many aspects of enchainment, the one most relevant here is its ability to enable people to presence absent people, objects and places. What this chapter has sought to demonstrate is that the objects embodying enchained relations across the landscape were often broken objects that could have been re-fitted to fragments from the same once-complete object that were deposited in another place. This claim is supported by two kinds of evidence: (a) the deposition in two different places of re-fitting fragments from the same object; and (b) the dispersion of fragments of objects from one place to (an)other(s), documented on completely excavated sites with good to excellent recovery rates and containing many orphan fragments. In both cases, it is hard to resist the conclusion that fragment dispersion across the landscape was one of the important social practices through which enchained relations were maintained at the local and sometimes wider level. There is currently an increasing acceptance – based upon isotopic evidence for the sourcing of people – of greater mobility among prehistoric individuals. If for persons, why not for things and fragments of things?

We are now in a position to identify a variety of forms of enchained relations, some of which being more relevant to specific cultural contexts than others. Here, it is worth emphasising the important point that fragment dispersion implicates temporal as well as landscape distance. The fragmentation of objects for use as tokens implies a temporal distance until validation occurs through the re-presentation of the token. On perhaps a longer time-scale, local curation strategies can ensure the availability of fragments for exchange or deposition at significant events, such as keeping sherds broken from vessel fragments buried with a household leader for a later burial of a cherished relative. The circulation of items of ancestral veneration is closely related to such a practice. Moreover, long-lasting curation of vessel or necklace fragments can convert enchained items into heirlooms, while relics would have a more distant social relationship to the person and a closer relationship to a generalised past. A final case concerns the collection of items from the abandoned site of another ethnic group – a case with implications for temporal as well as ethnic distance bridged by enchained object relations. It is important to develop ways of distinguishing between these forms of enchainment in future case studies supporting deliberate fragmentation.

The documentation of fragment dispersion raises certain interesting issues and problems. First, inter-site re-fitting is beginning to give us an idea of the spatial scale of this practice: several studies indicate re-fitting up to a 5-km radius of a site. Secondly, even after inter- or intra-site re-fitting, the conjoint object is still often incomplete – suggesting an even more complex object biography than we can currently document. Thirdly, there are tantalising hints that, after the break, fragments follow separate biographical pathways before they are re-united, often in a burial. Fourthly, the direction of movement of the fragment dispersion is still relatively resistant to analysis, both for the domestic and the mortuary domains, with the exception of lithic re-fitting in which micro-sequencing can be determined. Each of these issues merits greater attention in future research.

Now that we have reviewed the general evidence for re-fitting, it is appropriate to examine in more detail site assemblages from well-excavated sites with the aim of isolating intra-site re-fits and orphan fragments. Three cases of *Spondylus* shell rings are examined in chapter 7; we first turn to the fired clay anthropomorphic figurines from the Dolnoslav tell.

# 6.  The biographical approach – fired clay figurines from the Late Eneolithic tell of Dolnoslav

(with contributions by Ana Raduntcheva and Bistra Koleva)

## Planning and sequence

The site of Dolnoslav is a tell located 3 km North of the village of Dolnoslav, on the Southern edge of the Thracian plain, almost 30 km South of the river Marica. The tell measures 6.25 in height and has an oval form, with the base of the tell measuring 105m in length (NNW – SSE) by 64m in width (NNE – SSW). There are two main prehistoric horizons – the earlier, dating to the Early Neolithic, has not been investigated at all, while the Late Eneolithic horizon has been almost totally excavated by A. Raduntcheva and B. Koleva over nine seasons (1983–1991) (Raduntcheva 1996, 2002; Koleva 2001, 2002). In the following discussion, the NNW direction will be termed "North" and the SSE "South.

In the Late Eneolithic (Fig. 6.1a), the tell was enclosed by a low dry-stone wall of river pebbles, the remains of which scarcely attained 0.30m in height. Immediately inside the enclosing wall was an open area, partly explored, whose flat clay surface was coloured black through the admixture of manganese. This was separated from a second zone with clays of different colours in different phases by a narrow zone of fine river pebbles. Inside the open area was a zone of buildings, part of whose internal space was dug into the soil up to 0.30m in depth. Within this zone was a group of buildings that were built upon the flat cleared surface of the tell. Finally, there were some structures in the centre of the site that were built upon an artificial platform 0.60m in height. In this reading of the site plan, we can see a concentric pattern of structures, with an increase in the vertical dimension as people moved towards the centre of the site. This must have produced a very striking visual pattern of a relatively low mound in the plain with increasingly visible and dominant central structures.

When the Late Eneolithic group who re-settled Dolnoslav came to the site, they would have seen a low, ancestral mound that, in modern terms, had been abandoned for about a millennium. The excavators recognized three phases within the overall Late Eneolithic occupation but the very first act of the new settlers was

the construction of a platform measuring a maximum of 40 × 20m in the centre of the mound. The platform was 0.60m in height and constructed from pure earth that included many Late Eneolithic sherds, presumably collected specially for the purpose of this initial deposit. This operation could be termed the Pre-A Phase.

The platform acted as the foundation for seven structures – the central Shrine, Structures K-1 (complex 1), K-2 and K-3 and B4 (building 4), B5 and B7. These structures were built in the first phase of occupation (Phase A), together with 21 other buildings that were constructed on the flat surface of the mound – B1, B2, B3, B6 and B8–B24. Only B1, B2, B3 and the central Shrine were fully investigated in their earliest phase (Phase A) of use. The plans of the buildings were generally rectangular or trapezoidal, with only one single circular structure (B18). The buildings were mostly one-roomed; only two are two-roomed. The Central Shrine was divided into rooms by an inner clay wall, surviving to a height of 0.85m, and by two posts on the same alignment as the wall. The structure K-3 had two rooms at different heights, with the South room possibly open.

The total settled area on the top of the Phase A mound was cca. 3,000m²; there was a Built: Unbuilt space ratio of 1:2.3. It is not clear whether or not the dry-stone enclosure wall was constructed in this phase but this is probable. It is also not clear whether the surface of the open area near the perimeter of the mound was plastered with distinctive colours in this early phase.

In the second phase (phase B), all of the 28 structures in the site continued in use, with a similar Built: Unbuilt space ratio of 1:2.3. A stone cobbled surface was laid down East of B10. The site was carefully planned to ensure easy access to each building. There was a path running East – West that divided the site into equal halves. The path was constructed of stamped clay that included some stones and many Late Eneolithic sherds. The surface of the encircling open area was plastered with a black clay near the wall and a yellow clay towards the interior; it is believed that the dry-stone enclosure wall was by then in existence. These surfaces could be best viewed from the

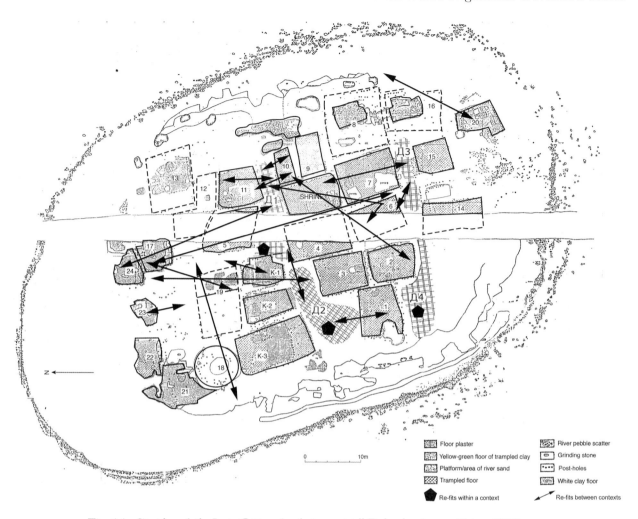

| | | | |
|---|---|---|---|
| ▨ Floor plaster | | ▨ River pebble scatter |
| ▨ Yellow-green floor of trampled clay | | ▭ Grinding stone |
| ▨ Platform/area of river sand | | ▦ Post-holes |
| ▨ Trampled floor | | ▨ White clay floor |
| ⬟ Re-fits within a context | | ⟋ Re-fits between contexts |

*Fig. 6.1a Site plan of the Late Copper Age features at tell Dolnoslav (source: Koleva 2002)*

higher parts of the central part of the site. The arrangement of the buildings suggests an entrance on the East side of the enclosure wall. There is a possibility that there was an entrance on the North West side, based on the occurrence of the most monumental part of the wall – three separate sectors each built on a terrace cut into the slope of the mound.

A major change in the arrangement of the structures took place in the third phase (Phase C). In the South East part of the mound, three buildings (B14, B15 and B20) were dismantled and burned, with their remains, including their Phase B finds, covered with a deposit of earth mixed with daub, much charred grain and much other material culture besides (*e.g.*, a bone bead necklace). Covering an area of cca. 15 × 15m, this deposit has been termed D3; in Deal's typology, it constituted the first abandonment phase on the site. On previously published plans, the area of D3 has been shown as much reduced because of the drawing convention to allow the definition of the houses

that it covered (*e.g.* Koleva 2002, Fig. 1). The removal of these three buildings meant a lower Built: Unbuilt space ratio – now reduced to 1:2.9 – and a large open area in the South East part. This is thought to have resulted in the construction of a new entrance on the South side of the enclosure wall. Despite these changes, the majority of buildings in the inner area continued in use – *i.e.* a total of 25 structures. In this phase, the inner open areas between the houses were plastered with a mixture of red ochre and clay to produce a striking red surface. The surfaces of the outer open areas near the enclosure wall were plastered with a grey-green clay with various other coloured nuances, that was shaped into various bas-relief shapes (Raduntcheva 2003), with the black manganese-rich clays still between this zone and the enclosure wall.

After some time had elapsed, all of the remaining 25 buildings were deliberately burnt down, together with their rich and varied contents. This could be termed the Post-C, or abandonment, phase. The mass of burnt building

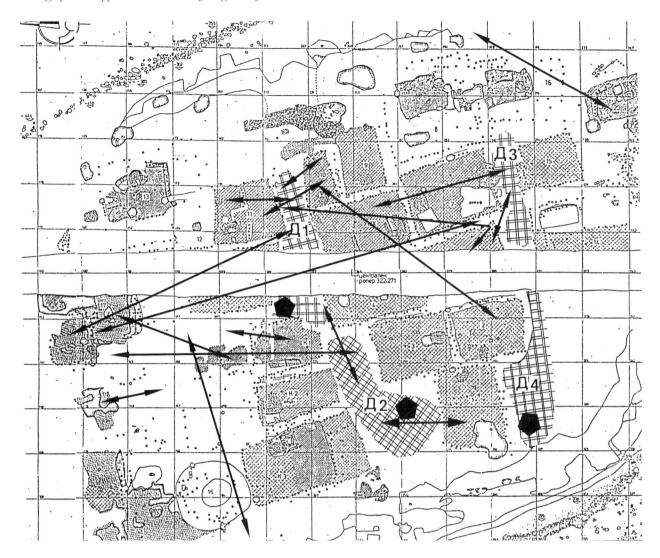

*Fig. 6.1b Re-fitting of figurines at Dolnoslav: lines with arrows = re-fits between fragments from different contexts; pentagons = re-fits between fragments from the same context*

materials created a destruction deposit that was up to 1.5m thick in some places. Part of this ritual closure of the site included the deposition of large quantities of earth mixed with daub and containing much material culture in three parts of the inner area: D1 and D2 were deposited on the East-West path, while D4 was deposited South of B1 and B2. The excavators believe that, after this act of closure, the building remains were covered with soil and the mound was plastered with white mineral.

While the overall site plan refers to a series of concentric ovals, there is also evidence from the plan and from excavated features for groups of buildings. The position of the unexcavated central baulk makes the definition of all house groups difficult but B1, B2 and B3 appear to form one group, while K-1, K-2 and K-3 another. This second group was reinforced by the construction of all buildings, and even their internal clay

altars, on the same alignment. There was also a common alignment linking the two parts of K-3 with the circular structure B18. The South room of K-3 was higher than the North room, which was in turn higher than B18 to which it was connected by a post-lined entrance. A second type of evidence concerns common foundation trenches. One such, with a minimum depth of 1,2m, was made for the Shrine, B7 and B9, suggesting an overall plan for the three structures. A similar common foundation trench was used for the construction of B2 and B3. There is also the plan evidence for a line of more or less parallel buildings on each side of the East – West-running path: on the North side, K-3, K-2, K-1, B5 and B11; on the South side, B3, B4, the Shrine and B10. While the existence of building groups may be accepted, it should be remembered that at least five buildings cannot be said to form parts of building groupings – B14–B17 and B20.

Much of the details recorded in the excavation therefore refer to the abandonment and closure of the site – the destruction of the Phase C structures and internal features, as well as the destruction of B14, B15 and B20 and their closure under D3.

In terms of the general distribution of finds, 54% of all finds were deposited in the built area, leaving 46% for the unbuilt areas (middens + open areas). Thus, in overall numerical terms, it would appear that the built and unbuilt areas were treated equally in terms of deposition.

In the built area, 31% of the antler objects were found, together with 36% of the figurines and 80% of the whole (restorable) vessels. A total of 667 restorable vessels was deposited on the site, with ceramic concentrations in the eight buildings of 30 to 100 vessels (B2, B13, K-1, K-2 and K-3, the shrine, B5 and B11). Totals of up to 30 vessels were found in the remaining 20 buildings. All of the vessels had traces of heavy wear, indicating long use-lives, even the numerous miniature vessels. A total of 1,112 tools was deposited in the built area, many with traces of long use and some with signs of secondary use. Antler was deposited as unused raw material, together with half-finished tools.

In the unbuilt area, 321 figurines were deposited, together with 165 pots that had been deliberately broken. Sherds from one and the same vessel were deposited in different middens and there were numerous miniature vessels. A total of 1,176 tools was deposited in the unbuilt areas, with generally the same characteristics as the tools found in the built area.

In terms of the five phases of the sequence at Dolnoslav – the pre- A construction of the platform, the three Phases A – C and the post-C abandonment –, the vast majority of artifacts was deposited in Phase C, with the destruction of the buildings transforming them into a series of more or less sealed "death-of-building" assemblages. For example, from a total of over 500 figurines, only a handful were deposited in pre-abandonment contexts – four in the first phase and fewer than 10 in the second phase, with over 480 in the third phase. One major exception was the large quantity of pottery mixed with the earth to form the initial building platform in the Pre-A Phase.

Several general interpretative comments may be advanced at this juncture. First, the visual aspects of the Late Eneolithic use of the tell were important, both in terms of verticality and colour. The most central buildings were also the highest, given their construction on the clay platform, with lower buildings nearby, partly-dug-in buildings further from the centre and clay surfaces further from the central area. This concentric spatial arrangement is likely to be a metaphor for the cosmological organization of the life of the Dolnoslav community. It is also likely that the differential access to the zones and the

buildings would have reinforced the social power of those with preferential access to central places.

It is now increasingly recognized in archaeology that colour symbolism is one of the most potent sources of visual communication using material culture. Colour was used at Dolnoslav in at least three ways – in the material culture in daily usage, in the surfaces on which people walked and moved across the site and in the buildings (including the building materials) themselves. A wide range of colours appeared in daily usage, from artifacts such as *Dentalium* (white), manganese (black) and graphite decoration (silver) on painted vessels, red ochre on Crusted painted wares, long blades made of flint from North East Bulgaria (yellow and grey), and green (malachite, as well as copper tools exposed to oxidation). These colours were contrasted with, or reinforced by, the colour of the enclosure wall (light grey), the black of the manganese-rich clay surface, those on the outer open areas (yellow in Phase B, grey-green in the third Phase) and those on the inner area surfaces (principally red). Although no fragments of painted wall plaster have survived the deliberate firing of the Phase C buildings, a wall painting of a schematic anthropomorphic face (0,48/0,42) was found on the party wall of the central shrine. On a bright red background, white, dark-red and black colours were used to model human face features (it is probable that at least some of the outer and inner walls of the buildings were differentiated from the earth hues of brown, beige, ochre and yellow). The use of a special white mineral pigment from the Rhodope Mountains (Belen Tash) should be noted for colouring the floors of some of the central buildings. White colour was also used as crusting and incrusting material, mainly clay figurines. The final point about colour was the emphasis on the red of the burnt daub and the black of the charred seeds in D3, making a strong colour-based statement about destruction, deposition and closure.

Thirdly, there is very little grounds for believing that the finds made in the destroyed buildings of the second and third phases constituted in any way a "living assemblage" of artifacts that "reflected" the social and economic activities of the inhabitants of the Dolnoslav mound. Most of the finds represented deliberate collection of objects for deposition. The time dimension of the collection of such assemblages should not be under-estimated. For example, the mixing of many Late Eneolithic sherds in the initial building platform meant either the making of large numbers of new vessels on or near the mound or the carrying of many vessels and sherds from somewhere else (perhaps previous occupation sites) on to the mound to make a foundation deposit. Similarly, the deposition of many litres of cereal grains in D3 could not have been achieved without careful forethought, storage and transport across the site. The middening and

| Figurine type | Abbreviation | Figures in text |
|---|---|---|
| Standing | ST | Figure 6.10 |
| Standing, hollow | SA | Figure 6.21 |
| Seated | SE | Figure 6.13 |
| Star-shaped | SS | |
| Star-shaped with anthropomorphic head | SSAH | |
| Anthropomorphic pot | AM | |
| Arm | ARM | |
| Head | HD | Figures 6.26, 6.28 |
| Head with a top-knot | HTK | Figure 6.22 |
| Head with perforated ears | HPE | |
| Head with perforated ears and top-knot | HPT | |
| Bust | BU | |
| Hole-arm figure | HAF | |
| Leaning figure | LE | |
| Torso | TO | Figures 6.12, 6.25–28 |
| Torso with legs | TOLE | Figures 6.22, 6.25, 6.27 |
| Bottom | BO | |
| Bottom with legs | BOLE | |
| Foot | FOOT | |
| Leg | LEG | Figures 6.11, 6.29 |
| Torso with bottom | TOBO | |
| Ear | EAR | |
| Thinker | TH | |
| Boot | BOOT | |

*Table 6.1 Types of figurines according to their morphological characteristics*

house-closure deposits at Dolnoslav incorporated the memory of economic, social, ritual and technological practices in use before site abandonment but not necessarily taking place there and then on site.

A final interpretative comment concerns moving things on and off the site. No estimates have yet been made for the time necessary for preparing the clay and the other materials, including large quantities of water, for the building of the structures on the tell. Nor is it clear how many kilograms of special clay had to be carried onto the site from nearby alluvial zones to form the outer unbuilt coloured surfaces. Just as white mineral pigment was brought onto the site from the Rhodopes, red ochre from a nearby source, *Dentalium* shells from the Black Sea and copper from Ai Bunar and other sources, so objects may well have been moved off the site to other occupation sites. One specific interest of this study is the mobility of broken objects on and off the tell.

## The clay figurines

### The assemblage

Fired clay figurines comprised the third most common artifact type on the Dolnoslav tell, after the antler tools and the pottery. During the re-fitting study performed in the spring of 2004, 500 anthropomorphic figurines were analysed, omitting more than 200 clay zoomorphic, bone and marble figurines. They were divided into 24 "types" or body parts according to their morphological characteristics (Table 6.1). The assemblage as a whole is typical for the Balkan Late Copper Age, including some widespread types of figurines such as seated or standing figurines, as well as some less common types designed as single body parts, such as ears, busts or arms. The terms used to denote the types in the current study are based on visual recognition of body parts, instead of attempting to link the figurines to any of the existing classification schemes (*e.g.*, Vajsov 1992). Thus, if a body and legs are present, the figurine is assigned as TOLE (*i.e.* torso + leg/s) rather than either as standing or as "N 123 or class **fragment**, type *legs*" (Vajsov 1992, 41). The distribution of simplified types, in which the 13 types represented by less than 1% are unified under the heading 'OTHERS', is given below (Plate 16).

The most common body part is the leg, followed by SA figurines (standing examples with rounded belly), standing figurines and torsos with legs. Distributed between 5% and 10% are the seated figurines, the heads, the torsos, the star-shaped figurines and the lower parts of the body with legs.

In dimensional terms, there are three classes of figurine size: small (less than 5 cm), medium (5.1–10 cm) and large (more than 10 cm). According to their length/height, the majority is medium-sized (61%), followed by small figurines (34%), while only 5% are large. This pattern changes when the width is taken into account – then the small are dominant (74%), with 24% medium-sized and only 2% are large. Since this dimension reflects the "broadness" of the figurines, it may be inferred that the size of most fragments is proportional – medium-sized in length and small in width.

In the course of the study, the context of deposition of the figurines led to the division of the unbuilt area of the Dolnoslav tell into *middens* (D1, D2, D3 and D4) and *open areas*. The *middens* were associated with accumulation behaviour, in which masses of different materials (clay, bone, etc.) were literally packed into a restricted area. They occupied the open spaces between or next to the burnt buildings. On the contrary, the *open areas* cannot be clearly linked to any structure or indeed pattern of deposition. Figurines deriving from the *open areas* were found at different levels and spread all over the site – both on the same living surface as the middens and on the earth piled above the middens and the buildings. Insofar as the people of Dolnoslav decided to leave some of these figurines on the tell rather than to remove them off tell, their less formal deposition suggests a varied set of depositional practices. Therefore, there are three main contexts in which clay anthropomorphs were found. The majority of the figurines were deposited in the middens (n=208 or 41%), there were fewer figurines from the buildings (n=179 or 36%) and significantly fewer examples from the open areas (n=113 or 23%).

Altogether, 16 types were found in the middens. The dominant type was the leg (20,2 %), followed by very similar number of fragments consisting of torso-and-legs (14,9%) and standing figurines (14,4%). The third most common types – SA figurines and torso fragments – shared similar frequencies (10,6%). Three types were less commonly deposited – seated figurines (8,2%), star-shaped figurines (6,7%) and heads (4,3%).

Not all types were deposited in all of the middens, each of which, moreover, had differing preferences – legs in D1, standing figurines in D2 and torsos-and-legs in D3 and D4. The same is true for the second commonest types in the middens: SA figurines, standing figurines and torso-with-legs in D1, seated figurines, SA and torsos-with-legs in D2, legs and torsos in D3 and torsos and standing figurines in D4. These regularities suggest that people at Dolnoslav controlled the deposition of figurines of different types in each midden according to specific principles, to be discussed later.

The distribution of types in buildings showed at once a greater diversity and a higher concentration of rare types. The majority of body parts was represented by less than 11%, with only two types above 14 % – SA figurines (16,2%) and legs (14,5%). The relatively high percentage of heads – 10,6% – is noteworthy (see p. 136). The spread of types within individual buildings is summarized below (Table 6.2). The most widespread type was the SA, found in 17 buildings, while 7 types were found in only one building.

The number of figurines deposited in a building varied from 1 to 17, with a preference for 7 – found in five buildings. The number of figurine types deposited in one building varied from 1 to 9, with the most common being 5 types – found in 9 buildings. Altogether, 12 types of figurines were found in the open areas. Akin to the deposition in middens, the dominant type comprised legs (25%), with similar frequencies of three other types.

## Gender

The commonest category of figurine lacked any gender information (39%) – in other words, the preserved body part was unsuitable for expressing gender information (*e.g.* a foot). Female figurines comprised almost 1/3 of all body parts (31%), while males and hermaphrodites amounted to only 1% each (Fig. 6.3). An intriguing gender category was represented by the *unsexed* figurines, comprising 28% of all figurines and including examples of torsos and/or legs on which sexual attributes (incised pubic triangle, modeled breasts or penis, etc.) could have been shown but were not. The deliberate choice **not** to gender these particular figurines hints at a diverse process of gender categorization, participating in the negotiation of the perception and reproduction of some gender categories, such as androgyny. Alternatively, the gender-neutral figurines may have been deliberately designed to evoke people in different stages in their life, in particular

| Figurine type | Number of houses |
|---|---|
| SA | 17 |
| Seated | 16 |
| Head, leg | 15 |
| Torso | 11 |
| Standing | 10 |
| Torso with legs | 9 |
| Lower part of body and legs | 6 |
| Star-shaped | 5 |
| Head with top-knot | 4 |
| Anthropomorphic pot, HAF, foot | 3 |
| Torsos with lower part, SA2H | 2 |

*Table 6.2 Frequency of figurine types in number of houses*

the non-sexually active periods of childhood or (fe)male menopause. It is possible that, on some of the figurines, male/female information was present on the missing body part (see below). An important implication of such a pattern is that, once the figurine is broken, the initial gender association is lost for all but one of the fragments. Intentional changes of sex, namely from female to gender-neutral, with a possible association with androgyny, can therefore be related to fragmentation practices. However, it should be underlined that the majority of the complete figurines from Dolnoslav (see below) are also unsexed, which suggests that the production of this gender category was a deliberate social practice.

Half of the figurines with sexual information represented female examples. Their number was closely matched by the unsexed figurines, forming 46% of the sample, while males comprised 2% and hermaphrodites just 1%. It is important to point out the depositional clustering of male figurines – two in building 19, two in D2 and the other two are found elsewhere. A hermaphrodite was also found in D2, in the same grid square as one of the male figurines, which marks the area as the only concentration of "rare" gender types. In general and in three specific cases, the middens were dominated by unsexed figurines, while the buildings shared an overall prevalence of female figurines. This opposition of gender categories between contexts is extended in the open areas, where almost a half the figurines lacked gender information, with female examples significantly outnumbering the unsexed figurines.

The relation between type and gender shows a very complex pattern, summarized in Table 6.3. Star-shaped figurines have been excluded from all gender analyses.

The rare types were generally unsexed or contained no gender information. The majority of types included 3 of the possible 5 gender classes – male, female, hermaphrodite, unsexed and no gender information. Among them, female figurines were prevalent on anthropomorphic pots and torso fragments; unsexed figurines were dominant on BOLE and TOLE types; and unsurprisingly, figurines with no gender information were dominant among the legs and the heads.

Among the gendered figurines, 10 out of the 16 types were dominated by female representations but the percentage of unsexed figurines was still relatively high. The female association was more common for upper body parts.

**Fragmentation**

The high incidence of broken figurines (96%) can be conceptualised in terms of the life course of the anthropomorphs, as much as through the analogy of the human life course. The number, type and treatment of breaks is indicative of the length of an anthropomorph's life and the nature of its experience. But we should not ignore those figurines that have remained complete throughout their lives, even though they are not numerous. More than half of the complete examples showed a clustered deposition – 4 figurines in D1, 3 figurines in D3 and D2; and 2 figurines in B2 and B16. The remaining complete examples were scattered in B3, B5, B8 and B15, with 5 in the open areas. The ratio of complete/fragmented figurines was equal or very similar for the whole assemblage and for different contexts – the middens as a group, each separate midden, the buildings and the open areas. This proportional distribution of complete and broken objects suggests two shared messages about the importance of both integral and fragmented images in all parts of the site, as well as their relative importance in every zone.

It is very intriguing that the majority of whole figurines (68%) were unsexed – slightly more than 10% of all unsexed examples. The percentage of complete female figurines was 18%, less than 3% of all female figurines. The complete figurines with no gender information formed a relatively high percentage – 14% but, at the same time, they comprised fewer than 2% of all figurines with no gender information. Hermaphrodites and males were all broken. The whole figurines deposited in the middens and buildings followed the same general pattern of domination of unsexed over female figurines. The pattern is reinforced in the open areas, where all the complete examples were unsexed.

| Body parts with no gender info | Body parts with single gender representation | Body parts with 2 types of gender representation | Body parts with 3 types of gender representation | Body parts with 5 type of gender representation |
|---|---|---|---|---|
| foot, head with perforated years, head with perforated ears and top knot, ear and boot, arm | torso with lower part of the body, leaning, thinker and bottom | bust, HAF, head with a top knot | legs, torsos, heads, anthropomorphic pot, lower part of body with legs, torsos with legs | standing, seated |

*Table 6.3 Body parts according to number of gender representations*

The gender of the broken body parts was more varied. Here the most numerous were the fragments with no gender information (39%), while almost 1/3 were female figurines. Apart from hermaphrodites and males, that comprised 1% each, the rarest gender category was the unsexed figurines (27%). A similar pattern was valid for the body parts from the open areas (without gender information- 45%, female – 37%, unsexed –16%), while, in the buildings, fragments with no gender information (37%) were equally frequent as female figurines (36%) with the unsexed fragments at 25%. In the middens, however, while the fragments with no gender information were still dominant (37%), the next most common body parts were the unsexed figurines (31%), followed by the female fragments.

More than half of the figurines had two (28%) or three (31%) breaks. Fragments with one break were fewer (16%), which may be an indicator of the potential for further fragmentation activities. On the contrary, figurines with 4 breaks (15%) may have represented the final stages of the fragmentation chain. In addition, around 10% of the fragments had five or more breaks, suggesting that four to five breaks marked the end of the fragmentation cycle. It is possible that in some exceptional cases further fragmentation resulted in the few examples with six, seven or eight breaks. The same general pattern can be observed in all three contexts – the middens, the buildings and the open areas.

The relationship between the type of the figurines and the number of breaks is very complex.

Four types comprised only one break (boot, bust, TH and HPE), one had only 3 breaks (bottom) and 3 types had only 5 breaks (ear, leaning figurine and torsos with lower part of body). Since all of the types were rare types, it is unwise to overemphasize the link between these types and the number of breaks. The remaining 14 types displayed various combinations of figurines with breaks ranging from one to six – *e.g.* the foot included fragments with one, two and four breaks, while the torso showed fragments with one, three, four and five breaks (Plate 17).

Plate 17 shows that figurines of each type experienced different number of breaks. Each type had a different distribution of fragments with various breaks. Although the most numerous in general, figurines with three breaks are not necessarily the commonest fragments. Such patterns suggest an internal fragmentation dynamic, observable in the relationship between figurine type and the number of breaks, in which some types have more fragments in the initial fragmentation phase (one or two breaks), others comprise fragments in all stages of fragmentation; and some are dominated by fragments in the final phase of fragmentation. The SA figurines and the standing figurines are the only two types with the full range of breaks, from 1 to 6. A possible interpretation is

that some types were preferred for a longer fragmentation cycle or that these types offered more potential for negotiations involving persons' life course. The same pattern was valid for all three contexts of deposition – middens, buildings and open areas.

The majority of figurines with no gender information comprised fragments with 2 breaks, which, at 68, is the biggest total of cases in the whole analysis. There was also a large number of fragments with 1 break. Bearing in mind that these are body parts which were not suitable for gender representation, it is obvious that almost a quarter of the whole assemblage lost its gender affiliation at a very early stage of fragmentation. Most numerous among the fragments with 1 break were the head and leg fragments, which may be an indication that these particular body parts were not suitable for further fragmentation. It should be mentioned, however, that there were other types apart from heads and legs that experienced only one break, as well as heads and legs with more than 1 break. Most of the female fragments had 3 breaks, as did many figurines with no gender information. Therefore, there was an equal possibility for a fragment either to preserve or to lose its gender after the third break. In that sense, any fragment that passed the third break point without loss of gender may be considered as a body part with targeted gender preservation. There were only 15 figurines with no gender information that had more than 3 breaks, with gender lost after the fourth, the fifth or the sixth break. The second commonest female fragments had 4 breaks, which together with the body parts with 5 and 6 breaks, formed a substantial sample of female figurines (n = 64) that preserved their gender throughout a long life. In addition, there were two figurines with 7 breaks and even 1 figurine with 8 breaks that reinforce the claim for gender preservation after multiple fragmentation. However, a quarter of all female figurines had either 1 or 2 breaks and were deposited before any further gender modification, at an early stage of their potential fragmentation chain. Hermaphrodites had 1, 2 and 4 breaks. Two of the male figurines had 3 breaks, two had two breaks, and the remaining two had 4 and 5 breaks. The small number of male and hermaphrodite figurines does not allow any conclusive links between gender and number of breaks. The unsexed figurines were also dominated by fragments with 3 breaks, whose frequency exceeded that of female fragments with 3 breaks. It is worth recalling that these were fragments on which gender attributes were expected. After three breaks, the message of a deliberate denial of gender was still very clear: 60% of all unsexed figurines had their absence of gender deliberately maintained rather than transforming the figurines into fragments with no gender information.

It is very important to underline that the number of breaks did not affect the gender of the figurines. There are extreme examples of up to 7–8 breaks, where gender was preserved even after such intensive fragmentation, while at the same time there were cases of the loss of gender information after a single break. Therefore, it cannot be assumed that changes of gender were the only aim of fragmentation processes. The Dolnoslav pattern stands in contrast to the pattern of fragmentation of Hamangia figurines, where a single break to the neck caused a change of gender (see above, pp. 62 and 64).

## The re-fitting exercise

The backbone of our research into the processes of enchainment through fragments was a series of 2004/5 museum studies performed in three Bulgarian and one Greek museums. The most extensive refitting experiment involved 484 fragments of anthropomorphic figurines from the Dolnoslav tell that were tried for matching joins – all with each other. A few figurines were re-fitted during the excavation from fragments that were found in adjacent contexts. During the refitting study, another 25 joins between fragments were identified. From a total of 484 fragments, 52 fragments were re-fitted to 25 conjoint pieces, which is a relatively high percentage (11%). Twenty of the joins were direct re-fits. According to Bollong's (1994, 17) criteria (see above, p. 82), the remaining five re-fits are classed as either code 3 – no direct refit but with similar morphological characteristics (4151/3182; 3041/1534; 3070/3434) or code 4 – no direct re-fit but 50% chance of coming from the same figurine (4253/2834;

5211/212). The body parts that form the joins are 5HD, 9TO, 14LEG, 5ST, 1SA, 9TOLE, 2HTK, 5SE and 2 BOLE. None of the joins makes a complete figurine; there are three that show 95% completeness, with a head or an arm or both still missing.

Most of the contexts of the joins linked buildings and middens (n=7) (Table 6.4 and Fig. 6.1b). B6 had two joins – one with D3, the other with D1 and the central profile. Four of the joins occurred in D1, two in D3 and only one in D2. There were no joins between the buildings and D4. The joins between the building and the middens created a horizontal spatial link of deposition between the two contexts. There were two joins between fragments deposited in phase A (B1 4936 and SH 5477) and parts deposited in phase C (D2 1488 and D3 3183). The remaining 6 joins were deposited during the last phase C. Therefore, there was also a vertical spatial link of deposition through time, indicating curation of figurine fragments. The relatively small sample from D4 – only 28 figurines – was probably the reason for the lack of vertical and horizontal link of deposition with other contexts, as well as for the paucity of complete examples.

There were 6 joins deriving from the middens, none of which was from a cross-midden context (Table 6.5). It is important to note that, with one exception (see above, pp. 62 and 64), the only external link of the middens was with the built area. There were 3 joins within D1, two within D2 and one within D4. The only middening area without internal refits was D3; this may have been related to the fact that the midden covered destroyed buildings and any refitting link would have come from the remaining buildings.

There were four joins between the buildings and the open areas (Table 6.6). One of them was between a fragment deposited in phase B (B20 – No 5335) and a fragment deposited in phase C, again showing fragment curation.

Only three joins were found between buildings (Table 6.7).

There were no joins within one and the same building. Half of the buildings containing figurines (13 out of 26) had one part of a join. Three of them had more than 1 part – B10 has parts of three joins, B11 and B17 each have parts of 2 joins. It is important that the redundant four parts were not redistributed among the buildings

| Buildings | Depots |
|-----------|--------|
| 4936 (B1) | 1488 (D2) |
| 2697 (B6) | 2110 (D1) – 3973 CP |
| 4151 (B6) | 3182 (D3) |
| 2835 (B10) | 2302 (D1) |
| 3902 (B24) | 3357 (D1) |
| 2411 (B11) | 2919 (D1) |
| 4577 (SH) | 3183 (D3) |

*Table 6.4 Joins between depots and buildings*

| Depots | Depots |
|--------|--------|
| 544 (D2) | 588 (D2) |
| 587 (D2) | 590 (D2) |
| 2206 (D4) | 2207 (D4) |
| 2921 (D1) | 3049 (D1) |
| 3050 (D1) | 3042 (D1) – 3971 CP |
| 3041 (D1) | 1534 (D1) |

*Table 6.5 Joins between depots*

| Buildings | Buildings |
|-----------|-----------|
| 4371 (B17) | 4025 (B19) |
| 4353 (B2) | 2834 (B10) |
| 3070 (B11) | 3434 (B10) |

*Table 6.6 Joins between buildings*

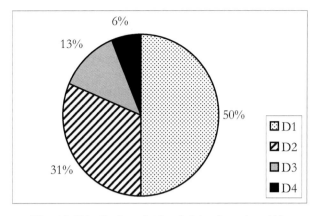

*Fig. 6.2 Distribution of joins deriving from the middens*

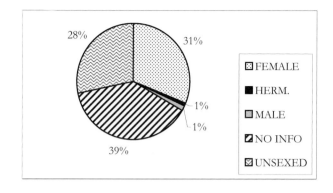

*Fig. 6.3 Figurines by gender from Dolnoslav*

without matching parts of joins but followed a clustering principle. This may symbolize that some households had more interrelated links than others. In five of the remaining 13 buildings, there are complete figurines, which may explain why there were no parts of joins. All but one of the complete examples from these 5 buildings were SA figurines, maybe forming a set, and it is possible that their deposition is based on the principle of accumulation of whole objects standing for a set of objects (Chapman 2000) and obviating the need for the additional reinforcement of enchained relations through deposition of matching parts. The exception to the mutual

| Buildings | Open areas/grid square | |
|---|---|---|
| 4307 (B17) | 3681 | M12 (trench) |
| 3891 (B23) | 4044 | U8 |
| 1584 (K-1) | 1698 | C9 |
| 5335 (B20) | 4688 | M16 |

*Table 6.7 Joins between buildings and the open areas*

| Depots | Open areas/grid square | |
|---|---|---|
| 674 (D2) | 229 | Q10 |
| 1522 (D2) | 2372 | F9 |
| 507, 508 (D1) | 241 | ? |

*Table 6.8 Joins between depots and open areas*

| Open areas/grid square | | Open areas/grid square | |
|---|---|---|---|
| 273 | ? | 2163 | O13 |
| 5211 | C5 | 212 | T9 |

*Table 6.9 Joins between open areas*

avoidance of complete figurines and parts of conjoint pairs was in B2; the fact that the whole examples were not of SA type probably necessitated the fragment enchainment. However, eight buildings have neither parts of matching joins nor complete figurines. It is possible that these buildings were related to other contexts on the tell through different objects (*e.g.* vessels) or that their enchained links were somewhere off the tell.

There were three two joins between middens and open areas – two deriving from D2 and one from D1 (Table 6.8). One of the joins constituted the only example of a direct refit between the middens and the open areas. The second join may have been an internal refit within D2, since the body part from the open areas was found very close to D2 and its findspot may reflect some post-depositional processes. The exact find spot of the third body part of the third join has been lost.

Half of the joins from the middens derived from D1 (n=8), followed by D2 (n=5), D3 (n=2) and D4 (n=1) (Fig. 6.2). The relative distribution of joins in the middens corresponded to the overall distribution of figurines in the middens.

Only two joins have both matching parts deposited in the open areas (Table 6.9).

There were two refits between fragments deposited in phase A and phase C, with only a single refit between phases B and C. All the remaining 22 joins are deposited during the last phase C. The fact that there were no refits between phases A and B suggests that the continuity between these phases of occupation was not negotiated through deposition of figurine joins. However, the links between phases A and C and phases B and C provided physical evidence for the enchained relationships of both earlier occupations to the latest phase of occupation. The joins between occupation payers represent a small part of the curation practices enabling the accumulation of the Phase C middens.

The conjoint figurines were coded as female in 15 cases, with 6 unsexed, 1 hermaphrodite and 3 with no gender information. Ten figurine fragments maintained their gendered identities through the act of fragmentation (five females, two unsexed and three lacking gender information). All the others suffered partial loss of gender information in four ways: (1) three female fragments transformed into one female fragment and one unsexed fragment; (2) seven female fragments into one female fragment and one or two fragments lacking gender information; (3) one hermaphrodite to hermaphrodite and no information; and (4) four unsexed to one unsexed fragment and one lacking gender information. This result reinforces the frequency of the unsexed figurines (Fig. 6.3) and stands in contrast to the pattern of Hamangia figurines' gender changes through breakage. More than 1/3 of the conjoint body parts had 2 breaks, followed by fragments with 3 breaks (30 %); relatively few fragments had only 1 or more then 3 breaks (Plate 19). In general, however, there are more parts of joins that revealed a developed or final stage of fragmentation. It is very important to underline that a relatively high percent of the refitted parts was deposited after 1 or 2 breaks – at a relatively early stage of their potential biographies.

The majority of breaks on re-fitted fragments were fresh, suggesting that the period between the breakage, the "use" and the final deposition of figurines was not very long. Alternatively, between fragmentation and deposition, the already broken parts were not treated in a way that left any traces of wear. However, six refitted parts had traces of wear on their breaks. Two of them were worn in more than one place, suggesting a complex life history (see below, pp. 130–135). Most traces of wear were on the extremities – particularly the feet (3 out of 6 body parts); one case on the heel, one case on both arms,

breasts and bottom; and one on the axis. Two three-part refits also had very worn feet. Furthermore, there was one body part with a very worn bottom and one with wear on the back of the head.

Wear was not necessarily connected with deliberate damaging activities. It may have come from repeated actions like rubbing, placing and moving – aspects of the figurine's life experience. More prone to wear were the edges of an object, which explains the worn breaks and worn extremities. The case of worn flat surfaces (*e.g.* the back of head) may indicate continuous or repeated holding or similar manipulations that have contributed to the partial wear of the fragments.

## Sidedness and wholeness

One of the main principles underlying the deposition of figurines in Dolnoslav proved to be the left – right opposition. The star-shaped figurines were excluded from the sidedness analyses, since the determination of left and right fragments was very difficult, if not impossible. Complete figurines – exhibiting an integration of both left and right – formed 4% of the assemblage. From the remaining fragments, the percentage of body parts that have no clear indication for sidedness was relatively high (37%). These are fragments that were either entirely neutral to sidedness, such as heads, or body parts that had both left and right sides – *e.g.* both legs. However, more than half of the figurines (59%) had some information for either the left or the right side. It was the distribution of these parts that proved to be very similar – 30% of left parts and 29% of right parts (Fig. 6.4).

Sixteen figurines belonged to the earlier phases (A and B) of deposition, leaving 454 figurines dating to phase C during more or less contemporary activities of deposition in all contexts – buildings, middens and open areas. Their general pattern of distribution, however, did not change during the last phase of occupation and followed the above-mentioned regularities – a dominance of neutral parts (neither left, nor right) and a similar distribution of left and right parts (compare Fig. 6.4 with Fig. 6.5).

All categories – left, right and neutral – were present in each context group – middens, buildings and open areas. The combination of left and the right parts was dominant in both the middens and in the open areas, with relatively similar frequencies (Fig. 6.6 and Fig. 6.7). A different pattern was observed in the buildings, where the combination of left and right parts hardly exceeded 50%, and there was a slight dominance of left over right parts (Fig. 6.8)

The largest number of neutral parts was found in the buildings – more than 40% of all neutral parts, which at the same time was the dominant sidedness category of all figurines deposited in the buildings (Fig. 6.8). If left and

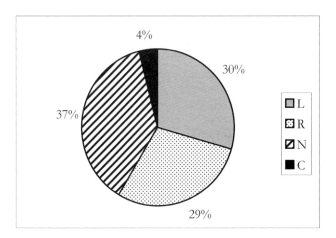

*Fig. 6.4 Distribution of left, right and neutral fragments: C = complete*

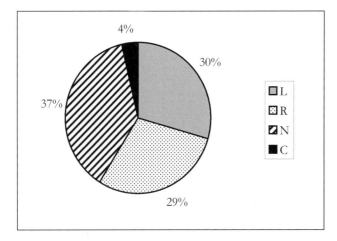

*Fig. 6.5 Distribution of left, right and neutral fragments, phase C*

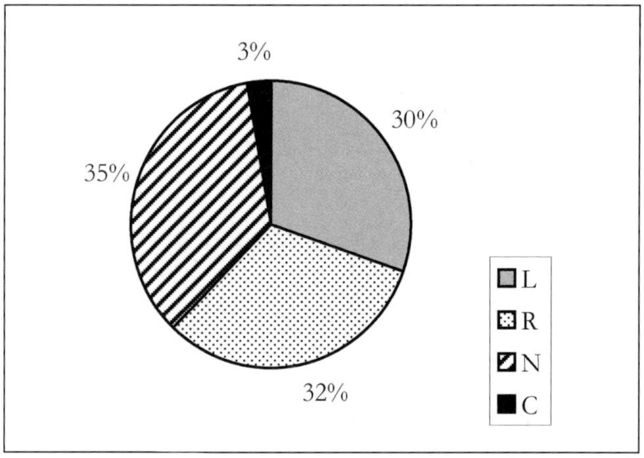

*Fig. 6.7 Distribution of left, right and neutral parts, open areas*

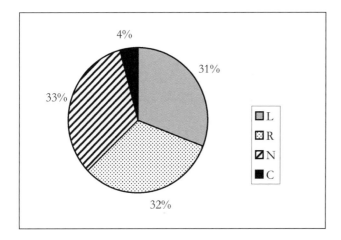

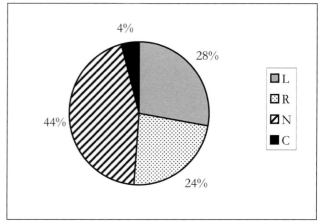

*Fig. 6.6 Distribution of left (L), right (R) and neutral (N) parts and complete (C), middens*

*Fig. 6.8 Distribution of left, right and neutral parts, buildings*

right parts are considered separately, then the neutral parts were the most numerous category; they prevailed in each context – middens, buildings, open areas, with a clear dominance in the buildings, while in the middens and the open areas they formed approximately 1/3 of all deposited figurines (Figs. 6.6 and 6.7).

The distribution of left, right and neutral parts in each of the middens was proportional to the total number of figurines in D1, D2, D3 and D4. The pattern of deposition showed a prevalence of right parts in D1 and D2 and left parts in D3 and D4, resulting in an overall balanced distribution of left and right parts in the middens (Fig. 6.6).

The preference for deposition of neutral parts in the built area (Fig. 6.8) was more obvious in the detailed distribution of body parts in the buildings (Fig. 6.9), where

15 were dominated by neutral parts. The pattern of deposition was very complex, similarities occurring as an exception (*e.g.* B4 and B7: Fig. 6.9). None of the buildings contained only left parts or only left and right parts.

During phase C, 23 of the buildings in which figurines were found were still in use, showing the same complex pattern of distribution. None of the buildings had only left or only right parts or only left and right parts and more than half buildings (n =14) were dominated by neutral body parts.

The overall pattern of distribution in the built area suggests that the left/right opposition was not the main depositional principle there or, more precisely, sidedness was allied to other depositional principles (*e.g.*, contrasts between upper and lower parts or gender) to produce this complex pattern (see below, pp. 128–129).

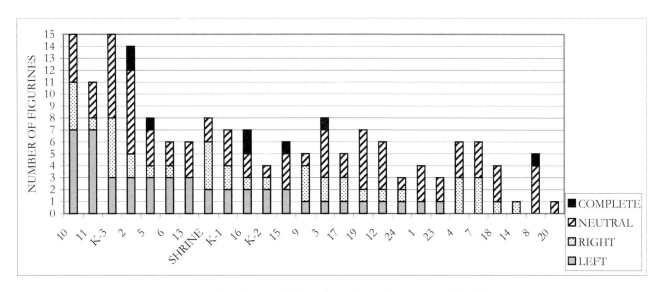

*Fig. 6.9 Distribution of left, right and neutral parts in each building*

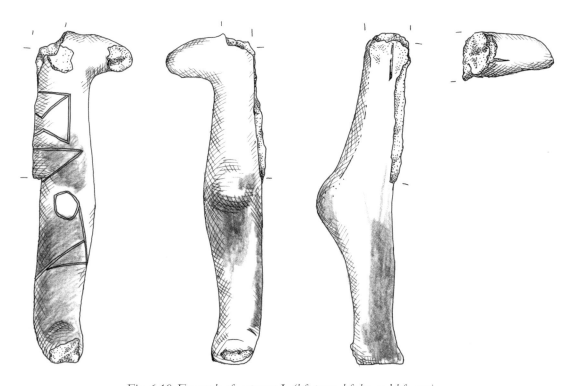

*Fig. 6.10 Example of category L (left torso, left leg and left arm)*

Although convenient for analyses of either left or right, the category *neutral parts* hinders the range of combinations of wholeness, leftness and rightness. Therefore, the assemblage was re-classified into eight new categories in attempt to grasp the whole variety of sidedness representations. In this classification, 'A' stands for ambiguous, 'L' for 100% left side (*e.g.* left torso and left leg, Fig. 6.10), 'R' for 100% right side (Fig. 6.11), 'W' for whole, indicating body parts indivisible into left and right (*e.g.* heads or torsos), 'LR' for left and right (*e.g.* both legs), 'WL' for the combination of whole part and left part (*e.g.* torso with left arm, Fig. 6.12), 'WR' for the combination of whole part and right part (Fig. 6.13), and 'WLR' for the combination of whole part, left and right parts (*e.g.* torso with both arms). In a simplification of this classification, some of the categories were unified, so

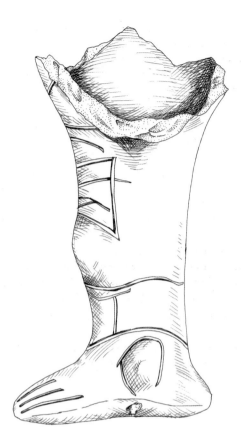

*Fig. 6.11 Example of category R (right leg)*

that 'L' stand for 'L'+'WL', 'R' stands for 'R'+'WR', and 'LR' stands for 'LR'+'WLR'. The majority of the new categories (43%) derived from the middens, one third is from the buildings and almost a quarter is from the open areas.

The symmetry of deposition of left and right parts (Fig. 6.4) is confirmed by the new categories (Plates 20 and 21). The next most common fragments (19%) were the whole (W) fragments, while the total percentage of the remaining categories varied between 15% (Plate 21) and 24% (Plate 20). These regularities did not change with the exclusion of figurines from the earlier phases (compare Plate 20 with Plate 22 and Plate 21 with Plate 23), suggesting that the deposition of figurines through time followed the same general pattern of sidedness.

The distribution of the new categories in the middens was proportional to the distribution of figurines in each midden. The distribution of each category, however, showed greater variation that was not always balanced (*e.g.* the LR category was most common in D2, but not in D1). However, the categorized fragments confirmed the pattern of the symmetrical left and right deposition of the whole assemblage (Figs. 6.4 and Plate 24). The other axis of repetition and reinforcement was the deposition of all categories in the middens, where again a comparable distribution is demonstrated (compare Plate 21 with Plate 25).

The first observable difference in relation to the deposition of left and right parts and the more nuanced

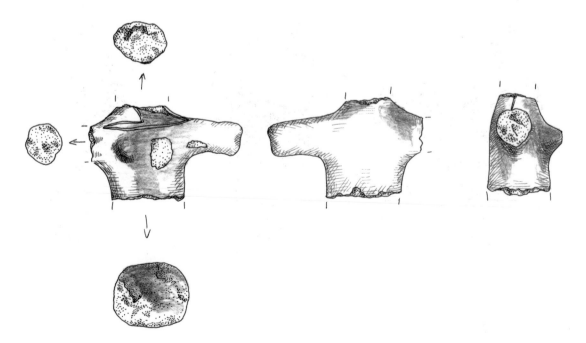

*Fig. 6.12 Example of category WL (whole upper torso and left arm)*

categories is on the level of deposition of categories in each midden. The distribution of categories in D1 and D4 repeated and even reinforced the pattern of deposition of left and right parts, in which there were more right parts in D1 and more left parts in D4 (see above, p. 125). In D2 and D3, however, the distribution of L and R categories was equal, in contrast to the pattern of deposition of left and right parts (see above, p. 125). In total, the distribution of categories in all 4 middens repeated the general symmetry of left and right deposition. Therefore, one may conclude that the re-classification of the sidedness of the figurines in five or indeed eight categories may have produced differences of detail but with a striking similarity in general depositional pattern.

The distribution of new categories in the open areas repeated the earlier pattern (compare Fig. 6.7 and Plate 26), except for a minor difference in the general distribution of categories and the distribution of the categories in the open areas, where the R category was slightly more common (compare Plates 21 and 27).

The distribution of categories in the built area corresponded to the distribution of left and right parts (compare Plates 28 and 29 with Fig. 6.8) – a further confirmation of the different depositional pattern in the building in comparison to the depositional pattern of the whole assemblage and those of the other two contexts – the middens and the open areas. A balanced distribution of all left (L, WL) and right (R, WR) categories was not strictly followed in the buildings, suggesting additional depositional constraints.

The detailed distribution of categories in each building presents a very complex set of combinations, in which is very difficult to claim any regularities (Plate 30). The same pattern is valid for the buildings from phase C.

Apart from the symmetries in the spatial distribution of the different body parts, there is a no less striking symmetry in left and right fragments as types (Appendix 3). Similarities occurred not only in the deposited left and right types but also in their number. As a major source of contrast on the human body, the left-right symmetry has been used to symbolize many aspects of cultural oppositions; we turn to the possible significance of these oppositions in our overall interpretation of the Dolnoslav figurine assemblage (see below, p. 137).

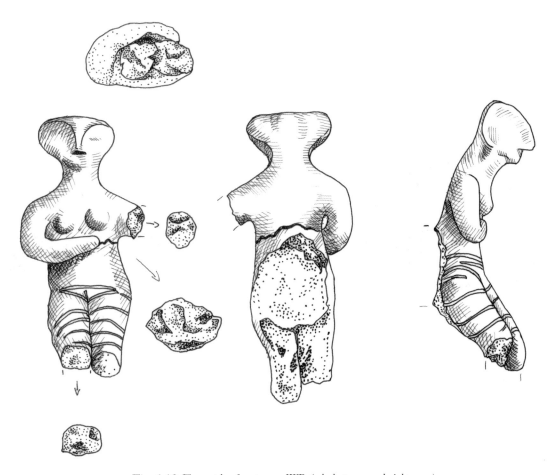

*Fig. 6.13 Example of category WR (whole torso and right arm)*

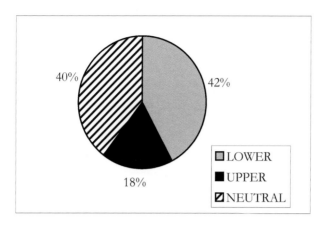

*Fig. 6.14 Distribution of lower and upper parts*

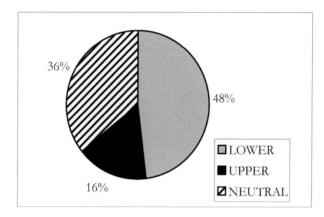

*Fig. 6.15 Distribution of lower and upper parts, middens*

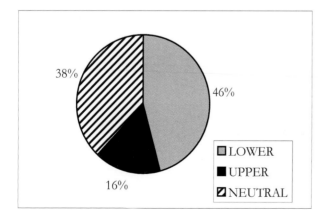

*Fig. 6.16 Distribution of lower and upper parts, open areas*

## Analysis of vertical dimensions

The regularity of the deposition of left and right body parts suggested an analysis of the other possible fragmentation pattern, in which the figurine body was divided into lower and upper parts. The star-shaped figurines and the complete examples were excluded from the analyses. The division line was accepted to be somewhere between the waist and the buttocks. Figurines that were broken around the waist or above that line but which also have a complete or fragmented lower part (buttocks, legs) are considered as neutral in respect of this opposition.

In contrast to the attempt to maintain a balance between left and right parts, there was a deliberate selection of far more lower than upper body parts (Fig. 6.14), although fragments neutral to lower/upper dimensions also had a relatively high distribution.

The distribution pattern of lower and upper parts was very similar in the middens and in the open areas – a clear dominance of lower parts, a high frequency of neutral parts (more than 1/3) and upper parts up to three times less common than the lower parts (Figs. 6.15–6.16). The distribution in the buildings, however, showed a very different pattern. The dominant body part here was the neutral category and the distribution of lower and upper parts was much more balanced than in the middens and the open areas (Fig. 6.17).

Almost half of all lower parts was deposited in the middens (Fig. 6.18). In contrast, most of the upper parts derived from the buildings (Fig. 6.19), which may manifest a major structuring principle, in which symbolism related to the upper body parts (heads, arms, chests/breast) should prevail in the built area, while symbolism related to the lower body parts (buttocks, legs, feet) should be dominant in the unbuilt areas. Such a principle is probably in constant re-negotiation, since there are both upper and lower parts in all types of context, if in differing proportions. An example of the symbolism of vertical differentiation comes from the African Oromo group (Megerssa and Kassam 1987), who define three ways of thinking: head thinking is patriarchal and hierarchical, emphasizing divisions and distinctions; heart thinking is prophetic, poetic, inspirational and oracular, with a female orientation to home and heritage; while abdominal thinking is concerned with the dissolution of boundaries, with unifying and harmonizing. These three ways of thinking exemplify the varying and alternating ways in which experience is lived (Jackson and Karp 1990, 16–17). The higher percentage of upper parts in the built area, often associated with female figurines, could be interpreted in this light. The variety of symbolic meanings of different body parts requires further exploration (Gaydarska *et al.*, in prep.).

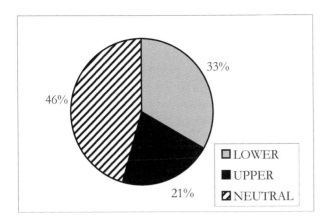

*Fig. 6.17 Distribution of lower and upper parts, buildings*

The usual pattern of minimal comparability was not entirely valid for the upper/lower part distribution on the level of individual buildings. There are only three pairs of buildings that shared the same pattern – B6 and B13; B15 and B17; and B23 and B24 (Fig. 6.20) – but an additional three groups of three buildings where the distribution of body parts was very similar (*e.g.* B9 to B6 and B13; B4 to B15 and B17; B8 to B23 and B24). The balanced deposition of upper and lower parts in each building was not so prominent, suggesting perhaps an idea of visibility on a general level of built space rather than for individual buildings.

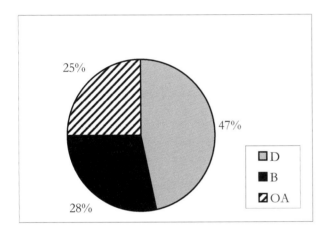

*Fig. 6.18 Distribution of lower body parts. Key: D – Middens; B – Buildings; OA – Open Areas*

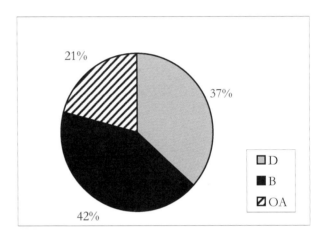

*Fig. 6.19 Distribution of upper body parts. Key: D – Middens; B – Buildings; OA – Open Areas*

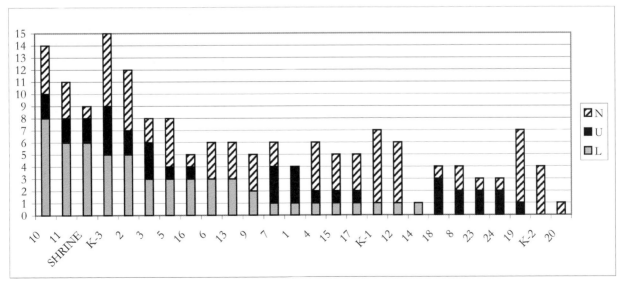

*Fig. 6.20 Distribution of upper and lower body parts in each building*

## *The life histories of figurines*

The study of artifact biographies is not new but rather an under-represented research topic in archaeology (Kopytoff 1986, Spector 1991). Recently, the life histories of artifacts has enjoyed a revival, with the metaphor of the life-cycle of the birth, life and death of objects used as a frequent interpretative tool (Skeates 1995; Jones, A. 2002, 83–144). Such an approach seeks to identify the social implications of the multiple activities performed on certain objects throughout their entire lives. While the birth and the death of a thing are more readily amenable to study, it was the gaps in the mid-life period that stimulated this investigation. Many figurines from Dolnoslav tell (n=213) have features that were the result of either pre-fragmentation or post-fragmentation treatment or both. While observations on the production of the figurines are discussed elsewhere (Gaydarska *et al.*, in prep.), the next pages summarize the evidence for those 142 figurines with traces of post-production treatment.[1] As will become apparent, the details provide a graphic account of figurine fragmentation, plus all of those experiences that figurines went through after their breakage.

### Pre-fragmentation activities

#### *Surface treatment*

A wide variety of activities can be traced on the body of a figurine between firing and fragmentation. Four figurines (TO, SE, ST, HTK) were burnished on the front and smoothed on the back. On one of them, there was additional burning on the back. Also four figurines (TO, SE, TOLE, TOBO) revealed exactly the reverse pattern – burnished on the back and smoothed on the front. On three of them, the contrast in surface treatment was reinforced by a colour contrast. The remaining 5 examples of specific surface treatment utilised the matt/gloss contrast. There were 2 fragments with a rough surface (on the bottom and the back) that contrasted with the remaining surface of the fragments; and there was one example of the reverse pattern – a smoothed, flat surface only on the side of the bottom and nowhere else. Another contrasting pair shows cases of combined treatments – rough on the front and smoothed on the back of head, as well as the reverse pattern. Smooth, sparkling and shiny surfaces were important properties of many prehistoric objects and were often used to characterize fine wares, as well as to establish contrasts between different parts of the same vessel (see above, pp. 49–51). The contrasts between colours are also reminiscent of the contrasts on Copper Age vessels and may be seen as a part of a wider practice of the categorization of difference through material culture. Additional insights into the meaning of high gloss and smoothness may be provided by considering the body parts to which they are applied (Gaydarska *et al.* in prep.).

#### *Decoration*

The traditional decoration style of incision and incrusting, together with their specific motifs, will be discussed elsewhere (Gaydarska *et al.* in prep.). There were two ways of providing special treatment for figurines – colour contrast and crusted painting. Altogether there are 9 examples of colour contrast applied to figurines or figurine fragments during firing: a black torso with a brown head; a black core with brown extremities; black and white contrast on the bottom and back of a leg; red and white contrasts on neck; two cases of black on the front and brown on the back, with one example of grey on the back as a variant; and 2 cases of SA figurines with black on the back and brown on the front.

The second treatment involving paint and colour was red and/or white crusting. There were two cases of crusting with both colours. In one of them, the red crusting was applied before the white crusting, where the decoration is very worn; in the other case, the sequence was reversed. In two cases, the white crusting was inside a hollow. In four cases, it was all over the figurines, with loss of crusting from one worn bottom. The last cases of white crusting comprised one fragment on the lower back and another under the arms and between the breasts (see below, p. 131).

#### *Secondary burning*

This is a relatively rare practice represented by 4 fragments – all legs, two of them forming a pair. They were exposed to secondary burning before their subsequent fragmentation.

### Post-fragmentation activities

#### *Secondary burning*

The commonest post-fragmentation activity was secondary burning – traceable on 30 fragments. They were found in all contexts – buildings, middens and open areas and the possibility that all of them were burnt during the last destructive fire was very low. The diversity of burning patterns and the fact that none of the fragments was entirely burnt suggest that the secondary burning on the fragments was a controlled process – only certain parts are affected by the fire and to an extent that does not change the texture of the clay, which was the case with many misshapen Dolnoslav vessels re-fired to red. Moreover the traces of burning were on the breaks of the fragments, which makes an explanation of accidental burning if not impossible then highly improbable. The majority of the breaks were on the left/right axis, leg or bottom (Table 6.10). There were only three fragments with secondary burning on torso breaks – one has additional burning on the lower torso, the other – over the incised and incrusted decoration, the third over the breast break. The number of fragments with burning on arm was similar (n=5), as with neck breaks (n=4) (Table 6.11). There was a single fragment with burning on the leg break and the leg itself. Two fragments with secondary burning revealed traces of multiple treatments and shall be discussed further below (see p. 132).

*Decoration*
Fourteen fragments were crusted with different colours of paint over their breaks: 3 of them show complex treatment and shall be discussed further below (see p. 132 & Table 6.14). On nine fragments, white colour was crusted onto a wide range of breaks – neck, base, leg, axis, right arm, foot, 2 arms of star-shaped figurine, torso, in the groove between legs and on one arm of a star-shaped figurine, whose top break was not crusted at all. The latter may present a case of complex treatment, in which the initial arm break was sealed with white paint and after that the top was removed from the figurine. Alternatively, there may have been a specific practice of crusting of certain breaks but not others. There was only one case of red crusting on an axis break, as well as one fragment with white and red crusting applied over the pubic break.

In addition to the undoubted fact that figurines were curated after the break, the secondary treatment of fragments poses the difficult question of the meaning of such treatment. Was such treatment meant to heal the break or maybe seal the break? Were these secondary manipulations intended to reinforce the fragmentation or mask it? And why were some breaks treated with crusting

and others with burning? These are important questions that only emerge with a recognition of the implications of deliberate fragmentation. However, it was not only on breaks that burning and crusting appeared, thus changing the emphasis from the practices themselves (burning and crusting) to the places where they were applied – breaks or other parts. In any case, fragments were kept and used in a number of inter-related social practices that resulted in the complex combination of different body parts with different secondary treatments. The possible interpretation of such complex patterns depends upon the identification of the manipulation sequence on each fragment that, although important, far exceeds the purposes of the present chapter.

## Activities that may have taken place either before or after the fragmentation

*Wear*
Thirty eight fragments had traces of heavy wear. The body parts with repetitive traces of wear are summarized in Table 6.12. One of the fragments with wear on the back of the head was also worn on the left ear and one of the fragments that was worn all over was especially worn on the bottom.

The remaining five fragments had wear on the head, the bottom and the back of the leg, the stomach and back, the lower back and the front torso. One of the fragments with a worn bottom had secondary burning on its left side and on the left leg. Most traces of wear were on body parts that symbolized a specific activity – *e.g.*, the foot, heel and sole, for walking; the bottom for sitting; or the

| Axis break – 3 |
|---|
| and top front leg |
| and back of   leg |
| and right      leg |
| and right side of leg and leg |
| and                   leg and bottom |
| and                          bottom – 7 |

*Table 6.10 Fragments with secondary burning on axis break*

| Body part | No. of fragments |
|---|---|
| Back of head | 4 |
| bottom | 8 |
| base | 3 |
| All over | 3 |
| foot | 11 |
| heel | 2 |
| sole | 2 |

*Table 6.12 Body parts with repetitive traces of wear*

| Arm break and left side of torso | Neck break and right arm |
|---|---|
| and bottom | and right arm and back |
| and bottom and back | and right ear and right neck |
| and on front after incised decoration | and right ear and face |
| and on front below face | |

*Table 6.11 Fragment with secondary burning on arm or neck break*

back of head for lying. In such cases, heavy wear may symbolize multiple performances of these activities, and hence the long life and experience of the figurine or person.

*Secondary burning*
Apart from the fragments with burning on breaks, there were 30 body parts with traces of burning that may have taken place either before or after the fragmentation or both (*e.g.*, the head fragment (No. 2454) burnt on the back of the head and on the ear break but not on the broken neck). Most often secondary burning was applied to the bottom – alone in 5 cases and in combination with other body parts in 5 cases (4 on legs, 1 on the back). Also frequent was the secondary burning on torsos and legs (Table 6.13). There were two star-shaped figurines with traces of fire – one on the top and bottom, the other on one of the arms. Five fragments were burnt on the back (HD, TO, TOLE and 2 SA), one of them with additional burning on the bottom break, another the above discussed

head (No. 2454) with complex traces of burning.

Despite the general uncertainty of the time of burning with regard to the fragmentation practice, there were some figurines to which secondary burning was applied before or after decoration. In one case, burning preceded incised and incrusted decoration; in other, it preceded white crusting on the top of a star-shaped figurine; and, in a third, the burning on the back and the left side of an SA figurine preceded incision. In four cases, burning was applied over decoration – two cases of incised and incrusted, and two cases of white crusting.

## Combined treatment

A combination of two manipulations regardless of its sequence vis-à-vis fragmentation was traceable on 24 figurines = two complete objects and 22 fragments. Table 6.14 is a summary of the possible micro-stratigraphy, including fragmentation at a certain point in the sequence of events.

| Upper | Torso not specified | lower | left | Legs not specified | right |
|---|---|---|---|---|---|
| right | left side | front | front | top | lower |
| | | left + bottom | | bottom | foot |
| | right side | | | all over | |
| | front base | | | | |
| | front and right side | | | | |

*Table 6.13 Fragments with secondary burning on torsos or legs*

| | |
|---|---|
| Surface treatment followed by | burning – 2 |
| | wear – 1 |
| | crusting – 3 |
| Burning followed by | decoration (white wash or crusting or incision) – 4 |
| Burning followed by | breakage followed by crusting – 1 |
| Burning followed by | incision + red & white incrustation, followed by breakage |
| | followed by white crusting – 1 |
| Crusting followed by | burning – 2 |
| | wear – 2 |
| Breakage followed by | fragmentation, with wear either before and/or after |
| | breakage and fragmentation – 1 |
| Breakage followed by | burning (torso break) and crusting (arm break) – 1 |
| Unclear sequence | burning and wear – 5 |
| | white wash and wear – 1 |

*Table 6.14 Number of figurines with combined treatment*

## Figurines with holes in the stomach

A specific variant on the twenty pregnant SA figurines was represented by six figurines with a hole in the stomach area (5SA and 1SE) (Fig. 6.21). All these figurines were females and five were in different stages of pregnancy. Four were found in buildings and two in the open areas. All of them were decorated with incision, with one further incrusted with white and one additionally crusted with red. Three figurines have traces of additional manipulations – two formed a join and are discussed further below (pp. 138 and 140–141), while the third suffered a burnt right bottom and burnt leg. It is likely that they represent the final stage of the birth cycle – the birth itself. However, there is one fragment whose perforation was made from the back, raising the possibility that some of them symbolized a kind of medical treatment comparable to trepanation.

## The life history of a conjoint pair

All of the joins provide valuable insights on the treatment of figurines before and after fragmentation. One particularly interesting example of how fragments are treated after the break is Join No. 5. The life histories of the remaining 24 joins are described in Appendix 4.

Join 5 consists of two fragments (Fig. 6.22) – a head with a top knot, upper torso and arms, found in building 17; and a left torso and left leg, found in building 19. Both fragments dispalyed gender information – breasts on the upper body and an incised pubic triangle on the lower body. The head had incised eyes, perforated ears and a stamped mouth, while the front and the back of the upper torso were incised with motif 167 (Fig. 6.23). The lower body part was also entirely incised with motif 172 (Fig. 6.24). There were traces of 4 breaks on the upper part – irregular fractures removing both ears and the tip of the right arm and angular at the axis of detachment from the lower part. No breaks were worn, which suggests that they were subject to minimal physical manipulation after the fragmentation. The lower part had three breaks – an irregular break at the axis of detachment from the upper part, a hinge fracture at axis of detachment from the right leg and a flake removed from the heel. The only break with no trace of any post-fragmentation treatment in this zone of the figurine was the break along the upper/lower axis. After the detachment of the flake from the heel, some physical activity such as rasping or filing or perhaps pre-depositional erosion, contributed to the heavy wear of the heel. The left/right axis break was secondarily burnt, as was the bottom.

Both fragments were found in buildings that were destroyed by fire. However, the fire did not have any affect on the upper fragment, and indeed on the lower fragment apart from the bottom and the left/right axis, which suggest that the secondary burning on the lower fragment probably pre-dated the final destructive fire. Therefore, regarding the lower body part, two activities have taken place after the separation of the upper and lower parts – special heel treatment and secondary burning. It is not possible to establish the primary activity – whether the heel was treated first (which raises the question of how the second heel was treated – the same or differently) or whether division of the lower part into left and right part preceded burning on the bottom and the axis. It is also

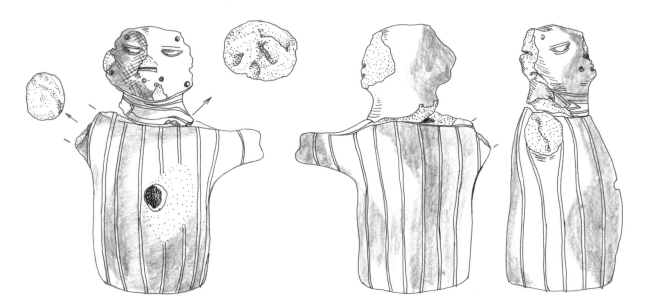

*Fig. 6.21 Figurine with hole in the stomach*

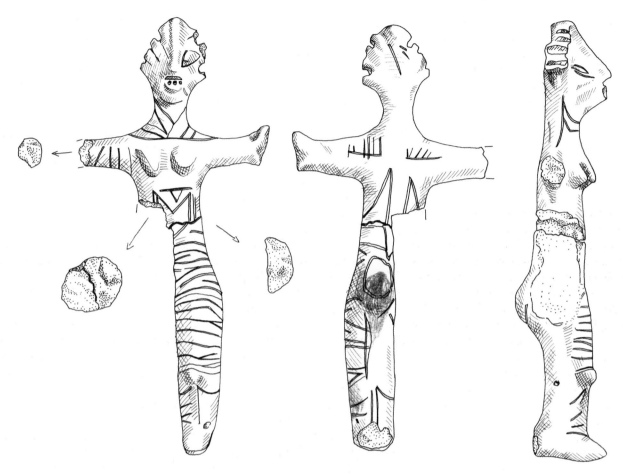

*Fig. 6.22 Join 5*

*Fig. 6.23 Decorational motif 167*

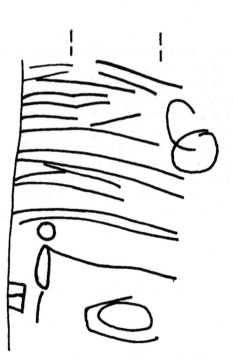

*Fig. 6.24 Decorational motif 172*

difficult to establish whether the right lower part was detached from the whole figurine or just from the left lower part. The same uncertainty is valid for the treatment of the upper body part – was it "trimmed" on the extremities (both ears and right arm) before or after the detachment of the lower part? The fact that the other extremity – the left heel – also revealed traces of manipulation plausibly suggests initial chipping of the extremities of the complete figurine. Despite the uncertainty of the fragmentation sequence, it is clear that the once complete figurine was divided into at least 3 fragments, each of which had its own biography. The upper part was either not specially treated or had minor changes before its final deposition in building 17. The left lower part was surely burnt after its separation from the right side. Either before or after this activity, the bottom was also burnt and the heel was manipulated. The end of the life-cycle of this body part was its deposition in building 19, located 5–10m from building 17 (Plate 18). The right lower part/s were not deposited on the site, thus enriching the biography of the once-whole figurine.

The fragments with complex life histories present concentrated principles of multiple post-production manipulations of the figurines at Dolnoslav. They illustrate better the issues of deliberate actions of burning, breaking, wear, etc. since they present a sequence of events. Together with the different life history of the separate parts of conjoint pairs (see Appendix 4), these fragments suggest that parts with traces of a single activity (*e.g.* either burning or breaking or wear, etc.) should also be perceived as items of special care and curation. While these examples are certainly important, we should not forget that, apart from 11 complete and untreated examples, every other Dolnoslav figurine has been the subject of some post-manufacture intervention or other, notably fragmentation itself. The diversity of figurine treatments, and their combination and re-combination, is echoed in the variety of cross-cutting categorizational principles valid for Late Copper Age ceramics and communities alike and is demonstrated in other examples of the current perception of material culture. The multiplicity of ways in which figurines were treated was surely a metaphor for the very varied life histories of Late Chalcolithic persons.

## Interpretation

If anything in Dolnoslav interpretation is certain, it is that Dolnoslav is an accumulation place for fragments. Whether fragments evoking either social memories or enchained social relations, or fragments that grew out of dividual persons, the emphasis is on the fragments. Another certain claim valid for deposition at Dolnoslav is that it would be unreasonable to believe that five or six

principles were all encompassed in one figurine, principles that at the same time formed the basis of the deposition of all 500 figures. We therefore believe that different figurines or fragments came and ultimately remained on the Dolnoslav tell, or were moved off the tell to other places, for different reasons. This explains why there are both complete and broken figurines; figurines with different numbers of breaks; figurines with no additional manipulations and with many, and, finally, multiple figurine refits. In order to understand the complex pattern of deposition on Dolnoslav, we have to differentiate the principles that governed the formation of the second most dramatic consumption of figurines yet known in the later prehistory of Southeast Europe.

The Dolnoslav evidence presents the greatest diversity of types of figurines deposited on a single site known so far. Their spatial distribution may be one way to explain the explicit use of such a variety of types. In the unbuilt areas (middens and open areas), there was an attempt to balance the deposition of different figurine types with the repeated finding of the same pattern – one commonest body part and three other less but equally common body parts. By contrast, in the built area, the emphasis was more on diversity and rare body types but, again, the principle of types competing in number underlay the main distributional pattern.

One principle for understanding the differential distributions of legs, torsos and heads is the idea that a diversity of figurine types conveyed the diversity of Late Copper Age society. We emphasise that we do not equate particular figurine types with particular social groups. Rather, we accept that the figurine diversity in Dolnoslav was a metaphorical perception of the people for their own society, comprising, as it did, different limited interest groups and different kinship groups. Figurine diversity points to an awareness of a diversified society, in which metaphorical representations of social variety may have been crucial in processes of social reproduction. The variety of kinds of people in the Late Copper Age related to the initial choice of making various types of figurines and what such a choice implied. Likewise, the final deposition of figurines completed and summarised social processes already in operation in prehistoric communities. The accumulation of all the figurine types, or only some of them, in different contexts was comparable to the Hamangia practice of depositing the full range of categories of figurines or raw materials in special pits in order to summarise all possible material relations in their world. We can, therefore, infer that deposition of different types of figurines was as important as their making.

The production and meaning of different figurine types is a topic of ongoing research (Gaydarska *et al.*, in prep) but two types are worth mentioning here in terms of their deposition at Dolnoslav. The first intriguing type is the star-shaped figurines. They cannot convey gender, do not (in most cases) convey vertical differentiation but they can convey bilateral symmetry (2 diagonal symmetries) and the principle of concentricity. This may have been the only artifact whose form, opposing inner core to concentric outer parts, related to the overall concentric spatial arrangement of the Dolnoslav tell.

The second important fragment type was the head. At Dolnoslav, there were fewer torsos than legs and fewer heads than torsos. If heads were perceived as the locus of personal identity, as in the Classic Maya concept of Bah (Houston and Stuart 1988), why were so few found in such an important accumulation place? Alternatively, if they were believed to be the locus of integration for opposed or perhaps complementary positions, such as male/female, left/right and front/back, the expectation is that they should have been much more frequent. A possible answer to these questions relies on the rarity of heads in comparison with other kinds of fragments; a figurine can be broken into many fragments but the head is always one. Thus, the presence of heads on different sites was probably dependent on a strategy of the re-distribution of heads, in which such a body part should have been present on each settlement – embedded in the everyday habitus of the people but yet retaining its great importance. Indeed, although few in number, figurine heads have been found on most, if not all, excavated sites. Heads appear to have been an irreducible element – broken off but rarely, and probably deliberately not, broken into further parts. Such pattern is in strong contrast to the practice of breaking Hamangia phallic necks (see Chapter 3) and points to a different understanding of heads. Furthermore, the special attention paid to this body part was reinforced by the presence of interchangeable heads, masked figurines and mask graves in Southeast European prehistory (Gimbutas 1986, 1989; Bailey 2005; Biehl 2003; Catuna, n.d.; Tallalay 2004) However, the weakness of these previous interpretations was that they missed the potential of head-related representations as constituting personhood on an individual level. That personhood can be created by "non-human" materiality is problematic only if viewed from the modern Western concept of self but, as we have already argued (see above, pp. 19–20), there is no ground to suggest that such concept was valid for the later prehistory of Southeast Europe (Chapman 2000; Jones, A. 2005) or even for Central and West/Northwest Europe (Whittle 2003; Fowler 2004, Jones, A. 2002a). On the contrary, the very nature of the diverse and abundant material culture of Southeast Europe is an outstanding but yet unexplored reservoir of principles for the creation of personhood. Head-related representations were just one part of the material world that constituted identities in the past. The gender-neutral images of heads and masks reveal that it is

less important what sex you are than who you are. The removable heads and the burials of masks are indicative of the key principle of fragmentation practice – *pars pro toto*. Therefore, figurine heads that are detached from the body functioned as any other fragment in an enchained relationship but, at the same time, retained the essence of a person for whom the categories of sex, age and status were not yet attributed.

The representation of gender and age is one of the most characteristic features in each figurine assemblage. Dolnoslav is no exception but it should nonetheless be recognized that 39% of all deposited figurines were lacking information about gender. This is a strong message from a society that was not totally pre-occupied with gender debates. Perhaps gender roles were negotiated and agreed on a household and/or communal level, later to be projected as one of the structuring principle of Dolnoslav figurine deposition. The paucity of male figurines at Dolnoslav sheds little light on the big question of why there were more female figurines than male. What it does, however, is to provide some understanding of the production of so many unsexed figurines. Earlier in this chapter, we suggested that the unsexed examples may have been associated with negotiation of androgyny or age-related statements. Insofar as the design of Late Copper Age figurines does not directly imply androgyny (contrary to the obvious case of Hamangia design!) and most of the complete figurines from Dolnoslav are unsexed, we would favour the interpretation of the gender-neutral figurines as age-related. There is no ground to believe that figurines, their makers and/or consumers would be associated only with sexually active men and women. Young pre-pubescent children, post-menstrual women and old men were a valued part of society and their social identity was also an important matter of negotiation and representation. It is plausible that the biography of the figurines was linked to the biography of the people. Thus, the unsexed fragments with 1 and 2 breaks (more than 30% of all unsexed fragments) may have stood for young people with few enchained relations, while unsexed fragments with 3 or more breaks (65% of all unsexed fragments) would have represented senior members of the community with multiple enchained relations. If we are correct in this interpretation, the life gendering process was a mirror image of Hamangia: at Dolnoslav it goes from gender-neutral to gendered to gender-neutral. The constitution of gender and age mediated through figurines was instrumental for the creation of household and communal identity, notwith-standing the contributions of other materialities, substances and practices to the formation of personhood.

One of the main depositional principles on Dolnoslav tell proved to be the balanced distribution of left and right parts. Sidedness is not a natural property of most materials and objects that prehistoric people used in their everyday life. The incorporation of different raw material (*Spondylus*, clay, etc.) could also have been seen in the light of a particular resistance to the value of sidedness. Objects such as the *Spondylus* shell could hardly have been transformed into an object with a left or a right part – even if that was the aim of the maker. *Spondylus* rings, however, had a residual sidedness from their manufacture out of either right or left valves. It is possible that there was a diachronic significance with changing uses of right and left valves: initially only the right valve, then both valves, and finally only the left valve (see below, pp. 146). Other materials such as wood, stone, leather facilitated more general production of both objects with left and right sides and objects void of sidedness. Sidedness was a property of a narrow range of artifacts that could be produced from different raw materials. Clay figurines were probably the most prominent example of the representation of sidedness, since they were replicas of the human body. They were also one of the best examples of the relation *pars pro toto*: even if only one part (left or right) was present, it is implicit that there was a matching part. Therefore, wholeness is most readily achievable by the complementary use of sidedness. Moreover, the bilateral symmetry of left and right favoured the notion that any pair of left and right parts stood for wholeness, even if the parts belonged to different figurines.

The left/right opposition can be explained in various ways. The structuralist approach was to attribute different categories to left and right and this was most often the gender/sex division. If we accept this approach, then left and right parts represented males and females and their final balanced deposition challenged the initial strategy of the production of more female figurines than male images. In the end, the man and woman were re-united in one complementary androgenous person on a society level. The weakness of this approach is that it does not yet explain the production of unsexed figurines. Left/right contrasts have nothing or very little to do with gender difference – all gendered organs are symmetrically placed. What relates to gender difference in a fragmentation chain is vertical differentiation: Hamangia figurines have a more complex up/down chain than do Late Copper Age figurines, where femaleness tends to be associated with the upper body part.

Another way to view the left and right contrast is the South Indian caste system, in which right-side castes are related to landowners and important social actors, and left-side castes are related to artisans and people making things with their own labour (Beck 1973). The introduction of metal (Renfrew 1969), changes in settlement planning (Chapman 1990), the appearance of extramural cemeteries and especially the Varna cemetery (Chapman 1983, 1991) leaves us in little doubt that Final Copper

Age society was a classic example of a complex society. Cross-cutting social divisions and diversifications may have been resulting in communities in which some people were predominantly (but not entirely) involved with cultivation, herding and food production, while other people were skilled in pottery production, flint knapping, figurine making and breaking, etc. This was not a rigid division of labour but, rather, a practical response to the intensification of subsistence strategies. Both groups were equally important for the biological and social reproduction of the society and such a division did not interfere with any other potential membership of the people. We suggest that this division was symbolically materialized by the left and right parts of the figurines. Akin to the left and right forming parts of an entity, the land-related group and the artisans were parts of a dialectic whole. There is no constraint on people to belong to either of the groups. More and less successful households could both have been members of one group (either left or right) and some members of one family could have been occupied with land processing, while others developed craft production. The symbolic social division into left and right would have been valid for the members of a small community but it also has an inter-regional significance, since the Late Copper Age was characterized by a well-developed exchange network based on production, consumption and distribution of objects, foods and exotica. Therefore, one may view the deposition of left and right parts of figurines on the Dolnoslav tell as a metaphor for the contrast between two widely shared identities: groups of people with land-oriented labour and groups of craftsmen, artisans and ritual specialists.

By this point in the book, it is probably clear that we accept the figurine fragments from Dolnoslav as strong evidence for deliberate breakage. The acknowledgement of the intentionality of such practices for ritual purposes is mentioned in the context of the Drama microregion (Lichardus *et al.* 2000) and more profoundly discussed for other Balkan Copper Age sites (Biehl 2003). Among other important insights on figurine production and meaning, Biehl (2003, 328–230 and Abb. 25–26) has identified points of normal and abnormal breakage of figurines. The former were usually focused on weak points in construction (head, arms and legs), while the latter concentrated on strong construction points, suggesting anything but accidental breakage. On the basis of the fragments with abnormal breakage, he proposes a cult of destruction that is part of a wider cult of transformation in which fragments, accidentally or deliberately broken, were major participants (2003, 340). The fact that no re-fitting parts were found on his sites (2003, 334) needs further clarification, since it is not clear whether any actual re-fitting study was performed or whether this information comes from the site/museum documentation; it is also unclear whether refits were tried between sites as well as within sites. However, Biehl (2003, 338) concludes that figurine fragments were a mobile class of artifacts used in exchanges and deposited (or destroyed) off-site.

The refitting exercise of the Dolnoslav figurine assemblage and, especially, the artifact biography approach have helped us to develop a methodology for the identification of the deliberate breakage of figurines. First of all, is the number of breaks traceable on a single figurine fragment. If one break can to some extent be explained by an accident, this can hardly be claimed for cases with multiple breaks. Moreover, preliminary experimental work on figurine breakage has proven accidental breakage to be very unlikely (Chapman and Priestman, in press). The majority of Dolnoslav fragments exhibits more than 1 break (84%). This is very strong evidence for further fragmentation after the first break or, as we call it, for the fragmentation chain. Indeed, in some rare cases, one can clearly recognize that a certain break could only have taken place after a previous break. More often, the sequence is not so clear but the close inspection of all breaks has yielded valuable information for the life cycle of figurines. Detailed discussion of each kind of break is the subject of another study (Gaydarska *et al.* in prep.) but what should not be omitted here is that most breaks would have required special fragmentation skills. Some breaks look like a "hole", as if the body part (usually the head) was drilled or bored out (Figs. 6.25–6.26 joins 11, 19). Others are a result of "snapping" (Fig. 6.13 N

2163) or from blows from two angles (Figs. 6.27–6.28 joins 14, 22). And finally, there are fractures on hollow figurines or fragments that if executed without care may have caused the total destruction of the object (Fig. 6.29 join10). Most probably, many of the breaks were performed by using special tools and therefore it is possible that only certain people – figurine knappers? – could have dealt with the sometimes delicate, sometimes tough, job of breaking a figurine. There is no doubt that the fragments deposited on the Dolnoslav tell were part of a widely practiced figurine fragmentation. The fragmentation chain can be related to separate acts of celebrating enchainment between owners of figurines or fragments of figurines. Being tokens of enchained relations, figurines were in constant move between sites and people. And indeed, on any average Late Copper site one would expect to find no more than 10–15 figurines deriving from a single occupation layer – which makes the deposition in Dolnoslav even more exceptional.

Before turning to a more general reconstruction of what people meant by the production, breakage and deposition of so many figurines, another key characteristic of the Dolnoslav assemblage is worth discussing in some detail. Almost 1/3 of the fragments revealed secondary treatment after detachment from matching part/s. They are burnt, or crusted, or worn or any combination of these activities. The first very important implication following from the evidence of secondary treatment is that it reinforces the notion of deliberate breakage of

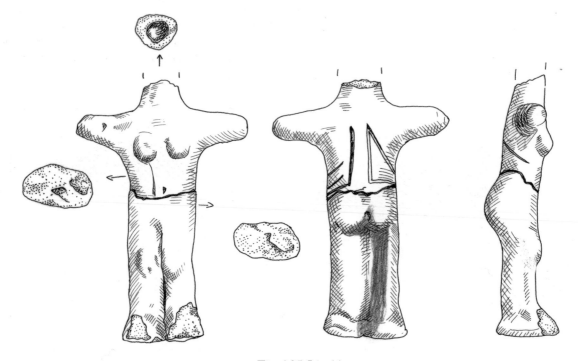

*Fig. 6.25 Join 11*

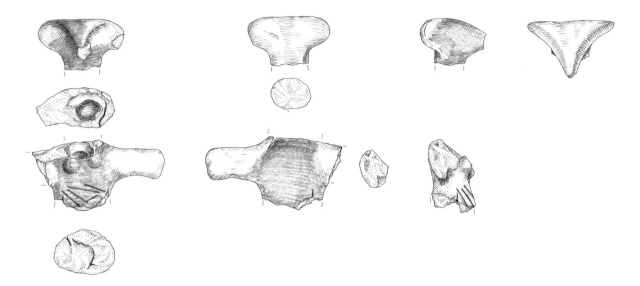

*Fig. 6.26 Join 19*

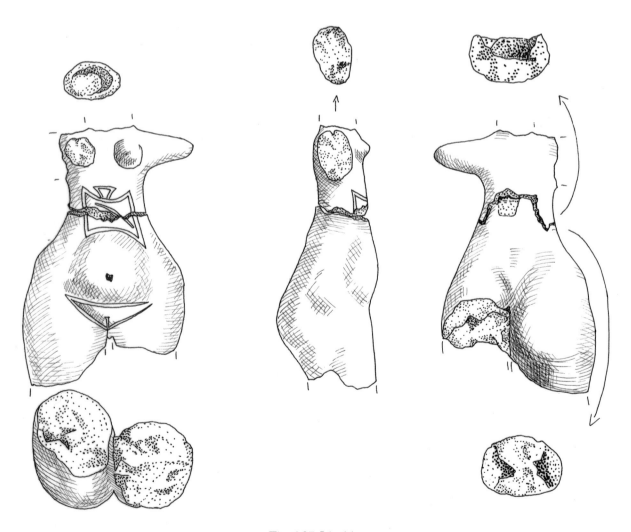

*Fig. 6.27 Join 14*

figurines and the subsequent keeping of the residual fragments, some of which for the purposes of additional manipulation. Especially explicit for the latter are the fragments with traces of treatment on the breaks. A second implication follows from the first that concerns the possible meaning of the performed operations –

burning, crusting and wear. One way of interpreting these manipulations relates them to the anthropologically attested associations between burning – purification and crusting – cleansing. Another approach involves close attention to the different body parts on which the secondary treatment took place. Most body parts were the

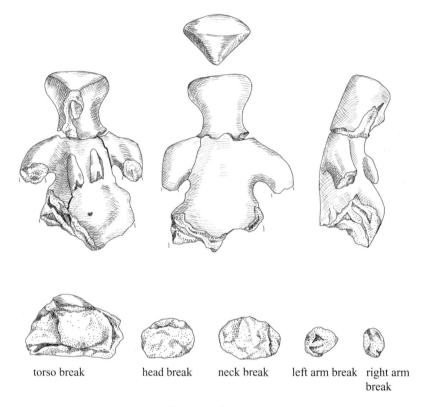

torso break          head break          neck break          left arm break     right arm break

*Fig. 6.28 Join 22*

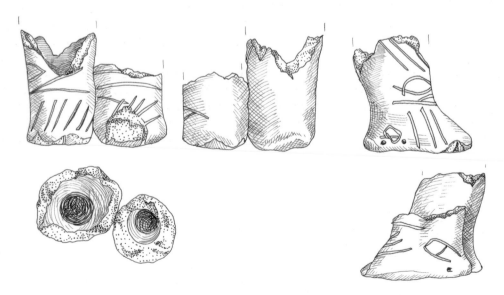

*Fig. 6.29 Join 10*

object of special manipulation, whether ears, nose, arms, feet, legs, bottom, breasts or stomach. If we accept the symbolic principle that each body part is representative of some state of being (*e.g.* the stomach – eating or pregnancy; the bottom – pollution or fertility), one may suggest that there is a direct link between the secondary treatment and these cultural phenomena. Such an approach does not, however, explain the burning, crusting and wear on the breaks. Therefore, most probably fragmentation and subsequent treatment of fragments as interrelated practices have operated in a dynamic non-constrained network of things, people and actions. Different quotidian and sacred issues were solved with different combinations of materiality and action (Gaydarska *et al.*, in prep.).

Post-Gimbutas studies of anthropomorphic and zoo-morphic images have been preoccupied with function, symbolism and meaning (Marangou 1992, Talalay 1993, Hamilton *et al.* 1996, Biehl 2003, Bailey 2005, Nanoglou 2005). Although most authors are cautious not to relate figurines to a single meaning or function, the final inter-pretation of figurines often relies on certain aspect of the imagery (*e.g.* posture and gesture; decoration, etc.), thus reducing the figurines to what may have been their most prominent but yet only one aspect of their multifaceted nature. The complexity of the patterns of making, break-ing and deposition is more consistent with the possibility that figurines were embedded in several overlapping social strategies. For the Dolnoslav figurines, we have identified three groups of strategies that cross-cut the principles of gender, sidedness and up-down-ness, and which can be best discussed within the framework of the figurine's life course. However, the key point for the understanding of figurines is that they embody different sorts of categorization principles at different stages of their lives.

## Birth

The first group of strategies involved the process of making a wide variety of figurines, whose variety is mediated by type, size, shape, decoration and surface finish. Such a process is very clearly manifested by the diversity and number of figurines deposited on the Dolnoslav tell, unprecedented except at one other site – the Vinča tell (Srejović 1968). Skourtopoulou (in press a) has made out a strong case for non-specialized production of lithics, deeply embedded in the everyday life of the Late Neolithic settlement at Makryalos. Biehl (2003) reaches similar conclusions for figurine production on the basis of their shape and decoration. The Dolnoslav data reinforce the notion of an even closer link between the objects and their makers. The figurines were born as babies into different households, with different circumstances and purposes. Their different decoration

and form represented not so much individuals as the social context and interest groups of that individual.

## Life

As they grew up, figurines developed in the context of everyday things happening. The creation of a figurine's biography led to either a simple or a complex life-history. This was **not** dependent upon the type of complete figurine to start with – but related to the person that the figurine grew out of. The life-histories of still complete figurines showed that they were not treated differently from fragments – three whole figurines had traces of burning, while two more had traces of wear. Both complete and broken figurines were used in both private and public ceremonies, whose material citations (Jones, A. 2005) were the figurines with traces of burning, crusting and wear. The emphasis on the images with complex biographies should not undermine the figurines with little/or no interesting events in their life-history. They were deliberately chosen, perhaps to be kept clean or ritually pure. The presence or lack of secondary treatment, the differential breakage patterns and the striking variety of types of figurines confirms the notion that figurines were important media in more general social strategies rather than obeying some strict rules in specific local cults.

The important question of whether figurines were treated in their place of origin or in their final resting place (*e.g.* Dolnoslav) is still very difficult, if not impossible, to answer. The differential wear on the fragments may have been a sign of travel but equally a testament to intensive local use. Moreover, there are many unworn figurines that must have been used carefully and kept for the practice of "keeping-while-giving" *pace* A. Weiner (1992). What Dolnoslav does show us is that some figurine parts left their "original" domestic context to travel to new sites. Perhaps the figurines that remained were treated more intensively, or in different ways, to prepare them for travel. The fact that similar processes would have been occurring on other sites from which figurine fragments were brought to Dolnoslav does not make comprehension easier. Figurine fragmentation echoed the enchainment of household members to other social groups.

The strategy of breaking figurines was not necessary dependent upon the type of figurine, since all types of figurines were broken with variety of number of breaks, and possibly not dependent upon their previous life-histories up to the point of fragmentation, given that some fragments had traces of previous treatment and others had not. The wide variety of body parts (24 types – maximum number in one type – 98, minimum – 1) suggests that there must have been personal demand for figurines to be broken in specific ways and these were very varied demands. Whoever was responsible for the fragmentation of figurines – a figurine-knapper or the household head in each household – the task was carefully and meticulously performed. The only way to make sense of the multiple deliberate fractures is to view fragmentation as embodied practice and fragments as constituting and maintaining enchained relations. This is clearly demonstrated by the refitting fragments deposited on Dolnoslav. The implicit multiple relations concentrated in fragments were reinforced by the reunion of the matching parts. The enchained relations already in operation after the figurine fragmentation were once more to be manifested by the deposition of conjoinable parts. Different parts of figurines formed the different joins, thus underlying the diversity of figurine types and, hence, the diversity of types of person (see above, p. 50) taking part in the enchainment process. At the same time, however, a structured selection of joins can be detected, in which almost all body parts are represented. In this way, heads can match bodies, torsos can re-join legs, and left sides can match with right sides. There is only one case in which all 4 fragments of a figurine formed a complete example, representing the ultimate integrity of fragmented objects, and therefore, of the enchained people. Most of the joins have parts still missing, thus linking the people and objects from the Dolnoslav tell to other people, places and things.

**Death**

Eventually, the figurines died and, in their burial, summed up all of the enchained relations they embodied and all of the things they represented throughout their lives. If they were a left part, they embodied the left-sidedness of certain corporate groups; if right fragments, they embodied right-sided corporate groups. If a fragment was neutral to left/right, then it was probably a materialization of gender or age; if a head, it was the essence of a person. If complete, it was the integrity of their complete social *persona* – the sum total of all of their fractal relationships.

The burial of figurines at different stages in their lives was probably related to the different stages of the people's life. Following this very simple principle may have resulted in a very complex pattern of deposition if other characteristics such as gender, number of breaks and the type of figurines are also taken into account. Such complexity could have been further reinforced by the number of deposited objects. If, we accept that Dolnoslav was one of the rare cases of the deliberate concentration of cross-cutting principles through figurine deposition, then the complex pattern of deposition seems not so difficult to comprehend. The left and right fragments should be considered to represent negotiations over communal identity, complete figurines represent integrity

of complementary or opposed parts, while re-fits reinforced the enchained relations demonstrated by the predominant deposition of fragments. Such a huge accumulation of figurines and fragments was nothing less than an attempt to resolve the contradictions between diversity and integration in an increasingly complex domestic world.

In Dolnoslav, we see every principle and strategy in action because of the strategies of deposition, which help us to identify strategies in action. Everyday practices are there but difficult to identify by traditional archaeological methodologies. This is why the variety of deposition at Dolnoslav was so important – it materialized both more structured and less structured deposition. Most practices of structured deposition were actually a reinforced version of everyday practices such as eating (the reinforcement is feasting, producing middening), meeting with other people (the reinforcement demonstrates social interaction through fragmentation or other similar practices) and working (by the deposition of worn tools). In fact, the deposition at Dolnoslav embodied the full spectrum of social practices. The deposition on Dolnoslav presented two additional kinds of integration: on the tell, people deposited a balance of figurines by sidedness and by vertical differentiation; by the principle of keeping-while-giving, people maintained a spatially wider integration of fragments left on the burnt-down tell and fragments carried away with them from the tell. A mirror image concerned the relatives coming to participate in the final deposition, when they placed parts of some figurines in the tell-to-be-burnt, while keeping matching fragments at home on another site.

The question remains: would it have been possible for a moiety-type system of the type probably found in the Late Neolithic to develop into such a diverse categorization system without the need for new kinds of corporate groups? The answer must be "no", since the power differentials were too great. In an increasingly complex world, the old principles of categorization and perception of self must have been challenged by the steady discovery of the potential of different materials, including the appearance of new materials such as metal and the increasing development of cognitive processes and embodied skills. Such tensions may have been solved either by incorporating the new materialities into the old principles (*e.g.* through the shape and decoration of pots) or by shifting the emphasis in the concept of being from the dividual to the individual self.

***Note***

1  The join fragments are included in these 142 but their detailed discussion can be seen below (see p. 133–135 and Appendix 4).

# 7. Personhood and the life cycle of *Spondylus* rings

There has been a recent upsurge of research interest in the archaeology of marine shells, with a Cambridge Manual devoted to the topic (Claassen 1998), a major survey article (Trubitt 2003) and several articles on particular aspects of shell usage. There is now a general recognition of the significance of marine shells, whether as material symbols of interpersonal relations, as symbolic links to water and the sea, with all of their metaphorical qualities, or as a sign of inland people's differential access to distant and rare goods (Claassen 1998, 203–208; Trubitt 2003). Trubitt (2003, 262–3) summarises this research in her assertion that shell prestige goods are symbols of power and prestige associated with the exotic, to which Saunders (1999) and Glowacki (2005) would add the supernatural.

Three particularly interesting aspects of this recent research concern the relationship between the aesthetics of shells and their symbolism (Saunders 1999), the potential of *Spondylus* shells for producing hallucinogenic effects (Glowacki 2005) and the links between shells and personhood (Clark 1991). These studies of marine shells in Meso- and South America and in Papua New Guinea have utilised ethno-history and ethnology to create more lively biographical pictures of shells based upon their specific materialities. Saunders (1999) discusses the extent to which the materiality of the pearl-oyster acted as a bridge between the mental and physical worlds of pre-Columbian indigenous American peoples. These societies saw their world as infused with spiritual brilliance that was manifested in three ways – natural phenomena (the sun, moon, water, ice and rainbows), natural materials (minerals, feathers, pearls and shells) and artifacts made from these materials. He discusses how an aesthetic of brilliance was constructed differently in different cultures, emphasising that "making shiny objects was an act of transformative creation" (1999, 246). The ritual significance of shells was heightened if they were procured from the deep sea – an analogy to shamanistic activity, in which a diver visited the dangerous spirit world and returned with sacred matter (1999, 247). In more speculative vein, Glowacki (2005) seeks to document a link between the value of *Spondylus* to Andean elites and the hallucinogenic effects of eating the oyster at different seasons. Since the only creatures with digestive systems strong enough to eat poisonous oysters were the gods, this marine shell symbolised the food of the gods. However, the problem of transporting live shellfish for highland consumption is not satisfactorily solved.

In many ways the most fruitful of these biographically-based studies of marine shells is Clark's (1991) integration of the formation of Wiru personhood with the creation of value for the marine pearlshell. In Wiru personhood, it is females who create people's bodies, while the males give individuality to people's appearance. Throughout life, payment must be made to the women for their contribution to persons' bodies – and this payment is made in pearlshells that are thought to be 'of great antiquity'. As Clark says, "Pearlshells are durable male wealth given for perishable female substance….", so that the individuation of bodies corresponds to the personification of pearlshells (1991, 315–317). Clark advances a case that, in historical time, ornaments made from plants, birds and land-mammals were supplanted by those made from marine shell (1991, 328–9), because the basis of pearlshell value was the combination of aesthetic qualities usually found in different objects – durable and bright, unlike birds' feathers (bright but ephemeral) or cassowary shells (durable but dull). Interestingly for fragmenterists, in the early part of the AD 20th century, travellers to the New Guinea Western Highlands noted the common usage of shell fragments and mended shell ornaments as heirlooms (1991, 310–1).

These and other ethnological studies provide a basis for the inter-penetration of the categories of shell ornaments and persons, just as shells can be persons in the Ojibwa under certain circumstances (Morris 1994, 9). It is important to emphasise the potential tension between two relations embodied in shells: the close material links between shells and persons – whether as worn as ornaments close to the body or as bearing enchained relations between persons – and the links between shells and aspects of Otherness such as the deep sea, the realm of the supernatural or simply the sea coasts that were remote for inland communities trading in shells. When colour symbolism and the aesthetic of brilliance are added to such metaphorical potential, the reasons why so many societies have incorporated some of their key cultural values into marine shells become more understandable. Clark (1991, 311) is surely right to question factors of scarcity and exchange value as **the** 'explanation' of value in marine shells. It is important to account for the social value of shells **before** the development of a central role for shells in bridewealth and ceremonial exchange.

In the Neolithic and Copper Age of the Balkans and Greece, two species of marine shell were frequently selected for the making of ornaments and for trade over a wide area of both South East and Central Europe. The dominant species of the two is *Spondylus gaederopus* (the European spiny oyster), the less common *Glycymeris glycymeris* (the dog cockle). Both are currently local to the Mediterranean, especially the Aegean and the Adriatic, because of their warm water temperature and its medium salinity (Shackleton and Elderfield 1990). A Black Sea origin has been proposed (Todorova 1995, 2002d, 182–185) but the analytical and ecological evidence does not support this view (Shackleton and Renfrew 1970). Fossil *Spondylus* is available in Central Europe (Shackleton and Elderfield 1990) and in eastern inland Bulgaria (*p.c.* Aneta Bakumska) but there is little evidence that it was of sufficiently high quality for ornament production. The shells have contrasting habitats – *Spondylus* attached to rocky substrate, often in shallow water of 2–5m depth but known up to depths of 30m, and *Glycymeris* in fine shell or sandy gravels but also offshore in water of varying depths, up to 100m. Both shells are periodically washed up onto beaches but prehistoric beachcombers would soon have discovered that shells collected from underwater were of better quality, less brittle and often larger than those from the beach (Miller 2003, 370).

Previous research into *Spondylus* shell ornaments has concentrated on their distribution and typology, with the implications of their dissemination for local societies. In an early and successful example of archaeological science, Shackleton and Renfrew (1970) sought to demonstrate by isotopic analysis that the *Spondylus* rings of the Balkan and Central European Neolithic were derived from Mediterranean sources; these shell rings were the exemplar of what Renfrew (1973) termed the 'prestige chain' form of exchange, an indication that Neolithic communities sought exotic goods conferring status on their bearers. Whittle (2003, 120–121) has extended the interpretation of cultural distance by characterizing the *Spondylus* in the Bandkeramik as possessing 'an unusually mysterious quality' because of its derivation from a cultural world with whom the Bandkeramik had little other connection – their place of mythic origin in the far South-East. The

typological studies of Willms (1985), Müller (1997), Kalicz and Szénászky (2001) and Séfériades (1995, 2000, 2003) indicated the likelihood of local or regional consumption zones based upon different shell ornament forms. Séfériades (2003) used ethnographic analogies to interpret the shell ornaments as a form of special currency, similar to the cowrie shell. Müller *et al.* (1996) estimated the number of *Spondylus* ornaments consumed *per annum* in the Western Linearbandkeramik Flomborn-stage cemeteries as cca. 230, asserting the long-term, continuous exchange of these shell ornament as status goods between lineages in different *Siedlungskammern*. A useful comparative study of *Spondylus* shell rings from the North Aegean appears in Nikolaidou (2003, 337–341).

It is only more recently that attention has been paid to the *chaîne opératoire* of shell rings, especially the early stages of production. Tsuneki (1989, 10 and Fig. 7) identified five stages in the manufacture of shell rings, not always in the given order (!):

---

**Stage 1:** the ventral margin of the shell is ground down to smooth the rugged natural margin;

**Stage 2:** the outer surface of the shell is ground down to reduce the thickness of the shell;

**Stage 3:** the shell is pierced inside the pallial line and the hole is enlarged through tapping;

**Stage 4:** the periphery of the hole is ground down until it is large enough to form a ring; and

**Stage 5:** the hinge teeth, the ears and other projections are ground down and the sides are smoothed.

---

*Table 7.1 Tsuneki's* chaîne opératoire *for* Spondylus *shell rings (source: Tsuneki 1989)*

The same five stages are outlined by Miller (2003, 371–2), on the basis of ethnographic analogy with Hokoham shell production techniques. Tsuneki (1989, 10) further proposed that stone querns, drills, small hammerstones and a small hand-held grindstone were the tools necessary for this task, as well as water and sand as an abrasive. The same author (1987, 3–6 and Figs. 2–3) makes the vital point that the two valves of the *Spondylus* were of different thickness, protrusions and colour. There can be no doubt that the making of *Spondylus/Glycymeris* rings involved considerable skill and much effort: indeed, Trubitt (2003, 252) emphasises just how hard it is to work fresh marine shell. The question of local manufacture of shell rings has been investigated at four sites: Late Neolithic Dimini (Tsuneki 1989), Dikili Tash (Karali-Yannacopoulous 1992) and Dimitra (Karali 1991) and Neolithic – Copper

Age Sitagroi (Miller 2003; Nikolaidou 2003). The result of this labour would have been symbolic objects of great power and prestige, fine costume ornaments for display, as well as potentially valued objects for trade to inland communities.

The research by Tsuneki, Miller and Nikolaidou comes closer than do other researchers to the "biographical" approach for objects, current now in social anthropology for 20 years (Appadurai 1986). However, in each case, one has the impression that the objects are being studied in order to investigate an extraneous factor (trade, local production) rather than as things in their own right. We believe that a combination of the more technical aspects of the *chaîne opératoire* approach with the personal biographies of things will extend the interpretative possibilities of marine shell rings and their relations to prehistoric persons.

There are many aspects of prehistoric shell rings that are worth consideration as the form of the materiality in which the rings existed for past individuals and communities. The underlying concepts for making shell rings are twofold: transformation and revelation. In a stimulating discussion of the crafting, elite power and the exotic, Helms (1993) reminds us that native cosmologies regularly assert that realms outside are the ultimate source of the basic raw materials, energies, knowledge, ancestral creators and culture heroes that enabled the production of life and social living on the inside (1993, 7). This equation of physical with supernatural distance resonates with the marine source of *Spondylus* shells as places of existential power. Transformative crafting of the kind necessary to produce shell rings provides a means to channel existential power/energy into material goods that preserve this energy in a tangible form (1993, 9). In traditional societies, creativity refers to the ordering of nature for cultural purposes, not to individual artistic uniqueness but to transformations, to moving between outside and inside realms (Helms 1993, 19). In this way, transformation and revelation can be seen at every stage of the production of shell rings.

Collection of the shells would have been a seasonal or discontinuous practice requiring considerable effort for coastal communities. It may seem obvious but the inhabitants of inland communities would have had no reason to develop skills in diving – this was a special and highly embodied skill for certain persons living only on or near the coast. It seems highly probable that the acquisition of each shell was an individual act, since the social practice of diving 5 m or more under the sea to retrieve a shell firmly attached to the rock would have required a sharp blow to dislodge it, suggesting an individual approach to the shell without the "interference" of other shells in bags or nets. The overcoming of the resistance of the shell to "capture" implies the develop-

ment of specific skills. Thus, from the outset of its "domestication", the shell would probably have been linked to a particular individual – the diver who brought the shell from the deep, dark, supernaturally charged and potentially dangerous water into another medium – the light, airy, warm, quotidian Mediterranean beach. This initial transformation from live shell in its natural habitat to an unnatural location in a settlement provided a tasty food, perhaps for feasting, at certain seasons but a poisonous food at others (cf. Glowacki 2005). The eating of oysters led to the incorporation of another group of persons with the shell's biography. Only then did the shell move into the domain of skilled crafting for the creation of artificial finery.

Examination of a large collection of unmodified *Spondylus* and *Glycymeris* shells indicates such a wide variety of shapes and sizes (Plate 31) that, even from the time of discovery, shells may have had their own distinctive character – their individual differentiated features, in terms of colour, length of spines and spikes and overall dimensions. To an experienced shell-ring maker, this first impression would have spoken of the potential of a particular shell for making a large, splendid ring, a medium-sized attractive ring or a small ring fit only for an exchange supplement rather than with a chance of having its own distinguished career.

One feature of shell rings that has attracted much attention (*e.g.* Shackleton 2003, 363) is their small size (interior diameter), which makes it impossible for many rings to be worn by anyone, even a young child (cf. experiments with a 6-year-old: Gaydarska *et al.* 2004). The implication is that, at an early stage of selection of a shell, which direction the shell can follow in a divergent biographical pathway – bracelet for wearing or ring for display – will be known. It is also possible that a young person who fits a small shell ring onto their arm would not have been able to remove it after the growth of their hand bones, so that, unless it is broken, the ring remains on the forearm (cf. the discussion about how to wear different types of copper bracelet, Sofaer Derevenski 2000). These choices are equivalent to three different variants on the theme of personhood – direct participation in the costume of one or many individuals; linkage through production and/or exchange with one or more individuals; or coercive identification with an earlier stage of personhood for the rest of an individual's life. These comments underline the importance of the initial choice of a *Spondylus/Glycymeris* shell from their rocky habitat.

The second transformation concerned the grinding of the outer surface of the shell – the removal of the spines, spikes, ridges and protuberances that make the *Spondylus* so distinctive a species in and out of the water. There are two elements in this multiple-stage transformation – symmetry out of often strong asymmetries and

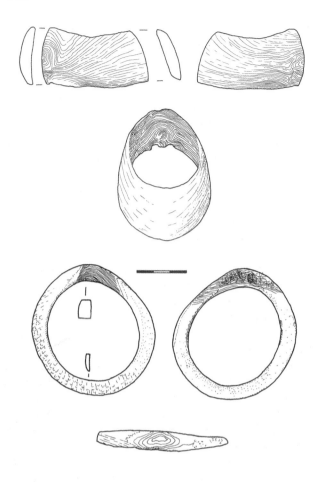

*Fig. 7.1 Left-valve ring (bottom) and right-valve ring (top), Durankulak cemetery*

smoothness out of roughness. There are four asymmetries in the left *Spondylus* valve – the left and right shape of the outer surface, the top and bottom shape of the outer surface, the section through the valve and the much greater roughness on the outside of the valve in comparison with its inner surface (Plate 31). The making of a shell ring gives a real sense of the one valued aspect of skilled crafting – the creation of a harmonious cultural order out of a chaotic natural shape (Helms 1993, 70–75). The resultant shape seeks bilateral symmetry in three dimensions: left – right, top – bottom and overall thickness of ring section. Even though there is a roughness or natural pitting remaining on the surface of many rings, there is a far greater degree of smoothness after manufacture than on the original raw shell surface. The right valve is much larger, so the shape of right-valve rings is less symmetrical than that of left-valve rings (Fig. 7.1). Nonetheless, there is a strong tendency to right-to-left symmetry and smoothness on both inside and outside surfaces. The decision to use a right- or a left-valve was fundamental to all subsequent selections; there was a strong chronological trend in this choice (Fig. 7.2).

The second transformative process is also a process of revelation insofar as different degrees of grinding and polishing can reveal a variety of natural features that may well be prized for their inherent aesthetic attraction as much as for "bringing out" the distinctive qualities of each shell ring. Just as the excavation of a 2-cm layer across a site may obscure or remove distinctive features, so the grinding of an additional 2 mm from a shell surface may well destroy a layer of red colour but uncover a

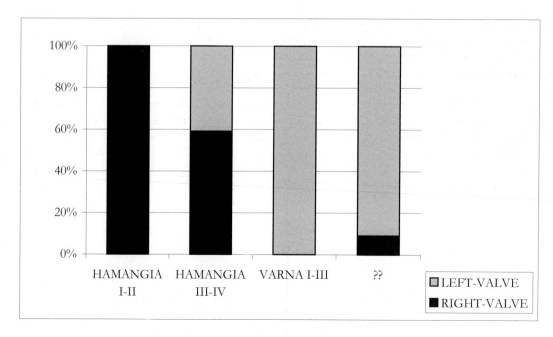

*Fig. 7.2 Type of rings by period, Durankulak cemetery*

lustrous, porcelain-like surface. Thus, making a shell ring involves prediction, from past experience and current practice, of the results of further grinding for the appearance of the shell. In this sense, there is an analogy between shell ring-making and flint-knapping, with experience-led prediction of the results of the next grinding/blow the basis of the craftsperson with high skill levels. It is easy to appreciate that the differential grinding away of successive surface shell layers can produce remarkably divergent "natural" features that go a long way to defining the unique character of a shell ring. There are, in addition, other, non-revelatory traces of the process of making a ring, including perforation, extra polishing and grooving.

This biographical approach to the transformation of marine shells, the revelation of their "natural" features and the addition of artificial features emphasises the reflexive processes of individuation characterising both the shell and the social actor. What appears to be a reductive, homogenizing process of manufacture is in fact an endlessly varied series of choices of what to reveal and what not to reveal, starting from an individual shell recovered by a specific diver from a known place. By the time that a shell ring has been created, its materiality has already been defined by a series of individual choices. The individual biography of the shell has already become intertwined with the biographies of several persons. The makers would have internalised an appreciation of two of Keightley's four key values – the precision required to reveal only what was needed to produce an attractive natural pattern and the varying symmetries of the right- and left-valve rings. Compartmentalisation did not enter the shell ring-makers' world, where variation was so highly prized that standardisation was not an important value.

The next part of the shell's biography concerns the main period of its life. Five specific traces of use can be recognised – fragmentation, wear, burning, chipping and the laying down of a deposit. These different traces often interact with each other to form a sequence of events, indicating a more complex life for the shell ring. The first is the overall subject of this book. Little needs to be added here, other than to emphasise that fragmentation extends the spatial and often the temporal biography of the shell ring to other people and places, thereby adding complexity to the narrative. Signs of burning or wear over an earlier fracture provides evidence of a multi-stage use life, demonstrating that there is still life in a deliberately fragmented shell ring. As we shall see in the study of the Dimini shell rings, it is possible that deliberate burning was practiced to enhance the aesthetic brilliance and patterning of the shell ring. The sedimentation of a deposit on a ring prior to other traces of use-life may well be an indication of short- to medium-term curation, before another more active phase in the ring's biography.

A critical stage in the use-life of a ring was the final stage – its death, whether through discard or deliberate deposition. Deposition of shell rings in contexts, such as houses, that were to be intentionally burnt could have led to dramatic changes in the ring's appearance.

In other words, any use-life marks on the shell ring made a visual statement about the object and its biography, leaving room for negotiation over whether or not the marks increased the value of the ring through a diversified suite of relations to more people or devalued the ring through aesthetic damage. This stage in the biographies of shell rings offers more possibilities for individuation of shell ring life histories, adding to the revelation of natural features and the presentation of artificial making-marks.

A final stage in the shell ring biographies is the post-depositional traces that accrete to the ring during and/or after burial. These marks are relevant to the prehistoric life history of the objects only if the rings are disinterred or robbed from the grave and brought back into an active "second life".

The important general point here is that, because of the materiality of objects, aspects - perhaps many diverse aspects - of their life stories are recorded on the objects themselves. The object thus contains its own self-referential cultural memory, embodying parts of its own experience and aspects of the foundations of its relations with different persons. A skilled 'reader' of a shell ring could have inferred the various processes of trans-formation and revelation that the individualised ring had passed through. Together with her knowledge of the persons linked to that ring's biography, the prehistoric person would have created a combined picture forming the basis for an appreciation of the ring – cultural, aesthetic and biographical – that interacted with its value.

## *The Varna and Durankulak shell rings*

The *Spondylus/Glycymeris* rings from the Durankulak and Varna cemeteries and the Late Neolithic settlement of Dimini offer examples of the creation of diverse object biographies. We begin with Durankulak and Varna. In a previous study of the *Spondylus* shell rings from the Varna and Durankulak cemeteries, an overall survey was presented of *Spondylus* (and *Glycymeris*) mortuary deposition in terms of the social context of enchainment and fragmentation. Diachronic and inter-site differences were noted in the distribution of ornament graves, gender and age associations with shell rings, sidedness of shell ring placement, their fragmentation ratio (the ratio of complete: fragmentary rings), the completeness index of each ring, the distribution of complete and fragmentary rings per grave, their associations with rings of other materials (copper and marble) and their frequency in

*Spondylus*-rich graves (Chapman 2004a). The conclusions were developed prior to any re-fitting exercise, and therefore based upon analyses of the Varna cemetery documentation (thanks to the kindness of Vladimir Slavchev) and the Durankulak cemetery publication (Todorova 2002). The three main conclusions were:

– a clear diachronic trend towards increasing ring fragmentation in the Black Sea Neolithic and Copper Age at Durankulak
– a quantum leap in ring fragmentation in the Varna cemetery
– a much larger quantity of shell fragments in graves, whether from the same or from different rings, in the Late Copper Age than before.

These general, archive-based conclusions did not take into account the state of the actual rings themselves. Nonetheless, these provisional conclusions were so interesting that a study of the original shell rings was considered to be an important aim of further research. This study included two basic elements – a detailed record of all the rings and a re-fitting exercise. A detailed recording was made of the *Spondylus/Glycymeris* rings in terms of their dimensions, completeness, type of fractures, condition, natural features, production traces, use traces and post-depositional changes. Sketches of all the rings are complemented by a photographic record of

a sample of rings and line drawings by Ms. Vessela Yaneva (Figs. 7.3–7.8). We should like to emphasise that the drawings of shell rings published here seek to portray as many traces of the biography of the shell ring as possible. It is only with such illustrations that readers can make an informed appreciation of the life history of objects (cf. Elena Georgieva's drawings of the Dolnoslav figurines: see above, Figs. 6.10–6.13, 6.21–22 and 6.25–6.29). The re-fitting exercise consisted of locating all of the shell ring fragments in the same room and seeking joins between each fragment and all of the other fragments. The potential results comprised three main possibilities - joins between fragments in the same grave; joins between fragments buried in different graves; and the absence of joins.

The length of time since excavation of these ornaments has led to a variable rate of shell ring discovery in the museum stores, with some fragments still unaccounted for. The total number of rings studied from Durankulak was 101, with 25 fragments "missing" as well as 47 complete rings on loan to other Bulgarian museums. The situation was clearer at Varna, with 246 rings studied and 26 fragments still unaccounted for. Since a primary purpose of the re-fitting study was the comparison of each ring with every other ring, these "absences" are regrettable; the re-discovery of the fragments may yet bring fresh results for this study.

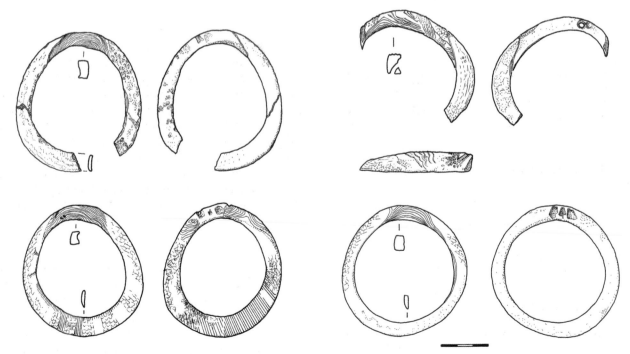

*Fig. 7.3 (top left) Natural features of Varna* Spondylus *ring*
*Figs. 7.4–6 (top right, bottom left, bottom right) Natural features of Durankulak* Spondylus *ring*

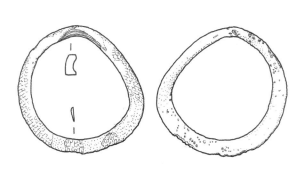

*Fig. 7.7 Natural features of Durankulak* Spondylus *ring*

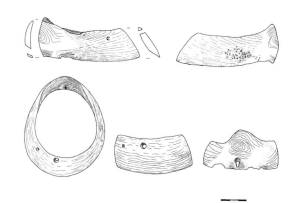

*Fig. 7.8 Natural features of Durankulak* Spondylus *ring*

| | | |
|---|---|---|
| Notch | | Pitting |
| Wear | | Burning |
| Polish | | Red colour |
| Groove | | Yellow colour |
| Lines | | Green colour |
| Deposit | | Sculpting lines |
| Rough surface | | Break |
| Perforation | | Thick hinge |

Key for *Spondylus* illustrations

The results of the detailed study of the shell rings for the purposes of reconstructing their individual biographies led to some interesting and important results. We shall consider these general results first, before turning to the more specific results of the re-fitting analysis.

## Ring biographies

A helpful starting point is the distinction between the choice of the right and the left valve for making rings. At Late Neolithic Dimini, Northern Greece, left valves were used exclusively to make small rings while right valves were broken down into smaller parts to make beads and pendants (Tsuneki 1989). This was not at all the case in the Black Sea zone. An analysis of the chronology of graves containing left-and right-valve rings indicates a slightly more complex pattern of choices (Fig. 7.2). While the Hamangia I–II rings were almost exclusively massive right-valve rings (Fig. 7.1), and the Late Copper Age (Varna–III periods) rings were formed almost exclusively from the slender left valve, the intervening period (Hamangia III–IV) at Durankulak made used of both right- and left-valve rings in similar frequencies. There is a systematic difference in ease of deliberate fragmentation of these two types of rings, with massive right-valve rings posing a major problem in neat breakage – a technique far simpler for the slender left-valve varieties.

The *Spondylus* rings from the Durankulak and Varna cemeteries fully illustrate the principles of transformation and revelation discussed above. The rings have been coded for the presence/absence of types of natural features, as well as the frequency of their occurrences. Traits relating to their production, their use-lives and any post-depositional features have been fully described for each ring. The term "pre-depositional feature" refers to the sum total of natural, production and use-life features – all of those traits that manifested the shell ring biography in all its simplicity or complexity. The following features, that are illustrated on the rings below (Figs. 7.3–7.8), have been observed (Table 7.2).

The revelation of natural features by incremental grinding of the shell's surface has produced a wide variety of natural decoration – many of them capable of producing striking visual effects (Figs. 7.3–7.8). In the Hamangia I–II period, the number of areas with (**not** types of !) natural features on the right-valve rings ranged from zero to six, with a tendency to reveal three features. In Hamangia III–IV, with a mixture of right- and left-valve rings, there is a normal distribution centered on four features and ranging from zero to 11, while in the

| Natural | Production | Use-life | Post-depositional |
|---------|------------|----------|-------------------|
| Notch | Polishing | Wear | Copper staining |
| Hinge | Perforation | Burning | Calcareous deposit |
| Holes | Groove | Flaking | Brown deposit |
| "Skin" | | | Other deposit |
| Sculpting | | | |
| Depression | | | |
| Pitting | | | |
| Heavy Pitting | | | |
| Lines | | | |
| Complex Lines | | | |
| Wavy Lines | | | |
| Garlands | | | |
| Red colour | | | |
| Yellow colour | | | |

*Table 7.2 Features of* Spondylus/Glycymeris *rings at Durankulak and Varna*

Varna–III periods, there is a much more complex pattern of features on the entirely left-valve rings, with a range of one to 13 and peaks at two, four, six and eight features. In the Late Copper Age, more care was taken than before in the selection of a large number and wide range of natural features, the effect of which was to increase the aesthetic value of the shell rings. In the Varna cemetery, there is a nearly normal distribution with a mean of two and a secondary peak at four features but a very long tail, ranging from zero to 12. This is one of the rare cases in which the Varna cemetery shows a less complex pattern than the Late Copper Age shell rings at Durankulak.

Given the extent of ring fragmentation, as well as the post-burial deposition of especially calcareous sediment on the shells' surface, it may be imagined that the statistics on natural features would have been dependent upon the completeness of the rings and the presence/absence of deposits. However, intensive investigation of these variables shows that neither the completeness index nor the extent of deposits have a major effect on the number of areas where natural features have been revealed. An evaluation of the frequency and intensity of deposit on pairs of rings in the same grave showed marked differences between the rings in almost every case, to such an extent that it raised the possibility that the deposit on one of a pair of rings had built up prior to final burial, in another place, while the other ring had not received such a deposit during its use-life.

Before considering production and use-life features, it is useful to turn to a method for investigating the overall selection of natural features – namely the biographical pathway. For this technique, the types of natural features listed above (Table 7.2) are grouped into six classes of

natural features:- Notch, Hinge, Holes, Pitting, Lines and Colours. All 63 possible combinations of these six classes were listed and the actual combinations on each ring were described and coded (Table 7.3). At Durankulak, a total of 20 combinations of natural feature classes were identified – seven in Hamangia I–II, 13 in Hamangia III–IV and 14 in Varna–III - in comparison with a total of 34 in the much larger sample from Varna (Fig. 7.9). There is a consistent preference for certain biographical pathways in all periods and at both sites – Pathway 19 (lines only) occurs most frequently in Hamangia I–II and Varna–III at Durankulak and at Varna, while Pathway 20 (lines + colour) is often preferred in Late Copper Age graves (Fig. 7.9).

The diachronic trends in the number of classes represented by the natural features on shell rings are rather confused and a little contradictory. The frequency of those shell rings without any natural feature classes peaks in the Hamangia I–II period at Durankulak and at Varna, with a big drop in the intervening periods at Durankulak, while the reverse is true for rings with two feature classes. High frequencies of rings with one feature class occur in all periods but Hamangia III–IV at Durankulak, while there is a low but steady occurrence of rings with four feature classes in all contexts. The sole location with rings with five feature classes is Varna. The selection of a shell ring without any natural features indicates the value attributed to a pure white lustrous surface, as close to a homogenous finish as can be found in shell rings. Conversely, those rings with four or five natural feature classes signify the value given to highly differentiated shells with a high level of individuality.

When it comes to the full range of pre-depositional features, there is a gradual increase in the range of classes

| NO. | COMBO | NO. | COMBO | NO. | COMBO | |
|---|---|---|---|---|---|---|
| 1 | N | 22 | N+HI+HO | 43 | N+HI+HO+L | |
| 2 | N+HI | 23 | N+HI+P | 44 | N+HI+HO+R | |
| 3 | N+HO | 24 | N+HI+L | 45 | N+HI+P+L | |
| 4 | N+P | 25 | N+HI+R | 46 | N+HI+P+R | |
| 5 | N+L | 26 | N+HO+P | 47 | N+HI+L+R | |
| 6 | N+R | 27 | N+HO+L | 48 | N+HO+P+L | |
| 7 | HI | 28 | N+HO+R | 49 | N+HO+P+R | |
| 8 | HI+HO | 29 | N+P+L | 50 | N+HO+L+R | |
| 9 | HI+P | 30 | N+P+R | 51 | N+P+L+R | |
| 10 | HI+L | 31 | N+L+R | 52 | HI+HO+P+L | N - NOTCH |
| 11 | HI+R | 32 | HI+HO+P | 53 | HI+HO+P+R | HI - HINGE |
| 12 | HO | 33 | HI+HO+L | 54 | HI+HO+L+R | HO - HOLES |
| 13 | HO+P | 34 | HI+HO+R | 55 | O+P+L+R | L - LINES |
| 14 | HO+L | 35 | HI+P+L | 56 | N+HI+HO+P+L | P - PITTING |
| 15 | HO+R | 36 | HI+P+R | 57 | N+HI+HO+P+R | R - COLOURS |
| 16 | P | 37 | HI+L+R | 58 | N+HI+HO+L+R | |
| 17 | P+L | 38 | HO+P+L | 59 | N+HI+P+L+R | |
| 18 | P+R | 39 | HO+P+R | 60 | N+HO+P+L+R | |
| 19 | L | 40 | HO+L+R | 61 | HI+HO+P+L+R | |
| 20 | L+R | 41 | P+L+R | 62 | N+HI+HO+P+L+R | |
| 21 | R | 42 | N+HI+HO+P | 63 | no features | |

*Table 7.3* Spondylus *combinations of natural features from Varna cemetery*

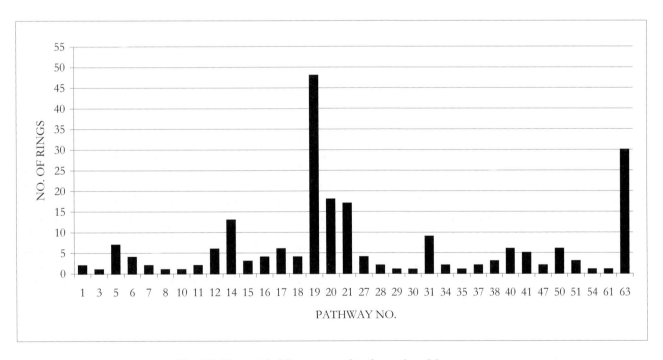

*Fig. 7.9 Rings with different natural pathways from Varna cemetery*

of natural features used with time at Durankulak, with a slight drop in range at Varna (Fig. 7.10–7.13). But while the Hamangia I–II values peak at three and four, and the Hamangia III–IV and Varna–III at three, the Varna peak is far lower – only one class of pre-depositional feature. This would suggest that the same, rather narrow range of natural "motif" classes is being used in far more parts of the average Varna shell ring than at Durankulak.

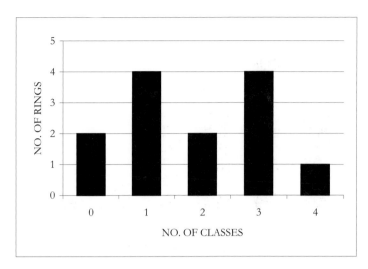

Fig. 7.10 *Classes of natural shell features, Hamangia I–II phases, Durankulak cemetery*

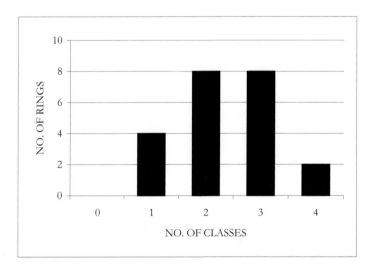

Fig. 7.11 *Classes of natural shell features, Hamangia III–IV phases, Durankulak cemetery*

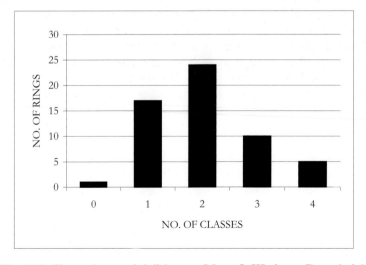

Fig. 7.12 *Classes of natural shell features, Varna I–III phases, Durankulak cemetery*

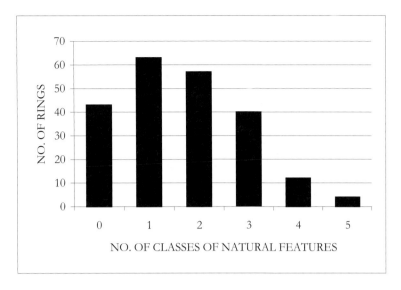

*Fig. 7.13 Classes of natural shell features, Varna cemetery*

## Fragmentation: the re-fitting exercises

At this point, it is important to consider the effects of fragmentation on the biographies of shell rings. Although Tsuneki (1989) has argued that the fragmentation of the Late Neolithic Dimini shell rings was the result of manufacturing mishaps, no evidence was adduced in support of this interpretation – a notion strongly criticized by Halstead (1993). Instead, it is more probable that fragmentary shell rings occur in Neolithic and Copper Age graves because the rings have been broken, either at the graveside or somewhere else. The re-fitting exercises for the Durankulak and Varna cemeteries give an indication of the extent of this social practice.

The first result of the re-fitting exercise was the modification of some of the 2003 conclusions on the number of complete and fragmentary shell rings in the graves (Chapman 2004a, Tables 3, 5, 9 and 13). While these differences are generally of a minor nature (see complete list in Appendix 5), the new results fully support the three main conclusions of the 2003 analysis. Nonetheless, the highest number of complete rings in any grave remains at four, from the earliest (Hamangia I–II) graves at Durankulak through to the Varna-period graves at Varna and Durankulak.

There is no better way of recognising the steady increase in the significance of fragment enchainment through the Black Sea Neolithic and Copper Age than by examining the regular increase in the percentage of fragmentary shell rings with time at Durankulak, with a still greater increase in incomplete rings at Varna, where fully 70% of all rings were deposited broken (Figs. 7.14–7.25). This quantum leap in fragmentation at the Varna

cemetery shows the differences in local social practices between cemeteries in the Late Copper Age.

The new studies also permit a more accurate assessment of the degree of completeness of the shell rings by period (Figs. 7.26–7.29). The sample sizes for the Hamangia I–II and III–IV graves at Durankulak are too small for a significant comment, with a range of 20–70% for the Hamangia III–IV rings. For the Varna-period ring fragments, the same range of completeness is found at both Durankulak and Varna but whereas the Durankulak rings peak at 30–40% and 60–80% completeness, the Varna cemetery shows the extent of deliberate fragmentation with its peaks between 10% and 40%. This means that fragmentation practices at Durankulak were based upon the deposition of both smaller and larger shell fragments in the graves, while, at Varna, the predominant practice involved the deposition of less than half of a shell ring in the grave, with the other, larger part kept outside that particular grave. Were these ring fragments deposited in other graves?

The main result of the re-fitting exercise at both the Durankulak and Varna cemeteries is that there was not a single example of a ring fragment re-fitting with another fragment of the same ring from another grave. While this would appear to be a negative result, it is nonetheless intriguing that the missing fragments of so many orphan ring fragments should be in circulation in the world of the living at the same time as their partner fragments were deposited in the world of the dead, or, alternatively, already deposited elsewhere by then.

As with the Dolnoslav figurines (see above, pp. 141–143), at least two scenarios can be envisaged to account for this very incomplete distribution of ring fragments.

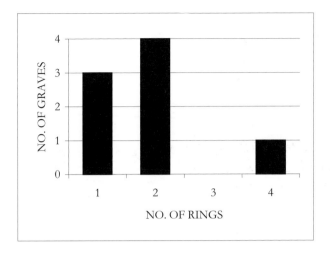

Fig. 7.14 *Complete rings in graves, Hamangia I–II*

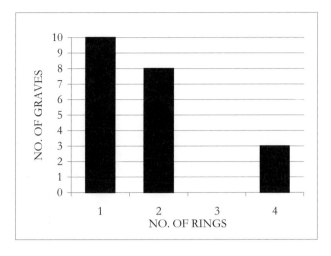

Fig. 7.17 *Complete rings in graves, Hamangia III–IV*

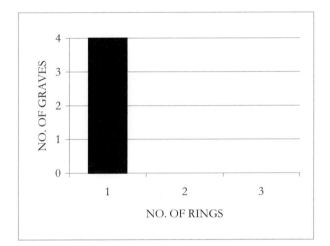

Fig. 7.15 *Fragmentary rings in graves, Hamangia I–II*

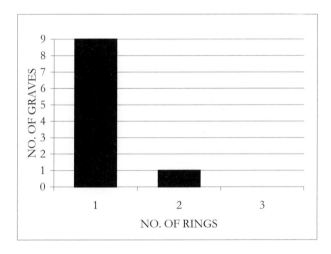

Fig. 7.18 *Fragmentary rings in graves, Hamangia III–IV*

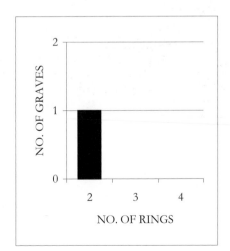

Fig. 7.16 *Complete and fragmentary rings in graves, Hamangia I–II*

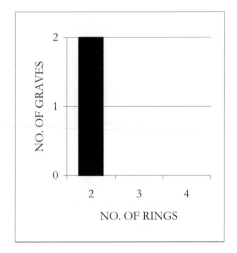

Fig. 7.19 *Complete and fragmentary rings in graves, Hamangia III–IV*

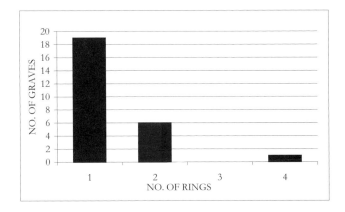

Fig. 7.20 Complete rings in graves, Varna I–III

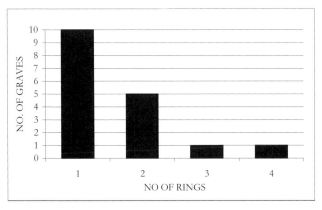

Fig. 7.23 Complete rings in graves, Varna cemetery

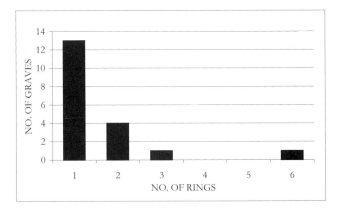

Fig. 7.21 Fragmentary rings in graves, Varna I–III

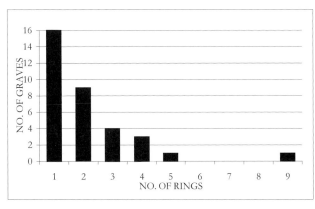

Fig. 7.24 Fragmentary rings in graves, Varna cemetery

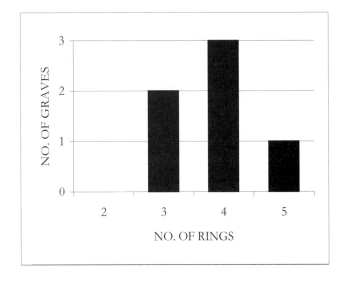

Fig. 7.22 Complete and fragmentary rings in graves, Varna I–III

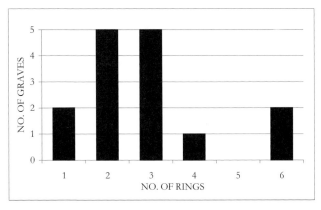

Fig. 7.25 Complete and fragmentary rings in graves, Varna cemetery

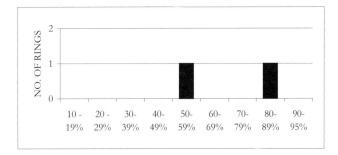

*Fig. 7.26 Completeness indices of shell rings, Hamangia I–II*

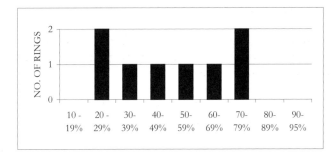

*Fig. 7.27 Completeness indices of shell rings, Hamangia III–IV*

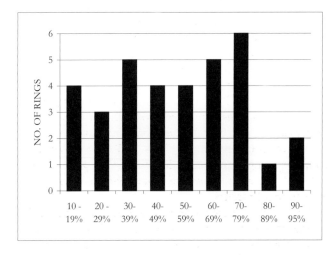

*Fig. 7.28 Completeness indices of shell rings, Varna I–III*

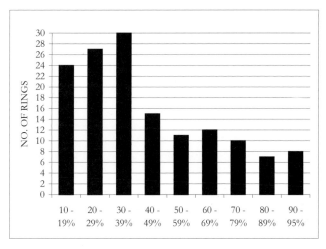

*Fig. 7.29 Completeness indices of shell rings, Varna cemetery*

the same ring. This custom has been recorded among the Kuma of Papua New Guinea, who use goldlip shells as bodily decoration and in the expression of male sexual prestige. When a man dies, his sons break up their father's shell ornaments and pile the fragments on top of his body, at the same time redistributing many of his other valuables (Reay 1959, 96–97). Either of these scenarios could account for the occurrence of one large fragment of a Varna-III vessel in Grave 584 at Durankulak, while the missing part of the vessel was deposited in a stone-built house on the tell on the Big Island (see above, pp. 95–96). In view of the different completeness indices for the shell rings at Varna and Durankulak, it seems likely that whole shell rings were more commonly brought to the Varna-period Durankulak than to the Varna cemetery, where only 59 complete rings are known out of a total of almost 250. Instead, perhaps as a reflection of the supra-regional contributions to burial at Varna, shell ring fragments played an important role in mortuary deposition. However, small slivers of shell found in several Varna cemetery graves suggest that at least some acts of shell ring fragmentation did in fact take place next to the grave.

The re-fitting study has also shown the number of fragments in each broken ring per grave and the number of fragments that have now (in 2004!) been re-fitted to make complete rings (Figs. 7.3–7.4). The two diachronic trends here are towards an increase in the number of fragments of the same broken ring in graves, as well as a higher number of fragments that can be re-fitted to re-create a complete ring. The Varna-period graves at Varna are the only graves where more than three fragments can be re-fitted to make up a fragmentary ring, with the highest value of eight fragments in a single grave. However, the re-fitting of fragments to make complete rings occurs in a quarter of the findings of complete rings in the

The first is that complete shell rings in circulation in settlements were deliberately fragmented in the settlement, with one fragment deposited in a grave and another taken as a token of the link between the newly-dead and the living, kept in the settlement or exchanged with another settlement. The second scenario represents the inverse, namely that the complete shell ring was present at the graveside and that one fragment was deposited in the grave, while the mourners took away other fragments of

Hamangia I–II graves at Durankulak – a higher frequency than in the other periods and sites! We shall return to the question of re-fitted complete shell rings in our examination of the possibility of different use-lives of ring fragments (see below, pp. 167–168.

In summary, the re-fitting studies at Durankulak and Varna have highlighted five new results:

– there is an increase over time in the deposition of broken shell rings at Durankulak and from Durankulak to Varna
– there is a far higher frequency of smaller shell ring fragments at Varna than at any period of the Durankulak cemetery
– there were no re-fits of shell ring fragments between graves at either the Durankulak or the Varna cemetery
– there is an increase over time in the number of fragments that could be re-fitted to make incomplete shell rings at Durankulak, as well as variation between the Late Copper Age cemeteries
– the highest percentage of shell rings that could be re-fitted within the grave occurs in the admittedly small sample of Hamangia I–II rings at Durankulak.

## Use-life of fragments

The establishment of the deliberate nature of shell ring fragmentation in Balkan prehistoric cemeteries leads to a further question: is it possible that shell fragments from the same ring laid to rest in the same grave have developed different biographies in their lifetimes? This notion implies that once-complete shell rings were deliberately broken and that fragments from the same ring were taken by (presumably) different people who used the ring fragments in different ways, only to re-unite the shell fragments with one another in the grave. Were this scenario to be supported by examples whose differential traces could not be otherwise explained, it would be very instructive in helping us to understand the social construction of personhood in the Balkan Neolithic and Copper Age.

There are six lines of evidence that could contribute to the exploration of this question (Table 7.4).

Any case where two or more fragments from the same shell show traces of obviously divergent use-lives would constitute strong evidence for the scenario of divergent life histories. This is rare in either cemetery, amounting to a single example from Varna. One of the three re-fitting fragments from the ring Museum Inv. 1193b differs markedly from the other two in terms of wear and sediment deposition – suggesting quite different life histories.

The variations in location and intensity of deposit on shell rings from the same grave make it improbable that the often carbonate material derives from the post-burial context. Instead, where there are re-fitting fragments with strikingly different deposit profiles, it is worth considering the acquisition of the deposit during the shell ring's pre-burial use-life. Only one such example has been identified – from Grave 733 in Late Copper Age Durankulak. Three cases from the same site/period are known where one of the ring breaks is coated with deposit, again probably acquired in their pre-burial lives. However, since the possibility that these deposits formed on the shell rings after deposition in graves cannot be excluded, this line of evidence cannot alone be considered as conclusive of different life histories for fragments of the same shell ring.

More convincing is any cases of differential wear and/ or polish on two or more re-fitting fragments from the same ring. A larger number of shell rings fits these criteria – a total of 14, comprising eight with polish, two with wear and four with polish and wear (Fig. 7.30–7.35). The chronological distribution of these traces is striking: no such pattern is found in Hamangia I–II and only one ring from a Hamangia III–IV grave is represented, in comparison to 13 Varna–III graves, more from Durankulak than from Varna. The alternative explanation for such patterning is that many of the complete shell rings have traces of wear and/or polish on part of their surfaces as part of the normal use-life of rings that have never been broken. Again, this line of evidence, on a stand-alone basis, is not compelling.

The final pair of lines of evidence are less convincing than the others. There are very few shell rings showing traces of burning- only two from Late Copper Age Durankulak – and both derive from complete rings that have never been broken (Fig. 7.30–7.35). The differential copper staining appears on only those shell rings deposited in Late Copper Age graves at Durankulak in association with copper bracelets.

Thus, few of these six lines of evidence is sufficiently strong to justify such an important inference as the differential use-life scenario posited above. However, when the same shell ring fragments testify to two or more lines of evidence, we are entitled to make a stronger inference about this scenario. This is the case with three shell rings – all from Late Copper Age Durankulak. The shell rings from graves 224 and 298 have a deposit on an old break and differential polish on one of the two fragments. The features on the ring in grave 447 combines polish on one of the three fragments with differential copper staining – *i.e.* evidence that is not so strong. The conclusion is that, after the break, fragments from two Durankulak rings and from one Varna cemetery ring are highly likely to have been involved in different social practices before their eventual re-union in the mortuary

| TYPE OF EVIDENCE | SITE | GRAVE / EXC. NO. / INV. NO. |
|---|---|---|
| different life histories | VEN | Exc. No. 1193b, with 3 re-fitting fragments |
| differential deposit | DUR | 733/k 1693 on 1/ 2 fragments |
| deposit on an old break | DUR | 298/k 0329 |
| | DUR | 763/k 1860 |
| | DUR | 224/k 0284 |
| differential polish &/or wear | DUR | 483/k 2154 (polish on 1/2 fragments) |
| | DUR | 733/k 1696 (polish on 1/3 fragments) |
| | DUR | 673/k 1620 (polish & wear on 1/3 fragments) |
| | DUR | 514/k 0960 (polish on 1/2 fragments) |
| | DUR | 447/F1 (polish on 1/3 fragments) |
| | DUR | 298/k 0329 (polish on 1/2 fragments) |
| | DUR | 267/k 0295 (polish on 1/2 fragments) |
| | DUR | 224/k 0284 (polish on 1/3 fragments) |
| | DUR | 223/k 0304 (polish & wear on 1/2 fragments) |
| | VEN | 207/ Inv. 2367 (wear on ventral/dorsal of 1/3 fragments) |
| | VEN | 158/ Inv. 2964 (wear on ventral/dorsal) |
| | VEN | 119/ Inv. 2951 (polish on ventral/dorsal of 1/2 fragments) |
| | VEN | 108/ Inv. 2942 (polish and wear on Dorsal of 1/3 fragments) |
| | VEN | 49/Inv. 2917 (ventral polish + ventral/dorsal wear on 1/3 fragments) |
| differential burning | DUR | 551/k 1107 on 70% of surface |
| | DUR | 558/k 1508 on small part of surface |
| differential copper staining. | DUR | 272/k 0582 on ventral/ edge of dorsal |
| | DUR | 447/k 0752 on polished surfaces |
| | DUR | 533/k 1031 on 1/2 fragments |
| | DUR | 763/k 1862 on inner cross-section |

*Table 7.4 Differential life histories on re-fitted shell fragments*

zone. There is less convincing evidence for such a scenario for another dozen or so Late Copper Age shell rings from both Durankulak and Varna. It is important to note the chronological regularity here – there is no evidence for such a scenario until the Late Copper Age.

In summary, the biography of a shell ring subsequent to the collection of the living shell by a specific diver is defined by a series of structured and consecutive choices by the shell ring-maker. The first choice is which valve to use – the right valve for massive rings or the left valve for more slender, more symmetrical rings. The cumulative effect of grinding and perforation is the production of what is likely to be an unique ring with its own specific range of natural features and production features. It is difficult to be sure of the aesthetic qualities valued most by prehistoric persons but combinations of colour, lustre, patterning and shape are the most probable qualities that a ring-maker would have considered.

In the Durankulak and Varna studies, a total of 14 natural features and three production features have been identified. While there is no diachronic trend in the number of classes of pre-depositional features found on the rings, there is a clear increase in the number of areas with such features on a given ring, including a peak in the Varna cemetery shell rings. This suggests increasing value is given to shell rings with a diversity of markings – a point borne out in the analysis of biographical pathways. Here, the emphasis is on diversity rather than on

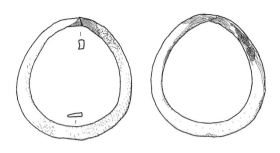

*Fig. 7.30 Rings with different life-histories from Varna*

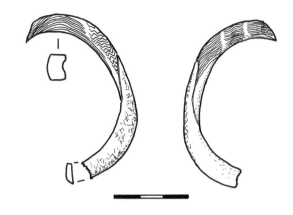

*Fig. 7.33 Rings with different life-histories from Durankulak*

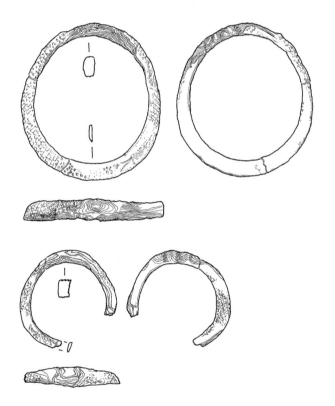

*Fig. 7.31 (top) and Fig. 7.32 (bottom) Rings with different life-histories from Durankulak*

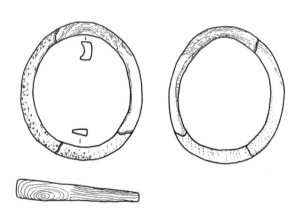

*Fig. 7.34 Rings with different life-histories from Varna*

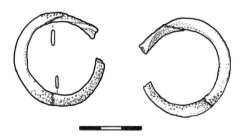

*Fig. 7.35 Rings with different life-histories from Varna*

standardisation, with the peak in diversity recorded for the Varna rings (34 pathways) in comparison to 20 pathways for all of the periods represented at Durankulak.

Any "experience" encountered by the shell ring would have added to its biography through the overlaying of new features on the natural and production markings. Four general use-life features have been recognised – wear, burning, flaking and possibly the accretion of a deposit. The fifth and arguably the most important use-life transformation concerns fragmentation itself. Several diachronic trends have been identified here – each with a quantum leap at the Varna cemetery: first, the increase in the percentage of fragmented rings deposited (as a percentage of the total ring assemblage); secondly, the decreased size of the completeness index of the broken rings; and thirdly, the increase in the number of fragments re-fitted to make still-incomplete rings. These trends, considered as a whole, indicate the increasing significance of deliberate fragmentation in the Late Copper Age and, in particular, at Varna.

That said, there was a total absence of re-fits between shell ring fragments from the same ring but deposited in different graves at both Durankulak and Varna. This indicates that, at the time of burial, the missing fragment(s) were either still in circulation in the domain of the living or else deposited elsewhere. Enchainment between the domains of the living and the dead is clearly attested in all phases at Durankulak and in a complex manner at Varna.

The most contentious issue raised by the re-fitting study concerns the possibility of a complex biography for some shell rings, during which fragments from the same deliberately broken ring were taken by different persons and treated in different ways before being re-united with their "lost" ring fragments in the grave. Despite the evidential problems associated with the claims for this type of narrative, this "lost and found" narrative cannot be definitively excluded from the biographies of Late Copper Age shell rings but neither can it be taken as well supported at present. Further research is necessary for the continuing evaluation of this form of complex life history, which, if documented, would offer a fascinating metaphor for the life histories of the people of the West Pontic Late Copper Age.

### The Dimini shell assemblage

An additional study of a *Spondylus* shell assemblage was undertaken to answer one research question thrown up by the re-fitting studies of shell rings and figurines and to seek to shed light on the conflicting interpretation of the Dimini shell rings (Tsuneki 1989; Halstead 1993, 1995; Kyparissi-Apostolika 2001; Souvatzi and Skafida 2003; Souvatzi, in prep.). Our first question revolved around

the absence of inter-grave re-fits at the Durankulak and Varna cemeteries in comparison with the frequent re-fits between fired clay figurines from different contexts at the Dolnoslav tell (see Chapter 6). Was the discrepancy in intra-site re-fits connected to the material – fired clay vs. shell – or was it related instead to the context of discard – domestic vs. mortuary? For this reason, it became essential to find a sizeable assemblage of *Spondylus* rings from a totally or nearly totally excavated settlement. No such settlement existed in the Balkans but one candidate emerged from Central Greece – the Late Neolithic settlement of Dimini, where almost 100 shell rings had been recovered in three separate excavations, dating from 1901 (Stais), 1903 (Tsountas 1908) and 1974–6 (Hourmouziades 1979).

The interpretation of the shell rings at Dimini forms part of a wider debate about the nature of Late Neolithic society at Dimini and in Thessaly overall. All participants to the debate agree that the site of Dimini was on or near the prehistoric coastline, even if the dating of past coastline changes remains insecure (Zangger 1991). By contrast, several interpretations have been proposed for the large number of broken *Spondylus* rings at Dimini. The third excavator – Hourmouziades (1979) – did not recognise any evidence for craft specialisation at Dimini but favoured a series of self-sufficient Domestic Activity Areas, each producing its own food, tools and shell rings. To the contrary, Tsuneki (1989) maintained that the high frequency of shell pre-forms and half-finished pieces indicated specialised on-site making of rings, especially likely in House N, and beads and buttons, especially in Open Area Γ, arguing that the rings were broken in the final stages of manufacture. The large number of fragments suggested to him large-scale production, mostly for export to inland Thessaly and perhaps the Balkans. Halstead (1993, 1995) agreed with Tsuneki that the two main *Spondylus* concentrations were not produced by sampling bias but noted that ring-making débitage was widespread in many parts of the site (1993, Fig. 2). Thus the concentrations were produced after manufacture, for, as Halstead (1993, 606) notes: "there is no reason to doubt that most of the shell ring fragments found at Dimini are from finished objects". Halstead focused on the high frequency of burnt ring fragments, suggesting that they were "not burnt with other discarded objects in the course of normal refuse disposal but were deliberately destroyed by fire" (1993, 608), as one form of inter-household competition (1995, 18). This potlatching behaviour allegedly countered the inflationary tendency inherent in wealth accumulation and allowed the conversion of wealth to prestige. Hence, for Halstead, unequal access to *Spondylus* was one basis for the emergence of social inequality in Late Neolithic Thessaly, accompanied as it was by the emergence of hoarding from sharing.

Kyparissi-Apostolika (2001) supports the ascription of prestige to *Spondylus* rings at Dimini.

This version of a prestige goods economy underpinned in part by shell rings is criticised by Souvatzi (2000, 118–120: in prep.), who questions the evidence for shell rings denoting intra-site prestige and proposes instead that craft goods were symbols of social integration (see also Souvatzi and Skafida 2003). Building on her standardisation of the terminology for the site through her useful definitions of the terms 'House' and 'Open Area', Souvatzi accepts Tsuneki's notion of specialised shell object production, arguing that two phases in the life of House N possessed all stages in the shell ring *chaîne opératoire* and that Area Γ was a workshop since wealth accumulation would not have occurred in open areas. Her claim that the shell rings in House N were burnt in the course of the burning of the house is supported by the claim that other organic remains were also burnt there – a claim directly contradicted by Halstead (1993, 608), who found unburnt animal bones in this house. What can a re-study of the *Spondylus* shell rings from Dimini add to the already existing welter of opinion and counter-opinion? Is it possible to shed new light on shell ring discard through a study of ring biographies and fragmentation?

The first point about the Dimini shell ring assemblage is its high rate of fragmentation; the shells are much more incomplete than those in the mortuary groups from Durankulak and Varna. While one-quarter of the Varna cemetery shell rings are complete, there is only one complete ring at Dimini. A Completeness Index (Fig. 7.36) shows a similar percentage of rings with an Index of 20–40% to that of Varna but with fewer of the smallest fragments (10–20%) than at Varna. The principal difference is the paucity of large fragments (>50%) at Dimini, indicating not necessarily that fragmentation has been much more intense at Dimini (since many small fragments were re-fitted in Varna graves to make complete or large fragments) but that the settlement context was not a context for accumulation of re-fittable fragments. Since the Completeness Indices of the Dimini settlement and the Varna cemetery are complementary distributions, a hypothetical Dimini cemetery would perhaps contain the large shell ring fragments that are missing from the Dimini settlement. In this sense, the Dimini settlement may have differed from Balkan Copper Age sites with burnt houses, such as at Dolnoslav (see above, p. 114–116).

Any contextual analysis of the Dimini shell rings must start from the overall distribution of the shell rings – concentrations in one House (House N) and one closed area (Area RHO), with a few ring fragments in Other Houses (*p.c.* L. Skafida). There is a strong association between *Spondylus* rings and the vicinity of hearths (*p.c.* S. Souvatzi). The main exceptions to this association comes from the second phase of House N, where a group of 19 shell rings was kept in a built-in stone cupboard and a second group of 3 rings was stored on a stone shelf (Souvatzi 2000, 118–120 and Tables 1, 2 and 4).

The contextual analysis by completeness is based upon a division into three ranges: low (10–20% complete), medium (25–30%) and high (35–55%). There are different completeness patterns for different Houses: some Houses have a dominance of medium completeness, with high completeness least represented, while there is an equal incidence of each completeness range in other houses.

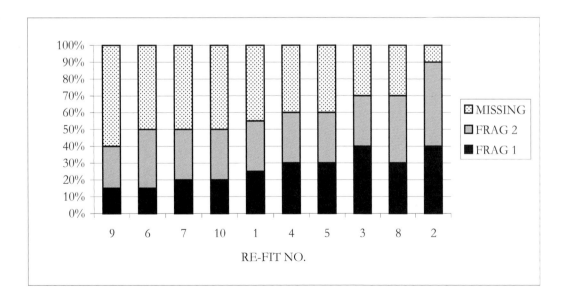

*Fig. 7.36 Completeness index for refitted shell ring fragments from Dimini*

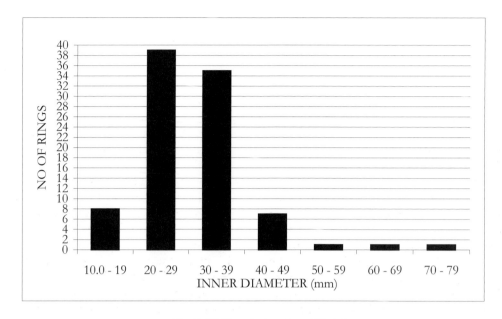

*Fig. 7.37 Size of rings from Dimini*

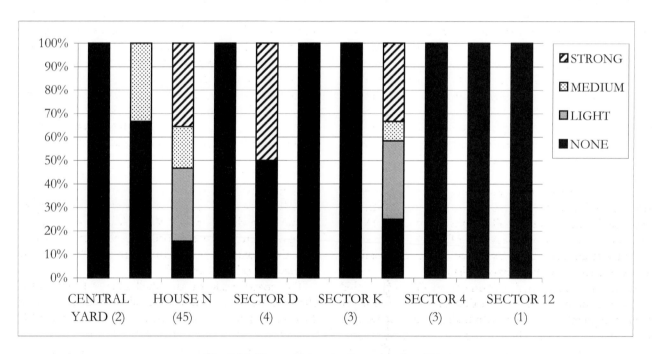

*Fig. 7.38 Rings with burning by context from Dimini*

A second characteristic of the Dimini shell rings is their small size, as measured by the inner diameter. Within a total range of 12–73 mm, 80% of the ring diameters peak between 20–39mm (so-called Medium size), with similar proportions of Small and Large fragments (Fig. 7.37). This means that only one in ten shell rings could have been worn as bracelets when complete, with the others sewn to clothing, tied round the neck or arm or placed on the figurine shelf along the long walls of houses, as in House N (for figurine shelves, Skafida in prep.). A contextual study of size shows that both large contexts have all size ranges but that smaller contexts are dominated almost entirely by Medium-sized rings. This result supports the idea that the two large accumulations were, in some sense, sets of rings, containing all possible categories of shell rings recognised at Dimini.

The third and very visual characteristic of the Dimini shell rings is burning – a point made by all other commentators. Almost two-thirds (64%) of the shell rings had been burnt but to different strengths (termed 'slight', 'medium' and 'strong') and over different areas of the ring surfaces. It is important to note that burning of shell rings does **not** occur in most contexts but only in four Houses. The large contexts contain rings with no burning, as well as with all strengths of burning, in similar proportions (Fig. 7.38). However, there is by no means a good correlation between burnt contexts and the proportion of burnt rings, while the same is true for unburnt contexts and unburnt rings. The most interesting discrepancy is that all of the *Spondylus* rings – many heavily burnt – found in House N were deposited in the unburnt first or second phases of the house's life rather than in the burnt house phase (Phase 3). While House Ksi was burnt at the end of its life, two unburnt rings were deposited there but only one burnt ring. A similar combination of burnt and unburnt rings was deposited in the burnt clay zone of Area D. Only in the burnt clay layer in House Rho did a large group of burnt rings occur – four slightly, one medium and four strongly burnt rings – but even there three unburnt rings were deposited (for all contextual details, *p.c.* S. Souvatzi). This means that, *contra* Halstead (1993) and Souvatzi (in prep.), it is improbable that all of the shell rings were burnt *in situ* in the course of a house fire; rather, there has been a deliberate selection of a wide range of rings – some burnt, some unburnt – for discard. We shall return to the implications of this finding when we look at individual ring biographies (see below, pp. 167–168).

The high rate of fragmentation of the Dimini shell ring assemblage suggested the value of a re-fitting exercise, in which every available fragment (n = 93) was tested for re-fits against every other fragment. This study would give an idea of the extent of enchained relations across the site, as well as characterising the proportion of "orphan ring fragments" missing from Dimini. At this point, it should be underlined that the site has not yet been completely excavated, with bedrock not yet reached in many sectors. Thus, this study cannot define the status of "orphan ring fragments" with any certainty but can provide a snapshot, in 2005, of the state of the shell ring assemblage.

The results of the re-fitting exercise were very interesting, showing one physical re-fit between two fragments and varying probabilities of nine further pairs deriving from the same shell ring. In Chapter 5, we referred to Bollong's (1994) criteria for the probability of re-fitting sherds (see above, p. 82). We adopted Bollong's criteria to the case of shell rings, using five measures of ring fragment similarity: (1) colour; (2) inner diameter; (3) special natural features; (4) polish; and (5) thickness/

width. In this manner, we could make realistic estimates of the likelihood of fragments deriving from the same ring, despite the absence of a physical re-fit. The single physical re-fit and the nine postulated re-fits are listed below (Table 7.5).

The postulated re-fits share the characteristic that a small fragment of missing ring separated the two fragments. It seems probable that this missing part was the débitage of shell ring breakage and that it was missed in the 1970s excavations, which did not use sieving. Such small pieces have been found in several graves in the Varna cemetery, suggesting "local" breakage of shell rings at the graveside (cf. the Bronze Age and Iron Age practice of 'trizna' in respect of pottery; Gaydarska 2004, 70 and Chapter 6).

If all of these re-fits are accepted, two obvious inferences can be drawn. First, the re-fitting of the shell ring fragments has managed to join 21.5% of all the fragments – a higher proportion than has ever been achieved with fired clay figurine re-fitting (cf. above, Chapter 6) or with inter-grave shell ring re-fitting (see this chapter, p. 153). Secondly, this still leaves a potential 73 "orphan ring fragments" incomplete and without any re-fits within the excavated deposits. Given the unknown proportion of the site as unexcavated, with the high probability of foundation deposits in the lower parts of the stratigraphy, it would be unwise to speculate on the likelihood of "orphan ring fragments" linking up with other fragments off the site, although this practice can be documented for figurines at Dolnoslav. But what is the Completeness Index of the re-fitted rings?

In each and every case, the re-fitted rings produce an incomplete shell ring, with the missing part(s) ranging from 10–60% (Fig. 7.36). There is a modal tendency for fragments to cluster around 30–40%, perhaps indicating a ring division into three broadly equal parts. Thus, even with ring fragment re-fits, there are still "orphan ring fragments" to be discovered!

The spatial scale of the shell ring re-fitting within Dimini shows considerable variability (Plate 18). Four of the re-fitted pairs were discarded in the same context (Re-fits 1, 2, 9 and 10). Two re-fits were discarded in different sectors: one part of Re-fit 7 was discarded in Sector A in the Central Yard, the other in Area 10 – a minimum distance of 270m (maximum of 380m) along the outside of enclosure wall 3, along the radial entrance passageway to the Central Yard and across two more spaces in the Yard. The different parts of Re-fit 8 were discarded in Areas 10 and 4 – a minimum of 130m apart (maximum of 220m) across two or three open areas. One re-fit (Re-fit 5) links a House and an Area – House N and Area ETA, a minimum of 100m apart (maximum of 180m) and separated by House X and two open areas. There are no re-fits between different houses. Of the three re-fits

| OUR RE-FIT NO. | FRAGMENT 1 Inv. No/Context | FRAGMENT 2 Inv. No/Context | SHARED CRITERIA | PROBA- BILITY |
|---|---|---|---|---|
| 1 | O 312 / House N | O 315/ House N | physical fit | 100% |
| 2 | O 444/ House RHO | O 446/ House RHO | 1/2/3/3/4/5 | 90% |
| 3 | BE 908.2/ surface | O 344/ Central Yard | 1/2/3/4 | 80% |
| 4 | O 561.4/ ??? | O 561.5/ ??? | 1/2/4/5 | 80% |
| 5 | O 325/ House N | O 327/ House ETA | 1/2/3/4/5 | 70% |
| 6 | O 561.10/ ??? | O 320.6/ House N | 1/2/3/3/4 | 60% |
| 7 | O 353/ Central Yard | O 546/ House 10 | 1/3/4/5 | 60% |
| 8 | O 488/ House 10 | O 510/ House 4 | 1/2/3/4/5 | 60% |
| 9 | O 477/ House RHO | O 468/ House RHO | 1/3/4 | 50% |
| 10 | O 474.1/ House RHO | O 474.2/ House RHO | 1/2/3 | 50% |

*Table 7.5 Physical and postulated re-fits between pairs of shell ring fragments, Late Neolithic Dimini*

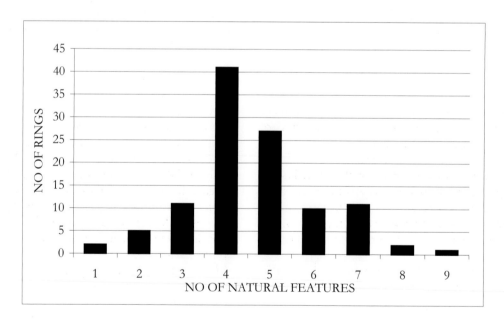

*Fig. 7.39 Natural features on rings from Dimini*

with incomplete contextual data (Re-fits 3, 4 and 6), there is a high probability that the two parts of Re-fit 6 derived from different contexts, since one part was excavated by Stais/Tsountas and the other from House N by Hourmouziades. In terms of the Domestic Activity Areas defined by Hourmouziades (1979) and used by Halstead (1993), the three cross-contextual re-fits linked DAAs A and B (Re-fit 5), C and the Central Yard (Re-fit 7) and C and D (Re-fit 8).

There can be no doubt that the shell ring re-fits provide

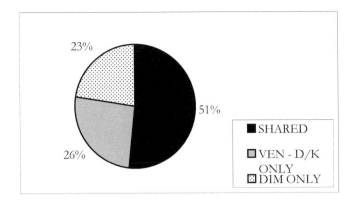

*Fig. 7.40 Representation of natural features on rings from Varna, Durankulak and Dimini*

an element of dynamism and mobility in the account of the settlement's artifact distributions that has hitherto been missing. The basic pattern of the re-fitted fragments and the orphan fragments is more in tune with the notion of activities cross-cutting household areas (Souvatzi, in prep.; cf. Skourtopoulou, in press a and b) rather than the domestic self-sufficiency of the Hourmouziades model. Instead of examining in detail the biographies of the re-fitted ring fragments, we now turn to a broader study of all of the shell ring biographies to gain further insights into use and depositional practices current at Dimini.

The study of shell ring biographies follows the approach defined above (see pp. 149–152) for the Durankulak and Varna assemblages. There is a striking distribution of natural features in the Dimini assemblage, approximating closely to that of a normal distribution (Fig. 7.39). The frequency of natural features is, however, affected to some extent by the presence/absence of post-depositional deposits on the surface of the rings. There is a similar approximation to a normal distribution for the pattern of areas with natural features. However, there is no relationship between the degree of completeness of a ring fragment and the area of, or number of, natural features.

As at Durankulak and Varna, it was found useful to categorise the many and varied natural features into a series of "biographical (or natural feature) pathways", linking the individual features into six groups and then investigating the combinations of these groups in each shell ring. The principal natural features and traits resulting from use found on the Dimini shell rings are illustrated below (Plate 32–43, with descriptions in captions).

It is important to note that the natural feature pathways found at Dimini show marked differences from those used at Durankulak and Varna – indicating overlapping technological traditions which, at the same time, express regionally specific choices – at least partly based upon different kinds of natural shells (Fig. 7.40). The main new feature emphasised at Dimini was the sculpted depression on the inner side of the ring (Fig. 7.34) – always polished away at Varna and Durankulak – while perforated holes were very rare at Dimini. The number of feature pathways selected at the three sites was proportional to the sample size. The four principal combinations were based on lines (Plates 40–41), pitting (Plates 40 and 42) and sculpting (Plates 43–44) (Fig. 7.41). A consideration of natural feature combinations by context shows that each group of contexts selected a very varied suite of combinations, with rings with a wider range of natural features in combinations being deposited in some Houses than in others (Fig. 7.42). The variety of biographical pathways was minimally affected by the degree of completeness of the ring fragment. It is important to underline the contribution of shell rings to the creation of different regional identities in Northern Greece and the West Pontic zone. Whatever variations in shell ring costumes relating to age, sex and status, these personal markers were nested within the broader, regional identities.

The next, and most important, phase in the investigation of biographical pathways was the establishment of micro-stratigraphies for each shell ring fragment – the sequence of events – natural and cultural – that changed the lives of the rings. There are five main events in the life of a shell ring: (termed 'natural': Plates 33–44); breaking the ring (Plates 34–37); burning (Plates 39 and 44); polishing (Plates 34, 36 & 41); and 'final' events (including wear (Plates 37, 40 & 42), stress cracks (Plates 37 & 40 and post-depositional deposits: Plates 41 & 43). Because of the high incidence of burning, we have the unusual possibility of sequencing these events more precisely, in a way that was not possible at Varna or Durankulak with shell rings, or even at Dolnoslav with the fired clay figurines. We have found that, far from being a wholly negative force of destruction, burning of shell rings can have a pleasing aesthetic effect, highlighting natural features such as complex lines. The main difficulty has been in deciding whether/how the rings have been polished after burning.

The distribution of 'phases' (the stratigraphic equivalent of an individual event) in the shell ring micro-stratigraphies ranges from three to seven, with a predominance of 3 stages, in comparison to a narrower range for the micro-stratigraphies of the re-fitted ring fragments (3–5, with a predominance of 4 stages) (Fig. 7.43). Eleven specific micro-stratigraphies have been identified, which for simplicity have been clustered into four Groups:

– Group 1: burning after the break(s) (*e.g.*, Figs. 7.57 & Plate 38)

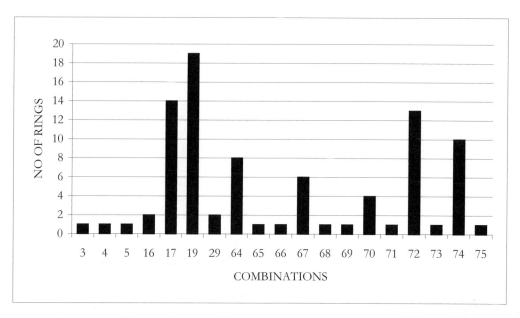

*Fig. 7.41 Rings with different natural pathways from Dimini*

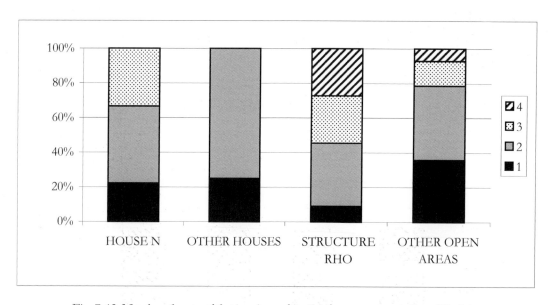

*Fig. 7.42 Number of natural features in combination by context group from Dimini*

– Group 2: first break – burning – second break (*e.g.,* Plate 35)

– Group 3: break(s) after the burning (*e.g.,* Plates 32 & 43)

– Group 4: unburnt rings (*e.g.,* Plates 34, 39–42)

The distribution of these micro-stratigraphical groups indicates that, of the two-thirds of burnt rings, 39% (or 35) rings (Groups 2 + 3) have been broken after burning – *i.e.* more than all of the unburnt rings. Within this total,

17 rings (18%) have been broken twice – once before burning and once after, indicating a complex life history prior to final deposition. In the unburnt ring group (Group 4), there is one case of a ring which is broken once before, and once after, the laying down of brown deposit, while, in another example, a deposit was formed after the break which followed the accumulation of use-wear. This result has two clear implications – that life 'after the break' was quite normal for a reasonably high proportion of the Dimini shell rings and that burning was only sometimes the final social act prior to, if not part of, deposition.

A contextual analysis of the micro-stratigraphical groups shows a clear distinction between the large contexts and the rest – all the sequence groups are found in rings deposited in House N and House RHO, while rings belonging to the unburnt Group 4 dominate all other houses. There are three exceptions to this latter trend – breaks either side of burning in rings deposited in House KSI and Areas D and D7.

One unsatisfactory aspect of the analysis is the grouping under one Phase ('final') of the results of three different processes – wear from usage, stress marks from

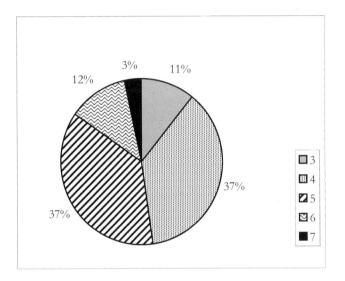

*Fig. 7.43 Phases in rings microstratigraphy*

burning or another such practice, and deposits from post-depositional soil processes. Several interesting trends emerge with the unpackaging of these three different elements. The lowest proportion of rings with wear falls in Group 1, where the last Phase is therefore generally the burning Phase. Thus, for 21/23 rings in Group 1, burning is the last social act prior to deposition. This result stands in strong contrast to up to 1/3 of the rings from the other Groups, on whom use-wear traces appear "stratified" over the last break (Fig. 7.44). Thus, in some cases, there are two phases of life history for rings after they were burnt. This finding makes it hard to support the deliberate potlatching of shell ring fragments by burning postulated by Halstead (1993) and Souvatzi (in prep.).

The final analysis concerns the biographical pathways and micro-stratigraphies of the two parts of the ten pairs of re-fitted shell rings. Each re-fitted pair was compared in terms of negative matches (the mutual absence of a natural feature, a production feature, a usage feature or a post-depositional trace), positive matches (the co-presence of such a feature) and discrepancies (differences between the two fragments). First, there was no relationship between the percentage probability of the fragments re-fitting and the number of discrepancies in biographical pathway. Secondly, most of the discrepancies related to different natural features, some of which were specific to particular parts of a shell (n = 20 cases). However, there were six pairs with discrepancies in use-life (presence vs. absence of burning on Re-fit 2; presence vs. absence of wear on Re-fit 6; wear on one fragment, with flakes detached from the other on Re-fits

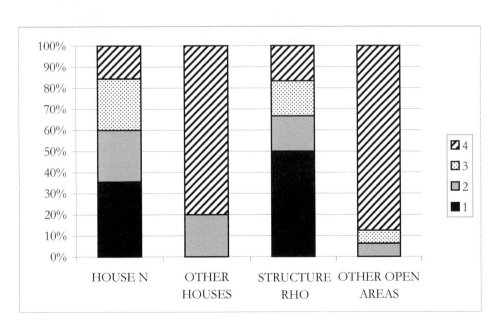

*Fig. 7.44 Microstratigraphic sequence groups by context groups from Dimini*

3, 4 and 7; and flakes detached from one fragment, with burning on the other on Re-fit 8). Each of these cases raises the possibility that the fragments went through different life experiences, perhaps subsequent to the original breakage. The three discrepancies related to post-depositional deposits confirm the different depositional contexts in which two of the pairs (Re-fits 3 and 5) were found but does not explain the same depositional context for the two fragments comprising Re-fit 10.

A detailed comparison of the micro-stratigraphical groups of re-fitted pairs indicates that a majority of cases shared the same micro-stratigraphy (n = 6). However, in four cases, there were discrepancies (the presence vs. absence of burning on Re-fit 2; reversal of the order of breakage and burning on Re-fits 4 and 6; and the reversal of the order of breakage and deposit on Re-fit 8). As at Varna and Durankulak, these findings suggest the possibility of a different mid-life experience for these fragments after initial breakage.

In summary, this study has not shed new light on the question of the local, on-site making of *Spondylus* rings at Dimini – this is taken as agreed by all commentators. What the fragmentation, re-fitting, biographical and micro-stratigraphical studies have shown is the multiple material linkages between the household activity areas at Dimini and the very complicated life histories of the shell rings. Such complexity does not equate with Tsuneki's interpretation of the breakage of most shells during the final stage of manufacture, since, prior to final deposition, the shells had already experienced long and diverse lives. Neither do our findings support Halstead's interpretation

of the deliberate destruction of the shells as a levelling mechanism practised by the Dimini élite, since the burning was often used for aesthetic enhancement and often one or two Phases prior to the final act of deposition. What the findings suggest is that not only complete but also fragmentary items of material culture could be used not only in personal or household display but also for fragment enchainment. The practices of which the shell ring fragments were part included wearing as a costume item, deliberate fragmentation, deliberate burning usually accompanied by polishing, the creation of use-wear through heavy usage, the exchange of fragments between household activity areas and the deposition in small or large groups in a wide variety of settlement contexts. Any notion that the shell rings were **simply** ornaments should surely be treated with extreme caution: the life historical approach demonstrates a far wider range of practices in which *Spondylus* shell rings played an important role than we had hitherto anticipated.

### Inter-site comparisons

The biographical and re-fitting studies of the five assemblages of *Spondylus* shell rings from the three phases of the Durankulak cemetery, the Varna cemetery and the Dimini settlement provide a rich pattern of variability in which the main differences are related to the contextual contrast between a settlement site and a set of mortuary arenas and diachronic changes in social practices in the mortuary domain. Recent AMS dates for the Durankulak cemetery indicate a duration of 200 years for the

| FEATURE | DIMINI | DURANKULAK | VARNA |
|---|---|---|---|
| Peaks in Inner Diameter | 20 – 40% | 50 – 70% | 50 – 70% |
| No. of Natural Features | 14 | 9 – 10 | 19 |
| No of Feature Pathways | 19 | 20 | 34 |
| % of Complete rings | 1% | 46 – 86% | 30% |
| Peak(s) in Completeness Index | 20 – 40% | 20 – 30% + 70 – 80% | 10–30% + 60–70% |
| % rings + inter-context re-fitting | 9% | 0% | 0% |
| % rings + intra-context re-fitting | 11% | 9–33% | 24% |
| % of rings + burning | 64% | 2% | 0.5% |

*Table 7.6 Differences between the Dimini settlement* Spondylus *ring assemblage and the Durankulak and Varna mortuary assemblages*

Hamangia I–II (5100–4900 Cal BC), a shorter period for the Late Copper Age graves (4500–4400 Cal BC) and an as yet poorly defined span for the Earlier Copper Age (Hamangia III–IV) (Higham *et al.,* submitted; Honch *et al.,* 2006). New AMS dates for Dimini indicate partial contemporaneity with both the Middle and Late Copper Age on the Black Sea zone (4790–4500 Cal BC, Souvatzi and Skafida 2003). These dates suggest the chronological sense of making direct comparisons between Dimini and the Hamangia III–IV and Varna–III phases at Durankulak and the Varna Late Copper Age graves.

The biggest difference between Dimini and the cemeteries is the presence of unworked shells and shell-making débitage at the former compared to its absence at the latter. But Dimini is not only a production site – it has just as much evidence for consumption as do the cemeteries! There is so far remarkably little evidence in Eastern Bulgaria for unworked *Spondylus/Glycymeris* shells or for production debris relating to shell ring-working. It is therefore a justifiable inference that finished shell rings were imported into Eastern Bulgaria, probably via the Aegean – Dardanelles – Black Sea route (cf. Gaydarska *et al.* 2004, Fig. 1). What follows is an account of the differences between the settlement and the cemetery assemblages – differences that far outweigh the similarities (Table 7.6).

In summary, the Dimini shell rings turn out to be substantially smaller than the Durankulak and Varna rings, with regional differences in preferred natural features and natural feature pathways, despite the numerical overlap. The Dimini assemblage reveals far fewer complete rings and a very small proportion of large fragments, with the high proportion of burnt rings at Dimini further differentiating it from those of Durankulak and Varna. But perhaps the most striking difference is the large number of re-fitting pairs of ring fragments linking various settlement contexts at Dimini, in contrast with no re-fitting between graves in either cemetery. The principal practice of re-fitting of mortuary fragments was within graves, while relatively few re-fits were made within houses or open areas at Dimini. What do these differences mean?

The difference in ring size takes us back to the very beginning of the shell ring biography – the selection of the shell for making the ring. If we assume that the Durankulak and Varna communities did not receive any or many their shell rings directly from the Dimini Bay area, there is a possibility that the divers in the source area (perhaps the North Aegean coast or islands) selected larger shells to make more impressive rings. However, the degree of overlap in shell size between the Dimini shell rings and those from another shell ring-making community – Sitagroi (data in Nikolaidou 2003) – suggests that this was not the case. In any case, there is no empirical evidence

for a systematic size difference in *Spondylus* shell populations in different zones of the Aegean. Thus, it is more likely that the Black Sea communities valued larger shell rings and sought them for mortuary rituals. A size comparison of the small sample from Agia Sofia Magoula in Thessaly (data in Tsuneki 1987) – another inland village importing shell rings from the coast – indicates a similar size range to that of Durankulak but not such large shell rings as at Varna. Thus what we have is a contrast between shell ring-making sites, where a full range of shell rings would have been made but only smaller rings were deposited, and shell ring-importing groups, who exchanged valuables for the larger rings (or ring fragments?) so vital to their social reproduction. Some of the largest left-valve shell rings known derive from the greatest mortuary accumulation yet known in the Balkan Peninsula.

But the importing groups were concerned not only with ring size but also with the quality and diversity of natural features that had been revealed through grinding and polishing. The Durankulak and Varna communities showed preferences for rings with certain natural features although, interestingly, rings with **no** additional features beyond their natural colour and brilliance were also popular. Whereas at Dimini, rings with lines, pitting and sculpture, singly or in combination, were preferred for deposition, the features prized by the Black Sea communities were lines and colour combinations - usually red and white. The striking appearance of linear patterns in multiple lines, garlands and other complex forms was enhanced by the delicate shades of red, usually in lines or small zones rather than covering the whole shell surface. The shell ring features complement or reinforce many features of the Black Sea ceramic assemblages at Durankulak and Varna – especially those reflecting brilliance, enhanced by burnishing and polishing. In the earliest cemetery phase at Durankulak (Late Neolithic – Hamangia I–II), the main fine wares presented black burnished surfaces – an opposition to the pure white of the massive, right-valve shell rings. In the Late Copper Age, the importance of the white – red colour contrast in the Varna and Durankulak cemeteries was denoted by its frequent appearance on pottery and shell rings (Chapman 2002; see above, pp. 45–48). Multiple fine linear incision is the closest analogy to natural shell decoration and it was also a feature of Black Sea coastal Earlier Copper Age ceramic assemblages, if less so in the Late phase (*e.g.* Early phase, or Hamangia III: Todorova *et al.* 2002, Abb. 114 and 117; Middle phase, or Hamangia IV: 2002c, Abb. 121; cf. Late phase, or Varna I–III: 2002c, Abb. 124–125). In both media, colour and sheen were exploited to create a world of aesthetic finery. The relationship of the natural features on the Dimini shell rings to its distinctive pottery will be the subject of a further study.

The importance of complete shell rings in the four mortuary assemblages is itself very variable, with the lowest fragmentation rate (14%) found in the earliest cemetery phase – Hamangia I–II at Durankulak and a increasing proportion of incomplete rings with time until Varna, with two in three rings broken and incomplete. We suggest that two competing practices were in tension – the custom of integrating the totality of relations embodied in the object deposited in the mortuary domain and the practice of emphasising the partible nature of the relationship between the newly-dead and the living by keeping ring fragments in separate contexts. The integrating practice was also visible with those Hamangia figurines placed in graves, all of which were dated to the Hamangia III phase. Moreover, this principle was incorporated into the notion of cemetery itself, in which the relations of those buried there were grounded in the wider community contributing to and forming the cemetery. It seems that, in the Late Copper Age at Varna, greater emphasis was placed upon the multiple enchained relations between the newly-dead and the living, as a way of representing the complexities of social relations that characterised this period. What this means for Dimini, with its single complete ring, is the significance of enchained relations between residents and others living away from the site as embodied in the high proportion of orphan shell fragments. The importance of fragment enchainment was also recapitulated at Sitagroi, where four out of 186 shell rings (or 2%) were complete (Nikolaidou 2003, 337), and in the small assemblage of shell rings at Agia Sofia magoula (n = 12), none of which is complete (Tsuneki 1987).

This interpretation is further supported by the low completeness index of the vast majority of the Dimini shell rings – also paralleled at Agia Sofia magoula. The recurrence of ring fragments measuring approximately 1/3 of the ring circumference suggests that rings were perhaps being regularly divided into three parts at or near Dimini, possibly as a means of systematizing enchained relations between three types of person. The breakage of rings into two unequal parts – often 20–30% / 70–80% – appears to typify the Black Sea communities, with both Completeness Indices occurring in graves at both sites. This practice may be the result of the tension between the integration (the larger fragment) and the fragmentation (the smaller fragment) principles in individual rings.

The total absence of inter-grave re-fits for the shell rings at Varna and Durankulak is puzzling. One suggestion would be that the enchained relationships requiring emphasis for the newly-dead were not with their dead kin but with those still living. The grouping of graves in the Varna and Durankulak cemeteries still requires further analysis but the burial of the newly-dead with their dead kin may have obviated the need for the further

material expression of the validity of their relationships. The identification of inter-context re-fits in the Dimini shell ring assemblage demonstrated that it was the mortuary context that was responsible for the absence of ring re-fits at Varna and Durankulak rather than the shell material itself. Although it seems that day-to-day interactions would also have reduced the need for materialisation of inter-household relations at Dimini, the existence of inter-context re-fits suggests either that children moved ring fragments between spaces or that a more structured practice linked two spaces and their habitual occupants. The latter is more likely in view of the social, ritual and possible cosmological significance of the shell rings. Such fragment dispersions could have occurred in the course of the often lengthy use-lives of the shell rings, which show several stages of change after the selection of the final form of the natural features. Thus, after the breakage of one shell ring, the fragments were taken into different households and each used in different ceremonies, leading to different biographies that took the ring fragments into different final places of deposition. At Dimini, such ceremonies were much more frequently linked to burning than in the Black Sea cemeteries – burning that sometimes resulted in the enhancement of the surface patterns in black – a symbolic reversal of the *Spondylus'* normal colour. There is also the possibility that the shell rings were burnt in the course of cremation practices, as attested in the Thessalian Late Neolithic at Soufli magoula and Platia Zarkou magoula (Gallis 1996). By contrast, the rarity of burning on the Durankulak and Varna shell rings matches the pronounced scarcity of cremations in the Balkan Neolithic and Copper Age (Chapman 1983; Băčvarov 2003). The possibility that the Dimini shell rings were presencing a mortuary ritual involving the deaths of important members of the community brings the Dimini rings contextually closer to those from the Black Sea zone. The other similarity between the Thessalian and Pontic rings derives from the Durankulak and Varna cemetery practices of re-uniting fragments from the same ring which had possibly experienced different biographical events but which were re-united in the grave. What should be emphasised, however, is the lack of evidence from the shell ring micro-stratigraphies at Varna and Durankulak for such prolonged stages of use-life as was common at Dimini. It is this difference that, in the end, indicates most convincingly the magnitude of the differences between the Thessalian shell ring assemblage and those from the Black Sea coast.

Whatever narratives that could be told of the Varna and Durankulak shell rings probably did not include the variety of social practices that the shell rings experienced at Dimini. This lack of biographical experience was more than compensated for by the long voyages from the North

Aegean to the shores of the Black Sea, which began in the earliest Hamangia period (late 6th millennium Cal BC) and continued until the demise of the communities burying at Varna and Durankulak. During these voyages, the symbolism of the origins of the *Spondylus* shells on rocky coastlines near Volos Bay or East of Chalkidiki, itself linked to the divers who retrieved the shells and brought them back from such dangerous zones, was magnified by the skill of the shell ring makers whose selection of techniques and mastery of revelation brought forth the natural features that were so attractive and so different in each shell ring. This combination of origins and fine crafting contributed a prestige association to an already exotic material, whose transport to the Black Sea relied on long-distance specialists whose status, in turn, depended upon the completion of trips from home and hearth to remote and dangerous areas and to communities speaking a different language. For every shell ring that reached the East Balkan coastline, a minimum of three specialists – and perhaps several different users – contributed to the ring's biography. Each person had their own biographical fame to offer an enchained relationship materialised through the *Spondylus* shell ring. Just as every contribution was different, so the physical form and characteristics of each ring was different, forming a basis for differentiation of the histories that were recounted of each shell ring. It is in this way that we can gain some insights into the personalisation of the shell ring and the objectification of each person contributing to its biography.

# 8. Re-fitting the narrative: beyond fragments

## Introduction: parts and wholes in context (reprise)

We are nearing the end of a long traverse across prehistoric Europe, in which we have examined more fragments of things than was good for us, with insufficient compensation by way of complete objects for such an effort. It was not enough to be confronted constantly by parts of wholes – we have moreover been bombarded by absences – the 'missing parts' of broken objects that we have not been able to find, all those items of refuse that have been thrown away, all the artifacts exchanged out of the community never to return, the places that have been long abandoned, the memories of the past that have faded …. Is there any escape from the world of fragmentation and the consequent proliferation of fragments?

According to philosopher David Bohm (1980), there is not and cannot be any escape, since, ironically, fragmentation is the one thing in our lives which is universal. Bohm identifies the roots of fragmentation in human consciousness as being very deep and pervasive. For Bohm, to divide up is to simplify – to make manageable the totality of the world and our experience of it. The innocent beginning of the process is to regard conceptual divisions as a useful way of thinking about things. The problems arise when those fragments of consciousness take flight and become independent entities with their own separate existence. The habit of seeing and experiencing the world as composed of fragments can lead to a way of thinking based upon such fragments. The response of acting in such a way as to try to break themselves and the world up to correspond with such a way of thinking can clearly lead to the proof of the correctness of such a fragmentary worldview (1980, 3–4). The Golden Age of wholeness stands as a desired absence on which to look back and contemplate how good things once were. Without it, there is only, *pace* Munro (1997), endless labour of division.

Bohm's perspectives on human consciousness works equally well for our consideration of things. Breakage, loss and absence would have been part and parcel of prehistoric lives and everyone would have become used to seeing fragments of once-whole things lying around their living area. The opportunistic use of broken objects became part of a way of life – a re-use of things that was in fact an extension of their biographies. Discarded blunt knives were re-used as scrapers, sherds were used as scoops or to dig out pits. This was the first step in the realisation that parts of things could be useful – could be used as separate entities in their own right. The utility of fragments also confirmed the idea that whole and part could somehow be related – that the object that is now in pieces was once whole. Away from their own home, people visiting a place where tribal lore had it that once people lived would have seen fragments of unknown antiquity and identity lying there, attracting their attention because they were already accustomed to the re-use of fragments in their own places. The thought that these fragments could be useful may also have been supplemented with the notion that these fragments once belonged to someone else – that there was anOther identity somehow implicated in the fragments. The presencing of past persons through the re-use of fragmentary material culture was, in itself, a small step but had enormous and surely unintended consequences for future social practices. To the extent that people in the past made variable uses of objects and monuments from **their** past (Bradley 2002), those people would have developed an appreciation of both the practical and the symbolic potential of broken things. The spreading role of fragments in past lifeways would have altered people's perceptions of wholeness and divisibility, not only in the sense of wholeness being effective and useful (who needs a broken water-jar?) but also by an acceptance of both parts and wholes as separate entities. Under certain circumstances, perhaps character-ised by changing views about the nature of relations between persons, the well-known utilitarian idea of fragments being connected to past whole objects could have been linked to another concept – that fragments could have been linked to past persons – to produce a metaphorical link between parts and wholes – that the part somehow stood for the whole object (representational logic) or that the fragment grew out of the whole object (dividual logic). Both forms of logic were probably important, in varying degrees, in each prehistoric society; each form of logic could have led to the further step of linking persons and objects in the creation of things not only out of people but also as representing people. The increasing recognition of not only the usefulness but also the power of fragments led to an acceptance of worldviews in which fragments took their place as one class of entity amongst many.

While objections may be raised to this narrative as relying on post-hoc logic and a generalised account of an undated and undatable sequence of conjectural changes, our reply is that we are simply sketching a possible set of relationships between human consciousness, social practice and the material world – relationships that would have matured during the *longue durée* of the Palaeolithic and onwards into the Holocene. This account underlines the important point that, even from the earliest times, it was impossible to separate the practical and the utilitarian from the symbolic and the metaphorical in a consideration of things and people. The increasing intensity of production and use of material culture invariably led to the creation of more and more fragments. How likely was it that their ubiquity went unnoticed and unexploited for so long?

Is there a possibility of a co-evolution of the fragmentation of consciousness and of objects? It is worth recalling that four of the key activities of Palaeolithic social life were all implicated in repeated acts of fragmentation. First, tool making usually proceeded by the reduction of larger stones to smaller objects of the appropriate form. Secondly, animal carcasses required butchery for consumption as smaller pieces. Thirdly, in the absence of tree-felling technologies, timber for fuel was usually collected as small pieces or in pieces chopped into firewood. And, perhaps most significantly, the social group itself may well have undergone seasonal changes in composition, nucleating for summer feasts, dispersing to survive winter famine. The cognitive basis of fragmentation as one of the principal means of problem-solving, whether for making hand-axes or surviving winter resource scarcity, may well have become fused into the way Palaeolithic people thought about the world and its mysteries.

To contextualise the ubiquity of fragments, let us return to Balkan prehistory and picture the kind of living space, on the top of a tell, on which countless generations lived. Judging by the micro-morphological data, the high organic content and the wealth of artifacts from deposits known as 'cultural layers', the living surface of the typical settlement was an uneven surface full of discarded refuse, where people had placed animal bones, mussel shells, hazelnut shells and broken objects, often treading them

into the surface, where they would have been partially covered after the next heavy rain had washed mud off the houses. The term 'Concentration Principle' has been used in a more social sense than that of Schiffer ("trash attracts trash" 1987, 62) to express the idea that people discarded much of their refuse near to the place where it was created and used/consumed (Chapman 2000b). On the rare occasions when small pits were dug into the ancestral mound in the restricted open spaces between houses, ecofacts and artefacts were placed there as an exchange between the ancestors and the present residents. Many objects – broken or whole – would have been kept inside the houses in between-use episodes, some highly visible on shelves for display, others concealed in the corners of often dark rooms. Some of the refuse produced by households on the tell would have been taken off the tell for disposal on flatter, less densely occupied areas, as was found at Omurtag and Podgoritsa (Gaydarska *et al.* 2005; Bailey *et al.* 1998). Children wishing to play with interesting fragments would also have taken them off the tell, as would adults re-using large pieces. But walking across the top of the tell could have been a hazardous business, with sharp edges ready to cut through leather shoes or bare feet. The smells of fires and decaying remains would have mingled with the sounds and smells of adults, children and household animals. The frequent discovery of human coprolites in 'cultural layers' on the Late Neolithic tell of Polgár-Csőszhalom, in Eastern Hungary tells its own story. And fragments, fragments and more fragments – relentlessly part of the habitus – standing for a once-whole object, still 'alive' and waiting for re-use, whether as children's toys, useful containers or symbols of enchained relationships.

There is an extraordinary contrast between the geometrical precision and centralised planning of tells such as Polyanitsa and Ovcharovo, with their highly ordered division of space (Todorova 1982), and the picture sketched here of the realities of walking over the living surface of such places. If this discrepancy was to be overcome, again and again, on an everyday basis, there can be little doubt that much work was necessary to maintain even a degree of cultural order in such messy, smelly and externally disorganised living places as tells. As Munro (1997) puts it, a consistent labour of division was required to separate matter that was out of place from matter that was indeed meant to be where it was. The conduits of disposal often used by archaeologists in their contextual analysis of finds – houses, pits and the cultural layer – may profitably be supplemented by off-tell disposal to provide the main axes of variation in the placement of refuse and fragments-in-transit. But to what extent can the contexts of refuse and fragments-in-transit be used to make direct inferences about past social practices? Clearly, there are two issues in an evaluation of on-site contexts: first, taphonomy and site transformational processes and, secondly, fragment mobility.

The assemblages of objects from sites in the Balkan Peninsula which we have studied have undergone taphonomic modification and object dispersion to varying degrees. It will be helpful to begin by differentiating three classes of context by security of depositional inference (Table 8.1).

The closed finds contexts in the two cemeteries at Durankulak and Varna comprise the individual burials, which, for the most part, are placed in pits dug into the subsoil. Although shallow pits in both cemeteries have often been disturbed, occasionally by burials from later periods, such intrusions have been identified by the excavators. Careful comparisons between the preservation of objects in graves located in varying parts of each cemetery indicate that neither the soil conditions at Varna nor the high lake-influenced water table at Durankulak have had any effect on finds preservation. Object mobility is considered minimal at both Durankulak and Varna, where there is no evidence for the kind of grave robbing that was prevalent in Bronze Age flat cemeteries such as Branč (Shennan S. 1975).

Burnt houses represent a characteristic feature of later Balkan prehistory, not only in the Copper Age of the East Balkans but also in the Neolithic, as at Baia-Goloviţa.

The closure of the houses was effected by the piling of substantial quantities of house rubble over the floors, on which often stood large accumulations of complete and fragmentary objects. The sealing of the assemblage by house rubble prevented not only taphonomic damage but also removal of artifacts. However, it may not be assumed that the finds on a burnt house floor were necessarily the 'living assemblage', since items could be added from, or removed to, other houses prior to the conflagration and almost certainly were so transformed.

As their name implies, semi-closed contexts ('semi-open' if the archaeologist is a pessimist!) are more subject to both kinds of transformation. The debris piled over the floor of an unburnt house is by no means as massive as in a burnt structure, more often taking the form of a low mound of trampled mud. This deposit was therefore susceptible to damage by pit-digging, whether accidental some time after abandonment or for intentional removal of artifacts from the 'dead' house. A more robust type of unburnt house than the Bulgarian Neolithic examples – some of the houses at Dimini – were constructed with dry-stone walls, presumably supporting light superstructures. The floors were covered in a low mound of stones, resembling a ploughed-out cairn. Nonetheless, the cairn had the effect of preserving finds placed on the floor.

| CLOSED CONTEXTS | Graves | Varna cemetery |
| | | Durankulak cemetery |
| | Burnt houses | Baia-Goloviţa, |
| | | Azmak |
| | | Dimini |
| | | Dolnoslav |
| SEMI-CLOSED CONTEXTS | Unburnt houses | Rakitovo |
| | | Chavdarova Cheshma |
| | | Nova Zagora-Hlebozavoda |
| | | Dimini |
| | Pits | Rakitovo |
| | | Chavdarova Cheshma |
| | | Nova Zagora-Hlebozavoda |
| | | Durankulak-Nivata |
| | | Medgidia |
| | | Tîrgşoru-Urs |
| | | Baia-Goloviţa, |
| | Middens | Dolnoslav |
| OPEN CONTEXTS | Open spaces in settlement | Dolnoslav |
| | | Dimini |
| | Extra-mural in the landscape | Balchik |

*Table 8.1 Context classes for the assemblages under investigation*

Pits form a semi-closed context type because of the process of their filling-in, which may take a very short time or cover a period of weeks or months. There were evidently opportunities to remove material deposited in a half-empty (?? half-full) pit – opportunities taken by children or by other residents seeking re-usable fragments. We cannot exclude the occasional removal of one or more fragments of a group of parts of the same object from the context in which both (all) were placed and its subsequent dispersal into other site contexts. On the basis of cultural value, we suggest the following ranking of the probability of occurrence of such fragment dispersal: highest probability – sherds; medium probability – figurine fragments; lowest probability – shell ring fragments.

The third type of semi-closed context is the midden, exemplified at only one site – the Final Copper Age tell of Dolnoslav. Here, the key formation process is retention and curation of large quantities of material culture for deliberate accumulation in four large piles of mixed finds – complete vessels and figurines, sherds, figurine fragments, food remains (animal bones, burnt grain and shells), as well as other small finds. Although the excavators identified a capping of burnt material on the top of each midden as a sign of closure at the abandonment of the site, it would still have been possible for later visitors to remove artifacts from the middens, perhaps for symbolic re-use elsewhere. However, the huge quantities of material culture preserved in each of the four middens suggest that this opportunity for scavenging was not strongly exploited.

The two types of open context form a strong contrast – open settlement spaces at two sites and the deposition of a fragmentary figurine in a cleft in a rock in the cliffs at Balchik. While the latter context was a liminal place that was hard to reach, any determined visitor could have removed any finds associated with the figurine. Contexts of deposition were widely used in the unbuilt spaces at both Dimini and Dolnoslav. Any object or object fragment left on the surface outside a building could have been either moved there from another context – perhaps by adults re-using the fragments or as part of children's play – or could have been the only surviving member of a group of fragments the majority of which have been taken elsewhere.

This assessment shows that, while several important site assemblages derived from secure contexts (burnt houses or graves), the majority of assemblages were deposited in semi-secure contexts (unburnt houses, pits and middens), while a few finds groups came from contexts whose stability cannot be assumed. These differences have been taken into account as far as possible in the individual site analyses and the comparison of results.

## The premise

We are now in a position to re-assess the primary premise of the book – deliberate object fragmentation and the significance of the re-use of the ensuing fragments in an extended life 'after the break'. It has been the contention of much recent research that deliberate fragmentation is a fundamental feature of not only later Balkan prehistory but also of communities living in many other times/places. The evidence for deliberate fragmentation is increasing each year, both at the level of inter-site data and intra-site data, such that the social practice can no longer be ignored by anyone seriously interested in material culture. Even such a sceptic as Bailey now admits (2005, 179) "the possibility that, even after breakage, figurines were re-cycled and re-circulated". But is this only a possibility? And how frequent was that possibility?

The arguments that we advance for the reality of deliberate fragmentation and re-use of fragments are based upon five kinds of data:- (1) inter-site re-fits (pp. 106–111); (2) intra-site re-fits between closed contexts (pp. 84–93, Chapters 6 & 7); (3) orphan fragments from settlements with total excavation, good recovery methods and other caveats (pp. 88–93, 100–105, Chapters 6 & 7); (4) orphan fragments from closed contexts, plus other caveats (pp. 95–100, Chapters 6 & 7); and (5) unambiguous evidence of further treatment of fragments on the fragment break (Chapters 6 & 7).

The physical matching of different fragments of the same broken object found in different sites provides strong evidence for the re-use of parts after deliberate breakage of the whole. This form of re-fitting is the hardest to find, since it is by no means obvious which sites to target; it is therefore likely that the handful of cases found so far is the tip of the iceberg. While the majority of such re-fits may well be restricted to local areas, up to 10km in radius, it is unwise to preclude re-fits over longer distances. Those re-fits that have been identified so far were recognised mostly because of unusual forms or striking decorative motifs; the exceptions were systematic lithic re-fitting programmes that started from identical types of raw material, progressing to a reconstruction of the *chaîne opératoire* of a single nodule. The inter-site re-fits identified so far are listed below (Table 8.2).

While the excavator is correct in interpreting the Achtal Gravettian re-fits as the spatial disaggregation of stages of lithic production, it is not clear that the same group of people were responsible for moving around between the four different caves. Even if this were true, the social aspect of enchaining the places that a group occupied by material discard is an important part of the Achtal example. The excavator of the Gyrinos Lake faces the same chronological issue but maintains that there was

| SITES | DATE | MATERIAL | INTER-SITE DISTANCES |
|---|---|---|---|
| Achtal (4 caves) | Gravettian | flint | 5 km |
| Gyrinos Lake (6 sites) | Mesolithic – Neolithic | flint | 6 km |
| Aldenhovener Platte (2 sites) | LBK | flint | 0,5–3 km |
| Locmariaquer (3 sites) | Neolithic | decorated menhir | 5 km |
| Trent valley (2 sites) | Late Bronze Age | bronze sword | 5 km |
| Velsen fort (4 sites) | Early Roman | Samian bowls | 3–8 km |

*Table 8.2 Inter-site re-fits*

coeval occupation on at least some of the sites. Here, the sporadic nature of face-to-face contact prompted the emphasis of significant social relations by material means. Post-abandonment scavenging from some sites by later occupants cannot, however, be excluded. There can be no doubt of the deliberate nature of the enchained relations between people, places and decorated menhir fragments in the Breton Neolithic case – the largest example of fragment re-fitting yet identified in prehistoric Eurasia. Equally, the Ewart Park sword fragments – still missing a third part – could hardly have been lost on two different but inter-visible hilltops: this is a clear case of deposition of object parts by groups connected by enchained relations that were extended to the places and the objects. The links between fragments of rare Samian bowl types between the Velsen fort and three other non-Roman sites indicate an inter-ethnic dimension to fragment dispersion, whatever its precise mechanism. Only precise dating of the relevant deposits can distinguish between non-Roman scavenging after the abandonment of the fort and an enchained relationship based upon exchange of Samian bowl fragments between the Roman garrison and their non-Roman neighbours.

The second line of support for the premise concerns intra-site re-fits of fragments deposited in secure, closed contexts – defined here as graves and burnt houses in which there is a high degree of intentionality in the depositional practices. It is also worth looking critically at claims for intra-site re-fits of fragments deposited in pits and other semi-closed contexts, since, in some cases, the degree of closure is higher than in others. What we exclude from consideration here is the large number of

lithic re-fitting studies that can be interpreted to demonstrate enchained links between different spaces within the same site. The examples of intra-site re-fitting are as follows (Table 8.3).

This list of 23 sites is by no means complete but it is illustrative of the range of contexts between which re-fits have been made. The most secure examples linking mortuary to mortuary context, burnt house to burnt house or burnt house to mortuary context are still relatively few but are important for demonstrating the incidence of deliberate fragmentation and the re-use of fragments at the site level. It is also highly probable that the far larger total of cases of re-fitting fragments linking semi-closed contexts, mostly pits, also supports deliberate fragmentation practices rather than children's play or other mechanisms of fragment dispersion because the fragments were often found in deep, sealed layers of different pits. If deliberate dispersion following fragmentation is not accepted for these cases, there is a strong probability of at least the curation of material before dispersed discard, as at Windmill Hill. Moreover, deliberate fragmentation and dispersion is highly likely in such cases as the Jomon figurine re-fitting, based as they are on fragments forming part of highly structured ritual pit deposition. In summary, there is strong support for the fragmentation premise from examples of intra-site re-fitting.

We now turn to the cases of parts missing from settlements that have been totally excavated using good recovery methods. This study has been conducted using lithic re-fitting for several decades. Indeed, data on the *chaîne opératoire* have been used to estimate the quantities of blades detached from cores discarded in one place and

| SITES | DATE | MATERIAL | TYPE OF CONTEXT |
|---|---|---|---|
| Endrőd 119 | Early Neolithic | pottery | S (pits & unburnt houses) |
| Ovcharovo-Gorata | Middle Neolithic | figurines & altars | S (pits) |
| Dimini | Late Neolithic | shell rings | S-O (unburnt house – Open area) |
| Durankulak | Late Copper Age | pottery | C (house – grave) |
| Shlyakovsky | Late Copper Age | flint | C (grave – grave) |
| Dolnoslav | Final Copper Age | figurines | C-C (burnt houses) C-S (house – midden) C-O (house-open area) |
| Gubakút | LBK | pottery | S (pits) |
| Frimmersdorf 122 | LBK | pottery | S (pits) |
| Molino Casarotto | Middle Neolithic | pottery | S (unburnt houses) |
| Rocca di Rivoli | Late Neolithic | pottery | S (pits) |
| Windmill Hill | Earlier Neolithic | pottery | S (ditch levels) |
| Kilverstone | Earlier Neolithic | pottery/flints | S (pits) |
| Hekelingen | Late Neolithic | flint | S (unburnt houses) |
| Barnhouse | Late Neolithic | pottery | S (unburnt houses & pits) |
| Chalain Site 2C | Final Neolithic | pottery | S (unburnt houses) |
| Shakadô | Middle Jomon | figurines | C (sealed ritual pits) |
| Phylakopi | Late Bronze Age | pottery & figurines | S (rooms in shrines) |
| Itford Hill | Middle Bronze Age | pottery | C-S (grave – unburnt house) |
| Runnymede Bridge | Late Bronze Age | pottery | S-S, S-O (mostly between open areas) |
| Speckhau cemetery | Early Iron Age | pottery | C (contexts in tumuli) |
| Nørre Fjand | Early Iron Age | pottery | C (burnt houses) |
| Wyszogród Site 2A | Early Medieval | pottery | S (pits) |
| Awatovi | Western Pueblo | pottery | S (rooms in houses) |

Key to Types of Context (Tables 8.3 – 8.5): C – closed; S – semi-closed; O – open.

*Table 8.3 Intra-site re-fits from closed and semi-closed contexts*

exported to other places (Torrence 1982, Healan *et al.* 1983). For ceramics and other non-lithic finds classes, the identification of fragments with no re-fitting parts on such settlements prompts the fragmenterist's question "where are the missing parts?" If is possible to demonstrate the absence of conditions of poor preservation of fired clay objects, as well as practices that could have consumed large quantities of orphan sherds, such as manuring, which removes sherds from manure heaps, and the grinding-down of sherds for chamotte in further pottery production, a serious alternative answer to the question must be fragment dispersal away from the site. Given that information on manuring practices and the use of chamotte in pottery is readily available for most regions, we can generally rule in or rule out these causes of sherd destruction. The post-depositional conditions favouring sherd preservation vary in a structured way according to regional climate, with drier zones (Arizona, South East Bulgaria) favouring survival of ceramics (Arnold 1985).

The question arises as to whether the high precipitation in Atlantic Europe, combined with the generally poor firing conditions of pottery in British prehistory, are the only, or even the dominant, factors responsible for the absence of 80–85% of sherd bulk in four assemblages from totally excavated sites (Kilverstone Earlier Neolithic, Tremough Late Neolithic/Early Bronze Age, Runnymede Bridge Late Bronze Age and Tremough Romano-Cornish)? The contexts of preservation for these assemblages is rather varied (pits at Kilverstone, pits, ditches and open areas for Tremough and largely open areas for Runnymede Bridge), with open areas offering least protection for the ceramics. Yet the sealing of the Runnymede Bridge deposits by alluviation may well have provided a set of long-term contexts for good artifact preservation. Equally, the pits and ditches at the other sites have given preferential conditions for survival over the open areas, where pottery was rare. Thus, special pleading would be required to accept that the total missing sherd bulk was destroyed by post-depositional climatic factors. It begins to look probable that one of the factors in the diminution of these assemblages was the deliberate removal of sherds from the site, whether to local middening areas or to other sites further away.

The alternative practice involves bringing sherds from vessels already broken on other sites onto these sites. One of the most serious problems for re-fitting of sherds – often avoidable for lithic re-fitting studies - is the direction of movement of the fragments. This is an issue for orphan figurine fragments on a range of totally excavated sites in the Balkans. But whatever the direction of movement of the enchained fragment, the important point to be underlined is the movement of fragments between sites. Thus, the orphan fragment argument complements the

cases of inter-site fragment re-fitting without the precision of being able to identify both places of deposition. The logistics and sampling frameworks of this type of research requires further attention. Nonetheless, a number of examples can be presented that fit the criteria outlined above (Table 8.4).

This group of 20 sites or assemblages comprises a consistent set of examples where there is a high probability of orphan fragment dispersion either away from the site or onto the site. At three of these sites, there have been positive interpretations of the movement of sherds from previously fragmented vessels onto a site: the Sonoran Desert Site 205, where sherds were introduced for a special purpose (in this case, agave-processing); the Rocca di Rivoli, where single decorated sherds with no other vessel parts present have been seen as sherd enchainment to underline important social relations with material culture; and the Dolnoslav tell, where figurine fragments (and possibly potsherds) were brought onto the site in a process of accumulation, probably preceded by extensive middening. One approach to the direction of movement of orphan fragments is a reading of the Completeness Index (see above, Figs. 5.1 & 5.6) to differentiate places with a high proportion of very incomplete fragments from those places with large orphan fragments, perhaps including complete profiles. The former would probably support inward movement of fragments, the latter outward dispersion. However, this issue remains for future resolution.

There is another category of orphan fragments to consider – those found in closed contexts. Everything said about the movement of orphan fragments from settlements, with their wide range of sometimes problematic contexts, can be stated more definitively for the closed contexts boasting the deposition of once-whole but now incomplete objects. The examples listed below (Table 8.5) represent just a sample of the wide range of especially (but not only) mortuary contexts that have been investigated.

These examples provide strong evidence for the widespread nature of enchained relations between the mortuary domain and the land of the living in European prehistory. The two cases of metalwork deposits are also indicative of wider relations across the landscape, perhaps proving the norm in times/places where so-called 'scrap-metal' hoards – rich in orphan fragments – have been deposited.

The final form of evidence for the continued use of fragmented objects 'after the break' depends upon unambiguous evidence of further treatment of fragments on the fragment break, achieved only through detailed examination of assemblages of broken objects. This kind of investigation has been attempted on one figurine assemblage (Dolnoslav) and three groups of *Spondylus*

| SITES | DATE | MATERIAL | TYPE OF CONTEXT |
|---|---|---|---|
| Gyrinos Lake | Mesolithic / Neolithic | flint | S, O |
| Endrőd 119 | Early Neolithic | pottery | S |
| Dimini | Late Neolithic | shell rings | C, S, O |
| Parţa tell I | Late Neolithic | pottery | C |
| Ovcharovo | Copper Age | figurines | C, S, O |
| Goljamo Delchevo | Copper Age | figurines | C, S, O |
| Vinitsa | Copper Age | figurines | C, S, O |
| Sedlare | Late Copper Age | figurines | C, S, O |
| Dolnoslav | Final Copper Age | figurines | C, S, O |
| Rocca di Rivoli | Late Neolithic | pottery | S |
| Kilverstone | Earlier Neolithic | pottery/flints | S |
| Tremough | Late Neolithic/ Early Bronze Age | pottery | S, O |
| Runnymede Bridge | Late Bronze Age | pottery | S, O |
| Tremough | Romano-Cornish | pottery | S, O |
| AZ I:1:17 (Anasazi) | AD 11th | pottery | S, O |
| Shoofly Village, AZ | AD 12th–13th | pottery | S, O |
| Sonora Site 205 | Hokoham | pottery | sherds brought onto site |
| Little Egypt, Georgia | AD 16th–17th | pottery | S, O |

*Table 8.4 Orphan sherds from settlement contexts*

shell rings (Durankulak, Varna and Dimini). In each case, there is extensive evidence of further life stages after the deliberate breakage of the object. At Dolnoslav, it has been possible to sequence the changes to figurines into pre-fragmentation and post-fragmentation. Post-fragmentation activities comprise frequent secondary burning and decoration on breaks as well as traces of wear, often heavy, on breaks. The commonest post-fragmentation activity is the secondary burning traceable on 30 fragments. Fourteen fragments were crusted with different paint over a variety of different breaks – mostly using white paint but occasionally red paint and a

combination of red and white. Wear over figurine breaks can be demonstrated to have occurred in several cases, indicating long and/or intensive usage after the break. It is clear that fragmentation is by no stretch of the imagination the final phase of a figurine's life history.

Similar results have been found with the three *Spondylus* shell ring studies. At Durankulak and Varna, a dozen or so rings show possible evidence for involvement in different social practices after their breakage but before their eventual re-union as re-fitting fragments in the same grave and there is convincing evidence from three more rings – two from Durankulak, one from Varna. There is

| SITES | DATE | MATERIAL | TYPE OF CONTEXT |
|---|---|---|---|
| Durankulak cemetery | Late Neolithic – Late Copper Age | shell rings, figurines, pottery | C (grave) |
| Varna cemetery | Late Copper Age | shell rings, pottery | C (grave) |
| Tiszapolgár-Basatanya | Early – Middle Copper Age | pottery | C (graves) |
| Nissehøj | Middle Neolithic | pottery | S (courtyard outside megalith) |
| Knowth | Neolithic | decorated stones | C (burial mound) |
| Lockington | Late Neolithic / Early Bronze Age | pottery | C (grave) |
| Mušja Jama | Late Bronze Age | metalwork | C (karst sink-hole) |
| Trent Valley | Late Bronze Age | bronze sword | S (hilltop deposits) |
| Speckhau cemetery | Early Iron Age | pottery | C (contexts in tumuli) |

*Table 8.5 Orphan fragments from closed contexts*

no evidence for such a scenario until the Late Copper Age. The profusion of burning on the Dimini shell rings enables the investigation of biographical pathways through the establishment of micro-stratigraphies for each shell ring fragment. Five main events could have defined the life of a shell ring: the selection of natural features (termed 'natural'); breaking the ring; burning; polishing; and 'final' events (including wear, stress cracks and post-depositional deposits). In fact, eleven specific micro-stratigraphies were identified, which comprised rings with burning after the break(s), rings with a sequence of first break – burning – second break, rings with break(s) after the burning and unburnt rings. Two-thirds of burnt rings were broken after burning and many were broken twice – once before burning and once after, indicating a complex life history prior to final deposition. These results have two clear implications – that life 'after the break' was quite normal for a reasonably high proportion of the Dimini shell rings and that burning was only sometimes the final social act prior to, if not part of, deposition.

The biographical approach confirms the conclusions of the studies of orphan fragments, intra-site re-fits and inter-site re-fits. Moreover, this conclusion is supported by the limited experiments on fragmentation, which demonstrated the difficulties in achieving accidental breakage of replica pottery, figurines, altar-tables and pintaderas on surfaces that were frequent in European prehistory. We invite readers to refute the overall conclusion of these lines of argumentation, viz. that there is widespread and reliable evidence to support the premise of deliberate fragmentation of objects and their re-use 'after the break'. We believe that these data conclusively demonstrates the principal fragmentation premise. In the remaining part of this concluding chapter, we accept the premise at face value in an exploration of the implications of this result for Balkan prehistory, in the wider fields of European prehistory and in the most general perspectives of archaeology as a discipline vitally concerned with fragments.

## The implications of the premise

We are now ready to examine the many and varied implications of the fragmentation premise and relate them to the other results of our investigation of Balkan prehistoric societies. We have chosen to structure the main implications in four sections, relating to the nested socio-spatial contexts of (i) persons, (ii) households, (iii) corporate groups in the settlement context and (iv) regional settlement networks and beyond. Because the inter-relatedness of each context prevents discussion of, for example, all facets of personhood at the outset, readers will find cross-references to narrower socio-spatial contexts in subsequent commentary on broader contexts. We cannot ignore the fact that the smallest social action can presence past histories and social structures as much as present power structures and enchained relations.

## Personhood and the everyday

The dynamic nominalist approach has been proposed to understand the construction of identity through self-categorisation. In this approach, agency and structure come together in the formation of identities, which may be described as the process of self-description through categorization. This leads to the emergence of new kinds of persons at the same time as their materialization. We have approached the cognitive structures that would have informed persons' social practices through our categorical analysis of pottery, which highlighted notions of symmetry, precision, compartmentalisation, standardisation, as well as forms of appropriate and inappropriate behaviour. Different persons embodied and applied these notions and routine practices to a greater or lesser extent but their visual materialisation made them part of the habitus for everybody. Other factors, too, would have shaped personhood – not least the place and household into which a person was born, their age and gender trajectory and their relations with others. Just as the daughter of a community leader living at Durankulak in a large stone house would have enjoyed different life possibilities from the son of a fishing family in a small wattle-and-daub house on the Black Sea coast, we can expect a degree of variation in the life experiences of prehistoric persons, leading to the emergence of **different** people whose identities mapped onto the kinds of person that formed their society in a complex way. Some of these other factors are discussed when we consider the household and the settlement context (see below, pp. 187–196).

One aspect of personhood whose existence follows from the fragmentation premise is fractal personhood, in which a person emerges out of other people, places and things, materialising relations of enchainment with these other entities through broken as well as complete objects. While the use of complete objects for enchained exchange was re-discovered in recent Melanesian societies, fragment enchainment there was much rarer. The fundamental difference in Balkan prehistory was that different persons held different parts of the same object at the same time. We have seen, for example, how fragments of the same object linked the newly-dead and the land of the living as often as enchained links were maintained between households and between settlements. The conceptualisation of the fragments of broken things as non-human dividuals helps us to understand the relationship between individuals, seen as complete objects, and dividuals that has been so important since LiPuma (1998). In this way, the 'individual' aspect of personhood stood for the sum of all of the parts of the person's social identity or, as Binford (1971) put it, the social persona.

The mapping of Gamble's (2005) insights into enchainment and accumulation onto these concepts of personhood creates the following scheme for the formulation of our understandings of personhood, structure and social action (Table 8.6).

What is important about these pairs of relationships is that they are each in tension in everyday practices. So, for example, and *contra* Fowler (2004), representational logic (the ability of things to stand for people and vice versa) can occur in the same social formation as the fractal logic that pertains particularly to the emergence of things from people and vice versa. The changing relative significance of these contrasting practices, processes and principles forms a fundamental part of the long-term prehistoric narrative.

Each of our studies of prehistoric objects from the Balkan Peninsula has yielded insights into important principles of personhood that are materialised in these objects. The two studies of anthropomorphic figurines provide us with a diachronic perspective on some of the

| PRACTICE | Fragmentation | Consumption |
|---|---|---|
| PROCESS | Enchainment | Accumulation |
| PRINCIPLE OF PERSONHOOD | Fractal | Individual |
| FORM OF SOCIAL LOGIC | Fractal | Representational |

*Table 8.6 Relations between key entities*

changes in the ways that people created and represented personhood, although we do emphasise that other aspects of personhood were also important. The current relative chronology of the Hamangia group confirms the existence of two contrasting principles of personhood in both the Late Neolithic and Early – Middle Copper Age. The first principle defines the life-cycle of the Hamangia person in three stages: birth as an androgynous person who has grown out of both parents and their respective genders; a gradual shedding of one gender with personal growth and maturation to become a single-gendered person, presumably in adolescence; and a stage in old age when the return to androgyny marks the integration of all gendered identities of the life-course, with full androgyny realised with death. These three stages are materialised in the biographies of those figurines representing this principle of personhood. The complete Hamangia figurine is androgynous, with female traits such as breasts, swollen hips and pubic triangles and a male, phallic neck with testicles symbolised by breasts. Breakage of this form of figurine changes the gender of the figurine through its life course, with the phallic neck fragment representing the male identity and the torso/hips representing the female part. While the vast majority of fragmentary figurines were discarded in the settlements, where they were used in everyday negotiations over gender relations, a high proportion of complete figurines was found in graves, symbolising the integration of gendered identities in androgyny as the culmination of an age trajectory.

This principle of personhood was the dominant principle found in Hamangia communities, if we can believe the strong numerical preponderance of this figurine type. The subordinate principle concerned the creation of a non-androgynous personhood as material-ised in the few complete figurines that have been found in four variant forms: the so-called 'Thinkers' – gendered figures with intact heads on short necks, other forms of single-gender figurines and gender-neutral forms, including miniature shell *astragalus* figures with no obvious gender. The fragmentation chain of these figurines stood as a metaphor for the life course of Hamangia persons, introducing only one change in gender status – the loss of gender in broken heads and legs of gendered figurines, in contrast to the maintenance of gender in 'torso + hip' fragments. This principle of personhood is similar to that found in the Final Copper Age figurines from Dolnoslav and represents a marked difference from the androgynous concept that was dominant in Hamangia groups.

The Final Copper Age Dolnoslav figurines also comprise a dominant and a subordinate principle of personhood – but the two are the exact obverse of the Hamangia situation. The subordinate principle was based upon the rare complete androgynous figurines whose gender status would have changed with the fragmentation

symbolising the life course, just as in the Hamangia case. The life course of the main principle, however, comprised three stages: the birth of a person without gender characteristics; the gradual growth of one gender – predominantly female – during maturation; and the gradual fading of that single gender for post-menopausal women and older males. The large group of gender-neutral figurines materialised both younger and older persons, while the single-gender females and males stood for the mid-life period. The number of breaks and extent of wear on gender-neutral figurines would have differentiated younger from older persons. This concept of personhood is radically different from the dominant Hamangia principle in at least two ways: the emphasis on taking on gender as a characteristic of growth and personal maturation rather than on the inheritance of both genders from birth – nurture rather than nature? – and a higher value placed upon age.

The different, but equally fractal, ways in which fragmentation transformed age and gender in both Hamangia and the Final Copper Age contrasted with the consumption of figurines manifesting the full range of gendered identities in Hamangia pits and birthing huts as much as in Dolnoslav structures or middens – a practice reinforced by the final re-integration of gender and the summation of the life course in complete androgynous figurines placed in Hamangia graves.

The development of personhood as illuminated by figurines from the Black Sea Late Neolithic and Copper Age and the South Bulgarian Final Copper Age can be seen as two points in a longer cycle of Neolithic – Copper Age developments in the Balkan Peninsula – a cycle that we have approached through the categorical analysis of pottery and a comparison with other material media. How does Hamangia and Dolnoslav personhood relate to other long-term changes in the creation of personhood? In this discussion, we continue with figurines and then turn to some important parallel cognitive developments.

The other figurine assemblages in the Balkan Neolithic and Copper Age divide into those whose representations of personhood resemble the Hamangia cycle and those more similar to the Dolnoslav cycle. The only other period in the sequence when androgynous figurines are important is the earliest farming period, through the inter-regional distribution of standardised rod-head figurines with their phallic necks and female body traits. It is tempting to propose the Hamangia androgynous conception of personhood for the earliest farming communities in other parts of the Balkans, even though figurine deposition in graves was very limited indeed. The dual-gendered nature of rod-head figurines was reinforced through their manufacture in two lateral parts. Requiring precision to make a good fit between the two symmetrical halves, this technique enabled relatively easy lateral fragmentation, although such a breakage could not have changed the figurine's gender – an aim requiring horizontal snapping across a strong part of the object that was frequently achieved. As in Hamangia, the early farmers produced other forms of figurines that were at the same time more regionally differentiated and sometimes special in form, colour or material. These figurines manifested a subordinate, non-androgynous principle of personhood akin to the second Hamangia principle. Overall, figurines in the early faring period showed low indices of standardisation but rod-head figurine-making required right-left symmetry, some precision and a degree of compartmentalisation. It is interesting that the periods in which the androgynous aspect of personhood was underlined were the earliest phases when farming became the subsistence mainstay – whether in the Central – West Balkans and Hungary (Karanovo I–II, Starčevo – Körös – Criş) or the Black Sea coast (Hamangia) – a development linked to major changes in the kinds of person living on early farming sites.

The apparent relationship between an essential approach to personhood involving androgyny and its dominance among the earliest farming groups merits comment; after all, why should a form of personhood centred on gendered life-changes have been so significant? While there are few categorical differences between early farming groups and the later mature farmers, the tendency towards dispersed homestead settlement present everywhere except Thrace would have validated the importance of the family unit as well as its gender complementarity. On the Thracian tells, tensions between communal principles of personhood and family-based principles for nuclear families living in the small houses may have stimulated the adoption of gender complementarity for household rituals to counteract the effects of other examples of community-wide material culture (pottery and lithics).

In the early part of the mature farming period (Karanovo III), we can detect a steady increase in both the frequency and diversity of fired clay figurines (Todorova and Vajsov 1993, 196–215), showing a decrease in standardisation. The continuing local tradition of figurines based on the rod-head design (rod-heads perched on larger, often rectangular bodies) occurred alongside those images more akin to human body shapes with abstract arms, legs and sometimes heads, closer to the core figurine zone in that period – the Vinča group. The concept of personhood in the latter was based upon an age-gender cycle similar to the Dolnoslav example, with the gradual accretion and subsequent loss of single-gender characteristics through the life course. These contrasts in design and notions of personhood were thus rooted in both cultural geography and traditions; choice of figurine designs meant identification with a more local

tradition rather than an exotic aesthetic. This choice relied on left-right symmetry but, otherwise, low levels of precision, compartmentalisation and standardisation. There was an even stronger selection of the West Balkan figurine tradition in the Late Neolithic and Early Copper Age, leading to a consolidation of non-androgynous facets of personhood well before the Late Copper Age. This latter phase was characterised by a strong emphasis on the discourse of difference, not least in figurine making, where variety was created by sizes, shapes, materials, surface colours, decoration and contexts of use and deposition. Here, left-right symmetry is allied to increased precision of design, especially of decoration, and a strong degree of standardisation.

The production of pottery offered the widest range of possibilities for the manifestation of the key principles people used in categorisation. The aspect most significant for our understanding of personhood concerns the cognitive developments implicit in the creation of material forms (Keightley 1987). Not only would the people making pottery or macroblades have embodied the principles and practices of symmetry, precision, standardisation and compartmentalisation necessary to produce certain material forms but those seeing and using such forms would have become familiar with the materialisation of those principles, accepting them into their habitus. These four principles will be considered as evidence for cognitive complexity among the society making the range of vessels.

In the earliest farming period, despite the mastery of firing conditions necessary for painted wares and, later, dark burnished wares, there was a low level of cognitive complexity in the pottery. While precision was evident in the fine detail of the painting, standardisation of design was minimal, while compartmentalisation was limited to low feet and rarely lids. This changed dramatically in the mature farming period (Karanovo III), with the making of multi-part vessels, often using inversions to attach the legs and featuring varied handles and lugs and tight-fitting lids, betokening a major increase in compartmentalisation and precision. The incidence of lugs, handles and high feet decreased in the following Karanovo IV phase, although this was offset by the increased precision and standardisation of interior and exterior decoration. These trends were mirrored in the Hamangia ceramics associated with the figurines. Different contrasts were found in the Early Copper Age (Karanovo V) assemblage, with its big increase in the diversity of forms, showing lower levels of standardisation but an increase in precision and compartmentalisation, notably in lids and the new compartmentalised 360° design fields, which included decoration on the base as well as everywhere else. The diversification of forms continued in the Late Copper Age, with the Varna cemetery showing a particular emphasis on precision and compartmentalisation in horned stands and well-fitting lids and many sites showing standardised but very varied forms and a peak in use of 360° design fields – in short, indications of a second peak in cognitive complexity.

A survey of the long-term lithic sequence provides further comparanda for the figurines and the ceramics. In the earliest farming period, macro-blades made on high-quality raw materials showed signs of symmetrical design, precision of core preparation and pressure-flaking and consequent standardisation of blade production (Gatsov 2004; Gurova 2004; Tsonev 2004). Three aspects of compartmentalisation can be noted – the different stages of the *chaîne opératoire*, the creation of standarised inserts for composite tools and the differentiation of raw material qualities between exotic materials good enough for macro-blades and local flints and cherts good enough for smaller tools. In the mature farming period, lithic industries are less diversified, with few macro-blades on most settlements. The domination of new lithic assemblages by local raw materials (Gurova 2004) meant that exotic materials were special and rare. The majority of chipped stone tools made on local materials showed less symmetry, precision and standardisation than in the earlier macro-blade technology. In the Climax Copper Age, the extension of lithic techniques and embodied skills in this phase produced a wider range of chipped stone tools than ever before. At one extreme was the household making of end-scrapers for scraping skin in the yard – at the other, the 41cm-long superblade deposited in Grave 43 in the Varna cemetery, a blade so curved that it could never possibly have been used for practical activities. The superblade technology developed in this phase represents the apogee of lithic technology in Balkan prehistory, with evident characteristics of distinctive colour symbolism, symmetry, precision and standardisation. We can therefore specify peaks in cognitive complexity in lithic production in the earliest farming period and the Climax Copper Age, with a decline in the mature farming period.

The final material medium for consideration comprises metal objects. The few metal objects, and types of metal object, in the earliest farming phase (Kalicz 1992) betokened early, fumbling steps in metallurgy, using a new and relatively unfamiliar material. None of Keightley's concepts can be seen to apply to the awls, fish-hooks, beads and rings – with the possible exception of a symmetry that is basic to the design of most objects. In the mature farming period, there was a moderate increase in the number of known metal objects, especially at Topolnitsa (*p.c.* H. Todorova). Metal objects were still rare on most settlements but were a defining feature of some places, again differentiating local materials from the exotic and exhibiting a basic symmetry of design. In the Late Copper Age, the production of a wide range of

copper tools, ornaments and weapons relied upon technical innovations such as the melting and casting of copper, as well as alloying, smelting and soldering. Ottaway (2001) has underscored the fundamental role of compartmentalisation in the *chaîne opératoire* of metal production. It may be thought that the introduction of mould-based casting of essentially symmetrical copper objects marked the attainment of new heights of standardisation and precision. However, this technique led to a greater diversification, based partly on regional but also on communal choice (Schubert 1965, Jovanović 1971, Vulpe 1970, 1975 and Todorova 1981). The other principal metallurgical highlight of the Late Copper Age was the development of early goldworking as exemplified in the Varna cemetery (Éluère and Raub 1991). The twin techniques of gold wire and sheet gold led to the creation of an enormous range of ornament forms, most of which have never been paralleled anywhere else in the Balkan Late Copper Age. The Varna gold assemblage shows different tendencies from those of copper metallurgy: symmetry and precision in the ornaments but a marked lack of standardisation in their production. Balkan metallurgy indicates a gradual increase in cognitive complexity with time throughout the Neolithic and Copper Age.

A consideration of the cognitive complexity material-ised in these different forms indicates a complex and shifting pattern, with a sole chronological regularity – the peak of cultural complexity in all material media in the Climax Copper Age (Fig. 8.1). By contrast, the increase in cognitive complexity from the early farming period to that of the mature farmers shown for pottery, figurines and metallurgy was not shared in lithic, specifically macroblade, production. Comparison of these trends with the aspects of personhood – androgynous or non-androgynous – emphasised in the figurine sequence shows no clear relationship, perhaps indicating a disjunction between those aspects of personhood related to age and gender and those aspects formed through the embodiment of cognitive complexity. We shall return to this possible disjunction later.

For the moment, it is important to note that there is evidence for cognitive complexity in all three periods, whichever the preferred form of personhood emphasised in the figurine images. Those early farmers who made, used or admired symmetrical objects or precisely-made things gradually incorporated an approach to the material world that would set the scene for the creation of other kinds of precise or symmetrical objects in other material media. The more widespread these embodied attitudes, the more likely it was that new material forms would have been accepted as part of their social world if the innovative forms exhibited precision, symmetry, bright colours or brilliance. We can think of these attitudes to

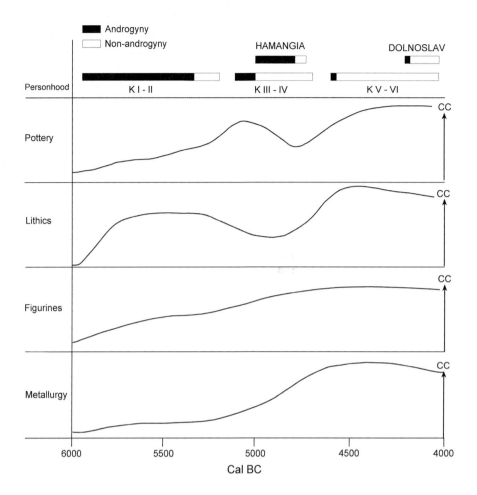

*Fig. 8.1 Schematic representation of cognitive complexity in later Balkan prehistory*

form in two ways – in terms of an incremental embodiment of skills and perceptions and in terms of cultural values. The spread of these skills and perceptions through a household or the wider settlement context increased the likelihood that they would be culturally valued. This would have influenced the development of such skills and perceptions in the household for each new generation, so that their embodiment would have occurred in increasing numbers of young persons, each one passing through similar learning stages as the others, with varying degrees of proficiency. Those with greater aptitudes towards the perception of symmetry, precision, compartmentalisation and standardisation may have been self-selecting for the next generation of craftspeople. Moreover, there is an interesting relationship between one of the key principles – compartmentalisation – and fragmentation practices. It is not only by abstract comparison that we can observe that the two terms stand in opposition to each other. Making a Karanovo III footed

bowl by the addition of four long clay legs to a pre-formed, inverted bowl was the exact reverse of the breakage of the complete footed vessel into bowl and legs – analogous to the breaking of a complete figurine into body and legs. A similar claim can be made for a composite flint tool and the fragment dispersion of a macro-blade into several blade segments. We would have expected a mutual and alternating influence of these two principles at a practical level of work on objects, rather than any mono-causal chain of thought.

Returning to personhood, the two aspects materialised in figurines may have had rather different relations to the development of self through the embodiment of incremental skills and perceptions. If the dominant form of Hamangia personhood is seen as essential, with androgyny present at birth and death, the dominant Late Copper Age form of personhood relied on the addition of single-gender characteristics during the life course – an incremental form of gendering. It is possible that, together with other gendered practices, the growth in cultural values of such embodied skills and perceptions may have modified approaches to personhood, leading to a gradual preference for created gender over essentialist principles.

The final aspect of the changes in material form in the long-term sequence concerns the way that objects teach people what to do with them (Wagner 1975; Chapman 2000, 29–30). Even though a tell Azmak ceramic lid resembled a carinated bowl, insiders would have known that it functioned as a lid and **not** as a bowl. It may have been taboo to place anything but sacred medicinal herbs on Varna horned stands. The differentiation of material forms would have led to disparities between appropriate and inappropriate forms of behaviour, though whether or not Karanovo I bone spoons had to be held in the right hand, as an early example of the bias against left-handers, cannot yet be definitively stated (!). The transmission of these values-in-practice would have reinforced the correctness of certain acts and actions, in turn reflecting upon the kind of person who would know what to do and what not to do in specific contexts. Refusal to perform appropriate actions would have been a normal response among many persons- perhaps mostly children – but even rejection of standards would have reinforced what was defined as deviant and acceptable action. In this way, the diversified embodiment of cultural values of everyday behaviour would have been sustained by the increasingly wide range of material forms that peopled everyday lives in the Neolithic and Copper Age.

We have identified three aspects of personhood from our studies of a variety of material forms – age-gender principles governing the life course, the incremental embodied skills and perceptions forming an approach to material forms, and the development of discrimination between appropriate and inappropriate forms of action in relation to those material forms. It will also be informative to consider other important aspects of personhood, such as the wider context of enchained relations between the person, other persons, places and things, in the following sections. We now turn to the household context to examine the dialectic of everyday dwelling practices and the categorisation principles used to materialise changing social structures.

## The household context

Houses and households have been central to many debates in Balkan prehistory, whether as the embodiment of symbolic principles for living (Hodder 1990), as living entities enfolding social practices (Bailey 1990), as the basic decision-making unit for economic and social practices (Tringham and Krstić 1990), as places for gendered encounters (Tringham 1991), as the material framework structuring settlement space (Chapman 1989, 1990; Kotsakis 2001) or, most recently, as places incorporating relations of a new kind typical of Neolithic lifeways (Jones, A. 2005). Here, insights from these approaches are synthesised in an attempt to view the house as an equal agent in fractal relationships, from which both persons and households reflexively emerged in processes that both created and materialised cultural values.

It is difficult to identify the persons living in houses but there is a widespread presumption (Tringham 1991, 1994; Bailey 1990) that, at most stages of their biography, households would have contained the elderly, the middle-aged and children of both genders. Living together and interacting much of the time, the persons in their variety of combinations – perhaps never the same in two houses or over long periods of time in a single household - would have created the personality of their own house, at the same time developing their own forms of personhood according to household and wider, corporate principles. But the ways in which these principles of personhood were worked out in daily practice were strongly grounded in household practices and relationships, only some of which required materialisation. It was largely out of the household setting that gendered (in)dividuals emerged through reiterated practices of cultural transmission.

The construction of the average two-roomed prehistoric house required considerable communal labour, estimated to be comparable to that needed to build a small megalithic tomb of Western European type. The improbability of a household erecting their house unaided sets house construction within a broader communal framework of shared labour that created and maintained wide social relations. In a fractal perspective, where emergent properties are vital, the house would have grown out of the wider group of persons as an objectification of both their dividual identities and their combined social *personae*. With the building of the house, an important aspect of the inhabitants' continuing biographical pathways would have been their growing out of the house, which sustained them in multiple social and physical ways but, especially, through the framing of the most intimate of their social relations and daily practices. The life courses of the inhabitants could rarely have been separate from that of the house where they spent much of their lives.

Just as with people and objects, the sharing of the same principles of categorisation and cultural order between houses and other material media provided the basis for fractal relations, in the course of which objects grew out of houses and vice versa. Those aspects of geometric order shared between houses and objects – precision, symmetry and compartmentalisation – are therefore of great importance in creating wider, mutually reinforcing perceptions of valued cultural order. There are many examples in typical timber-framed houses. The location of most entrances symmetrical to whichever wall they cut through – whether the gable end (*e.g.* Dimini House N; Hourmouziades 1979) or the long wall (Dolnoslav Structure B1: Raduntcheva 1996) – created a left-right, back-front symmetry upon entry that could have been drawn upon to frame social relations and action inside the house. The carpentry of the main posts and beams of the house involved precision both in their cutting and assembling, while the same was true of the coppiced wattling and other minor timbers. The division of the interior house space into rooms and other subdivisions revealed varying degrees of compartmentalisation, whether vertical or horizontal. Finally, the standardisation of houses can be seen at many sites (*e.g.*, Karanovo I houses at Karanovo; Hiller and Nikolov 1997) through markedly similar ratios of length: width, number of rooms and layout of internal fittings. While most of the measures of spatial order characterising these houses work at the settlement level (see below, pp. 190–191), others apply to individual houses (Chapman 1989; 1990). The regularities in the lengths and widths of houses at sites such as Lepenski Vir, Targovishte, Radingrad and Poljanitsa (Chapman 1989, Fig. 12), indicate the time and effort spent on the careful reproduction of traditional design, based upon ancestral practices materialised in the successive phases of dwelling on the tell. Whatever the details of house construction, there is a long-term continuity in these fundamental principles of geometric order which, in a fractal perspective, cannot but have exerted a strong influence on the persons growing out of these houses.

We should not over-stress the degree of standardisation in houses, any more than in objects: diachronic differences in size, shape, building techniques and construction materials are well attested (Bailey 2000). However, houses in many different social contexts shared much at the level of overall design principles. In contrast to the typically irregular or sub-circular form of working pits or the oval or circular shapes of settlements, houses were normally rectangular, whether built of stone, as on the Durankulak tell and at Dimini, or of wattle-and-daub, as at most settlements. The principle of rectangularity contrasts with the long-lived principle of circularity governing the design of monuments and houses in the Neolithic, Bronze Age and Iron Age of Britain (Bradley 1998, Part II). The regularity of a rectangular internal space allowed further regularity in spatial sub-divisions, partly mediated by the upright posts within the house. The rectilinear design principle also allowed for the possibility of adding extra rectangular rooms – a potential rarely utilised until the Climax Copper Age (Poljanitsa and Ovcharovo; Todorova 1982) or the Hungarian Late Neolithic (Gorzsa; Horváth 1987). Houses were also vertically differentiated from all other structures in their settlement, exceeding the height

of any palisades and fences so as to be clearly visible from within as well as outside the settlement. The emphasis on the vertical and visibility was especially marked in the case of two-storey constructions (*e.g.* on the Csőszhalom tell; Raczky *et al.* 2002), which also allowed a vertical as well as the more usual horizontal differentiation of spatial practices. Moreover, the house provided a counterpoint of order and tidiness to the disorder of the external spaces of a typical prehistoric site, where walking over a surface with exposed sharp ends of animal bones or sherds could have been a dangerous enterprise. In short, the house emerged from, and was consistent with, a geometric logic with which we are already familiar in our studies of objects. This logic was embodied in the many examples of miniature house models known from the Balkan Peninsula and Eastern Europe, ranging from the simple one-roomed models typical of Thessaly (Toufexis and Skafida 1998) to the more elaborate images of structures from Tripolye – Cucuteni (Videiko 2004).

The everyday practices of people living in houses and visiting other houses led to a wide variety of relations, some of which were materialised and made visible through deposition. At Late Neolithic Dimini, for example, the homogeneity of painted wares, lithics and animal bones deposited in most households contrasted strongly with the variable deposition of *Spondylus* shell rings, both in terms of their frequency and shell ring biographies. The basic pattern of shell ring fragments re-fitted between contexts and orphan shell ring fragments fits the notion of activities cross-cutting household areas proposed by Souvatzi rather than the domestic self-sufficiency of the Hourmouziades model. Similar inter-household dispersion of re-fitting fragments – this time of fired clay figurines – was found at tell Dolnoslav, where the picture of households showed persons making whole figurines embodying different stages of their life course, with an increasing likelihood of figurine wear, re-use and fragmentation with increasing age. In a fractal perspective, figurines were born into different households, emerging out of the houses and their occupants. The accumulation of figurine collections in and by each household told the story of the persons of that household and perhaps, following Biehl (2003), addressed an additional narrative of the household's own biography. In turn, this materialisation of persons created different kinds of person through their embodiment in different forms and through the highly contrasting kinds of fragmentation affecting different figurines. The most important enchained relations between persons living in separate households were mediated by re-fitting figurine fragments deposited in different houses; the three examples known from Dolnoslav exhibited three different principles of opposition. The fragmentation of pieces that later could be re-fitted emerged out of these enchained relations between households.

The final stage of some Neolithic, and many more Copper Age, houses was their deliberate destruction by fire, in some cases as a consequence of the death of a household or village leader. The variable accumulation of objects for inclusion in such burnt houses materialised the sum total of enchained relations out of which the leader, and/or their family, had emerged through their life course. Both the emotions spilling over from bereavement and the memories of the person who was lost to the household found potent symbolic evocation in the dramatic, transformative ceremony of house burning, out of which emerged a distinctive ancestral identity for the newly-dead and the beginnings of a healing process for the ruptured society. Moreover, added symbolic value emerged out of the memory of the specific forms of material culture burnt with the house – memories to be overlain on similar material forms to be made and used in different contexts in the future.

Needless to say, the visual spectacle of a house burning ceremony would not have been restricted to the affected household but would have symbolised the transformation of a community-wide nexus of enchained relations. It is to the wider community level that we now turn.

## The settlement – community and corporate groups

There was a complex relationship between community structure and fractal aspects of personhood, often mediated by the household. Community-level relations were based upon relationships of sociality and conviviality between people from different houses. As Peter Wilson (1988) has observed, to the extent that houses were independent spaces excluding other people, domestic architecture created neighbours and the concomitant need to renew social relations with neighbours through hospitality. This notion identifies one type of enchainment as the everyday, face-to-face practice of exchange between neighbouring households, whether of household products or the secondary movement of exotic items. Although Dalla Riva (2003) has maintained that, except for food exchange, many face-to-face interactions within a settlement do not require validation by material tokens, the fractal perspective suggests that (in)dividual persons emerged precisely out of face-to-face contacts and exchanges within the community, just as fractal objects emerged out of the quotidian enchainment of (in)dividuals.

Whatever the size, permanence and structure of communities living in Neolithic and Copper Age settlements, the community represented something more than the total of fractal relationships emerging within its boundaries. This 'something more' is, in the first place, an integrated whole – the symbol of a supra-household and trans-generational entity, materialised through accumulation. Moreover, the community guaranteed a shared identity for its members that anchored a person in a moral and juridical framework: a statement that a certain woman was born in the village of 'Rakitovo' presenced relationships with other known and respected members of that community and validated her social identity. In addition, the social reproduction of both persons and individual households was inextricably linked to the community as a whole because it was at the community level that the values of social practices and the principles pertaining to cultural order were underwritten and likewise reproduced. Finally, it was the social structure of the community as a whole that supported the level of institutionalisation of limited interest groups, in some cases setting limits on the extent of possible social differentiation.

The personal identities based upon membership of a community emerged out of the settlement's specific qualities and characteristics. The relative importance of the house and the overall community depended initially on its settlement context. For an extended family living in an isolated homestead, the house was the central focus of identity as symbol and practice – far more so than for a household in a village community. In the former, there were tensions between the potential to create the household's particular local set of material culture and the need to exchange appropriate objects betokening personal identities and membership of the breeding network linking the household to another 30 or 40 homesteads. The spatial dispersal of labour into enchained homesteads constrained the intensified production of relations-and-things. In the village, the multiplication of identical elements (house, oven, storage area, sleeping platform) gave the settlement a coherence that reinforced the identities of each separate household. It also framed the enchained relations within and between households in a consistent way, supporting communally accepted principles of personhood and identity in the wider landscape.

The settlements that have attracted archaeologists have largely been the successful, long-lived places where continuity of dwelling has resulted in accumulations of material on flat sites or mounds. But, alongside the 'successful' sites, there were many shorter-term lowland or upland sites that did not develop into tells and upland seasonal sites (Chapman 1997a; Kotsakis 2005). The place that any person lived in and especially the size of co-residential group would have been a strong influence on their sociality and the development and nature of their identity in other places (Chapman 1988a; 1989). Just as it is inconceivable that a settlement mound could have developed without long-term commitment to place from a village-based community (Chapman, in press b), so the place-based identities of people from long-established tells would have been more elaborated and deep-rooted than for those people dwelling in smaller and/or less permanent sites with less stable breeding networks, more affected by random demographic fluctuations. The twin poles of permanence and flux lay at the heart of personal and communal identity. Put at its simplest, living on an isolated homestead would have offered individuals far more possibilities for incorporation of personal characteristics into personhood than would living on a tell, with its strong communal life, identities and tensions.

The principles of cultural order, together with the cultural values given to them, were strongly expressed at the community level in terms of settlement coherence – the outgrowth of principles of planning and practices of spatial order. The vast majority of horizontal settlements betrayed few signs of deliberate planning in terms of following a pre-agreed template of order. The exceptions show that the lack of ordering principle was not the result of a lack of constraint on expansion! In this sense, the rectangularity of the timber-framed house stood in contrast to the layout of other settlement features and the absence of geometric planning on most flat sites. The most obvious exception was the concentric principle used to structure Tripolye settlements such as Kolomiishchina and Talljanky (Videiko 1996): even if the number of concentric rings of houses was unknown at the outset, there was a socially accepted way of adding houses to the settlement core. The large scale of recent motorway rescue excavations has provided excellent opportunities for the examination of settlement planning but the grid pattern of houses built along parallel paths, recognised in geophysical survey of Vinča sites such as Grivac (McPherron and Srejović 1971), is apparently still a rarity on horizontal sites. Instead, a loose agglomeration of household clusters represented the main ordering principle in the 30 ha. excavated at the horizontal site of Polgár-Csőszhalom (Raczky *et al.* 2002).

Tells were a different matter. The initial size restrictions and diminishing occupation size with vertical growth defined ideal conditions for pre-determined planning of house layouts. While this choice produced settlement plans of remarkable geometric order on a few tells (especially Polyanitsa and Ovcharovo; Todorova 1982), many other tell communities rejected the geometric option in favour of loose structuring that resembled the spatial structuring found on nearby horizontal sites (*e.g.* Vinča-Belo Brdo: Chapman 1989). The strict separation between tells and off-tell places has been broken down through the discovery of off-tell activities and buildings when looked for (*e.g.* Podgoritsa, Bailey *et al.* 1998; Omurtag, Gaydarska *et al.* 2005). The geometric order of some tells was differentiated at the level of houses, as well as interior

and exterior access patterns (Chapman 1990). Two patterns were discerned on completely excavated tells. Pattern A, found at Radingrad and Targovishte, revealed simple 1- to 3-room houses, with one entrance and one oven and concomitantly simple access pathways throughout the occupations. In the contrasting Pattern B, found at Poljanitsa and Ovcharovo, houses had up to 11 rooms, often with multiple entrances and several ovens; other differences include the very high ratios of built to unbuilt (BUB) space which increased with time, cyclical patterns through time in house dimensions (length and width) and markedly similar minimum inter-house spacing (for explanation of terms and methods, see Chapman 1989, 1990). It was inferred that the practices that produced Pattern B were indicative of both spatial and social complexity of the kind not normally found on tells, based upon the differentiation of house space, with larger families controlling access to rooms more carefully and the development of specialised uses of rooms – for hospitality, domestic ritual, food preparation, food storage, tool making and sleeping. But even the Pattern A social practices betoken a more developed sense of spatial coherence and continuity over time than we have found on horizontal sites. All of Keightley's four principles of symmetry, precision, compartmentalisation and standardisation can be readily identified in the village planning and house construction of Copper Age tells.

There was another fundamental division for tell-dwellers, arising out of the high BUB ratios – the impossibility of locating certain activities on a tell occupation surface full of houses. The list of activities is long and includes the growing of legumes or herbs in a garden, the herding of sheep or cattle, the organisation of outdoor rituals or dances, the smelting of copper ores or the firing of ceramics. In principle, all of these activities were sustainable within even a planned open village such as Grivac. But, for tell-dwellers, there were strong spatial associations between appropriate and inappropriate practices, ensuring the ubiquity of off-tell activities and structuring everyday life in particular ways. What did all these differences mean for social relations, personhood and social categorisation on tells and flat sites?

The combination on certain tells of ordered village space, carefully observed regularities in both the location of houses and their dimensions and the division between what was possible and impossible on the tell itself placed strong constraints upon social practices, leading to a well-developed sense of the forms of appropriate and inappropriate behaviour. The perception of geometric order in the built environment supported similar insights into the production of objects. Traditional practices were built into the fabric of tell villages, producing certain kinds of persons who probably would have found living in a less ordered horizontal settlement disorienting and bewildering. The social relations between neighbours in densely packed villages must also have been subject to positive inducements to hospitality as well as negative constraints on potential 'polluting' behaviour, such as loud music, smelly refuse and violence. But did tell lifeways really provide a cocoon of safe, predictable social relations for the residents?

The nucleation of people in such a village had two main positive effects: the availability of communal childcare and other shared labour and an intensity of social interaction found but sporadically on dispersed homesteads. The downside was the frequency of disputes within the household and between neighbours. The forager's strategy of mobility for dealing with disputes was useful but the options were limited – to move to another densely packed tell with fewer relatives and friends or to live in an off-tell hut and join in tell activities less frequently. Given the moral and political links between persons and their settlement of origin, moving off into unknown areas would have been a high-risk response. If a group of people collectively rejected high dispute levels, budding-off to found another settlement would have led to the reproduction of geometric order on a smaller scale on what was, at first and for some time, a flat site. The general point is that all of the advantages and drawbacks of life in a nucleated settlement (Chapman 1988a) were concentrated under tell conditions, which appears to have limited the scope for (in)dividual agency. It will be interesting to investigate the messages from the objects of the Neolithic and Copper Age in comparison with those principles clearly underlying the changing versions of the built environment.

The horizontal settlements of the Early Neolithic at Rakitovo and Chavdarova Cheshma are marked by organic growth with little indication of planned design. The houses are both rectangular and trapezoidal, with considerable variation in size (Raduntcheva *et. al.* 2002, Abb. 1–2) but the quality of space between houses meant few constraints on social practices and the absence of a strongly polarised set of appropriate and inappropriate practices. One regularity in practice was the deposition of painted fine wares and unpainted medium fine and coarse wares in every household context at Rakitovo. The ubiquity of both wares indicates a unified communal identity within the settlement, also noted at the regional level. The difference in colour, brightness and decorational complexity between painted and unpainted wares could have been used to support a binary categorisation at the household and settlement levels that may well have been gender-related through task differentiation. The spread of dark burnished fine wares across the southern Balkans in the late phase of the early farming period (Chapman 1981, 33–39) replicated the basic division of early farmers' material culture between things either rooted in local

tradition, such as painted wares, or enshrined in an exotic aesthetic, *viz.*, the dark burnished wares. A preference for one fine ware rather than the other shaped personal as much as more inclusive identities, perhaps leading to the emergence of a dual social structure of two corporate groups in each community.

The virtual disappearance of painted wares at the start of the mature farming period (Karanovo III) was perhaps a sign of the decisive strengthening of one corporate group over the other. Further support for a hierarchical form of dual structure came from the categorical analysis of Karanovo IV ceramics, with its stronger emphasis on oppositional categorisation incorporated into strict rules on form and decoration and on form and colour contrasts. However, the oppositional principle was not strongly supported in the increasingly common non-tell settlements in this phase, where the main contrast in spatial order was between rectangularity of houses and less organised pits and working areas, with no obvious exclusion of social practices from the core of occupation.

Moreover, whatever categorisational contrasts were found in material culture in the Neolithic would have been softened by the everyday association of different persons with the contrasting types of figurines, pottery and stone tools, leading to the reinforcement of identities created through the emergence of these objects out of people. It is likely that these varied associations led to the gradual increase of cross-cutting relationships in the Neolithic that built on gender differences but were not exclusively related to them. The expectation would be that the greater the emphasis on cross-cutting relations rather than hierarchical or oppositional categorisation, the more important would enchained relations based upon fractal personhood have become; conversely, the individual aspect of personhood would have been favoured through oppositional categorisation principles. Thus, in the Neolithic, the existence of both cross-cutting and oppositional categories led to tensions between fractal and individual means of creating personhood, mediated by marked differences between the local and the exotic, the quotidian and the special. Tell dwelling reinforced the ancestral basis for personhood and reinforced the spatial division between tell and off-tell with social practices limited to one or other zone. By contrast, reinforcement of the differences in social practices through spatial differentiation was much weaker on horizontal sites.

In the Copper Age, the messages from the objects and from the built environment were curiously contradictory. Both villages, houses and their respective patterns of access embodied geometric order and Keightley's qualities of symmetry, precision and compartmentalisation to a high degree, creating stronger constraints upon social practices than in the Neolithic. But, in Copper Age material forms in all media, the explosion of diversity and differentiation threatened the principle of standardisation which was not so strongly expressed in the built environment as the other geometric principles, thus creating tensions with the continued embodiment of symmetry, precision and compartmentalisation. The paucity of rules governing aspects of Copper Age ceramic production, allowing, for example, the placement of any decorational style on any vessel form, emphasised the limits on the representation of principles of integration – perhaps a temporary response to the inherent tensions between diversity and integration. What was widespread was the cross-cutting method of categorisation, which celebrated and reinforced diversity. The significance of the cross-cutting principle of categorisation underlined the fractal aspect of personhood, which was expressed in the multiple combinations of persons in a diversity of limited interest groups. The proliferation of limited interest groups, whether household units, kinship groups, occupational units or age-sets, was a principal aspect of Copper Age identity. While persons grew out of these groups, the increasingly complex ceramic assemblages grew out of these new identities through their material-isation. It is interesting that it was only at Varna – the place of greatest material differences between mortuary sets – that there were signs of the hierarchical structures which were one way to resolve issues of how to integrate societies characterised by increasing complexity and diversity. The tensions between cross-cutting and oppositional categories found in the Neolithic continued in the Climax Copper Age, leading to further tensions between fractal and individual means of creating personhood. To the extent that increasing numbers of Copper Age persons lived on tells, the influence of a dwelling perspective based upon geometric order and a spatially-reinforced segregation between appropriate and inappropriate behaviour were strong influences on personhood, producing different kinds of persons from those in the earliest farming period.

One key element of community structure concerns the summary statements made by a community about itself. We have studied two examples of this form of communication – the Durankulak cemetery and the destruction deposits of the burnt structures and middens at tell Dolnoslav. These object-rich places betoken the reflexive relations between the processes of enchainment and accumulation – both the (in)dividual artifact enchained to persons, things and places within and outside the place of deposition and the material legacy of accumulation that requires negotiation for the community to move on. We begin with the mortuary zone.

Many aspects of fractal relations are characteristic of the mortuary domain – the arena for the most public display of the deepest human emotions, as well as for the most public negotiation of tensions between the processes

of enchainment and accumulation, remembrance and forgetting. The commitment of a community to a mortuary zone separate from their settlement creates a new distance between the living and the dead as much as the necessity to bridge that gap – akin to the importance of hospitality between neighbours separated by house walls. The cross-citation of settlement and cemetery has been a major theme in archaeology, with, for example, analogies between the forms of the houses of the living and the dead (Hodder 1994), the introduction of shared cosmological principles into each (Parker Pearson and Richards 1994) and the shared principle of circularity (Bradley 1998). Olivier's (1999) illuminating study of the rich Early Iron Age Hochdorf burial shows how multiple timescales were vital for the preparation of the grave goods and the monumental barrow that linked the mortuary and the domestic arenas. But these studies miss an important effect of the fractal principle that unites the two arenas even more closely – the notion that the cemetery as place grew out of the places familiar to the community just as the persons buried there grew out of other persons, things and places. The example of Durankulak will be used to support this facet of (in)dividual relationships.

In the Durankulak complex, the earliest settlement, dated to the local Late Neolithic, was located on the shore of the lagoon. The absence of traces of above-ground houses suggests that occupation may have been intermittent but repeated. The principal remains were the large pits, some containing post-holes for some form of temporary shelter, and with several containing production débitage and the remains of consumption episodes. Worn figurine fragments and the post-cranial bones of the steppe ass were also placed in pits together with many decorated sherds. The residues in the pits possessed mnemonic qualities because of the social relations embodied in the practices that created them. At the same time, the first few graves were dug in a location less than 250m from the settlement, also on the shore of the lagoon. The outgrowth of the burial place from the settlement can be seen in the excavation of pits of similar depths into the same kind of soil, the deposition of similar decorated ceramics as orphan sherds and the complementary offerings of steppe ass crania. The greater regularity of the usually rectangular graves was perhaps an echo of the rectangular form of the timber-framed houses that Early Hamangia communities built in their longer-term settlements. The existence of a separate mortuary domain suggests the start of an uncoupling of ritual practices from their traditional household context.

In the Late Hamangia phase, a dramatic change in settlement location occurred, with the movement of the site to one of the very few islands on the Black Sea coast (for details, see Chapman *et al.*, in press). This rocky island was the source of building material for large, permanent drystone-walled houses that have been found from the earliest occupation levels on the island (Todorova 1997) and continued as the main house form until the end of the Late Copper Age occupation (Boyadžiev 2004). This change marks a seismic symbolic shift from small, short-term, wattle and daub structures and pits on the soft shoreline to large, permanent, stone-built houses on the rocky island. In contrast, the cemetery on the shore showed continuity in use, with grave forms mostly emerging out of the earlier burial rites but with an important addition – the construction of grave chambers or roofs using the same stones from the island that were used to build houses. Drystone graves formed an increasing proportion of the graves from the Late Hamangia into the Late Copper Age, echoing the sense of permanence that marked dwelling on the island. Enchained relations between the land of the living and the domain of the dead have been demonstrated by the re-fitting of sherds from the same vessel from a grave and a house on the island (see above, p. 95–96). Although no re-fitting programme has yet been established to connect the many other orphan sherds from graves to their missing fragments, the widespread extent of such fractal relations cannot be in doubt. This is confirmed by the placing of nine orphan figurine fragments in Hamangia III graves, as well as by the results of the re-fitting programme of *Spondylus* shell rings at Durankulak. Here, the discovery of orphan ring fragments in all phases of the cemetery's use is underlined by a diachronic change, with increasing proportions of incomplete ring deposition with time but with continuing deposition of complete rings. It would seem that two competing practices were in tension – the custom of integrating the totality of relations embodied in the object deposited in the mortuary domain and the practice of emphasising the partible nature of the relationship between the newly-dead and the living by keeping ring fragments in separate contexts. There is some unconfirmed evidence for the practice of re-uniting fragments of long-since broken rings in some Durankulak graves after different life courses experienced by each fragment. If confirmed, this may have been a fractal version of the practice at Hamangia funerals of re-establishing androgynous personhood in the transition from newly-dead to ancestor through the deposition of complete dual-gender figurines. Such a practice was transformed in the Late Copper Age into the deposition of gender-neutral images – complete or fragmentary – in either burnt houses (Dolnoslav) or graves (Durankulak). The very separation and diversification of ritual practices in the mortuary domain from household rituals could explain the importance of enchained relations in re-integrating the different domains.

The mortuary arena stimulated each household, in the light of their fractal relations with the newly-dead, to make decisions about which objects to bring to the grave and which to leave at home. Much of the variability in the incidence of grave goods may well have related to this practice, since potential grave goods evoked the memories of past people, places and things, participating in their history and ancestral qualities as well as their places of origin and routes to the cemetery. While fragments of locally produced ceramics may well have materialised very local histories and everyday enchained links, exotic marine shell fragments were more likely to have recapitulated long-distance relationships and the political histories of entire corporate groups. The longer the Durankulak community dug graves for the newly-dead by the shore of the lagoon, with households placing appropriate grave goods in often surprising quantities, the more unlikely – perhaps even impossible – it became to choose **another** place for mortuary ceremonies. The cumulative significance of the Durankulak cemetery was rooted in the value of the place and the objects deposited there, as well as the fame of the persons buried there and the enchained biographies of all three fractally-related elements – people, objects and place.

Different things were happening ten or more generations later at Dolnoslav, where there was a long-running tension between the everyday scale of exchange, use and deposition of material culture and the three massive consumption events defining the beginning, the late phase and the end of Final Copper Age activities on the tell. The tension between what some would unhelpfully term 'profane' and 'sacred' was mediated by the fact that it was the products of everyday life, perhaps including seasonal meetings at the tell, that were regularly curated in preparation for the grand events of consumption – a pair of figurine legs here, a burnt end-scraper there or a carinated bowl over there. We can see how the results of small-scale enchained relations within and between households built up through the passage of social time to create the basis for the large-scale processes of accumulation that marked critical events in the life history of the site. Although we cannot glimpse in isolation the groups of things emerging out of enchained ties in the same way that we can define (in)dividual graves at Durankulak, the cumulative result of curation was not dissimilar. The dense distribution of pottery in the earliest structure – the central platform – was matched by the finds densities in the three burnt houses sealed by Midden D3 and greatly exceeded by the objects placed in the three middens and the 25 structures at the end of the occupation.

We can observe the signs of curation on objects in two ways: the re-fitted figurine fragments found in different phases of occupation and the treatment of figurines after the break. Two joins have been found to link Phases A and C, with one re-fit between fragments deposited in Phases B and C. While there were no joins between buildings sealed by midden D3 and other buildings, nor between D3 and the three other middens, there were two re-fits linking midden D3 and Phase 3 buildings and one re-fit between a building under D3 and an open area. The joins between these stratified figurine fragments indicate the division of the life course of a broken figurine, one part for rapid deposition, the other for a new lease of life in another context, as a more mature, more fragmented figurine. The occurrence of post-fragmentation treatment on as many as 1/3 of all broken figurines shows the importance of the curation of individual figurines through special treatment (wear, crusting of paint and/or burning) as part of an elaborated life history.

These communal acts of foundation and closure were also enchained to persons not living at Dolnoslav, who brought their own curated things and fragments of things made in other places to the tell for ceremonial deposition. The large number of orphan figurine fragments in the final deposition, as well as the numerous orphan sherds previously identified (Chapman 2000, 58–9 and Fig. 3.1), indicate either fragment dispersion away from Dolnoslav or fragment concentration onto the tell. The overwhelming evidence for accumulation processes at Dolnoslav would perhaps support the latter, with numbers of people from other sites enchaining their own sites and objects to the Dolnoslav centre through the deposition of fragments of figurines whose missing parts were in these persons' homes. The fact that, even after re-fitting, most conjoint figurines still lacked a part suggests that these missing parts were indeed taken off the tell in return. This interpretation suggests that, like Durankulak, Dolnoslav was a local centre at the heart of its enchained network, with deposition of curated objects sustaining the central process of accumulation.

In addition to their prominent role in these acts of consumption, figurines manifested the complexity of Final Copper Age society by at least five different categorisational schemes – their age-sex identity, their scale of completeness, from complete to highly fragmentary, the body part represented, their left – right siddeness and their position on the vertical (up-down) scale. These five schemes make the best sense if we think of figurines as representations of the life cycle of persons – not as individuals (an interpretation finally rejected by Bailey 2005) but as categories of persons framed in multi-dimensional social contexts.

Thus a figurine's age-sex identity would delineate a phase in the communally-defined cycle of three stages – younger unsexed – gendered – older unsexed. The social practices in the household would provide the figurine with life experiences consistent with the various categories of person living there. While an unsexed figurine would remain unsexed throughout their lives, a female figurine may have maintained its sexual identity through multiple breaks or had it divided into two parts – sexed and unsexed – at the first fragmentation. The predominance of unsexed figurines in the complete examples and in deposition in the middens underlines the significance of age for Dolnoslav personhood.

The rarity of complete figurines and their concentration in a few buildings, and those never containing conjoint fragments, emphasises their importance as a statement about the integration of personhood over and above age-sex identity, left-right siddeness and vertical differentiation. The relationship between complete and fragmentary figurines is the first example of regularities in their overall distribution that have no obvious explanation. Not only did complete and broken figurines receive similar treatments (burning, crusting or wear) but the ratio of complete: broken figurines was very similar in all contexts – all the middens together, each separate midden, all buildings together, all open areas together and hence the total assemblage as well. We shall return to this problem later. What is clear at this juncture is the importance of the highly fragmented figurines as tokens of enchained relations.

The considerable variety of body parts found at Dolnoslav would have been consistent with the notable social diversity characteristic of the Final Copper Age. The depositional patterning of figurine body parts indicates complex preferences, probably related to the symbolism associated with different zones of the body. The main depositional contrast was that a wider range of body parts was placed in the buildings, especially the rarer types, with a distinct preference for a different body part in each midden. The pattern in buildings is reminiscent of the collection of the (almost) complete set of Hamangia age-sex categories in pits at Medgidia and Durankulak-Nivata. Particular body-part preferences, *e.g.*, the high frequency of torsos+legs in Midden D4, may well have referenced a specific limited interest group symbolised by the chosen body part. A different meaning for heads, as the essence of the person, if not personhood itself, would have moderated a weak relationship of heads to age, gender and status classes.

One of the most puzzling features of the Dolnoslav figurine assemblage is the balanced distribution of left and right-sided fragments. This balance was found repeatedly, using different principles of classification, in the total sample, in middens, buildings and open areas taken as a whole and in many of the body parts. If the distinction between left and right referred to occupational differences, such as agriculture vs. craft production, the balance in siddeness would represent an important communal identity principle. However, we should not ignore fragments neutral to siddeness, which were preferentially deposited in buildings. The more intriguing question, however, relates to how this balance was achieved in so many different contexts; an identical question was raised for the ratio of complete: broken figurines. There would appear to be two possible solutions.

The first idea is simple chance – the figurines were deposited in isolated acts by a wide range of persons, including neighbours and outsiders bringing an unknown proportion onto the site in already fragmented form. The objection to a cumulative balance produced by unrelated events is the multiple patterning found not only for left and right-sidedness but also for complete and broken figurines. The second solution favours a longer-term practice of multiple figurine curation over a period of time, perhaps years rather than weeks. The slow build-up of figurine fragments provided some opportunities for leaders to determine contrasts between, for example, left-sided figurines in buildings and right-sided figurines in middens. The final stage in this scenario would have been the ultimate deposition in one cataclysmic social event covering the whole of the settlement. The second explanation is perhaps preferable, given the clear evidence for curation and accumulated deposition at the tell.

The final categorisational scheme refers to the vertical differentiation of figurines into upper and lower parts and vertically-neutral segments. In each type of context, the lower fragments exceed the upper, with neutral parts as numerous as lower fragments. The distinction was reinforced by the context of deposition – a majority of upper fragments was placed in buildings, while a majority of lower fragments was placed in middens. Since sexual identities were more specific to up-down contrasts than to left/right-sidedness, vertical differentiation may have had sexual associations as well as the representation of limited interest groups.

These cross-cutting principles of categorisation matched those that applied to the Dolnoslav ceramic assemblage in the portrayal of a complex social structure comprising many parts, integrated to a lesser or a greater extent. The consumption of the Dolnoslav figurines represents the tensions existing between diversity and integration in a complex world. The integrative principle was represented in two ways: within the tell and between sites. On the tell, the complementary distributions of complete and broken objects, left- and right-sided fragments and upper and lower fragments provided a global integration between the diverse social groupings associated with the divisions. The fragment dispersion between sites integrated people, places and things over the long-term, with curation strategies the key to the accumulation of large quantities of material culture. (In)dividual diversity in the figurine repertoire remained as a key principle of the Copper Age world, perhaps referencing the (in)dividuality of persons in the multi-

dimensionality of social life. It was in everyday practices that (in)dividuality dominated. In the massive acts of consumption, the community stood as an integrated whole – the symbol of a supra-household and trans-generational entity, materialised through accumulation.

Let us return briefly to general perspectives on the development of new community structures. The dynamic nominalist principle of new kinds of persons emerging simultaneously with their description would have been of major importance at the start of the Neolithic and the Copper Age. The people of each period would have been transformed by the impact of new raw materials and new kinds of social groupings. With the emergence of farming, new types of person were created, in particular the 'farmer' and the 'herder' but also the 'potter', the 'polished stone tool-maker' and perhaps the 'brewer'. These new types of person co-emerged fractally with new foodstuffs and objects, such as flour, bread, lamb chops, barley beer, pottery and axes – the one could not have occurred without the other. Notions of personhood would have been influenced by the wide range of new relations, not least gendered relations, based upon these identities, as well as by their interplay with traditional types of person – 'hunter', 'shellfish-collector', 'flint-knapper' and 'leather-worker'. The communal values of the new products went hand in hand with the status of their creators. It is probable that, while those dwelling in dispersed homesteads would have included some of these new classes of people, meeting others seasonally, tell villagers would have included the full range of types of persons, with everyday contacts for most people. The discovery of secondary products would have ushered in new episodes of person-creation, with 'dairy producers' producing milk, cheese and yoghurt and 'ploughmen' harnessing animal traction, as well as the diversification of traditional persons such as weavers, now making woollen textiles, and carpenters, now shaping wooden wheels, planks and complex joints for carts. The values assigned to the new things transformed the traditional system of communal values, itself confirming new statuses for new types of person.

Before flint and copper mining, there would have been no need to characterise such a person as a 'miner'. Raduntcheva (2003, 48–60) has enumerated the wide range of Late Copper Age persons needed for the successful development of intensive copper mining. The picture that Rauntcheva paints is of the co-ordination of a large number of persons, as well as many **types** of person, each with complementary skills. While some crafts, such as carpentry, basket-making and rope-making, represented the development and intensification of traditional tasks, other interest groups comprised persons with wholly new skills. The introduction of metal finishing tools, as deposited in grave 4 in the Varna cemetery

(Ivanov 1988, Abb. 22; Marazov 1988, 74–75), changed the embodied skills on which a carpenter relied. The novel interest group of 'miners' would have been united by a shared practice of communal labour and a communally validated system of rewards for the production of a valued material. The same would have been true of 'gold-panners', 'copper smelters', 'mould-makers' and potters with gold-painting skills. At the same time, some persons involved with bone tool making may have also been specialists in pottery decoration. The interests of these groups of skilled persons were probably not identical and may have overlapped very little with, for instance, the interests of those farmers who provided seasonal supplies for those concerned with making copper axes. The cross-cutting interests of such groups would have created such a differentiated society that complex and powerful practices of integration would have been required. The possibility of hierarchical differentiation is supported by the evidence from several Climax Copper Age tells and cemeteries for both personal and household differen-tiation, suggesting a degree of personal and corporate indebtedness. Yoon (1989) has demonstrated how the in-corporation of Korean villages into wider socio-economic structures in the 1980s led to the decentring of the identities of villagers from the agnatic household, raising questions about both individual and communal identity. While the wider socio-economic structures of the Late Copper Age were on a far smaller scale than those in recent Korea, social differentiation may have posed similar challenges to personal identities in tell villages.

The institutional basis of Neolithic and Copper Age lifeways revolved around the family, the limited interest groups, the corporate groups and the community as a whole. The key issue of power relations is strongly implicated in community integration and intra-settlement differentiation. The domination of alternative interest groups by the agendas of the community head or the corporate group leaders would have led to a scenario of greater community integration. An alternative scenario whereby household heads or limited interest group leaders wielded greater power, using it to reduce the influence of corporate groups or the whole community, would have favoured differentiation, unless the household possessed the structure of the entire community writ small, as Sahlins proposed for the domestic mode of production (Sahlins 1974). What we can see represented in Climax Copper Age material culture is the tension between integration and diversity. This is consistent with a varied and complex picture of institutional differentiation, with several potentially competing power bases seeking to integrate the varied households and limited interest groups to their own benefits.

This is a narrative that cannot be told in isolation from the wider context of exchange networks across a landscape offering an extraordinary range of materials for the enchainment of persons, things and places. We now turn to the wider context of social and (in)dividual relations.

## Enchained relations across the landscape

The social relations of a person living on a prehistoric site may be conceived in terms of a network of nested sets of contacts, most intensive near the home settlement and decreasing in intensity with distance. The most frequent off-site contacts between prehistoric people were meetings between those living in neighbouring settlements. If these settlements were dispersed homesteads, any communal labour would have meant helping neighbouring families in exchange for future labour or gifts. Larger, seasonal festivals would have brought together extended families from many homesteads – perhaps an entire local entire breeding network – providing a regular context for enchained exchange and marriage negotiations. Deposition of everyday objects from each homestead, with occasional exotics emphasising even wider enchained relations, would have marked these occasions, material-ising their membership of a wider group. The larger groups of people living on East Balkan tells also formed part of overlapping breeding networks, perhaps linking a tell to four or five other tells more closely than with other tells. For a variety of possible biographical reasons, one of these tells would have emerged as a local centre for seasonal festivals. In the West Balkans, the development of either tells or larger nucleated settlements among groups of related smaller sites meant a self-selection process of the place for seasonal ceremonies. In each type of network, low-level 'centres' emerged, perhaps for decades or longer, as focal points for the communal identity of kin networks dispersed over the landscape.

The choice of place for such an accumulation of communal memories was a vital decision for the local network. Examples from the dispersed networks included the foraging centre at Lepenski Vir, with its concentration of locally produced and exotic things (Chapman 2000, Chapter 6); Dolnoslav or Smjadovo, with their con-centrations of ceramic and figurine fragments, occupied central places in dispersed tell networks; Makriyalos, with its evidence for communal feasting on a massive scale (Papa *et al.* 2004), the Vinča-Belo Brdo tell, with its ritual innovations in the early phase of occupation (Chapman 1981; 1998) and the large horizontal site of Turdaş, with its rich pit deposits (Chapman 1981) exemplified such central sites in nucleated networks. The evidence for inter-site re-fittings (see above, pp. 106–111) supports the movement, exchange and deposition of fragments of a variety of forms of object in such local networks, with the identification of a spatial scale of up to 10km. The even stronger evidence for inter-site exchange of parts of things from orphan fragments (see above, pp. 88–105) is consistent with the local 10-km scale of enchained exchange. The implications of the fragmentation premise at the level of the local network is the validation of personal links between sites through the enchainment and deposition of not only complete objects but also of fragments. Thus, there was a spatially dispersed aspect of personhood, with (in)dividuals growing out of fragments of objects not made locally by a member of the immediate family but on another site 6km distant by a second cousin. Some households would have developed wider enchained relations with many others, just as other households' relations were more constrained; the same was true for persons. Difference between persons or between households grew out of small-scale local variations in everyday enchained practices. Those exchanging or depositing objects at a festival would have developed an extra layer of enchained relations to their personhood – a more intense experience than for those merely witnessing the ceremony.

An important factor in local networks was the density of settlement (Chapman 2000, 34–7 and Fig. 2.2). While the distance between Early Neolithic tells was sometimes as little as 10 km (the Struma valley), although it could be as much as 25 km (North Bulgaria) (Todorova and Vajsov 1993, Karta 10), the densification of the Late Copper Age settlement network meant that people on a tell rarely lived more than 5–8 km from their neighbours (Dennell and Webley 1975, Fig. 3; Todorova 1978, 56 and Map 3). Increased densification had four principal implications for enchained networks. First, and most importantly, neighbours were simply closer than before. An inter-tell distance of 5 km represented an hour's walk either way for people from each tell, hardly 20 minutes outside the maximum subsistence territory (Gaydarska 2004). This led to a far higher degree of informal contacts between neighbours than was possible in the Neolithic, where a 15–20 km spacing meant more widely spaced overnight visits of higher social intensity. It also meant a greater likelihood of the formation of limited interest groups with members from more than one settlement. Secondly, the wider choice of social relations, not least marriage partners, amongst a larger local population led to more differences between people, each of whom could have been enchained to a varying group of (in)dividuals. This meant more complex relations of enchainment within each household and each corporate group, leading to tensions and perhaps clashes of loyalty. Thirdly, the increasing densification of relations stimulated increasing demand for objects to materialise these relations – both locally made objects growing out of local persons and places and exotic things with complex biographies. Fourthly, the shrinking spatial scale of what were once

overlapping breeding networks led to the intensification of **local** enchained relations among small groups of tells, with the possible emergence of closed networks. The prioritisation of the local required validation by exotic as well as by locally made objects. The overall impact of densification undoubtedly led to a growing social complexity – materialised in the design of Climax Copper Age ceramics, figurines and metalwork.

However, the negative side of increasing densification and complexity was the increase in tensions between (in)dividuals and groups. There is no anthropological evidence that cross-cutting relations between members of different settlements would have reduced the potential for violence: as Harrison (1989, 586) states, "in many of the New Guinea Highland societies, much warfare seems to be simply a violent form of sociality …" (cf. Shaw and Wong 1988, Haas 1990, Knauft 1991, Ferguson and Whitehead 1992). The failure to reciprocate an enchained gift with an object of suitable fame, the theft of another's sexual partner or copper axe, the excessive usage of an inter-communal resource and a host of similar everyday irregularities could have readily triggered inter-group tensions that would have escalated into hostility in the absence of appropriate compensation. It is significant that there was a steady increase in the quantity and diversity of weapon-tools, tool-weapons and defensive structures in later Balkan prehistory from the early farming period until the Climax Copper Age, when there was a quantum leap in defences and the first appearance of true weapons (Chapman 1999a). Local use of weapons is the obvious alternative to their use against Gimbutassian Kurgan invaders. The emergence of a new kind of person – the 'warrior' – depended upon the frequency and success of inter-group military conflict. That such a person had emerged in the Late Copper Age is supported by the deposition of sets of high-status weapon-tools in some of the richest Varna graves (Chapman 1999a). These warrior sets in turn confirm the importance of local warfare, whose probability increased with the scale of breeding network closure.

At the regional scale of exploration and contacts, people would have discovered the environmental diversity of the Balkans, not least in terms of the complementary resources offered by lowlands and adjacent uplands. The dynamics of local and exotic material culture in local social networks created changes in the relations of those dwelling in lowland settlements towards the upland zone. The people living in the South Balkans in the 6th and 5th millennia Cal BC were clearly familiar with both the uplands and the lowlands. Although we know more of their lives in the lowlands of the Thracian valley or the Plain of Thessaly, these groups also settled in inter-montane basins in the Rhodopes and the Pindhos, making seasonal visits to even higher zones to bring lowland material culture for deposition in rocky places such as Pchelarovo. Conversely, lowland dwellers regularly brought a part of the mountains to the lowlands through the collection of lithic raw materials, fine stones and occasionally pigments. The enchainment of these places not only related the two zones but also mediated the duality, contrast and opposition that the two zones offered as a metaphor for social relations within the communities who lived there. But there was also exchange between different lowland zones; the abundance of exotic, high-quality, honey-coloured flint for macro-blade production was as much as a marker of the start of the Neolithic as was painted pottery over much of the South Balkans. Lowland copper sources were also used on a small scale by early farmers. Thus, one opposition regularly drawn on to structure social relations was the distinction between local things and exotic objects, whether from the uplands or the distant lowlands. The abundance of shiny and colourful exotic raw materials and objects not only lent visual diversity to lowland settlements but could also have been drawn upon as a basis for ritual power through a demonstration of people's control over the exotic (Chapman, in press c).

Later expeditions for metal took mature farming groups far outside the lowland zone. The discovery of such a remote and small-scale source of copper as Rudna Glava (Jovanović 1982), high in the mountains south of the Iron Gates Gorge, implies systematic prospection of the uplands by local groups – a social practice probably occurring all over the mountain ranges of South East Europe. Such visits to the uplands would have led to the cumulative discovery of many other lithic sources for tools and ornaments. For example, an increased range of raw materials was used more intensively by Vinča groups in comparison with the Starčevo early farmers (Chapman 1981, 77–83). The people involved in such regular expeditions would have constituted a limited interest group, with its own dynamic, sense of enchained identity and specialised knowledge and practices. Not every member of a lowland tell community would have joined the seasonal expedition to the hills; perhaps no-one from some of the dispersed homesteads could have been spared for a journey lasting perhaps two or more weeks. Only some group members would have possessed the knowledge needed for the voyage – recognition of the signs of weather appropriate to an expedition, the routes into the uplands, the communities living there and the gifts they preferred, as well as the precise locations of all of the raw materials that were targeted. The importance of the group's contribution to social reproduction increased the status of each member as well as the interest group itself.

There was an intensification of the enchainment of increasingly wide groups of people through the exchange of exotic materials in the Climax Copper Age, whether for pigments for pottery decoration (for graphite, see Leshtakov 2006), stone ornaments and figurines (Georgiev 1955), salt (Chapman and Gaydarska 2003), marine shells (Gaydarska *et al.* 2004) and especially flint and metal objects. The mines and surface exposures of North East Bulgaria provided high-quality flint for macro-blade production for settlements over much of the South Balkans, as well as in the North Pontic and Eastern Carpathian zones (Manolakakis 1996; Chapman 2003, in press a). The difference between such exotic flint and local flints and cherts amplified the contrast between the local and the exotic on which everyday social reproduction was increasingly based. The lead isotope analyses of Late Copper Age metal objects indicated the use of many separate copper sources in all parts of the Balkans (Pernicka *et al.* 1993, 1997; Gale *et al.* 2000). The absence of copper objects made of Ai Bunar copper on sites closest to the mine underlined the importance of the exotic. In fact, despite the large-scale labour invested in the Ai Bunar mine, the locally deposited objects were mostly made of copper derived from North West Bulgaria and Eastern Serbia (Pernicka *et al.* 1997); Ai Bunar was thus at the heart of an 'export-led' exchange network. All of these cases point to the overall conclusion that the entanglement of the exotic in the identities of local people reached its apogee in the Climax Copper Age. It was probably only in this period that specific classes of exotic object became common enough on a typical tell settlement for their re-categorisation and institutionalisation as a necessary part of key social transactions.

However, the demand for exoticity brought another kind of object into the local context – an object so rare and well-travelled that it could not ever change categories to become marriage- or child-payments but only represent significant value for the entire community. As Gell (1992, 148) put it, "The exotic import is at a premium because it is bound up with a transactional mode (commodity exchange) which is positively valued and which confers value upon commodities." This class of object derived from so far away that it probably signified the appearance of another type of person – the 'long-distance specialist' – who betokened the increased spatial scale of exotic acquisition. This person was capable of making long voyages, often far beyond the adjacent upland zone, in the course of which s/he met strange peoples speaking unfamiliar languages, with different habits from those known at home, materialised in objects utterly unknown to her/his tribal ways. Mary Helms (1993, 4) has summarised the acquisition of the long-distance exotic objects as usually falling to élites in hierarchical or non-hierarchical societies, such acquisition being comparable to acts of artistic or craft production through the transformation of things from outside society into socially significant goods. Moreover, for Helms, skilled crafting, art and long-distance acquisiton went together as a "package" for the production of élite values. Helms (1993, 93–94) differentiates between two-way exchange, which emphasised the qualities of the relationship, from one-way acquisition, which emphasised the qualities of the things. While one-way acquisition could reach further than two-way exchange cosmologically and spatially, two-way exchange occurred within the boundaries of an entity, perhaps defining the boundaries of ordered society.

It is important to note that, even though such special long-distance objects became more significant in the farming period, they were already part of hunter-gatherer personhood (Gamble 2004). In the earliest farming period, highly polished, brightly coloured objects were the principal form of long-distance objects, whether the nephrite sceptre and ornaments from Gălăbnik (Kostov and Bakamska 2004) or the necklace of paligorskite beads from Lepenski Vir III (Srejović 1969). The patchy distribution of the marine shell *Spondylus gaederopus* in the Early Neolithic cannot mask its long voyage to the Middle Danube basin – a precursor to the continental-wide exchange network taking *Spondylus* shell ornaments as far North as southern Sweden in the fifth millennium Cal BC, a network subsuming the shorter but still long-distance traditional exchange into the Middle Danube basin (Chapman 1981; Séfériades 2003). In the Climax Copper Age, an object such as the pumice in the Omurtag hoard (Gaydarska *et al.* 2004) is now thought to derive from Lipari, since it pre-dates by more than two millennia the eruption of Santorini – the earliest mechanism for the spread of pumice within the Aegean (*p.c.* K. Kotsakis and S. Andreou). The probable distance travelled by this unique piece exceeds 2,000 km; whatever route actually taken would have involved several maritime and several land stages. A similarly long voyage is materialised in the carnelian beads found in the Varna and Durankulak cemeteries – perhaps deriving from Armenia (Kostov *et al.* 2004). These long-distance items are so rare and valued that they could not have become part of even important social transactions but remain as inalienable treasures held by and for the community. As Godelier (1999, 8) says, it is vital for any society to have fixed points – sacred objects constituting realities that are excluded from gift-exchange or trade.

As with Munn's (1986) Gawa menfolk, whose fame was inextricably linked to the prestige of the shell ornaments that they traded, Neolithic and Copper Age people manifested the diversity and reach of their enchained regional networks through the display of exotic objects connected to a long chain of persons. To the extent that exotic objects underpinned social reproduction as marriage- or child-payments, those unable to participate directly in the exchange network would have been impelled to enter debt relations to acquire these socially vital things. It is difficult to estimate the proportions of tell households lacking the enchained resources necessary to acquire exotic objects from their region: participation in key ceremonial practices would have been harder for people at certain stages in their life (*e.g.* older females and males, parents with young children, etc.). There must have been many families from dispersed homesteads who would have found participation so problematic that they would have entered a category of indebted relations. It is probable that a new kind of relationship co-emerged with a wider variety of personal wealth in the Climax Copper Age – the 'patron – client' relationship. Characterised by the provision of the client's labour for the patron's projects, whether building, ploughing, harvesting or the gathering of a diversity of resources, the relationship formed the basis for initially small-scale inequalities that could eventually have become institutionalised. Such a development created a wedge in the hitherto seamless web of enchained relations, opening up the possibility that formerly inalienable objects could become the equivalent of labour. The possible co-existence of a practice-based hierarchical relationship between persons and the essentialism of a fractal relationship in which a person grows out of another person must have introduced tensions into both the traditional concept of personhood and the ancestral egalitarianism characteristic of tell-dwelling communities. It is likely that this crisis reduced the emphasis on the fractal aspects of personhood in favour of the more individual aspects, just as the validation of the new 'patrons' would require the possibility of displaying tokens of that new status. The inter-community cemetery at Varna may be viewed in the context of such a development.

The greatest concentration of exotica known in the Balkan Neolithic and Copper Age derives from the Varna cemetery. The wide-ranging but ultimately unsuccessful search for adjacent settlements closely related to the Varna cemetery suggests a primary characteristic of Varna as a mortuary space not only conceptually separated from, but also adjoining, the domestic arena – as at Durankulak or Vinitsa – but conceptually and spatially separated from any place of dwelling. This greater distancing of the mortuary from the domestic domains indicates a parallel and deeper decoupling of ritual practices, leading to the more intense ritualisation of mortuary practices than was evident in household mortuary ritual (cf. Yoon 1989, 5).

Not surprisingly, the greatest emphasis in studies of Varna has been placed on the richest graves. Here, we shall explore the full range of grave goods in burials, from no grave goods at all to the richest graves in the cemetery, so as to define the total role of the mortuary zone in social reproduction. Our starting point is that **all** grave goods evoked the memories of past people, places and things, participating in their history and ancestral qualities as well as their places of origin and routes to the cemetery.

One contrast headlined at the complex accumulation place of Varna is the difference in social relations underpinning 'lavish' 'rich' and 'poor' graves. At one extreme lay the 10–15 lavish graves, with thousands of individual objects, many in sets, betokening corporate groups negotiating for social power positions, demonstrating their multiple enchained relations through the accumulation of exotic mortuary gifts. At the other extreme lay the poor graves (*i.e.* graves with no grave goods), where we see not an expression of corporate group practices but rather the burial of a member of a household or a small family with no possibility to express the accumulation process through exotic objects. In the middle were a large number of rich graves with a far smaller number of objects and a somewhat narrower range of types of objects than in the lavish graves. What do these differences in grave goods signify?

One way of understanding this contrast expresses the tension between the fractal and individual aspects of personhood. We have already underlined the contrast between individual personhood, with its emphasis on the integration of complete persons, places and things, achieved by accumulation processes and through consumption practices, and fractal personhood, whereby processes of enchainment create persons out of (often broken) things and vice versa. It is plausible that the burial of the newly dead with few grave goods marked the denial of the dominant values sustained by accumulation and the consumption of exotica in favour of the less spectacular values underpinning fractality. The total absence of grave goods in many graves at Varna left only the spatial relation between such graves and other nearby burials intact as a token of communal relationships and a minimal membership of the Varna mortuary community, while simultaneously denying both material accumulation and material enchainment. Alongside the various forms of accumulation attested at Varna – material accumulation, the accumulation of memories and the accumulation of object biographies (Chapman 2000, 174–9) – the most lavish graves materialised the accumulation of the most spatially diverse and the most socially differentiated set of enchained social relations.

The contrast between fractal and individual aspects of personhood at Varna goes some way to an identification of the social practices at work but it hardly addresses the central problem of the magnitude of the difference in grave good deposition. Here, we return to the emergence of patron-client relations in the Climax Copper Age. Already 60 years ago, Childe (1945) identified unusually lavish displays in the mortuary domain not as a reflection of societal wealth but rather as a sign of social tensions at

a time of major social change. The new AMS dates for the Varna cemetery (Higham *et al.*, submitted) indicate that burials started in the early 5th millennium Cal BC, at the very beginning of the Pontic Late Copper Age, only a few generations after the opening of the Ai Bunar copper mine and therefore in a period of increasing regional exchange. These enchained regional exchange networks were able, perhaps for the first time, to provide each tell settlement with a number of prestige copper objects not so great that every household could possess one or more but sufficient for several, if not many, households to keep one. This differential control of marriage- and child-payments gave power to certain households on a tell to control key social transactions. It also differentiated homesteads lacking access to exchange networks for copper objects from tells that were connected by traditional gift-exchange relations. The other novel development arose from the intensification of regional exchange, which itself led to greater contact between regional élites and a more homogenous expression of the new status. This allowed, for perhaps the first time, the development of an inter-regional paramountcy in which the more intensive interaction between regional leaders created a new kind of person – the 'paramount chief' – someone whose power was based on prestige gift exchange and the possession-in-trust of exotic sacred objects central to the identity of the lineage.

The generation of new patron-client relationships and a new inter-regional paramountcy created two social crises for the Late Copper Age – a crisis in the communally accepted form of personhood and a threat to the egalitarian basis of ancestral dwelling on the tell from a new level of conspicuous, competitive consumption that could not be contained within the traditional ancestral domestic arena. It was the emergence of these social crises that led to the establishment of a new arena of social power to validate the newly-developed patronal roles as well as the new role of paramount chief – the mortuary domain (cf. Chapman 1991). The earliest and most important of such mortuary arenas was created at Varna. There, members of those families with client relationships to the local and regional patrons were buried in the graves with no or very few grave goods, while the large number of wealthy graves outside of the core of the cemetery symbolised patrons displaying their regional exotica as a sign of new social roles as patrons. The most lavish graves at Varna were reserved for those members of the inter-regional élites whose lineage was supporting their claims to succeed the newly-dead paramount – in short, to assume the position of the next paramount chief.

The lavish, wealthy and poor graves at Varna stood for three new types of person – the paramount chief, the patron and the client. Each type of grave combined the fractal and individual aspects of personhood. In lavish graves with human remains, those complete bodies symbolised the integration of the fractal persona in death, while the exotic grave goods marked the inalienable ritual goods at the heart of a paramount chieftainship, as well as symbolising a complex web of enchained exchange relations criss-crossing much of the South Balkans. The lavish mask graves emphasised the fractal aspect of personhood, with the mask related to the mobile figurine heads and figurine masks that often constituted orphan figurine fragments. The lavish cenotaph graves lacking clay masks underlined the absence at the heart of fractality – the missing body whose social persona was presenced by the grave goods. The elimination of female bodies from the core area of the Varna cemetery demonstrated the success of the male ideological ploy to dominate the mortuary domain.

The wealthy graves at Varna were articulated extended inhumations, including adult males, adult females and children. The mostly complete bodies were accompanied by mostly complete objects, with the exception of marine shell ornaments, whose fractal relations were linked to the domain of the living rather than to that of the dead. Many objects comprised the rare regional exotica required for key rites of passage that the newly-dead had already experienced – in other words, a memory of the very rituals that had enabled the emergence of this type of person in the first place. Similar rich graves from other published cemeteries, such as Devnja, Goljamo Delchevo and Vinitsa, showed strongly gender-based divergences in the construction of personhood, with males emerging out of copper tools, weapons and ornaments and females developing out of household tools and non-metal ornaments (Chapman 1996).

The poor graves represented another type of absence – the denial of the traditional materially enchained relationships that had been superseded by the new type of hierarchical, patron-client relationship. What is truly striking is that some persons were buried without a single personal object – not even a shell bead or a flint flake: surely a sign of a deliberate decision to eschew fractality in the mortuary context.

The limited number of lavish graves at Varna, representing no more than ten generations of paramount chief, or a maximum of 300 years, suggests a stabilisation of the new social structure by the middle part of the Late Copper Age. The presence of both rich and poor graves in other smaller cemeteries (Chapman 1996) suggests that the patron-client system had become integrated into the social structure as an unproblematic part of everyday practice. However, the structural implications of hierarchical relationships for fractal personhood were severe, leading to increasing tensions in the later part of the Climax Copper Age.

There is scope for the investigation of the relationship between such tensions and the end of Climax Copper Age societies and their transformation into a significantly less complex group of communities. Two trajectories could be sketched in as divergent responses to such tensions. In the first, the values of the hierarchical basis of patronage were successfully challenged by clients still trying to maintain the fractal side of personhood. The resultant decrease in complexity stemmed from the weakening of those hierarchical relations that had become an important way of maintaining social cohesion. These changes led to the increasing importance of fractal aspects of personhood as symbolised by fragmentation practices and enchainment processes. In the second trajectory, hierarchical relations become more dominant than before, leading to a decline in social complexity through a further weakening of fractal relations and also signalled by the declining importance of cross-cutting modes of social categorisation. These two proposals provide signposts along a road leading to further research into the end of Climax Copper Age societies.

In summary, it is our claim to have provided such strong, if not unequivocal, support for the fragmentation premise that no fair-minded person can ignore this aspect of material culture studies any longer. The implications of the fragmentation premise – for the creation of personhood, for the *modus operandi* of artifact biographies and for changes in categorical principles throughout the life course of an object – open up many new and hitherto unacknowledged pathways through later Balkan prehistory, while also, more generically, setting a new research agenda for future research in material culture. It is to the future that we turn in a short concluding chapter.

# 9. Concluding pointers towards future research

The authors hope that readers have found the investigation of the fragmentation premise to have been a challenging voyage through later Balkan prehistory, with some interesting and relevant detours to, *inter alia*, Arizona, North Italy, Scandinavia and Brittany. We need hardly stress that the voyage is by no means over. We should like to conclude this contribution to fragmentation research by presenting what we see are the main issues framing the research agenda of the future – both for Balkan prehistory and more generically – from the viewpoint of the fragmenterist.

## Issues for the Balkan Neolithic and Chalcolithic

– The documented cases of inter-site re-fitting and the high frequency of orphan fragments have shown that fragmentation can be studied on the landscape level. The high level of object and fragment mobility – documented on several sites by objects missing as much as 80% of their body mass – unsettles the Balkan Neolithic and Copper Age far more than any claims for settlement mobility (Bailey *et al.* 2005). It will be important to find a method of characterising local (10km-radius) groups with small-scale central places in the Balkan Neolithic and Chalcolithic. The effort to define and understand fragment mobility and its spatial scale and settlement context will require a major research re-orientation that must stand at the highest level of research priorities.

– The study of objects, persons, architecture and places has led to the identification of two schemes for the creation of personhood in Balkan prehistory – a Hamangia mode and a Dark Burnished Ware mode. It is a high research priority to identify further possible modes in other times/places, for example the relationship between tensions in personhood and the fall of the Climax Chalcolithic.

– The understanding of pit-sites and middening practices remains in its infancy in the archaeology of the Balkan Peninsula. Both social practices have important implications for the creation of place and personal identity, making this a high research priority.

## Issues for prehistory

– A number of sites widely separated in time and space, and thus with very different post-depositional environments, have produced the same empirical results that 80% of sherd material was missing. How widespread is this absence and is it related to poor conditions of preservation, fragment dispersion both to and from the site in question, or a combination of the two? If there is widespread repetition of this pattern, we must think very seriously about a far higher degree of object mobility than is currently under consideration. Related to such mobility is the question of how to discern the direction of travel of fragments and whole objects.

– We claim that all objects have the potential for biographical study, especially when in large assemblages and with contextual information. In this work, we make the strong claim that we can study personhood through the emergence of persons from places, objects and other persons. In particular, a high incidence of deliberate fragmentation should be a good sign of the fractal aspect of personhood. It will be important to extend such research efforts to other times/places.

– The significance of enchainment can be summarised in four main points – the first three global, the fourth local:

  • enchainment mobilises the identity triad of persons, places and things through presencing;
  • enchainment comprises the best, and sometimes the only, explanation for deliberate fragmentation;
  • enchained relations subsume concepts such as curation, tokens, ancestral veneration, heirlooms and relics.

  • **but**
  • enchainment remains at the general level of social practice – the challenge is to refine the links between persons and things for each specific cultural context.

— The *châine opératoire* approach has made steady and considerable progress on the technical front but little movement in the direction of integrating the results into a social archaeology. We propose the development of a more socially attentive *châine opératoire* for all kinds of material, not just lithics.

— There is a large number of site classes where intensive, systematic re-fitting studies would produce revealing results. These classes of sites include barrow cemeteries, large flat cemeteries, so-called 'founders' hoards and, especially large-scale or complete settlement excavations. It is also worth biting the bullet to establish a research framework for an efficient and effective means of finding inter-site re-fits.

— More experimental work on fragmentation is urgently required, both to seek wider confirmation of patterning found in accidental and deliberate fractures and to extend the range of materials beyond ceramics.

— Finally, the fragmentation of trees remains a theme in search of a researcher. Following on from the fascinating research by Gordon Noble (Noble, 2006), it is apparent that trees, timber and wooden objects may have been a material that was fragmented as early as stone and animal carcasses and so would offer a very promising field for future research.

Six years after the first book on fragmentation, we are convinced that this is a research theme of increasing importance. There is a growing body of theory relating to enchained relations of various kinds and an emerging suite of methods for the identification of fragment re-fitting. Although taphonomic issues are the starting-point for any site-based analysis, they should no longer be considered as the end-point. The evidence for deliberate object (and body) fragmentation can no longer be overlooked or dismissed as an irrelevant and time-consuming curiosity. The horizons for fragmentation and re-fitting studies are broad and open – and much can be achieved using this perspective in archaeology.

# Appendix 1  Summary of files deposited with AHDS/ Archaeology, York

URL: http://ads.ahds.ac.uk/catalogue/resources.html?partwhole_ba_2006

| | |
|---|---|
| AHDS COVER DOC .doc | Word file providing details of the Project, background information on the sites, details of the files and keys to all of the Excel spreadsheets and captions for all illustrations |

**DOLNOSLAV FIGURINES**

| | |
|---|---|
| DOLNOSLAV FIGURINE DATABASE.xls | Excel spreadsheet with basic data on all the Dolnoslav figurines |
| Descriptions of joins.doc | A Word file with full descriptions of all joins between figurine fragments made during our investigations |
| Folder – Dolnoslav illustrations | 50 illustrations of the Dolnoslav figurines |
| Folder – Dolnoslav motifs | 230 decorative motifs found on the figurines |

**DURANKULAK SHELL RINGS**

| | |
|---|---|
| DUR SPOND DATA.xls | Excel spreadsheet with basic data on Durankulak *Spondylus* shell rings |
| DUR SPOND FEATURES.xls | Excel spreadsheet with data on natural features n shell rings at Durankulak |
| Folder – Durankulak illustrations | 28 illustrations of Durankulak shell rings |

**VARNA CEMETERY**

| | |
|---|---|
| VEN SPOND DATA.xls | Excel spreadsheet with basic data on Varna *Spondylus* shell rings |
| VEN WORK1.xls | Excel spreadsheet with data on natural features n shell rings at Varna |
| Folder – Varna illustration | 28 illustrations of Varna shell rings |

# Appendix 2

## The reinforcement index

Each vessel has a score based upon the number of reinforcements to the basic criterion of decorational zoning. Hence, a carinated bowl with unreinforced vertically-zoned decoration would score '0', while a dish with colour and matt/gloss contrasts and a combination of decorative techniques would score '3'. The calculation of an overall reinforcement measure for the whole assemblage is based upon the division of the sum of all vessel scores by the total number of vessels.

### Example: the Varna cemetery

To calculate this index, all those vessels without decoration are removed from the analysis (n = 55). There are 5 vessels with unreinforced decorational zonation (scoring '0' points); 17 vessels with one reinforcement to their zonal decoration (scoring '1' point each: a total of 17); 10 vessels with two reinforcements to their zonal decoration (scoring '2' points each: a total of 20); 17 vessels with three reinforcements to their zonal decoration (scoring '3' points each: a total of 51); 4 vessels with four reinforcements to their zonal decoration (scoring '4' points each: a total of 16). This produces a grand total of 104 points for 53 vessels, giving a mean reinforcement index of 1.96 (rounded up to 2.0).

## The index of decorational intensity

The index of decorational intensity measures the diversity of decoration on a class of vessels. For each decorated vessel, the number of vertical bands and horizontal registers are added to the techniques of zonal reinforcement to produce a vessel score; the mean of vessel scores for each shape class gives an index of decorational intensity for that class. The mean of the indices for all the shape classes at a single site produces an overall site decorational intensity index.

### Example: the Varna cemetery

Seven classes of forms have been defined for the Varna cemetery: bowls (number of decorated surfaces (interiors + exteriors) (n) = 25), dishes (n = 2), jars (n = 1), lids (n = 12), stands (n = 6) and miniature vessels (n = 2). Vessels in the 'Other' category (a 'refuse' category) (n = 23) were exclude from the calculation. The scores for each bowl sum three measures: the number of exterior decorational zones, the number of the interior decorational zones and the number of contrasts reinforcing either of these. The count for all bowls was 161; division by the number of decorated surfaces (n = 25) produces a decorational intensity for bowls of 6.44. This measure ranged from 2.5 for dishes to 7.4 for stands. The total counts for all decorated vessels came to 261; with the total number of decorated surfaces being 42, the overall index of decorational intensity for the whole assemblage was 6.2.

# Appendix 3
# Combination of body parts according to sidedness

Identical body parts found on both sides are joined by an underline

| LEFT – 100% | RIGHT – 100% |
|---|---|
| ST – left side, 2SA – left torso (3735 is upper) | ST – right half |
| 2ST – left torso, left arm and left leg (one is with left bottom) | ST – right torso, right arm and right leg |
| L. torso and l. arm (TO) | R. torso and r. arm (2TO, HAF) |
| L. bottom and l. leg (7BOLE, 3LEG, 3SE, ST) | R. bottom and r. leg (7BOLE, 2LEG, 3SE, ST) |
| L. bottom and upper l. leg (4BOLE) | R. bottom and upper r. leg (2BOLE, ST) |
| L. foot (2FOOT) | R. foot (FOOT) |
| L. leg (21 LEG, 2SE) | R. leg (30 LEG, TOLE) |
| L. lower leg (15 LEG) | R. lower leg (15 LEG, FOOT) |
| L. lower leg and l. foot (4FOOT) | R. lower leg and r. foot (LEG) |
| L. lower torso and l. leg (8TOLE, 4BOLE, 2SE) | R. lower torso and r. leg (9TOLE, ST, SE) |
| L. lower torso and upper l. leg (6TOLE, LEG) | R. lower torso and upper r. leg (8TOLE) |
| L. torso, l. bottom and l. upper leg (TOLE, ST is with upper torso) | R. torso, r. bottom and l. upper leg (TOLE, ST is with longer leg) |
| L. torso and l. leg (5TOLE, LEG) | R. torso and r. leg (4TOLE, 3LEG, ST-one LEG is upper) |

| | |
|---|---|
| L. bottom (BOTTOM) | R. arm (ARM) |
| L. neck and l. torso (2TO) | R. knee (LEG) |
| L. neck, l. torso and l. arm (ST) | |
| L. torso, l. arm and l. upper leg (TOLE) | |
| L. upper leg (2LEG) | |

| LEFT – not 100% | RIGHT – not 100% |
|---|---|
| Head, torso and L. arm (SA) | Head, torso and R. arm (SA, ST) |
| Head, upper torso and L. arm (2 HD/TO) | Head, upper torso and R. arm (HD/TO, HD) |
| Neck, torso and L. arm (2TO, ST, SA is with upper torso) | Neck, torso and R. arm (4TO – 2TO are upper) |
| Torso and L. arm (2TO, SA) | Torso and R. arm (2TO) |
| Upper torso and L. arm (TO, SA) | Upper torso and R. arm (TO) |
| Torso, bottom and upper L. leg (SE) | Torso, bottom and upper R. leg (ST) |

| | |
|---|---|
| Head, neck, upper torso and L. arm (HD) | Torso, R. bottom and R. leg (ST) |
| Neck, torso, upper legs and L. arm (TO, SE is without neck) | Lower torso and upper R. leg (TOLE) |
| Torso, L. bottom and L. arm (TOBO) | Torso, R. arm and R. leg (SE) |
| | Torso, bottom and R. arm (HAF) |
| | Torso, bottom, upper legs and R. arm (TOLE) |

# Appendix 4
# Description of re-fitted joins, Dolnoslav figurines

**Join 1** has two parts – head deposited in building 1 during occupational phase A and upper torso and right arm deposited in D2, presumably during the last occupational phase C. The head is with incised eyes, perforated years and stamped mouth, additionally decorated on the neck with red crusting and incised and incrusted motif 112. The torso is with sign 17 on the back and 18 on the front and back; and incised and red incrusted motif 16 on the neck. The head has no information for gender and the torso is unsexed. There are 2 breaks on the head – flat at the neck and a flake was detached from the nose. The torso has 3 breaks – irregular on the neck, oblique and irregular at the point of detachment from the lower body and a flake was detached from the arm. The incised and incrusted decoration on both fragments was executed prior to the detachment of the head, while the white crusting may have happen either before or after the fragmentation.

After at least two transformations – detaching from the body, and detaching a flake from the nose, the head was deposited in building 1 during the initial phase of occupation. The torso was kept for two more occupational phases, either in the same building or somewhere safe from atmospheric influence or wear. It is possible that between phases A and C the torso still had its lower part and its left arm and was deposited after at least 2 more transformations in D2 during the last occupational phase. The remaining body parts could be either removed from the site or brought to the site during any of the phases of occupation – A, B or C.

**Join 2** consists of 3 fragments that form a pair of hollow legs. The fragment of the right leg found in building 6 was stuck to its matching part found in D1 during the excavations. The left leg (or rather foot) was found at the Central profile. All pieces have no information for gender. The right leg is incised all over with motif 101. The left leg is with incised decoration, too. Both legs each have one angular break on the point of detachment of the upper part. The legs belong to big hollow figurine, whose upper part/s was not found. Since the legs were not attached to each other, they could have been removed separately or at the same time. The left leg has more detached parts since it is only 8,2 cm high, while both parts of the right leg (24,5 cm in height) reach the point, where the lower torso of the figurine might have been. After the detachment of the right leg from the body, the leg was further fragmented into two parts and then deposited in contexts that are 15–20 m apart from each other (building 6 and D1). The left leg was also additionally broken after the detachment from the body but its upper leg was (as well as the rest of the figurine) not kept on the site. The foot was then deposited somewhere close to the other leg, since it was found in the central profile (see map).

**Join 3** consists of 2 fragments – a left and right lower torso with leg that were refitted during the excavations, found in building 6 and an upper torso and arms found in D3. Both fragments have female traits and incised decoration – motif 133 on the lower torso and motif 229 on the neck. In addition, the upper part was white crusted on front and back. The lower part has three breaks – angular at the point of detachment from the upper body and flat on both feet. The upper part has two breaks – complex at the point of detachment from the lower body and angular at neck/head break. Only the lower part was additionally treated – it was burnished on the front and smoothed on the back, there were patches of burning on the back and the foot breaks were worn. The two parts do not physically match but they have very similar technological and morphological characteristics. The missing link between the fragments and the restoration of the lower body parts prevents the reconstruction of the possible fragmentation sequence. However, it is clear that the lower part possessed a "richer" artifact biography than the upper part. The former was differently treated on the surface, it has passed at least 4 fragmentation cycles, two of the breaks were additionally manipulated, with secondary burning before its final deposition in building 6. The latter was deposited after two breaks in D3, 10–15 m from its matching parts. The remainder of the figurine was not deposited on the site.

**Join 4** consists of two fragments – the left side of a standing figurine found in building 10 and a right lower torso and right leg found in D1. The left part was unsexed, while the right had no information for gender. There are three breaks on the right side – irregular on the neck, hinged on the left/right axis and flat at the point of detachment of the lower leg. The left side has 2 breaks - flat at the point of detachment of the upper body and hinged on the left/right axis. The fact that the two sides were attached along the left/right axis suggests the following fragmentation sequence: first, the head was detached from the body and immediately or at a later stage was taken off the site; then the torso was separated to left and right side; both of which had one further transformation – the foot was detached from the right side, while the upper torso was detached from the left side. The right foot and the left upper body were taken off the site. The remaining 2 parts out of at least 5 from the once complete figurine were deposited in adjacent contexts, 5 m from each other.

**Join 6** consists of two fragments – a head with a top knot found in D1 and an upper torso found in building 24. The head has incised eyes and a mouth, the front neck is decorated with incised motif 108. The torso also has incised decoration on the front and back – motif 174. The head has no information for gender, while the presence of breasts on the torso indicates a female figurine. The head has only one irregular break at the neck, in contrast to the 7 breaks on the torso. Three of them are irregular – on the neck and on both arms, and three are just flakes detached from the back and both breasts. The seventh break, which is at the point of detachment from the lower torso is complex and worn.

Additional features on the fragments are graphite on front neck, traces of wear on the back of the head, a burnished front torso and a smoothed back torso. Therefore, at least four different activities were performed on the fragments from join 6 – graphite application, wear, burnishing and smoothing. There are visual overlaps between two of the treatments – the application of graphite and the burnishing both result in black shining surfaces. The fact that two techniques were applied to achieve similar effect suggests the possibility that these operations were executed after the head was detached from the body. Otherwise, it would be difficult (but not impossible) to perform either manipulation on one part (*e.g.* burnishing of the torso) without leaving any traces on the other. It is not to be excluded that different body parts *had* to be treated differently, in which case these techniques were performed on a more or less complete figurine. In any case, it is clear that the front of the figurine was deliberately treated to present a colour/matt contrast on one part. The other part consists of a relatively rough back (worn head and smoothed but not burnished back with detached flake) in opposition to a carefully treated front. Even if the body parts were treated as fragments (head and torso) rather than as a whole, the front/back opposition remains.

From the moment of its creation to the moment of its final deposition, the head has passed through three major manipulations – detachment from the body, the application of graphite and wear. Much more varied was the life history of the upper body part. It has been transformed at least 9 times – 4 major detachments from the head, lower torso and both arms, 4 minor detachments from the back and both breasts, burnishing, smoothing and wear. The only secure sequence of activities is that burnishing and smoothing took place before the detachment of the flakes. Otherwise the polishing activities would have covered the places of detachment. It is important to point out that the removal of the breasts does not change the gender of the figurine. Although the breasts are not there, the trace of their fractures are indicative for females. This is in contrast to the Hamangia figurines, where breakage wipes out any traces of previous gender. The question why the breasts were removed can be approached by putting the answer in the perspective of de-gendering by breakage – the most famous of which is the case of Hamangia figurines (see above, Chapter 3). Since the body morphology of the Dolnoslav figurines does not imply androgyny, a single or indeed a series of breaks cannot readily erase the initial gender. There are, however, some activities like smoothing and burnishing that may have aided the full de-gendering of the figurine. The fact that they were not undertaken suggests that full de-gendering was not sought before the final deposition of the upper body part in building 24, 5–7 m from the head, deposited in D1. There are at least 3 remaining body parts not deposited on the site.

**Join 7** has three fragments – a right leg found in D1, a left leg also found in D1 and the torso of a seated figurine found in the so-called open areas. Both legs have no information for gender, while the torso has breasts and a pregnant stomach, indicating a female. The right leg has 2 breaks – flat at the point of detachment from the body and at the right/left axis. The left leg also has 2 breaks – irregular at the point of detachment from the body and flat at the right/left axis. Both feet are very worn. The torso has 7 breaks – angular on the neck and the left and right stomach, irregular on the left arm and both legs; and flat on the right arm. All of the breaks are worn, that may have been the result of the long-term exposure or deliberate treatment.

The different type of break of the two legs at the point of detachment from the body suggests that they were removed from the body at different time. The legs are solid and it was possible to detach one of them from the other and from the body with one blow, although it may have required some special skills and experience. It is also possible that the legs were removed as a pair but later the break at the left leg has eroded and turned from a flat into an irregular break. The fact that both feet are worn is indirect evidence that the legs stayed as parts after the detachment of the body and the manipulation of the feet. The next moment in their life history was to separate the legs physically and to bring them together symbolically through joint deposition in D1 (they are found in one square grid).

The body had a different fate. After at least 6 fragmentation phases and the same number of natural or deliberate causes of wear, the body was left in the open area. It is difficult to establish the fragmentation sequence but wear on all 7 breaks suggests more or less contemporary detachment of the head and the extremities, after which the body was specially manipulated or neglected (left to erode), contributing to the wear on the breaks. The head and the arms were taken off the site or were never brought in.

**Join 8** consists of two fragments – a right lower torso and right upper leg found in D2 and a left lower torso and left leg, also found in D2. Both body parts are unsexed and have 2 breaks each. The right part has an irregular break at point of detachment from the body and at the point of detachment from the lower leg. The left part has a flat break at the point of detachment from the body and the left/right axis. The right part looked as if it was made as a single piece, pointing to a specific post-fragmentation activity aiming to mask the breakage. It is also possible that the legs were made separately and were conjoined at the final stage of the production of the figurine. The left part is not preserved to the same length and it is not possible to see if it was treated the same way. The flat breaks suggest that the left part was removed simultaneously from the body and the other leg with a tool. Otherwise, such a breakage pattern requires high skills and experience. After the detachment of the left part, the right part was removed and manipulated to look as if it was never part of a two-legged figurine. The part was further fragmented with its lower part removed. After the manipulations – one for the left part and at least two for the right part, both fragments were deposited close to each other (found in the same square grid). The upper part of the figurine was taken off the site.

**Join 9** consists of two fragments – a seated torso with upper right leg and left bottom found in D2 and a right leg found in the same grid square. The torso represents a hermaphrodite (penis and breasts) and the leg has no information for gender. There are four breaks on the torso

– flat on right arm, irregular on the left arm and complex at the point of detachment from both legs. The leg has only one angular break at the point of detachment from the body and had traces of burning over the axis break. Although rare as a gendered representation, the hermaphrodite body was not treated specially after its 4 breaks. The only secure evidence for the fragmentation sequence is that the legs were detached from the body at different times, as is visible from the types of break on both legs. Such a complex fracture is not possible (or at least it is extremely difficult) to achieve with a single blow. After the torso had reached its final fragmentation phase, it was deposited in D2. Its counterpart had one more manipulation before deposition – its axis break was burnt. The remaining parts of the figurine were not deposited on the site.

**Join 10** consists of two legs found in one grid square (D4) (Fig. 6.29). Neither contained any gender information. They were decorated with the incised motif 82 on the front. In addition, each had 8 incised toes. The right leg had 2 breaks – angular at the point of detachment from the upper leg and hinged along the left/right axis. The left leg had three breaks – irregular at the point of detachment from the upper leg, hinged along the left/right axis and a flake was detached from the foot.

The difference in the type of the fracture at the point of detachment from the upper leg and the different length of both legs suggests that they were not removed from the body by a single blow. On the other hand, however, they are hollow and originally attached to each other. It would have been very difficult to detach only one leg from the body and from the other leg at the same time and to leave both legs intact. Rather, we would assume that both legs were first detached from the body/upper legs and after that they were either separated and then more parts were removed from their upper surface or vice versa. In any case, there are at least three stages of transformation from what might have been a whole figurine to what was deposited in D4. A fourth transformation was made on the left leg, when a flake was removed from its foot. The body and the upper legs were not deposited on the site.

**Join 11** has two fragments – an upper torso found in D1 and a lower body with legs found in building 11 (Fig. 6.25). The upper part was decorated with incised motif 22 on the back and had a constructional hole for the head. The lower part was decorated with incised motif 149 on the upper legs. The upper part is female, while the lower part is unsexed. There are three breaks on the upper part – irregular on the neck/head break and angular at the point of detachment from the lower body. There are 3 breaks on the lower part – irregular on the bottom, flat on the left foot and a flake was detached from the right foot. The upper part has passed two transformations – detachment from the head and from the lower body and it was not clear which was the initial operation. The lower part had at least 3 treatments, which also may have taken place while the body was still attached to the upper part and the head (?) – a break at both feet and manipulation of the right foot that has caused heavy wear. It is not possible to establish the sequence of fragmentation but, at the end of it, two of the three large parts were deposited in adjacent contexts.

**Join 12** consists of 2 fragments –an upper torso and arms found in D1 and a lower torso with legs also found in D1. The upper torso has female features (breasts), while the lower is unsexed. There are two breaks on the upper part – both irregular at the head/neck axis and at the point of detachment from the lower body. The lower body has only one break – irregular at the point of detachment from the upper part. This once-whole figurine had a "simple" life history in comparison to the other figurines from the site. The parts that remained on the site had 2 breaks altogether – at the head/neck axis and at the point of detachment from the lower body – and were not specially treated after the fragmentation. It is possible that the missing head had further breaks and/or post-fragmentation manipulations. The final operation with the two body parts was their deposition in neighbouring square grids.

**Join 13** consists of three fragments – a torso with right arm found in D1, a left leg also found in D1 and a right leg that derives from the central profile. The body was decorated with incised motif 99 on the front and incised motif 100 on the back. The same motifs were used on the front and back of both legs. There was a hole in the neck, probably for the attachment of the head. Both legs had no information for gender, while the torso had an incised pubic triangle. The legs have two breaks each – flat at the point of detachment of the right leg from the body and the same at the right/left axis. The left leg has an irregular break at the point of detachment from the body and flat at the left/right axis. The torso has 5 breaks – concave on the neck, irregular at the point of detachment of right arm and the point of detachment of right leg and flat at the point of detachment of left arm and the point of detachment of left leg. The torso was the only body part with traces of secondary burning on the right side. There are no traces of fire in D1, which suggests that the body part was burnt before its final deposition. This post-production treatment may have taken place before, after or between the actions of multiple fragmentation. It is impossible to say whether the legs were still attached to the body when the head and the arms were removed.

What is more clear is that the legs were probably removed at different times, since they have different types of breaks at the point of detachment from the body. The situation is the same as in Join 7, where detachment of a single leg is not impossible but requires skills and experience. As with Join 7, it should not be excluded that both legs were removed at one blow but the left leg has suffered some kind of post-fragmentation wear or erosion that has produced the different breakage pattern at the point of detachment from the body.

After 6 manipulations – 5 breaks and secondary burning – the body of the once-whole figurine was deposited close to two of its other parts – both legs that have passed only two transformations. The head and the arms were taken off the site or were never brought in.

**Join 14** consist of two fragments – a upper torso with left arm found in building 17 and a lower torso found in the open area (Fig. 6.27). The upper part was decorated with incised motif 166 on the front and had a modeled hollow for attachment of the head. The lower part also had incised decoration – motif 234 on the front. Both fragments have female features – breasts and a pubic triangle respectively. The upper part has 4 breaks – irregular at the neck/head axis, flat at the point of detachment of right arm and at the right breast and angular at the point of detachment from the body. The lower part has 3 breaks – irregular at the point of detachment of right leg and complex at the point of detachment from the upper body and at the point of detachment from the left leg. The left part of the lower torso has traces of intensive burning and with no evidence for fire in the open areas, the secondary burning of the figurine has taken place before its final deposition. The fact that there are no traces of burning on the left side of the upper part is indirect evidence that the secondary treatment was performed after the detachment of the upper and lower body parts. Whether the leg/s were present during the firing is difficult to say with certainty. The lack of burning on the break with the leg suggests that at least the left leg might have been still attached to the body. In any case, the lower part has passed at least 4 manipulations – 3 breaks and a secondary burning before being left at the open areas. The upper part had also at least 4 manipulations – 4 breaks before its more targeted deposition in building 17. There are at least 4 parts from the once-whole figurine that are not present on the site.

**Join 15** consists of two fragments – a head found in building 23 and a torso found in the open areas. The head has no information for gender and has an incised nose, perforated ears and a stamped mouth. The torso has one female feature (a pregnant stomach) and incised decoration all over the body with motif 239. The head has 4 breaks – irregular on the nose and the right ear, angular on the left ear and convex at the neck/head axis. The body has two breaks – irregular at the neck/head axis and at the point of detachment of the right arm. Both parts have traces of additional treatment. The head was rough on the front but smooth on the back and had traces of burning on the face, the right ear and the neck break. The torso had a horizontal perforation in the stomach and was burnt on the front. This almost whole conjoint figurine (only the right arm missing) had a very complex life history. The torso was found in front of building 19, which means that the fire in this building may have contributed to the secondary burning on the front side. Therefore, the detachment of the right arm and the head and the stomach perforation preceded this final, not necessarily deliberate burning. However, there is no strong evidence to support such claim, which raises the question of whether the burning was not accidental and was somehow related to the stomach perforation. One possible explanation is that the burning was a cleansing/ purification operation after birth, symbolized by the hole in the stomach. Whether the head and the arm were still attached to the body during the burning is difficult to claim with certainty. The same is valid for the three missing parts from the head (both ears and nose) – whether they were still there when the head was removed from the body or removed before that is not clear. However, it is sure that the secondary burning on the head took place after its removal from the body as there are burning traces over the neck break. It is plausible that the same fire caused the burning on the face and the right ear. The burning may have been related to the roughness of the front part of the head as some kind of activity of erasing identity The smoothness of the back of the head reinforces the contrast with the front, where the effect of negligence was sought. It is possible that the burning on the torso and the head has happened in the same fire, when the head and the body were detached in some kind of deliberate post-natal manipulation in which the figurine stands for a type of person. After at least 7 manipulations on the head and 4 manipulations on the body, both parts were deposited closely to each other but in different contexts. The right arm was not found on the site.

**Join 16** consists of two fragments – a left lower torso with left leg found in K1 and a right lower torso and right torso with legs found in the open areas. Both parts are unsexed and bear incised decoration. The lines of left part are all over the fragment and are incrusted with red with motif 177. The lines of the right part are also incrusted with red. The left part has 3 breaks – irregular at the point of detachment from the torso, angular at the point of detachment of the foot and hinged at the left/

right axis. The right part has two breaks – irregular at the point of detachment from the torso and hinged at the left/right axis. Both breaks are worn. Therefore, the right part has fewer breaks but was additionally manipulated to erode the breaks before it was left in the open areas. The outdoor conditions may have also been the reason for the worn breaks. The possible fragmentation sequence of the left part is – initial detachment from the upper body part/s, followed by the separation of both legs, and finally detachment from the foot. After three stages of transformation, the left part was deposited in the K-1. The remaining part/s of the figurine were not present on the site.

**Join 17** has two fragments – a right torso, right bottom and upper right leg deposited in the central shrine during phase A and a left torso, left bottom and upper left leg found in D3, in a later phase. Both sides have an incised pubic triangle indicating a female. The right part is decorated with incised motif 195 on the front and side of the fragment. The left part is also decorated all over with incised motif 231. The right part has 4 breaks – irregular at neck/head detachment point, at the point of detachment of the right arm, and at the point of detachment of the lower leg; and finally a hinged break at the left/right axis. The left part has 3 breaks – angular at the point of detachment from the head and arm, hinged at the left/right axis and irregular at the point of detachment of the lower leg. The right part has a burnt bottom, while the left part is burnt on the side of the torso and on the left arm break. Both parts have a complex life history. Most probably a common break was the head break, in which the left upper part was more affected, and, when the arm break was performed, the final result was a very irregular break shape. Whether the legs were still attached to the body when the head break took place is not possible to establish. It is also very difficult to establish if the arms were still present during the left/ right axis break. Indirect evidence that the arms were removed prior to the axis break is the secondary burning on both fragments. The traces of burning on the left side are over the arm break and the side of the torso but not over the axis break; therefore this activity took place before the axis break. It is plausible that the traces of burning on the right bottom are from the same general burning activity, suggesting that the two body parts were still conjoint at that time.

After 4 major fragmentations and an act of secondary burning, the right part was deposited in the central shrine during the initial stage of occupation, while the left side was kept in use during the next two phases and was finally deposited in D3 during the final act of deposition in phase C. The remaining parts of the body were removed from the site or were never brought onto the site.

**Join 18** has two fragments – a left lower leg found in D2 and a left torso with left arm and left leg found in the open areas. The leg has no information for gender and is decorated with incised motif 69. The unsexed torso also has incised decoration. The leg has 3 breaks – irregular at the point of detachment from the upper leg, flat at the point of detachment of the foot and hinged at the left/right axis. The torso has 5 breaks – irregular at neck/head break, at the point of detachment of the left arm and at the point of detachment from the lower leg; and hinged at the left/right axis and along the left front torso. The hinge fracture on the axis of both fragments suggests that they were still conjoint when the left/right break took place. Otherwise, it would be very difficult (but not impossible) to detach the lower left leg from the remaining figurine and after that to remove the upper left part, or vice versa. After the left/right break, the lower left was detached from the upper leg and finally the foot break took place. It is also possible that the foot was fragmented when the whole leg was still intact. After three breaks, the lower leg was deposited in D2. The upper part has a much more complex fragmentation history. It is likely that the head was removed when the figurine was more or less complete. Whether the arm/s were present during this break is not possible to establish. After the head was removed, the body was split into left and right parts. The next two breaks, whose sequence is not possible to establish, are the detachment of the lower leg and the "trimming" of the front torso. One possible reason for the latter is the erasing of the gender of the figurine, which, if true, would be the only successful case in the whole assemblage of gender alteration through genital removal. After the end of the intensive fragmentation cycle, the torso was left in the open areas. The head and the right part of the body were not present on the site.

**Join 19** consists of 2 fragments – an upper torso with left arm found in D2 and a head found in the open areas (Fig. 6.26). The head has no information for gender, while the breasts on the torso are indicative for female. The torso has a hole for attachment of the head and is decorated on the front with incised motif 15. The head has 3 breaks – flakes were removed from the nose and the left ear, and there was an irregular break on the neck/head area. The torso also has 3 breaks – irregular at the point of detachment from the neck, flat at the point of detachment of the right arm and angular at the point of detachment from the lower body part/s. The flake breaks on the head were worn, which may be indirect evidence that the breaks on the torso were performed while the head was still attached to the body. During these activities, the surface of the flake scars was worn out and, after the final detachment of the body from the head, the latter was left in the open areas. The outdoor conditions may also be the reason for wear on the head but this does not explain the absence of wear on the neck break.

After 3 major but unsequenced transformations, the upper body was deposited in D2. The lower part/s of the body were removed from the site or alternatively were never brought to the site.

**Join 20** has two fragments – a left lower leg found in D1 and a seated torso also found in D1. The leg has no information for gender and is incised with motif 75. The female torso is incised and white incrusted with motif 221 on the front and 222 on the back. The leg has two breaks – irregular at the point of detachment from the upper leg and flat on the left/right axis. The torso has 5 breaks – complex at the point of detachment of the head, concave at the point of detachment of the right arm, angular at the point of detachment of the left arm and irregular at the left/right axis and the point of detachment of the right leg.

The pattern of fragmentation of Join 20 confirms the above-made suggestion that it is possible to detach one leg from the other and from the body at one blow (see Joins 7 and 13). It is not possible to establish what is the sequence of the five breaks but it is clear that the upper body and the right leg had to stay together even after fragmentation. Their physical separation was reinforced symbolically and, although they were deposited in D1, they are at least 10 m from each other. The head, the arms and the right leg were not present on the site.

**Join 21** comprises 2 fragments – a head with upper torso and lower torso and conjoint legs found in the open areas. Both fragments have female features. The upper part has two breaks – hinged at the point of detachment of the left arm and at the point of detachment from the lower body. The head is brown, while the body is black, suggesting some special regime of firing. The lower part has incised horizontal lines on both legs and is modeled with a seat. It has 4 breaks – complex at the point of detachment from the upper part, at the back right leg and the rear left leg; and a hinge fracture on the back. The latter is worn which suggest that it preceded the other breaks. While the complex fragmentation cycle, perhaps involving also the upper part, was performed, the initial back break was slowly becoming worn. Alternatively, this break was specially treated to achieve such a pattern. The fragmentation sequence on both parts is not possible to establish. After fragmentation, the two parts were left on the site although not in highly formalized places. The missing parts – at least 2 – were not deposited on the site.

**Join 22** consists of two fragments – a torso deposited in building 20 during occupation phase B and a head found in the so-called open areas (Fig. 6.28). The left arm of the torso was re-fitted during the excavations. The head has no information for gender, while the torso had female features - breasts and a pregnant stomach. The latter was decorated with incised motif 214. The head has 3 breaks – irregular and worn on the nose and the right cheek and complex and fresh on the neck. The torso has 5 breaks – irregular at the neck and both arms and angular at the left breast and bottom. All but the neck break has traces of wear, that points to some deliberate post-fragmentation activities. The body was made of several slabs of clay, smoothed on the front and burnished on the back. In addition, the areas between the breasts and under the arms were crusted with white. The head was also crusted with white and had an eroded cheek. Since the white crusting is over the burnished surface (Fig. 6.28), the polishing activities preceded the colouring. White crusting appears on both the head and the torso, which may indicate that the process was performed when the parts were conjoined. An additional argument that the different manipulations were made while the figurine was still unbroken is the fact that only the neck fracture was not worn. It is possible that, after all 14 operations – smoothing the back; burnishing the front; burning the back of the left ear; applying white crusting to the head, the underarms and the inter-breasts area; detaching the lower arms, the left breast and the bottom and finally filing the 4 breaks – the torso was detached from the head and deposited in building 20 before its destruction in phase B. The head was left in an open space for a long time before the final sealing of the site in phase C, explaining its eroded cheek. If the head was removed from the body soon after its production, the torso still had 13 stages of transformation, while the head has only 3. The remaining parts of the body were removed from the site, or alternatively were not brought on the site.

**Join 23** has two fragments – a left torso with legs found in building 2 and a left lower leg found in building 10. The torso with leg is unsexed and the lower part of the leg has no gender information. There are 3 breaks on the upper part – complex at the point of detachment from the torso, irregular at the point of detachment from the lower leg and flat at the left/right axis. The latter had traces of wear. The lower leg has 3 breaks, too – flat at the point of detachment from the upper leg and at the left/right axis, hinged at the point of detachment from the foot. The flat breaks of the lower leg at the point of detachment from the upper leg and at the left/right axis imply the use of some tool or highly skilled hand-breaking experience (for a similar breakage pattern, see Join 8). After the removal from the body and before final deposition in building 10, this part has passed though another fragmentation process – its foot was detached. The fate of the torso with leg was different. After the

detachment of the lower leg, the upper leg remained attached to the body for some time. It is possible that, during this time, the deliberate actions of wear on the left/right axis were performed as if to "erase" any visible link with the missing left leg. It is not to be excluded that the causes of wear may have taken place after the leg was removed from the body. In any case, after 3 breaks and deliberate manipulation of wear, the torso with leg was deposited in building 2 at a relatively large distance from the other part. The upper part/s of the body and the feet were not deposited on the site.

**Join 24** consists of a right bottom with attached leg found in building 11 and a left leg found in building 10. Neither fragment has information for gender. The right part is decorated with incised motif 152 on the leg. Also incised is the decoration of the left leg – motif 144. The right part has two breaks – irregular at the point of detachment from the body and flat at the left/right axis. There are traces of burning on the leg, the bottom and the axis break. The left leg also has 2 breaks – complex at the point of detachment from the upper leg and flat on the left/right axis. There is a burning patch on the top front leg and on the axis break.

One possible reconstruction of the fragmentation sequence identifies the right part as the first lower part to be removed from the once-whole figurine. As mentioned on several occasions, it is possible to remove one leg (in this case an extended leg) from the body, leaving the other leg intact at the same time. This would have left the left leg still attached to the body, enabling further fragmentation at the desired height. Both left and right lower parts were treated very similarly – with burning on the axis break and the legs which seems to be the last activity before their final deposition in adjacent buildings. The great similarity in the post-fragmentation treatment suggests that it was a result of deliberate rather than accidental firing, or indeed the fire that has destroyed the two buildings. The upper part/s of the body were not on the site.

**Join 25** consists of two fragments – a left bottom with leg and an upper left torso found in the open areas. The lower part is unsexed, while the upper part is female. The lower part is decorated all over with incised and white incrusted motif 49. The upper part has 5 breaks – angular at the neck/head point and the back of the arm, hinged on front of the arm and axis; and flat at the point of detachment from the lower body. The lower part has 3 breaks – irregular at the point of detachment from the body, flat at the right/left axis and hinged at the point of detachment of the foot. The two parts do not have a physical match, which explains the different breaks at their potential join point. They are, however, very similar in fabric and there is a more than 50% chance that they belong to one and the same figurine. After the major transformations (3 for the lower part and 5 for the upper part), the fragments were not deposited in a structured context but were also not removed from the site. The head and the right side of the once-whole figurine were not deposited on the tell.

It is very important to underline that a relatively large percent of conjoint parts was deposited after one or two breaks. Perhaps their shorter fragmentation cycle, and hence their low "enchained" value, was compensated by the presence of a matching part, since the join would provide additional enchained links. The value of the matching parts with one or two breaks was that they demonstrate joins on the Dolnoslav tell.

# Appendix 5
# Summary of *Spondylus* results, Easter 2004

**Pre-Easter 2004**

| | GRAVES + SPONDYLUS ORNAMENTS | GRAVES + SP BRACELETS | GRAVES + FRAG SP BR |
|---|---|---|---|
| DURANKULAK | | | |
| Hamangia I–II | 22 | 13 | 4 |
| Hamangia III–IV | 73 | 32 | 22 |
| Varna I–III | | 50 | 22 |
| VEN | 147 | 70 | 53 |

**Post-Easter 2004**

| | GRAVES + COMPLETE | GRAVES + FRAG | GRAVES + C + F |
|---|---|---|---|
| DURANKULAK | | | |
| Hamangia I–II | 8 | 4 | 1 |
| Hamangia III–IV | 21 | 10 | 2 |
| Varna I–III | 26 | 19 | 6 |
| VEN | 17 | 56 | 21 (+46 FRAGS) |

# Bibliography

Allison, P. M. (1992) Artefact assemblages: not "the Pompeii Premise". In Herring, E., Whitehouse, R. and Wilkins, J. (eds.) *Papers of the Forth Conference of Italian Archaeology*, 49–56. Accordia Research Centre, London.

Andreou, S., Fotiadis, M. and Kotsakis, K. (1996) Review of Aegean prehistory V: the Neolithic and Bronze Age of Northern Greece. *American Journal of Archaeology* 100, 537–597.

Anthony, D. (1997) Prehistoric migration as social process. In Chapman, J. and Hamerow, H. (eds.) Migrations and invasions in archaeological explanation. *BAR*, International Series 664, 21–32. Oxford.

Appadurai, A. (ed.) (1986) *The social life of things*. Cambridge, Cambridge University Press.

Arnold, B. and Murray, M. L. (2002) A landscape of ancestors in southwest Germany. *Antiquity* 76, 321–322.

Arnold, D. E. (1985) *Ceramic theory and cultural process*. Cambridge, Cambridge University Press.

Ascher, R. (1968) Time's arrow and the archaeology of a contemporary community. In Chang, K. C. (ed.) *Settlement archaeology*, 43–52. Palo Alto, National Press Book.

Astuti, R. (1998) "It's a boy", "it's a girl"! Reflections on sex and gender in Madagascar and beyond. In Lambek, M. & Strathern, A. (eds.) *Bodies and persons. Comparative perspectives from Africa and Melanesia*, 29–52. Cambridge, Cambridge University Press.

Băčvarov, K. (2003) *Neolitni pogrebalni obredi. Intramuralni grobove ot bulgarskite zemi v konteksta na Jugoiztochna Evropa i Anatolia*. Sofia, Bard.

Bailey, D. W. (1990) The living house: signifying continuity. In Samson, R. (ed.) *The social archaeology of houses*, 19–48. Edinburgh University Press, Edinburgh.

Bailey, D. W. (2000) Balkan prehistory. London, Routledge.

Bailey, D. W. (2001) book review of J. Chapman's 2000 Fragmentation in archaeology. *American Anthropologist* 103(4), 1181–1182

Bailey, D. W. (2005) *Prehistoric figurines. Representation and corporeality in the Neolithic*. London and New York, Routledge.

Bailey, D. W., Tringham, R. E., Bass, J., Stevanović, M., Hamilton, M., Neumann, H., Angelova, I. and Raduncheva, A. (1998) Expanding the dimensions of early agricultural tells: the Podgoritsa Archaeological Project, Bulgaria. *Journal of Field Archaeology*, 25/4, 375–96.

Bailey, D. W. ,Whittle, A. and Cummings, V. (2005) *Unsettling the Neolithic*. Oxford, Oxbow Books.

Bánffy, E. (1990/1) Cult and archaeological context in central and southeast Europe in the Neolithic and Chalcolithic. *Antaeus* 19–20, 183–250.

Bánffy, E. (n.d.) Intact and fragmented cult objects – a case study. Session on "*Fragmentation*", *5th Annual EAA Meeting*, Bournemouth, IX/1998.

Barfield, L. H. and Bagolini, B. (1976) *The excavations on the Rocca di Rivoli, Verona, 1963–1968*. Verona, Museo Civico di Storia Naturale di Verona.

Barley, N. (1994) *Smashing pots: feats of clay from Africa*. London, British Museum

Barrett, J. (1999) The mythical landscapes of the British Iron Age. In Ashmore, W. and Knapp, A. B. (eds.) *Archaeologies of landscape. Contemporary perspectives*, 253–265. Oxford, Blackwell.

Barrett, J. C. (1994) *Fragments from antiquity. An archaeology of social life in Britain, 2900–1200 BC*. Oxford, Blackwell.

Battaglia, D. (1990) *On the bones of the Serpent: person, memory and mortality in Sabarl society*. Chicago, Chicago University Press.

Battaglia, D. (1995) Problematizing the self: a thematic introduction. In Battaglia, D. (ed.) *Rhetorics of Self-making*, 1–15. Berkeley, University of California Press.

Bausch, I. (1994) *Clay figurines and ritual in the Middle Jomon period. A case study of the Shakadô site in the Kofu Basin*. Unpubublished M. A. dissertation, University of Leiden.

Bausch, I. (n.d.) Fragmentation practices in Central Japan: Middle Jomon figurines at Shakadô. Session on "*Fragmentation*", *5th Annual EAA Meeting*, Bournemouth, IX/1998.

Beausang, E. (2005) Childbirth and mothering in archaeology. *GOTARC Series B. Gothenberg Archaeological Theses No 37*. Department of Archeology, University of Gothenberg.

Beck, B (1973) The right-left division of South Indian Society. In Needham, R. (ed.) *Right and left. Essays on dual symbolic classification*, 391–426. The University of Chicago Press, Chicago and London

Bem, S. (1976) Probing the promise of androgyny. In Kaplan A. G. and Bean J. P. (eds.) *Beyond sex-role stereotypes*. Boston.

Berciu, D. (1960) Deux chefs – d'oeuvre de l'art néolithique en Roumanie: le "couple" de la civilisation de Hamangia. *Dacia N.S.*, 4, 423–441.

Berciu, D. (1966) *Cultura Hamangia*. București.

Biehl, P. (2003) *Studien zur Symbolgut des Neolithikums und der Kupferzeit in Südosteuropa*. Bonn, Habelt.

Biehl, P. (n.d.) Communicating with artifacts: the transformation and destruction of figurines in the Southeast European Copper Age. Session on "*Fragmentation*", *5th Annual EAA Meeting*, Bournemouth, IX/1998.

Binford, L. R. (1964) A consideration of archaeological research design. *American Antiquity* 29/4, 425–441.

Binford, L. R. (1971) Mortuary practices: their study and their potential. In Brown J. (ed.) Approaches to the social dimensions of mortuary practices. *Washington, D.C.: Memoir of the Society for American Archaeology*, 25, 6–29.

Binford, L. R. (1981) Behavioral archaeology and the "Pompeii premise". *Journal of Anthropological Research* 37/3, 195–208.

Blake, E. (1999) Identity mapping in the Sardinian Bronze Age. *European Journal of Archaeology* 2/1, 35–55.

Blau, P. M. (1977) *Inequality and heterogeneity*. New York, Free Press.

Bleie, T. (1993) Aspects of Androgyny. In Broch-Due, V., Rudie, I. and Bleie, T. (eds.) *Carved flesh/cast selves. Gendered symbols and social practices*, 257–278. Oxford, Berg.

Boast, R. (1997) A small company of actors. A critique of style. *Journal of Material Culture* 2, 173–198.

Bodu, P., Karlin, C. and Ploux, S. (1990) Who's who? The Magdalenian flintknappers of Pincevent (France). In Cziesla, E., Eickhoff, S., Arts, N. and Winter, D. (eds.) *The big puzzle. International symposium on refitting stone artefacts*, 143–164. Bonn, Holos.

Bogaers, J. E. (1968) Waarnemingen in Westerheem, I: In het spoor van Verritus en Malorix? *Westerheem*, 17, 173–179.

Bognár-Kutzian, I. (1963) The Copper Age cemetery of Tiszapolgár-Basatanya. *Archaeologia Hungarica* 42. Budapest, Akadémiai Kiadó.

Bognár-Kutzian, I. (1972) *The Early Copper Age Tiszapolgár Culture in the Carpathian Basin*. Budapest, Akadémiai Kiadó.

Bohm, D. (1980) *Wholeness and the implicate order*. London, Routledge and Kegan Paul.

Bökönyi, S. (1992) The early Neolithic vertebrate fauna of Endrőd 119. In Bökönyi, S. (ed.) *Cultural and landscape changes in Southeast Hungary I*: Reports on the Gyomaendrőd Project, 195–300. Archaeolingua 1, Budapest.

Bollong, C. A (1994) Analysis of the stratigraphy and formation processes using patterns of pottery sherd dispersion. *Journal of Field Archaeology* 21, 15–28

Bon, S. E. (1997) A city frozen in time or a site in perpetual motion? Formation processes at Pompeii. In Bon, S. E. and Jones, R. (eds.) *Sequence and Space in Pompeii*. Oxbow Monograph 77, 7–12

Bosman, A. V. A. J. (1994) Een onverwachte ontdekking bij de Ruïne de Brederode. *Velisena, Velsen in historisch perspectief* 3, 4–6.

Bosman, A. V. A. J. (1997) *Het culturele vondstmateriaal van de vroeg-Romeinse versterking Velsen 1*. Unpublished PhD, University of Amsterdam.

Boyad•iev, Y. (2004) Chalcolithic Stone Architecture from Bulgaria. *Archaeologia Bulgarica* VII/1, 1–12.

Boyad•hiev, Y (2004) Late Neolithic sunken houses in Thrace. In Nikolov, V., Bǎčvarov, K. & Kalchev, P. (eds.) *Prehistoric Thrace. Proceedings of the International Symposium in Stara Zagora, 2003*, 207–214. Sofia – Stara Zagora.

Braasch, O. (1995) 50 Jahre verloren. In *Luftbildarchäologie in Ost- und Mitteleuropa – Aerial Archaeology in Eastern and Central Europe*, 109–122. Potsdam.

Bradley, R. (1997) *Rock art and the prehistory of Atlantic Europe. Signing the land*. London and New York, Routledge.

Bradley, R. (1998) *The significance of monuments. On the shaping of human experience in Neolithic and Bronze Age Europe*. London and New York, Routledge.

Bradley, R. (2000) *An archaeology of natural places*. London, Routledge.

Bradley, R. (2002) *The past in prehistoric societies*. London, Routledge.

Bradley, R. and Ford, D. (2004) A long distance connection in the Bronze Age: joining fragments of a Ewart Park sword from two sites in England. In Roche, H., Grogen, E., Bradley, J., Coles, J. & Raftery, B. (eds.) *From megaliths to metal. Essays in honour of George Eogan*, 174–177. Oxford, Oxbow Books.

Brandt, R. (1983) A brief encounter along the Northern frontier. In Brandt, R. and Slofstra, J. (eds.) Roman and Native in the Low Countries. Spheres of interaction. *BAR I-184*, 129–143. Oxford.

Broch-Due, V. and Rudie, I. (1993) Carved flesh-cast selves: an introduction. In Broch-Due, V., Rudie, I. and Bleie, T. (eds.) *Carved flesh/cast selves. Gendered symbols and social practices*, 1–40. Oxford, Berg.

Brück, J. (1999) The nature of the upper secondary fill in the outer ditch, Trench B: the case for more rapid deposition and continued significance of the enclosure. In Whittle, A., Pollard, J. and Grigson, C. (eds.) *The harmony of Symbols. The Windmill Hill causeway enclosure*, 375–380. Oxford, Oxbow.

Brück, J. (in press) Fragmentation, personhood and the social construction of technology in Middle and Late Bronze Age Britain. *Cambridge Journal of Archaeology*.

Bueno Ramírez, P. & Behrmann, R. de Balbín (2000) Art mégalithique en plein air. Approches de la définition du territoire pour les groupes producteurs de la péninsule ibérique. *L'Anthropologie* 104, 427–458.

Buko. A. (1998) Pottery, potsherds and the archaeologist: an approach to the pottery analyses. In Tabaczyński, S. (ed.) *Theory and Practice of Archaeological Research* Vol. III, 381–408. Warszawa, PAN.

Buko, A. (n.d.) Pottery fragmentation as a source of archaeological evidence. Session on *"Fragmentation", 5th Annual EAA Meeting*, Bournemouth, IX/1998.

Burgh, R. F. (1959) Ceramic profiles in the western mound at Awatovi, North-eastern Arizona. *American Antiquity* 25, 184–202.

Burstow, G.P. and Holleyman, G. A. (1957) Late Bronze Age settlement on Itford Hill, Sussex. *Proceedings of the Prehistoric Society* 23, 167–212.

Busby, C. (1997) Permeable and partible persons: a comparative analysis of gender and the body in South India and Melanesia. *Journal of the Royal Anthropological Institute* 3/2, 261–278.

Calado, M. (2002) Standing stones and natural outcrops. The role of ritual monuments in the Neolithic transition of the Central Alentejo. In Scarre, C. (ed.) *Monuments and landscape in Atlantic Europe*, 17–35. London, Routledge.

Cameron, C. M. (1991) Structure abandonment in villages. In Schiffer, M. B. (ed.) *Archaeological Method and Theory* Vol. 3, 155–194. Tucson, AZ, University of Arizona Press.

Carr, C. (1984) The nature of organisation of intra-site archaeological records and spatial analytic approaches to their investigation. *Advances in Archaeological Method and Theory* 7, 103–222. New York, Academic Press.

Cassen, S. (2000) Funerary stelae reused in the passage graves of western France: towards a sexualisation of the carvings. In Ritchie, A. (ed.) *Neolithic Orkney in its European* context, 233–246. Cambridge, McDonald Institute for Archaeological Research.

Catuna, C. (n.d.) Fragmenting and hoarding the ancestors: an economy of enchainment in Gumelnița-Karanovo VI culture. Session on *"Fragmentation", 5th Annual EAA Meeting*, Bournemouth, IX/1998.

Cauvin, J (1972) *Religions Néolithiques de Syro-Palestine*. Centre de Recherches d'Ecologie et de Préhistoire, Saint-Andrée-de-Cruzières.

Chapa Brunet, T. (n.d.) Fragmenting images: some reflections about uses of fragmentation in the Iberian culture (VIth–Ist century B.C. Session on *"Fragmentation", 5th Annual EAA Meeting*, Bournemouth, IX/1998.

Chapman, J. (1981) The Vinča culture of South East Europe: studies in chronology, economy and society. *BAR, International Series 117*. Oxford.

Chapman, J. (1983) Meaning and illusion in the study of burial in Balkan prehistory. In A. Poulter (ed.) *Ancient Bulgaria Volume 1*, 1–45. Nottingham, University of Nottingham Press.

Chapman, J. (1988) Ceramic production and social differentiation: the Dalmatian Neolithic and the Western Mediterranean. *Journal of Mediterranean Archaeology* 1/2, 3–25.

Chapman, J. (1988a) From "space" to "place": a model of dispersed settlement and Neolithic society. In C. Burgess, P. Topping and D. Mordant (eds.) Enclosures and defences in the Neolithic of western Europe. *BAR. International Series* 403, 21–46, Oxford.

Chapman, J. (1989) The early Balkan village. *Varia Archaeologica Hungarica*, 2, 33–53.

Chapman, J. (1990) Social inequality on Bulgarian tells and the Varna problem. In Samson, R. (ed.) *The social archaeology of houses*, 49–98. Edinburgh, Edinburgh University Press.

Chapman, J. (1991) The creation of social arenas in the Neolithic and Copper Age of South East Europe: the case of Varna. In P. Garwood, P. Jennings, R. Skeates and J. Toms (eds.) Sacred and Profane, *Oxford Committee for Archaeology Monograph No. 32*, 152–171. Oxbow, Oxford.

Chapman, J. (1994) The living, the dead, and the ancestors: time, life cycles and the mortuary domain in later European prehistory. In J.

Davies (ed.) *Ritual and remembrance. Responses to death in human societies*, 40–85. Sheffield, Sheffield Academic Press.

Chapman, J. (1995) Social power in the early farming communities of Eastern Hungary – perspectives from the Upper Tisza region. *A Josa András Múzeum Évkönyve* 36, 79–99.

Chapman, J. (1996) Enchainment, commodification and gender in the Balkan Neolithic and Copper Age. *Journal of European Archaeology* 4, 203–242.

Chapman, J. (1997) Places as timemarks – the social construction of landscapes in Eastern Hungary. In Chapman J. and Dolukhanov, P. (eds.) *Landscapes in Flux,* 137–162. Oxford, Oxbow Books.

Chapman, J. (1997a) The origins of tells in eastern Hungary. In Topping, P. (ed.) *Neolithic landscapes,* 139–164. Oxbow, Oxford.

Chapman, J. (1998) 'Objects and places: their value in the past', in Bailey, D. W. (ed.) *The archaeology of prestige and wealth. BAR International Series* 730, 106–130. Oxford.

Chapman, J. (1998a) Fragmentation. *5th Annual Meeting, EAA, Abstracts Book,* Bournemouth, EAA, 153.

Chapman, J. (1999) Where are the missing parts? – a study of artefact fragmentation. *Památky Archeologické* 90, 5–22.

Chapman, J. (1999a) The origins of warfare in the prehistory of Central and Eastern Europe. In Carman J. & Harding, A. (eds.) *Ancient warfare. Archaeological perspectives,* 101–142. Alan Sutton, Stroud.

Chapman, J. (2000) *Fragmentation in archaeology: People, places and broken objects in the prehistory of South Eastern Europe.* London, Routledge

Chapman, J. (2000a). *Tensions at funerals. Mortuary archaeology in later Hungarian prehistory.* Budapest, Archaeolingua.

Chapman, J. (2000b) Rubbish-dumps' or 'places of deposition'?: Neolithic and Copper Age settlements in Central and Eastern Europe'. In Ritchie, A. (ed.) *Neolithic Orkney in its European context,* 347–362. Cambridge, MacDonald Institute.

Chapman, J. (2000c) Pit-digging and structured deposition in the Neolithic and Copper Age of Central and Eastern Europe. *Proceedings of the Prehistoric Society* 61, 51–67.

Chapman, J. (2002) Colourful prehistories: the problem with the Berlin and Kay colour paradigm. In Jones, A. and MacGregor, G. (eds.) *Colouring the past. The significance of colour in archaeological research,* 45–72. Oxford, Berg.

Chapman, J. (2003) Domesticating the exotic: the context of Cucuteni-Tripolye exchange with steppe and forest-steppe communities. In Boyle, K., Renfrew, C. and Levine, M. (eds.) *Ancient interactions: east and west in Eurasia.* McDonald Institute Monographs, 75–92. McDonald Institute for Archaeological Research, Cambridge.

Chapman, J. (2004) Categorical analysis of Neolithic and Copper Age pottery from Bulgaria. In Nikolov, V., Băčvarov, K. & Kalchev, P. (eds.) *Prehistoric Thrace. Proceedings of the International Symposium in Stara Zagora, 2003,* 46–66. Sofia – Stara Zagora.

Chapman, J. (2004a) '*Spondylus* bracelets – fragmentation and enchainment in the East Balkan Neolithic and Copper Age.' In Slavchev, V. (ed.) Festschrift für Prof. Dr. Habil. Henrieta Todorova. *Dobrudzha* 21, 63–87.

Chapman, J. (in press) Exploring Diversity in the Ceramic Assemblage from the 1992–1996 Excavations at Schela Cladovei, Romania (To appear in Bonsall, C. & Boroneanţ, V. (eds.) *The Mesolithic – Neolithic transition in the Iron Gates Gorge and the Schela Cladovei excavations*).

Chapman, J. (in press a) A seasonal Cucuteni occupation site at Silişte-Prohozeşti, Moldavia. (To appear in Monah, D., Dumitroaia, Gh., Chapman, J. and Weller, O. (eds.) *The human uses of salt.* Piatra Neamţ.)

Chapman, J. (in press b) Meet the ancestors. Settlement histories in the Neolithic. (To appear in Bailey, D., Whittle, A., and Cummings. V. (eds.) *Unsettling the Neolithic.* Oxford, Oxbow Books).

Chapman, J. (in press c) Engaging with the exotic: the production of early farming communities in South East and Central Europe. In Biagi, P., Shennan, S. and Spataro, M. (eds.) *A Short Walk in the*

*Balkans: the first farmers of the Carpathian Basin and adjoining regions.*

Chapman, J. and Dolukhanov, P. (1993) Cultural transformations and interactions in Eastern Europe: theory and terminology. In Chapman, J. and Dolukhanov, P. (eds.) *Cultural transformations and interactions in Eastern Europe,* 1–36. Aldershot, Avebury.

Chapman, J. and Gaydarska, B. (2003) The provision of salt to Tripolye mega-sites. In Korvin-Piotrovsky, A. (ed.) *"Tripolian settlement-giants", The international symposium materials,* 203–211. Kiev, Institute of Archaeology.

Chapman, J. and Gaydarska, B. with Hardy, K. (in press) Does enclosure make a difference? A view from the Balkans. To appear in Venclová, N. (ed.) *Enclosing and excluding in prehistoric Europe.*

Chapman, J. and Hamerow, H. (1997) (eds.) Migrations and invasions in archaeological explanation. *BAR,* International Series 664. Oxford.

Chapman, J. and Priestman, S. (in press) The Vădastra experimental fragmentation programme: preliminary results. (To appear in: Gheorghiu, D. (ed.) *Experiments in archaeology and society – The Vădastra Project.* Oxford, Archaeopress.)

Chapman, J., Shiel, R., Passmore, D., Magyari, E. et alii (2003) The Upper Tisza Project: studies in Hungarian landscape archaeology. E-book 1 (JCC – 80%) (available on: (http://ads.ahds.ac.uk/catalogue/projArch/uppertisza_ba_2003/index.cfm)

Chase, P. G. (1985) Whole vessels and sherds: an experimental investigation of their quantitative relationships. *Journal of Field Archaeology* 12, 213–218.

Childe, V. G. (1945) Directional changes in funerary practices during 50,000 years. *Man* 4, 13–19.

Childe (1956) *Piecing Together the Past: The Interpretation of Archaeological Data.* London, Routledge and Kegan Paul.

Claassen, C. (1998) *Shells.* Cambridge, Cambridge University Press.

Clark, J. (1991) Pearlshell symbolism in Highlands Papua New Guinea, with particular reference to the Wiru people of Southern Highlands Province. *Oceania* 61, 309–339.

Claßen, E. (1998) Der linearbandkeramische Siedlungsplatz Frimmersdorf 122, Erftkreis, Unveröffentlichte Magisterarbeit, Köln.

Claßen, E. (1999) Der linearbandkeramische Siedlungsplatz Frimmersdorf 122, Erftkreis. *Archäologische Informationen* 22/2, 361–366.

Claßen, E. (in press) Siedlungsstrukturen der Bandkeramik im Rheinland. In Lüning, J. and Zimmermann, A. (eds.) The Bandkeramik im 21 Jahrhundert.

Comşa, E. (1995) *Figurinele antropomorfe din epocă neolitică pe teritoriul României.* Bucureşti, Ediţie Academiei Rômane.

Conkey, M. (1990) Experimenting with style in archaeology: some historical and theoretical issues. In Conkey, M. and Hastorf C. (eds.) *The uses of style in archaeology,* 5–17. Cambridge University Press, Cambridge.

Conkey, M. and Tringham, R (1995) Archaeology and the Goddess: exploring the contour of feminist archaeology. In Stewart, A. and Stanton, D. (eds.) *Feminists in the academy: rethinking the disciplines,* 199–247. Ann Arbor, MI, University of Michigan Press.

Cooper, R. (1993) Technologies of representation. In Alionen, P. (ed.) *The semiotic boundaries of politics.* Berlin, Mouton de Gruyter.

Cressey, P., Stephens, J., Shepard, S. and Magid, B. (1982) The core periphery relationship and the archaeological record in Alexandria, Virginia. In Dickens, R. Jr. (ed.) *Archaeology of urban America: the search for patterns and process,* 143–173. New York, Academic Press.

Csikszentmihaly, M. and Rochberg-Halton, E. (1981) *The meaning of things: domestic symbols and the self.* Cambridge, Cambridge University Press.

Csordas, T. (ed.) (1994) *Embodiment and experience. The existential ground of culture and self.* Cambridge, Cambridge University Press.

Cziesla, E. (1990) On refitting of stone artefacts. In Cziesla, E., Eickhoff,

S., Arts, N. and Winter, D. (eds.) *The big puzzle. International symposium on refitting stone artefacts*, 9–44. Bonn, Holos.

Cziesla, E., Eickhoff, S., Arts, N. and Winter, D. (eds.) (1990) *The big puzzle. International symposium on refitting stone artefacts*. Bonn, Holos.

Dalla Riva, M. (2003) *Pottery fragmentation at two Neolithic sites in Northern Italy: Fimon-Molino Casarotto (Vicenza) and Rocca di Rivoli (Verona)*. Unpublished B. A. (Hons.) dissertation, University of Birmingham.

David, N., Sterner, J. and Gavua, K. (1988) Why pots are decorated? *Current Anthropology* 29/3, 365–389.

De Grooth, M. E. T. (1990) Technological and socio-economic aspects of Bandkeramik flint working. In Cziesla, E., Eickhoff, S., Arts, N. and Winter, D. (eds.) *The big puzzle. International symposium on refitting stone artefacts*, 197–210. Bonn, Holos.

Deal, M. (1985) Household pottery disposal in the Maya Highlands: an anthropological interpretation. *Journal of Anthropological Archaeology* 4, 243–291.

DeBoer, W. R. (1983) The archaeological record as preserved death assemblage. In Moore, J. A and Keene, A. S. (eds.) *Archaeological Hammers and Theories*, 19–36. New York, Academic Press.

DeBoer, W. R. (1984) The last pottery show: system and sense in ceramic studies. In van der Leeuw, S. E. and Pritchard, A. C. (eds.) *The many dimensions of pottery*, 527–572. Amsterdam, University of Amsterdam.

DeBoer, W. R. and Lathrap, D. W. (1979) The making and breaking of Shipibo-Conibo ceramics. In Kramer, C. (ed.) *Ethnoarchaeology: implications of ethnography for archaeology*, 102–138. New York, Columbia University Press

DeMarrais, E., Castillo, L. J. and Earle, T. (1996) Materialization, ideology, and power strategies. *Current Anthropology* 37, 15–31.

Dennell, R. and Webley, D. (1975) Prehistoric settlement and land use in Southern Bulgaria. In Higgs, E.S. (ed.) *Palaeoeconomy*, 97–109. Cambridge University Press, Cambridge.

Derrida, J. (1982) Signature, event, context. In Derrida, J. (ed.) *The margins of philosophy*, 307–330. Brighton, Harvester Press.

Dobres , M-A and Robb, J. (2000) (eds) *Agency in archaeology*. London, Routledge.

Domboróczky, L. (2003) Radiocarbon data from Neolithic archaeological sites in Heves county (North-Eastern Hungary). *Agria* XXXIX, 5–71.

Douglas, M. (1966) *Purity and danger: an analysis of concepts of pollution and taboo*. London, Routledge and Kegan Paul.

Douglas, M. (1973) *Natural symbols : explorations in cosmology*. London, Barrie and Rockliff

Douglas, M. and Baron Isherwood (1996) *The world of goods. Towards an anthropology of consumption*. 2nd edition. London, Routledge.

Douglas, M. and Ney, S. (1998) *Missing persons. A critique of the social sciences*. Berkeley, University of California Press.

Drew, R. (1988) Untersuchungen zur räumlichen Verbreitung von Scherben identischer Gefäßzugehörigkeit. In Boelicke, U., von Brandt, D., Lüning, J., Stehli, P. and A. Zimmermann (eds.) *Der bandkeramische Siedlungsplatz Langweiler 8, Gemeinde Aldenhoven, Kreis Düren. Rheinische Ausgrabungen 28*, 483–552. Köln/Bonn.

Dumitrescu, V. (1968) *Arta neolitică in România*. Bucureşti, Meridiane.

Durkheim, E. (1933) *The division of labour in society*. Free Press, Glencoe.

Elenski, N. (2004) Cultural contacts of North-Central Bulgaria with Thrace and the Marmara area. In Nikolov, V., Băčvarov, K. and Kalchev, P. (eds.) *Prehistoric Thrace*, 67–79. Sofia, Institute of Archaeology.

Ellen, R. (1988) Fetishism. *Man (N.S)*, 23, 213–235.

Ellis, L. (1984) *The Cucuteni-Tripolye culture. A study in technology and the origins of complex society*. BAR. Oxford.

Ellison, A. (1972) The Bronze Age pottery. In Holden E. W. A Bronze Age cemetery-barrow on Itford Hill, Beddingham. *Sussex Archaeological Collections* 110, 104–113.

Éluère, C. and Raub, C. R. (1991) Investigations on the gold coating technology of the great dish from Varna. In Mohen, J-P. (ed.) *Découverte du métal*. Picard. Paris.

Eogan, G. (1998) Knowth before Knowth. *Antiquity* 72, 162–172.

Ferguson, B. and Whitehead, N. L. (eds.) (1992) *War in the tribal zone*. Santa Fe, NM, School of American Research Press.

Fol, A. and Lichardus, J. (1988) Katalog der Ausstellung. In Fol, A. and Lichardus, J. (eds.) *Macht, Herrschaft und Gold*, 181–271. Saarbrücken, Moderne Galerie des Saarland-Museums.

Fontana, V. (1998) Procedures to analyse Intra-site pottery distribution, applied to the Neolithic site of Fimon – Molino Casarotto (Italy), House-site No 3. *Journal of Archaeological Science* 25, 1067–1072

Fowler, C. (2004) *The archaeology of personhood. An anthropological approach*. London and New York, Routledge

Gaffney, C., Gaffney, V. and Tringle, M (1985) Settlement, Economy and Behaviour? Micro-regional Land Use Models and the Interpretation of Surface Artefact Patterns. In Haselgrove, C., Millett, M. and Smith, I. (eds.) *Archaeology from the Ploughsoil*, 95–108. Sheffield.

Gale, N., Stos-Gale, S., Radouncheva, A., Ivanov, I., Lilov, P., Todorov, T. and Panayotov, I. (2000) Early metallurgy in Bulgaria. *Godishnik Nov Bulgarski Universitet*, IV–V, 102–168. ALEA, Sofia.

Gallis, K. (1996) Burial customs. In Papathanassiopoulos, G. (ed.) *Neolithic culture in Greece*, 171–174. Athens, N. P. Goulandris Fondation.

Gamble, C. (2004) Social archaeology and the unfinished business of the Palaeolithic. In Cherry, J., Scarre, C. and Shennan, S. (eds.) *Explaining social change: studies in honour of Colin Renfrew*, 17–26. Cambridge, McDonald Institute for Archaeological Research.

Gamble, C. (2005) Materiality and symbolic force: a Palaeolithic view of sedentism. In DeMarrais, E., Gosden, C. & Renfrew, C. (eds.) *Rethinking materiality: the engagement of mind with the material world*, 85–95. Cambridge, McDonald Institute for Archaeological Research.

Garfinkel, Y. (1994) Ritual burial of cultic objects: the earliest evidence. *Cambridge Archaeological Journal* 4/2, 159–188

Garrow, D., Beadsmoore, E. and Knight, M. (2005) Pit clusters and the temporality of occupation: an earlier Neolithic pit site at Kilverstone, Thetford, Norfolk. *Proceedings of the Prehistoric Society*, 71, 139–158.

Gatsov, I. (2004) Chipped Stone collection from Menteşe, NW Anatolia. In Nikolov, V., Băčvarov, K. and Kalchev, P. (eds.) *Prehistoric Thrace*, 94–98. Sofia, Institute of Archaeology.

Gaydarska, B. (2003) Application of GIS in settlement archaeology: an integrated approach to prehistoric subsistence strategies. In Korvin-Piotrovsky, A. (ed.) *Tripolian settlement-giants*, The international symposium materials, 212–216. Kiev.

Gaydarska, B. (2004) *Landscape, material culture and society in South East Bulgaria*. Unpub. PhD, Durham University.

Gaydarska, B. (2004a) Preliminary research on prehistoric salt exploitation in Bulgaria. In Slavchev, V. (ed.) Festschrift for Prof. H. Todorova *Dobrudzha* 21, 110–122.

Gaydarska, B. Chapman, J. and Angelova, I. (2005) On the tell and off the tell: the fired clay figurines from Omurtag. In Spinei, V., Lazarovici, C-M. and Monah, D. (eds.) *Scripta praehistorica M. Petrescu-Dîmboviţa Festschrift*, 341–385.

Gaydarska, B., Chapman, J., Angelova, I., Gurova, M. & Yanev, S. (2004) Breaking, making and trading: the Omurtag Eneolithic *Spondylus* hoard. *Archaeologia Bulgarica* 2, 11–34.

Gaydarska, B., Chapman, J. Raduntcheva, A. and Koleva, B. (in prep.) *The social life of images: late Copper Age figurines from Dolnoslav, Bulgaria*.

Gell, A. (1992) Inter-tribal commodity barter and reproductive gift-exchange in old Melanesia. In Humphrey, C. and Hugh-Jones, S. (eds.) *Barter, exchange and value. An anthropological approach*, 142–168. Cambridge, Cambridge University Press.

Geneste, J. (1985) *Analyse lithique d'industries moustériennes du Périgord: une* approche technologique du comportement des groupes humains au Paléolithique moyen. Unpublished PhD thesis, Université de Bordeaux.

Georgiev, G. I. (1955) Mramorna statuetka from Blagoevo, Razgradsko. *Izvestia na arheologicheskia muzei*, XIX, 1–13.

Georgiev, G. I. (1961) Kulturgruppen der Jungstein-und der Kupferzeit in der Ebene von Thrazien (Südbulgarien). In Böhm, J. and de Laet, S. J. (eds.) *L'Europe à la fin de l'âge de la pierre*, 45–100. Editions de l'Académie Tchechoslovaque des Sciences, Prague.

Georgiev, G. I. (1965) The Azmak mound in southern Bulgaria. *Antiquity* 39, 6–8.

Gheorghiu, D. (2006) The controlled fragmentation of anthropomorphic figurines. In Monah, D., Dumitroaia, Gh., Chapman, J. and Weller, O. (eds.) *Cucuteni. 120 de ani de cercetări*, 137–144. Piatra Neamţ: Centrul de Cercetare a culturii Cucuteni.

Giddens, A. (1984) *The Constitution of Society: Outline of a Theory of Structuration*. Berkeley, University of California Press.

Gilchrist, R. (1999) *Gender and archaeology. Contesting the past*. London, Routledge.

Gimbutas, M. (1982) *Goddesses and Gods of old Europe*. London, Thames and Hudson.

Gimbutas, M. (1986) Mythical imagery of Sitagroi society. In Renfrew, C., Gimbutas, M. and Elster, E. S. (eds.) *Excavations at Sitagroi. A prehistoric village in Northeast Greece*. Vol. 1. *Monumenta Archaeologia 13*, 225–302. Los Angeles, UCLA Press.

Gimbutas, M. (1989) Figurines and cult equipment: their role in the reconstruction of Neolithic religion. In Gimbutas, M., Winn, S. and Shimabuku, D. (eds.) *Achilleion. A Neolithic settlement in Thessaly, Greece, 6400–5600 BC. Monumenta Archaeologica, Vol. 14*, 171–227. Institute of Archaeology, University of California, Los Angeles.

Gkiasta, M., T. Russell, S.J. Shennan and J. Steele 2003. Origins of European agriculture: the radiocarbon record revisited. *Antiquity*, 77, 45–62.

Glowacki, M. (2005) Food of the Gods or mere mortals? Hallucinogenic *Spondylus* and its interpretive implications for early Andean society. *Antiquity* 79, 257–268.

Godelier, M. (1999) The Enigma of gift. Cambridge, Polity Press.

Gould, R.A (1978) (ed.) *Exploration in ethnoarchaeology*. Albuquerque, University of New Mexico Press.

Greenfield, H. J. & Draşovean, F. (1994) Preliminary report on the 1992 excavations at Foeni-Salaş: an Early Neolithic Starčevo-Criş settlement in the Romanian Banat. *Analele Banatului* Seria Nouă III: 45–85.

Grinsell, L. (1960) The breaking of objects as a funeral rite. *Folklore* 71, 475–491.

Grinsell, L. (1973) The breaking of objects as a funeral rite: supplementary notes. *Folklore* 84, 111–114.

Grøn, O. (1991) A method for reconstruction of social organization in prehistoric societies and examples of practical application. In Grøn, O., Englestad, E. and Lindblom, I. (eds.) *Social Space*, 100–117. Odense University Press.

Gurova, M. (2004) Evolution and retardation: flint assemblages from Tell Karanovo. In Nikolov, V., Băcvarov, K. and Kalchev, P. (eds.) *Prehistoric Thrace*, 239–253. Sofia, Institute of Archaeology.

Haas, J. (1990) *The anthropology of war*. Cambridge, Cambridge University Press.

Haită, C. (1997) Micromorphological study at Borduşani – Popină. *Cercetări arheologice*, X, 85–92.

Hall E. H. (1914) *Excavations in eastern Crete, Vrokastro*. Philadelphia, University of Pennsylvania Museum.

Hally, D. (1983) The interpretative potential of pottery from domestic

Halpin, C. (1984) Blewburton. *South Midlands Archaeology* (CBA Group 9) 15: 93.

Halstead, P. (1993) *Spondylus* shell ornaments from Late Neolithic Dimini, Greece: specialised manufacture or unequal accumulation?

*Antiquity* 67, 603–609.

Halstead, P. (1995) From sharing to hoarding: the Neolithic foundation of Aegean Bronze Age society? In Laffineur, R. and Niemeier, W-D. (eds.) *Politeia: Society and State in the Aegean Bronze Age* (Aegaeum 12), 11–20. Liège, University of Liège.

Halstead, P. (1999) Neighbours from hell? The household in Neolithic Greece. In Halstead, P. (ed.) *Neolithic society in Greece. Sheffield Studies in Aegean Archaeology* 2, 77–95. Sheffield, Shefield Academic Press.

Hamilakis, Y. (1998) Eating the dead: mortuary feasting and the politics of memory in the Aegean Bronze Age societies. In Branigan, K. (ed.) *Cemetery and society in the Aegean Bronze Age*, 115–131. Sheffield, Sheffield Academic Press.

Hamilakis, Y. (n.d.) Re-collecting the fragments of memory. Session on *"Fragmentation", 5th Annual EAA Meeting*, Bournemouth, IX/1998.

Hamilton, N., Marcus, J., Bailey, D., Haaland, G., Haaland, R. and Ucko, P. (1996) Can we interpret figurines? *Cambridge Archaeological Journal* 6/2, 285–291.

Hänsel, A. and B. (eds.) *Gaben an die Götter. Schätze der Bronzezeit Europas*. Berlin, Staatliche Museen zu Berlin.

Harding, A. (2000) *European societies in the Bronze Age*. Cambridge, Cambridge University Press.

Harrison, S. (1989) The symbolic construction of aggression and war in a Sepik River society. *Man* (N.S.) 24, 593–599.

Hartz, S. (1990) Artefaktverteilungen und ausgewählte Zusammensetzungen auf dem spätglazialen Fundplatz Hasewisch, Kreis Stormen, BRD. In Cziesla, E., Eickhoff, S., Arts, N. and Winter, D. (eds.) *The big puzzle. International symposium on refitting stone artefacts*, 405–430. Bonn, Holos.

Haşotti, P. (1985) Noi cercetări arheologice în aşezarea culturii Hamangia de la Medgidia – "Cocoaşă". *Pontica*, 18, 25–40.

Haşotti, P. (1986) Cercetările arheologice din aşezarea culturii Hamangia de la Tirguşor – punctual "Urs". *Materiale*, 16, 26–33.

Haşotti, P. (1997) *Epoca Neolitică în Dobrogea*. Constanţa, Museul de Istorie Naţională şi Arheologie.

Hatt, G. (1957) Nørre Fjand. *Arkæologisk-kunsthistoriske Skifter Danske Videnskabernes Selbskab* 2/2. København.

Hayden, B. and Cannon, A. (1983) Where the garbage goes? *Journal of Anthropological Archaeology* 2, 117–163

Healan, D. M, Kerley, J. M. and Bey G. L. III (1983) Excavations and preliminary analysis of an obsidian workshop in Tula, Hidalgo, Mexico. *Journal of Field Archaeology*, 10, 127–145.

Helms, M. W. (1993) *Crafts and the kingly ideal. Art, trade and power*. Austin, TX, University of Texas Press.

Herdt, G.H. (1982) *Rituals of manhood: male initiation in Papua New Guinea*. University of California Press, Berkeley and Los Angeles.

Hetherington, K. (1997) In place of geometry: the materiality of place. In Hetherington, K. and Munro, R. (eds.) *Ideas of difference*, 183–199. Oxford, Blackwell.

Hetherington, K. (2004) Secondhandedness: consumption, disposal and absent presence. *Environment and Planning D: Society and Space* 22, 157–173.

Higham, T., Chapman, J., Slavchev, V., Gaydarska, B., Honch, N., Yordanov, Y. and Dimitrova, B. (submitted) New AMS radiocarbon dates for the Varna Eneolithic cemetery, Bulgarian Black Sea coast (To appear in *Antiquity*).

Hill, J. D. (1995) How should we understand Iron Age societies and hillforts? A contextual study from Southern Britain. In Hill, J. D. and Cumberpatch, C. G. (eds.) *Different Iron Ages*, BAR International Series 602, 45–66.

Hill, J. D. (n.d.) Bits and pieces: the interpretation of parts of things and people in ritual deposits on Southern English later prehistoric settlements (c1000 BC–AD 43). Session on "Fragmentation in Archaeology", *5th Annual EAA Meeting*, Bournemouth, IX/1998.

Hill, J. N. (1970) Broken K Pueblo: prehistoric social organisation in the

American Southwest. *Anthropological Papers of the University of Arizona* 18.

Hiller, S. and Nikolov, V. (eds.) (1997) *Karanovo, Die Ausgrabungen im Südsektor 1984–1992. Band I.* Horn/Wien, Verlag Berger and Söhne.

Hillman, D. and Mazzio, C. (1997) Introduction: individual parts. In Hillman, D. and Mazzio, C. (eds.) *The body in parts. Fantasies of corporeality in early modern Europe,* xi–xxix. London, Routledge.

Hodder, I. (1982) *Symbols in action: ethnoarchaeological studies of material culture.* Cambridge, Cambridge University Press.

Hodder, I. (1990) *The domestication of Europe.* Oxford, Blackwell.

Hodder, I. (1991) *Reading the past.* 2nd edition. Cambridge, Cambridge University Press.

Hodder, I. (1994) Architecture and meaning: the example of Neolithic houses and tombs. In Parker Pearson, M. and Richards, C. (eds.) *Architecture and social order: approaches to social space,* 73–87. London and New York, Routledge.

Hodder, I. (1999) *The Archaeological Process. An Introduction.* Oxford. Blackwell.

Hodder, I (2001) A review of contemporary theoretical debates in archaeology. In Hodder, I. (ed.) *Archaeological Theory Today,* 1–13. Cambridge, Polity Press.

Hofman, J. L. & Enloe, J. G. (1992) (eds.) Piecing together the past: applications of re-fitting studies in archaeology. *BAR,* I-578.Oxford

Hofman, J. L. (1992) Putting the pieces together: an introduction to refitting. In Hofman, J. L. and Enloe, J. G. (eds.) Piecing together the past: applications of refitting studies in archaeology. *BAR,* I-578, 1–20. Oxford.

Holden, E. W. (1972) A Bronze Age cemetery-barrow on Itford Hill, Beddingham. *Sussex Archaeological Collections* 110, 70–117.

Holten, L. (2000) Death, danger, destruction and unintended megaliths: an essay on human classification and its material and social consequences in the Neolithic of South Scandinavia. In Ritchie, A. (ed.) *Neolithic Orkney in its European context,* 287–297. Cambridge, McDonald Institute for Archaeological Research.

Holtorf, C. (2003) Fra/gmen/te/d me/gal/th/s. *3rd Stone* 47: 26–31.

Honch, N., Higham, T., Chapman, J., Gaydarska, B. and Hedges, R. (in press). A Palaeodietary Investigation of Carbon (13C/12C) and Nitrogen (15N/14N) in Human and Faunal Bones from the Copper Age Cemeteries of Varna I and Durankulak, Bulgaria, *Journal of Archaeological Science.*

Hornsey, R. (1987) The Grand Menhir Brisé: megalithic success or failure? *Oxford Journal of Archaeology* 6/2, 185–217.

Horváth, F. (1987) Hódmezővásárhely-Gorzsa: a settlement of the Tisza culture. In Raczky, P. (ed.) *The Late Neolithic in the Tisza region,* 31–46. Budapest – Szolnok, Szolnok County Museums.

Hoskins, J. (1998) *Biografical objects. How things tell the stories of people's lives.* New York and London, Routledge.

Hourmouziades, G. (1979) *To Neolitiko Dimini.* Volos, Etaireia Thessalikon Erevnon.

Houston, S. D. and Stuart, D. (1988) The ancient Maya self: personhood and portraiture in the Classic period. *RES 33,* 73–101.

Hurcombe, L. (2000) Time, skill and craft specialisation as gender relations. In Donald, M. and Hurcombe, L. (eds.) *Gender and material culture in archaeological perspective,* 88–109. London, Macmillan.

Ingold, T. (1993) The temporality of the landscape. *World Archaeology,* 25, 152–174.

Ivanov, I. (1975) Razkopki na Varnenskiya eneoliten nekropol prez 1972. *Izvestia na Narodinia Muzei Varna* 11, 1–16.

Ivanov, I. (1988) Die Ausgrabungen des Gräberfeldes von Varna. In Fol, A. and Lichardus, J. (eds.) *Macht, Herrschaft und Gold,* 49–66. Saarbrücken, Moderne Galerie des Saarland-Museums.

Ivanov, I. (1991) Der Bestattungsritus in der chalkolitischen Nekropole von Varna (mit einem Katalog des wichtigsten Gräber). In Lichardus, J. (ed.) *Die Kupferzeit als historische Epoche.* Saarbrücker Beiträge zum Altertumskunde 55, 125–150. Saabrücken, Saarland

Museum.

Jackson, M. and Karp, I. (1990) Introduction. In Jackson, M. and Karp, I. (eds.) Personhood and agency. The experience of Self and other in African cultures. *Uppsala studies in cultural anthropology, 14,* 1–14.

Jallot, L (1990) Conservation et distribution du matériel céramique: de l'espace domestique à l'espace social. In Colomer, A., Coularou, J. and Gutherz, X. (eds.) Boussargues (Argelliers, Hérault). *Documents d'archéologie française 24,* 171–198.

James, A., Jenks, C. and Prout A. (1998) *Theorising childhood.* Cambridge, Polity Press.

Jażdżewski, K. (1955) Ogólne wyniki badań archeologicznych w Gdańsku w latach 1948–1952. *Wiadomości Archeologiczne* 3, 137–152.

Jenkins, R. (1997) *Rethinking ethnicity: arguments and explorations.* London, Routledge.

Johnson, M. H. (1989) Conceptions of agency in archaeological interpretations. *Journal of Anthropological Archaeology,* 8, 129–211.

Jones, A. (2002) *Archaeological theory and scientific practice.* Cambridge, Cambridge University Press.

Jones, A. (2002a) A biography of colour: colour, material histories and personhood in the Early Bronze Age of Britain and Ireland. In Jones, A. and MacGregor, G. (eds.) *Colouring the past. The significance of colour in archaeological* research, 159–174. Oxford, Berg.

Jones, A. (2005) Lives in fragments? Personhood and the European Neolithic. *Journal of Social Archaeology* 5/2, 193–224.

Jones, A. and Richards, C. (2003) Animals into ancestors: domestication, food and identity in Late Neolithic Orkney. In Pearson, M. P. (eds.) *Food, culture and identity in the Neolithic and Early Bronze Age. BAR. International Series 1117,* 45–52. Oxford, Archaeopress.

Jovanović, B. (1971) Metalurgije Eneolitskog Perioda jugoslavije. Beograd.

Jovanović, B. (1982) Rudna Glava: najstarije rudarstvo bakra na Centralnom Balkanu. Beograd, Arheološki Institut.

Joyce, R. (1988) Comment on David, N., Sterner, J. and Gavua, K. (1988) Why pots are decorated? *Current Anthropology* 29/3, 383–384.

Kaiser, T. (1990) Ceramic technology. In Tringham, R. and Krstić, D. (eds.) *Selevac. Monumenta Archeologica 15,* 255–288. Los Angeles, The Institute of Archaeology, University of California.

Kalchev, P. (2004) The transition from Late Neolithic to Early Chalcolithic in the Stara Zagora area. In Nikolov, V., Băčvarov, K. and Kalchev, P. (eds.) *Prehistoric Thrace,* 215–226. Sofia, Institute of Archaeology.

Kalchev, P. (2005) *Neolithic dwelling, Stara Zagora.* Exposition Catalog. Stara Zagora: Regional Museum of History.

Kalicz, N. (1992) A legkorábbi fémleletek Délkelet-Európában és a Kárpát-medencében az i.e. 6–5. évezredben. *Archaeológiai Értesítő* 119, 3–14.

Kalicz, N. and Szénászky, J. G. (2001) *Spondylus*-Schmuck im Neolithicum des Komitats Békés, Südostungarn. *Praehistorische Zeitschrift,* 76/S, 24–54

Karali, L. (1991) Parure en coquillage du site de Dimitra en Macédoine protohistorique. In Laffineur, R and Basch, L. (eds.) *Thalassa: L'Égée préhistorique et la mer. Actes de la troisième rencontre Égéenne internationale de l'Université de Liège, 23–25 avril 1990, 315–322. Aegaeum 7.* Université de Liège, Liège.

Karali-Yannacopoulous, L. (1992) La parure. In Treuil, R. (ed.), *Dikili Tash: Village préhistorique de Macédoine orientale I: Fouilles de Jean Deshayes (1961–1975), BCH Supplément 24,* 159–164. École française d'Athènes, Athens.

Keightley, D. (1987) *Archaeology and mentality: the making of China. Representations* 18, 91–128.

Kent, S. (1984) *Analysing activity areas.* An ethnographic study of the use of space. Albuquerque, University of New Mexico Press

Kent, S. (1987) (ed.) *Method and theory for activity area research. An Ethnological*

*Approach*. New York, Columbia University Press.

Kent, S. (1991) The relationship between mobility strategies and site structure. In Kroll, E. M. and Price, T. D. (eds.) *The interpretation of archaeological spatial patterning*, 33–60. New York and London, Plenum Press.

Kingery, J. and Friedman, J. D. 1974. The firing temperature of a Karanovo sherd and inferences about South-East European Chalcolithic refractory technology. *Proceedings of the Prehistoric Society* 40, 204–205.

Klepikov, M. (1994) Pogrebeniya pozdneeneoliticheskogo vremeni u hutora shlyahovskii v Nizhnem Povolzhie. *Rossiska Arkheologiia* 1994/3, 97–102.

Klíma, B. (1963) *Dolní Věstonice*. Praha, CAV.

Kloos, U. (1997) Die Tonware. In Lüning, J. (ed.) Ein Siedlungsplatz der Ältesten Bandkeramik in Bruchenbrücken, Stadt Friedberg/Hessen. *Universitätsforschungen zur prähistorischen Archäologie 39*, 151–255. Bonn.

Knapp, B. and Meskell, L. (1997) Bodies of evidence in prehistoric Cyprus. *Cambridge Archaeological Journal* 7/2, 183–204.

Knauft, B. M. (1991) Violence and sociality in human evolution. *Current Anthropology* 32, 391–428.

Kobayashi, T. (1974) Behavioural patterns in pottery remains. *Arctic Anthropology (Supplement) XI*, 163–170.

Kobyliński, Z. and Moszczyński, W. A. (1992) Conjoinable sherds and stratification processes: an example from Wyszogród, Poland. *Archaeologia Polona* 30, 109–126.

Kohl, G. and Quitta, H. (1966) Berlin radiocarbon measurements 2. *Radiocarbon* 8/1, 27–45.

Kokkinidou, D. and Nikolaidou, M. (1996) Body imagery in the Aegean Neolithic: ideological implication of anthropomorphic figurines. In Moore, J. and Scott, E. (eds.) *Invisible people and processes: writing woman and children into European archaeology*, 88–112. Leicester, Leicester University Press.

Koleva, B. (2001) Niakoi nabljudenia vurhu arhitekturata na kusnoeneolitnia kultov obekt pri Dolnoslav, Plovdivsko. *Godishnik na arheologicheskia muzei Plovdiv*, X, 5–19.

Koleva, B. (2002) Prostranstven model na inventara ot purvi stroitelen horizont na kusnoeneolitnia obekt pri Dolnoslav. *Godishnik na arheologicheskia muzei Plovdiv*, IX,1, 120–130.

Kopytoff, I. (1986) The cultural biography of things: commoditization as process. In Appadurai, A. (ed.) *The social life of things*, 64–91. Cambridge, Cambridge University Press.

Kostov, R. and Bakamska, A. (2004) Nefritovi artefakti ot rannoneoloitnoto selishte Galabnik, Pernishko. *Geologia i mineralni resursi*, 4, 38–43.

Kostov, R. Dimov, T. and Pelevina, O. (2004) Gemmological characteristics of carnelian and agate beads from the Chalcolithic necropolis at Durankulak and Varna (in Bulgarian). Geologia i mineralni resursi 10, 15–24

Kotsakis, K. (2001) Mesolithic to Neolithic in Greece. Continuity, discontinuity or change of course? *Documenta Praehistorica*, 28, 63–73.

Kotsakis, K. (2005) Across the border: unstable dwelling and fluid landscapes in the earliest Neolithic of Greece. In Bailey, D., Whittle, A., and Cummings. V. (eds.) *Unsettling the Neolithic*, 8–15. Oxford, Oxbow Books.

Kramer, C. (1985) Ceramic enthoarchaeology. *Annual Review of Anthropology* 14, 77–102.

Kreuz, A., Marinova, E., Schäfer, E. and Wiethold, J. (2005) A comparison of early Neolithic crop and weed assemblages from the Linearbandkeramik and the Bulgarian Neolithic cultures: differences and similarities. *Vegatation History and Archaeobotany*, 14/3, 1–33.

Kroll, E. M. and Price, T. D. (1991) (eds.) *The interpretation of archaeological spatial patterning*. New York and London, Plenum Press.

Küchler, S. (n.d.) Fragmentation: anthropological perspectives. Session on *"Fragmentation", 5th Annual EAA Meeting*, Bournemouth, IX/ 1998.

Kunchev, M and Kuncheva, T. (1988) Pozdneneoliticheskoe poselenie "Hlebozavod" u goroda Nova-Zagora. *Studia Praehistorica* 9, 68–83.

Kurz, S. (2001) *Siedlungsforschungen im Umland der Heuneburg*. Regensburg.

Kurz, S. and Schiek, S. (2002) *Bestattungsplätze im Umfeld der Heuneburg*. Stuttgart, Konrad Theiss.

Kyparissi-Apostolika, A. (2001) *Ta Proïstorika Kosmimata tis Thessalias*. Athens, Ministry of culture (TAPA).

L'Helgouach, J. & Le Roux, C-T. (1986) Morphologie et chronologie des grandes architectures de l'Ouest de la France. In Demoule, J.-P. & Guilaine, J. (eds.) *Le Néolithique de la France*, 181–191. Paris, Picard.

Laqueur, T. (1990) *Making sex: body and gender from the Greeks to Freud*. Harvard University Press, Harvard.

Larson, M. L. and Ingbar, E. E. (1992) Perspectives on refitting: critique and a complementary approach. In Hofman, J. L. and Enloe, J. G. (eds.) Piecing together the past: applications of refitting studies in archaeology. *BAR*, International Series 578, 151–162. Oxford.

Lazarovici, Gh. (1987) "Şocul" Vinča-C în Transilvania. *Acta Musei Porolissensis* XI, 33–55.

Le Premier Or (1989) *Le premier or de l'humanité en Bulgarie 5ème millénaire*. Paris, Réunions des musées nationaux.

Le Roux, C.-T. (1992) The art of Gavrinis presented in its Armorican context and in comparison with Ireland. *Journal of the Royal Society of Antiquaries of Ireland* 122, 79–108

Leibhammer, N. (2000) Rendering realities. In Hodder, I. (ed.) Towards reflexive method in archaeology: the example at Çatalhöyük. *McDonald Institute Monograph, BIAA Monograph 28*, 129–142. McDonald Institute for Archaeological Research, Cambridge.

Lemonnier, P. (1990) Topsy-turvy techniques. Remarks on the social representation of techniques. *Archaeological Review from Cambridge* 9/ 1, 27–37.

Lemonnier, P. (ed.) (1993) *Technological choices: transformations in material culture since the Neolithic*. London, Routledge.

Leroi-Gourhan, A. (1964) *Le geste et la parole. I. Technique et langue*. Paris, Albin Michel.

Leshtakov, P. (2004) Graphite deposits and some aspects of graphite use and distribution in Bulgarian Chalcolithic. In Nikolov, V., Băčvarov, K. and Kalchev, P. (eds.) *Prehistoric Thrace*, 485–498. Sofia, Institute of Archaeology.

Leshtakov P. (2006) The Sources and Distribution of Graphite as A Means of Decoration in the Bulgarian Chalcolithic In Monah, D., Dumitroaia, Gh., Chapman, J. and Weller, O. (eds.) *Cucuteni. 120 de ani de cercetări*, 293–297. Piatra Neamţ: Centrul de Cercetare a culturii Cucuteni, 198.

Lichardus, J., Fol, A., Getov, L., Bertemès, Fr., Echt, R., Katincharov, R and Iliev, I (2000) Forschungen in der Mikroregion Drama 1983–1999. Dr. Rudolf Habelt GMBH, Bonn.

Lindauer, O. (1992) Ceramic conjoinability: orphan sherds and reconstructing time. In Hofman, J. L. and Enloe, J. G. (eds.) Piecing together the past: applications of refitting studies in archaeology. *BAR*, International Series 578, 210–216. Oxford.

LiPuma, E. (1998) Modernity and forms of personhood in Melanesia. In Lambek, M. and Strathern, A. (eds.) *Bodies and Persons: Comparative Views from Africa and Melanesia*, 53–79. Cambridge, Cambridge University Press

Lubar, S. (1993) Machine politics: the political construction of technological artifacts. In Lubar, S. & Kingery, W. D. (eds.) *History from things. Essays on material culture*, 197–214. Washington, D.C., Smithsonian Institution Press.

Macfarlane, C. (1985) Analysis of the join linkages. In Renfrew, C. *The archaeology of cult. The sanctuary at Phylakopi*. Supplementary Volume 18, 453–469. London, Thames and Hudson.

Machnik, J. (1961) Winyki badań v latach 1953–1954. In *Igolomia. I.*

*Osada wczesnośrdniwieczna*, 11–112. Wroclaw.

Makkay, J. (1992) Excavations at the Körös culture settlement of Endrőd-Oregszőlők 119. In Bökönyi, S. (ed.) *Cultural and landscape changes in Southeast Hungary I*: Reports on the Gyomaendrőd Project, 121–194. Archaeolingua 1, Budapest.

Malmer, M. P. (1991) Social space in Alvastra and other pile dwellings. In Grøn, O., Englestad, E. and Lindblom, I. (eds.) *Social Space*, 118–122. Odense University Press.

Mandelbrot B. B. (2004) *Fractals and chaos: the Mandelbrot set and beyond*. New York, Springer.

Manolakakis, L. (1996) Production lithique et émergence de la hierarchie sociale: l'industrie lithique de l'énéolithique en Bulgarie (première moitié du IVe millénaire). *Bulletin de la Société Préhistorique Française* 93/1, 119–123.

Marangou, C. (1992) Eidolia. Figurines et miniatures du Néolithique Récent et du Bronze Ancien en Grèce. *BAR. International Series 576*. Oxford.

Marangou, C. (1996) Figurines and models. In Papathanassopoulos, G. (ed.) *Neolithic culture in Greece*, 146–151. Athens, Museum of Cycladic Art.

Marazov, I. (1988) Tod und Mythos überlegungen zu Varna. In Fol, A. and Lichardus, J. (eds.) *Macht, Herrschaft und Gold*, 67–77. Saarbrücken, Moderne Galerie des Saarland-Museums.

Marcus, J. (1996) in Hamilton, N., Marcus, J., Bailey, D., Haaland, G., Haaland, R. and Ucko, P. (1996) Can we interpret figurines? *Cambridge Archaeological Journal* 6/2, 285–291.

Margos, A. (1978) Les sites lacustres dans les lacs de Varna et la necropole de Varna. *Studia Praehistorica* 1–2, 146–148.

Marinescu-Bîlcu, S. (1981) Tîrpeşti: from prehistory to history in Eastern Romania. *BAR* I-107, Oxford.

Marinescu-Bîlcu, S. (2000) The pottery. Tradition and innovation. In Marinescu-Bîlcu, S. and Bolomey, A. (eds.) *Drăguşeni. A Cucutenian community*, 91–110. Bucureşti, Editura Enciclopedică.

Martin, P. S., Longacre, W. A. and Hill, J. N. (1967) Chapters in the prehistory of Eastern Arizona, III. Field Museum of Natural History, Chicago. *Fieldiana, Anthropology* 57.

Matthews, W., French, C. A. I., Lawrence, T., Cutler, D. F. and Jones, M. K. (1997) Microstratigraphic traces of site formation processes and human activities. *World Archaeology* 29/2, 281–308

Mauss, M. (1936) Les techniques du corps. *Journal de Psychologie* 32.

Mauss, M. (1985) A category of the human mind: the notion of person, the notion of self. In Carrithers, M., Collins, S. and Lukes, S. (eds.) *The category of the person: anthropology, philosophy, history*, 1–25. Cambridge, Cambridge University Press.

McOmish, D. (1996) East Chisenbury: ritual and rubbish at the British Bronze Age-Iron Age transition. *Antiquity*, 70, 68–76.

McPherron, A. and Srejović, D. (1971) *Early farming cultures in Central Serbia and East Jugoslavia*. Belgrade.

Megerssa, G. and Kassam, A. (1987) *Oromo thinking: towards a folk model of cultural interpretation with particular references to trees*. Paper presented at the Symposium on African folk models and their application. Uppsala University.

Meskell, L. (1995) Goddesses, Gimbutas and "New Age" archaeology. *Antiquity* 69, 74–86.

Midgley, M. (1992) *TRB culture. The first farmers of the North European Plain*. Edinburgh, Edinburgh University Press.

Milisauskas, S. (2002) Interpretations and narratives of the Neolithic of southeast Europe. *Antiquity* 76, 887–889.

Miller, D. (1985) *Artefacts as categories. A study of ceramic variability in Central India*. Cambridge, Cambridge University Press.

Miller, D. (1987) *Material culture and mass consumption*. Oxford, Blackwell.

Miller, M. (2003) Technical aspects of ornament production at Sitagroi. In Elster, E. & Renfrew, C. (eds.) *Prehistoric Sitagroi: excavations in Northeast Greece, 1968–1970*. Volume 2: the final report, 369–382.

Los Angeles, Cotsen Institute of Archaeology.

Millett, M. (1979) How much pottery? In Millett, M. (ed.) *Pottery and Archaeologist*, 77–80. London, Carbon.

Mills, B. J., Eileen, L. C. and Wandsnider, L-A. (1992) Spatial patterning in ceramic vessel distributions. In Hofman, J. L. & Enloe, J. G. (eds.) Piecing together the past: applications of re-fitting studies in archaeology. *BAR*, I-578, 217–237. Oxford.

Monah, D. (1992) Grand thèmes religieux reflétés dans la plastique anthropomorphe Cucuteni-Tripolye. *Memoria Antiquitatis*, XVIII, 189–197.

Monah, D. (1997) *Plastică antropomorfă a culturii Cucuteni-Tripolie*. Piatră Neamţ, Centrul de Cercetare a culturii Cucutenii.

Moore, H. (1994) *A passion for difference*. Cambridge, Polity Press.

Morris, B. (1994) *Anthropology of the self. The individual in cultural perspective*. London, Pluto Press.

Mosko, M. (1992) Motherless sons: "divine kings" and "partible persons" in Melanesia and Polynesia. *Man* 27, 697–717.

Mosko, M. (2000) Inalienable ethnography: keeping-while-giving and the Trobriand case. *Journal of the Royal Anthropological Institute* 6, 377–396.

Müller, J. (1997) Neolitische und chalkolitische *Spondylus*-Artefakte. Anmerkungen zu Verbreitung, Tauschgebiet und sozialer Funktion. In Becker, C. et alii (eds.) *Hronos. Beiträge zur prähistorischen Archäologie zwischen Nord- und Südosteuropa. Festschrift für Bernhard Hänsel*, 91–106. Espelkamp, Marie Leidorf.

Müller, J., Herrera, A. & Knossalla, N. (1996) *Spondylus* und Dechsel – zwei gegensätzliche Hinweise auf Prestige in der mitteleuropäischen Linearbandkeramik? In Müller, J. and Bernbeck, R. (eds.) *Prestige – Prestigegüter – Sozialstrukturen. Beispiele aus dem europäischen und vorderasiatischen Neolithikum*, 81–96. Bonn, Holos.

Munn, N. (1986) *The fame of Gawa: a symbolic study of value transformation in a Massim (Papua New Guinea) society*. Cambridge, Cambridge University Press.

Munro, R. (1997) Ideas of difference: stability, social spaces and the labour of divison. In Hetherington, K. and Munro, R. (eds.) *Ideas of difference*, 3–24. Oxford, Blackwell.

Murray, P. (1980) Discard location: the ethnographic data. *American Antiquity* 45, 490–502

Myers, O. H. (1958) 'Abka re-excavated. *Kush* VI, 131–141.

Nanda, S. (1990) Neither man nor woman: the Hijras of India. Belmont, CA, Wadsworth.

Nandris, J. G. (1972) Relations between the Mesolithic, the First Temperate Neolithic and the Bandkeramik: the nature of the problem. *Alba Regia* XII, 61–70.

Nanoglou, S. (2005) Subjectivity and material culture in Thessaly, Greece: the case of Neolithic anthropomorphic imagery. *Cambridge Archaeological Journal* 15/2, 141–156.

Needham (1996) The Late Bronze Age pottery: style, fabric and finish. In Needham, S., Spence, T., Serjeantson, D. and Sorenson, M-L. S. (eds.) *Refuse and disposal at area 16 east Runnymede. Runnymede Bridge research excavations, 2*, 106–164. British Museum Press.

Needham, S. and Spence, T. (1997) Refuse and the formation of middens. *Antiquity* 71, 77–90.

Needham, S., Spence, T., Serjeantson, D. and Sorenson, M-L. S. (1996) *Refuse and disposal at area 16 east Runnymede. Runnymede Bridge research excavations, 2*. London, British Museum Press.

Nikolaidou, M. (2003) Catalog of items of adornment. In Elster, E. & Renfrew, C. (eds.) *Prehistoric Sitagroi: excavations in Northeast Greece, 1968–1970*. Volume 2: the final report, 383–401. Los Angeles, Cotsen Institute of Archaeology.

Nikolov, V (1993) Spätneolitische Siedlungen in Thrakien: das Problem Karanovo IV. *Saarbrüker Studien und Materialen zur Altertumskunde* 2, 157–190.

Nikolov, V. (1997) Die neolithische Keramik. In Hiller, S. and Nikolov,

V. (eds.) *Karanovo, Die Ausgrabungen im Südsektor 1984 – 1992. Band I*, 105–146. Horn/Wien, Verlag Berger and Söhne.

Nikolov, V. (2002) *Rannoneolitna risuvana ornamentatsija.* Sofia.

Ninov, L (1990) Animal bones from boreholes of early neolithic settlement near village Kovahevo, Blagoevgrad. *Studia Praehistorica*, 10, 197–199.

Noble, G. (2006) *Neolithic Scotland: timber, stone, earth and fire.* Edinburgh, Edinburgh University Press.

Olivier, L. (1999) The Hochdorf 'Princely Grave' and the question of the nature of archaeological funerary assemblages. In Murray, T. (ed.) *Time and archaeology. One World Archaeology 37*, 109–138. London, Routledge.

Olivier, L. (n.d.) Breakage, dismantling and separation in the Iron Age of Western Europe. Session on "Fragmentation in Archaeology", *5th Annual EAA Meeting*, Bournemouth, IX/1998.

Orton, C. (1993) How many pots make five? *Archaeometry* 35/2, 169–184

Orton, C., Tyers, P. and Vince, A. (1993) *Pottery in archaeology. Cambridge manuals in archaeology.* Cambridge, Cambridge University Press.

Ottaway, B. (2001) Innovation, production and specialization in early prehistoric copper metallurgy. *European Journal of Archaeology* 4/1, 87–112.

Papa, M. Halstead, P., Kotsakis, K. and Urem-Kotsou, D. (2004) Evidence for large-scale feasting at Late Neolithic Makryalos, Northern Greece. In Halstead, P. and Barrett, J. (eds) Food, cuisine and society in prehistoric Greece. *Sheffield Studies in Aegean Archaeology*, 5, 16–44. Oxford, Oxbow Books.

Parker Pearson, M. (1999) *The archaeology of death and burial.* Stroud, Alan Sutton.

Parker Pearson, M. and Richards, C. (1994) (eds.) *Architecture and order: approaches to social space.* London and New York, Routledge.

Parker Pearson, M. and Richards, C. (1994) Architecture and order: spatial representation and archaeology. In Parker Pearson, M. and Richards, C. (eds.) *Architecture and social order: approaches to social space*, 38–72. London and New York, Routledge.

Peebles, C. (1979) *Excavations at Moundville, 1905–1951.* University of Michigan Press, Ann Arbor.

Perlès, C. (2001) *The Early Neolithic in Greece.* Cambridge, Cambridge University Press.

Perlès, C. and Vitelli, K. D. (1999) Craft specialisation in the Neolithic of Greece. In Halstead, P. (ed.) *Neolithic society in Greece*, 96–107. Sheffield, Sheffield Academic Press.

Pernicheva, L. (1990) Le site de Kovatchevo, néolithique ancient, dans le département de Blagoevgrad. *Studia Praehistorica* 10, 142–196.

Pernicka, E., Begemann, F., Schmitt-Strecker, S. and Wagner, A. (1993) Eneolithic and Early Bronge Age copper artefacts from the Balkans and their relation to Serbian copper ores. *Praehistorische Zeitschrift*, 68/1, 1–54.

Pernicka, E., Begemann, F., Schmitt-Strecker, S., Todorova, H. and Kuleff, I. (1997) Prehistoric copper in Bulgaria. *Eurasia Antiqua* 3, 41–180.

Pétrequin, P., Pétrequin, A., Giligny, F. and Ruby, P. (1994) Produire pour soi, la céramique de Chalain 2C au Néolithique Final. *Bulletin de la Société Préhistorique Française* 91/6, 407–417

Petrie, W. M. F. (1899) Sequences in prehistoric remains. *Journal of Royal Anthropological Institute*, 29, 295–301.

Petrova, V. (2004) The ceramic assemblage of the Late Chalcolithic Karanovo VI culture. In Nikolov, V., Băčvarov, K. and Kalchev, P. (eds.) *Prehistoric Thrace*, 421–432. Sofia, Institute of Archaeology.

Pigeot, N. (1987) *Magdaléniens d'Étiolles: économie de débitage et organisation sociale.* Gallia Préhistoire Supplément 25. Paris, CNRS.

Price, T. D. (1991) Postscript: the end of spatial analysis. In Kroll, E. M. and Price, T. D. (eds.) *The interpretation of archaeological spatial patterning*, 301–305. New York and London, Plenum Press.

Prigogine, I. (1987) *The end of certainty: time, chaos and the new laws of nature.* London, The Free Press.

Raczky, P. et al. (16 authors) (2002) Polgár-Csőszhalom (1989–2000): Summary of the Hungarian-German excavations on a Neolithic settlement in Eastern Hungary. In Aslan, R. et al. (eds.) *Mauerschau. Festchrift für Manfred Korfmann. Band 2*, 833–860. Remshalden-Grunbach, Greiner.

Raduntcheva, A. (1976) Vinitsa. Eneolitno selishte i nekropol. *Razkopki i Prouchvania* VI. Sofia, Izdatelstvo na BAN.

Raduntcheva, A. (1996) Dolnoslav: a temple centre from the Eneolithic. *Godishnik na Department Arheologiya* (Nov Bulgarski Universitet) II/III, 168–181.

Raduntcheva, A. (2002). Eneolithic temple complex near the village of Dolnoslav, district of Plovdiv, and the system of rock sanctuaries with prehistoric cultural strata in Rodopi Mountains and outside its territory. *Godishnik na Arheologicheski Muzei Plovdiv* IX/1, 96–119.

Raduntcheva, A. (2003) Kusnoeneolitnoto obstestvo v bulgarskite zemi. Razkopki i prouchvania XXXII. Sofia, AIM BAN.

Raduntcheva, A., Matsanova, V., Gatsov, I., Kovachev, G., Georgiev, G., Chakalova, E. & Bozhilova, E. (2002) Neolitno selishte do grad Rakitovo. *Razkopki i Prouchvaniya*, XXIX. Sofia, Gal-iko.

Ray, K. (1987) Material metaphor, social interaction and historical reconstruction: exploring patterns of associations and symbolism in the Igbo-Ukwu corpus. In Hodder, I. (ed.) *The archaeology of contextual meaning*, 66–78. Cambridge, Cambridge Universtiy Press.

Reay, M. (1959) *The Kuma. Freedom and conformity in the New Guinea Highlands.* Melbourne, Melbourne University Press.

Renfrew, C. (1969) The autonomy of the South East European Copper Age. *Proceedings of the Prehistoric Society*, 35, 12–47.

Renfrew, C. (1973) *Before civilisation. The radiocarbon revolution and prehistoric Europe.* Harmondsworth: Penguin.

Renfrew, C. (1985) *The archaeology of cult. The sanctuary at Phylakopi.* Supplementary Volume 18. London, Thames and Hudson.

Renfrew, C. (2001) Symbol before concept: material engagement and the early development of society. In Hodder, I. (ed.) *Archaeological Theory Today*, 122–140. Polity Press, Cambridge.

Richards, C. (n.d.) The wonder of stone. Unpublished paper, *27th Theoretical Archaeology Group conference*, Sheffield, December 2005.

Roebroeks, W., De Loecker, D., Hennekens, P. & van Leperen, M. (1992) "A veil of stones": on the interpretation of an early Middle Palaeolithic low density scatter at Maastricht-Belvédère (The Netherlands). *Analecta Praehistorica Leidensia* 25, 1–16.

Roebroeks, W. and Hennekens, P. (1990) Transport of lithics in the Middle Palaeolithic: conjoining evidence from Maastricht-Belvédère. In Czielsa, E., Eickhoff, S., Arts, N. and Winter, D. (eds.) *The big puzzle. International symposium on refitting stone artefacts*, 283–296. Bonn, Holos.

Rowlands, M. and Warnier, J.-P. (1993) The magical production of iron in the Cameroon Grassfields. In Shaw, T., Sinclair, P., Andah, B. and Okpoko, A. (eds.) *The archaeology of Africa: food, metals and towns*, 512–550. London, Routledge.

Sahlins, M. (1974) *Stone Age economics.* Chicago, Aldine.

Sahlins, M. (1985) *Islands of history.* Chicago, University of Chicago Press.

Sahlins, M. (1991) The return of the event, again; with reflections on the beginning of the Great Fijian War of 1843 to 1855 between the kingdoms of Bau and Rewa. In Biersack, A. (ed.) *Clio in Oceania: toward a historical anthropology.* Washington, D.C., Smithsonian Institution Press.

Sanders, D. (1990) Behavioural conventions and archaeology: methods for the analysis of ancient architecture. In Kent, S. (ed.) *Domestic Architecture and the Use of Space.* Cambridge, Cambridge University Press.

Saunders, N. J. (1999) Biographies of brilliance: pearls, transformations of matter and being, c. AD 1492. *World Archaeology* 31/2, 243–257.

Scarre, C. (2002) Coast and cosmos. The Neolithic monuments of Northern Brittany. In Scarre, C. (ed.) *Monuments and landscape in Atlantic Europe*, 84–105. London, Routledge.

Schachermeyr, F. (1955) *Die altesten Kulturen Griechenlands*. Stuttgart.

Schaller-Åhrberg, E. (1990) Refitting as a method to separate mixed sites: a test with unexpected results. In Czielsa, E., Eickhoff, S., Arts, N. and Winter, D. (eds.) *The big puzzle. International symposium on refitting stone artefacts*, 611–622. Bonn, Holos.

Scheer, A. (1990) Von der Schichtinterpretation bis zum Besiedlungsmuster – Zusammensetzungen als absoluter Nachweis. In Cziesla, E., Eickhoff, S., Arts, N. and Winter, D. (eds.) *The big puzzle. International symposium on refitting stone artefacts*, 623–651. Holos, Bonn.

Schiffer, M. B. (1975) The effects of occupation span on site content. In Schiffer, M. B. and House, J. H. (eds) *The Cache River archaeological Project: an experiment in contract archaeology*, 265–269. Arkansas Archaeological Survey, Research Series 8.

Schiffer, M. B. (1976) *Behavioral Archaeology*. New York, Academic Press

Schiffer, M. B. (1985) Is there a "Pompeii premise" in archaeology? *Journal of Anthropological Research* 41, 18–41

Schiffer, M. B. (1987) *Formation processes of the archaeological record*. Albuquerque, University of New Mexico Press

Schiffer, M. B. (1989) Formation processes of Broken K Pueblo: some hypothesis. In Leonard, R. D. and Jones, G. T. (eds.) *Quantifying diversity in archaeology*, 37–58. Cambridge University Press, Cambridge.

Schlanger, N. (1996) Understanding Levallois: lithic technology and cognitive archaeology. *Cambridge Archaeological Journal* 6/2, 231–254.

Schneider, S. (2003) *Ancestor veneration and ceramic curation: an analysis from Speckhau Tumulus 17, South West Germany*. Unpub. M.A. dissertation, University of Wisconsin – Milwaukee.

Schubert, F. (1965) Zu den südosteuropäischen Kupferäxten. *Germania* 43, 274–295.

Schwarz, M. T. (1997) *Molded in the image of changing woman. Navajo views on the human body and personhood*. Tucson, The University of Arizona Press.

Séfériades, M. (1995) *Spondylus gaederopus*: the earliest European long-distance exchange system. A symbolic and structural archaeological approach to Neolithic societies. *Poročilo* 22, 233–256.

Séfériades, M. L. (2000) *Spondylus gaederopus*: some observations on the earliest European long-distance exchange system. In Hiller, S. and Nikolov, V. (eds.) *Karanovo Band III. Beiträge zum Neolithikum in Südosteuropa*, 423–437. Wien, Phoibos Verlag

Séfériades, M. L. (2003) Note sur l'origine et la signification des objets en spondyle de Hongrie dans le cadre du Néolithique et de l'Énéolithique européens. In Jerem, E. & Raczky, P. (eds.) *Morgenrot der Kulturen. Festschrift für Nándor Kalicz zum 75 Geburtstag*, 353–373. Budapest, Archaeolingua.

Seymour, D. and Schiffer, M. B. (1987) A preliminary analysis of pit-house assemblages from Snaketown, Arizona. In Kent, S. (1987) (ed.) *Method and theory for activity area research*, 549–603. New York, Columbia University Press.

Shackleton, J. C. and Elderfield, H. (1990) Strontium isotope dating of the source of Neolithic European *Spondylus* shell artefacts. *Antiquity* 64, 312–315.

Shackleton, N. (2003) Preliminary report on the molluscan remains at Sitagroi. In Elster, E. & Renfrew, C. (eds.) *Prehistoric Sitagroi: excavations in Northeast Greece, 1968–1970*. Volume 2: the final report, 361–365. Los Angeles, Cotsen Institute of Archaeology.

Shackleton, N. and Renfrew, C. (1970) Neolithic trade routes re-aligned by oxygen isotope analysis. *Nature* 228, 1062–1065.

Shanks, M and Tilley, C. (1982) Ideology, symbolic power and ritual communication: a reinterpretation of Neolithic mortuary practices. In Hodder, I. (ed.) *Symbolic and Structural Archaeology*, 129–154.

Cambridge, Cambridge University Press.

Shaw, R.P. and Wong, Y. (1988) *Genetic seeds of warfare: evolution, nationalism and patriotism*. London, Unwiun Hyman.

Shennan, S. (1975) The social organization at Branč. *Antiquity* 49, 279–288.

Sherratt, A. (1982) Mobile resources: settlement and exchange in early agricultural Europe. In Renfrew, C and Shennan, S. (eds.) *Ranking, resource and exchange*, 13–26. Cambridge

Sherratt, A. (1986) The pottery of Phases IV and V: the Early Bronze Age. In Renfrew, C., Gimbutas, M. and Elster, E. S. (eds.) *Excavations at Sitagroi. A prehistoric village in Northeast Greece*. Vol. 1. Monumenta Archaeologia 13, 429–476. Los Angeles, UCLA Press.

Singer, J. (1977) *Androgyny towards a new theory of sexuality*. Routledge and Kegan Paul, London.

Skafida, E. (in press) Symbols from the Aegean World: the case of late Neolithic figurines and house models from Thessaly, Hellas. (To appear in Inretnational symposium, The Aegean in the Neolithic, Chalcolithic and Early Bronze Age. Urla-Izmir 13–19 October 1997).

Skafida, E. (in prep.) The figurines of Neolithic Dimini. Social organisation and ideology of Neolithic communities in Thessaly.

Skeates, R. (1995) Animate objects: a biography of prehistoric "axe-amulets" in the central Mediterranean region. *Proceedings of the Prehistoric Society*, 61, 279–301.

Skibo, J. M., Schiffer, M. B. and Kowalski, N. (1989) Ceramic style analysis in archaeology and ethnoarchaeology: bridging the analytical gap. *Journal of Anthropogical Archaeology* 8, 388–409

Skourtopoulou, K. (in press a) Making things, creating communities: co-existing craft patterns in Late Neolithic Greece. (To appear in Boyd, B. and Sillar, B. (eds.) *Embedded technologies. Re-working technical studies in archaeology*. Oxford, Berg.)

Skourtopoulou, K. (in press b) Questioning spatial contexts: the contribution of lithic studies as analytical and interpretative bodies of data. (To appear in Papaconstantinou, D. (ed.) *Deconstructing Context: A Critical Approach to Archaeological Practice*. Oxford, Oxbow.)

Smith, C. (1992) *Late Stone Age hunters of the British Isles*. Routledge, London and New York.

Smith, W. (1971) Painted ceramics of the Western mound at Awatovi. *Papers of the Peabody Museum of Archaeology and Ethnology, 38*. Harvard University.

Sofaer Derevenski, J. (1997) Age and gender at the site of Tiszapolgár-Basatanya, Hungary. *Antiquity* 71, 875–889.

Sofaer Derevenski, J. (2000) Rings of life: the role of early metalwork in mediating the gendered life course. *World Archaeology* 31, 389–406.

Sørensen, M-L. S. (1996) Pottery evidence for formation process in the Late Broze Age deposits. In Needham, S., Spence, T., Serjeantson, D. and Sorenson, M-L. S. (eds.) *Refuse and disposal at area 16 east Runnymede. Runnymede Bridge research excavations, 2*, 61–77. British Museum Press.

Sørensen, M-L. S. (2000) *Gender Archaeology*. Cambridge, Polity Press.

South, S. (1977) *Method and theory in historical archaeology*. New York, Academic Press.

Souvatzi, S. (in prep.) *The archaeology of the household: examples from the Greek Neolithic*. Unpublished PhD thesis, University of Cambridge.

Souvatzi, S. and Skafida, E. (2003) Neolithic communities and symbolic meanings. Preceptions and expressions of symbolic and social structures at Late Neolithic Dimini, Thessaly. In Nikolova, L. (ed.) *Early symbolic systems for communication in Southeast Europe*. *BAR*, International Series 1139, 429–441. Oxford, Archaeopress.

Spassov, N. and Iliev, N. (2002) The animal bones from the prehistoric necropolis near Durankulak (NE Bulgaria) and the latest record of *Equus hydruntinus* Regalia. In Todorova, H. (ed.) (2002) *Durankulak Band II. Die prähistorischen Gräberfelder*, 131–324. DAI, Berlin – Sofia, Anubis.

Spector, J. (1991) What this awl mean: towards a feminist archaeology.

In Gero, J. M. and Conkey, M. (eds.) *Engendering archaeology*, 388–406. Oxford, Blackwell.

Srejović, D. (1968) Neolitska plastika tsentralnobalkanskog podruchia. In *Neolit Centralnog Balkana*, 177–240. Belgrade, Nadodni muzei.

Srejović, D. (1969) *Lepenski Vir: nova praistorijska kultura u Podunavlju*. Beograd, Srpska Kni•evna Zadruga.

Stallybrass, P. (1992) Shakespeare, the individual and the text. In Greenberg, L., Nelson, C. and Treichler, P. (eds.) *Cultural studies*, 593–612. New York, Routledge.

Stanislawski, M. (1978) If pots were mortal. In R. Gould (ed.) *Explorations in ethnoarchaeology*, 201–228. University of New Mexico Press

Stäuble, H. (1997) Häuser, Gruben und Fundverteilung. In Lüning, J. (ed.) Ein Siedlungsplatz der Ältesten Bandkeramik in Bruchenbrücken, Stadt Friedberg/Hessen. *Universitätsforschungen zur prähistorischen Archäologie 39*, 17–150. Bonn.

Stevenson, M. G. (1982) Towards understanding of site abandonment behaviour. *Journal of Anthropological Archaeology* 1, 237–265.

Stevenson, M. G. (1991) Beyond the formation of hearth-associated artefact assemblages. In Kroll, E. M. and Price, T. D. (eds.) *The interpretation of archaeological spatial patterning*, 269–300. New York and London, Plenum Press.

Strathern, A. and Stewart, P. J. 1998. Melpa and Nuer ideas of life and death: the rebirth of a comparison. In Lambek, M. & Strathern, A. (eds.) *Bodies and persons. Comparative perspectives from Africa and Melanesia*, 232–251. Cambridge, Cambridge University Press.

Strathern, M. (1988) *The gender of the gift*. Berkeley. University of California Press

Sullivan, A. P. (1978) Inference and evidence in archaeology: a discussion of the conceptual problems. In Schiffer, M. B. (ed.) *Advances in Archaeological Method and Theory* 1, 183–222. New York, Academic Press.

Sullivan, A. P. (1989) The technology of ceramic reuse: formation processes and archaeological evidence. *World Archaeology* 21/1, 101–114

Sullivan, A. P., Skibo, J. M. and van Buren, M. (1991) Sherds as tools: the role of vessel fragments in prehistoric succulent plant processing. *North American Archaeologist* 12/3, 243–255.

Svoboda. J., Lozek, V. and Vlcek, E. (1996) Hunters between East and West: the Paleolithic of Moravia. New York and London, Plenum Press.

Swogger, J. G. (2000) Image and interpretation: the tyranny of representation? In Hodder, I. (ed.) Towards reflexive method in archaeology: the example at Çatalhöyük. *McDonald Institute Monograph, BIAA Monograph 28*, 143–152. McDonald Institute for Archaeological Research, Cambridge.

Talalay, L. (1993) Deities, dolls and devices. Neolithic figurines from Franchthi Cave. Excavations at Franchthic Cave Fascicule 9. Bloomington IN, University of Indiana Press.

Talalay, L. ( 2004) Heady business: skulls, heads and decapitation in Neolithic Anatolia and Greece. *Journal of Mediterranean Archaeology* 17/2: 139–163.

Thomas, J. (1999) *Understanding the Neolithic*. London, Routledge.

Thomas, J. (2001) Archaeologies of Place and Landscape. In Hodder, I. (ed.) *Archaeological Theory Today*, 165–186. Cambridge, Polity Press.

Thompson, M. (1979) *Rubbish theory. The creation and destruction of value*. Oxford, Oxford University Press.

Todorova, H. (1972) Kolektivna nahodka ot idol i sud ot Balchik. *Izvestia na Arkheologicheskia Institut* 33, 39–45

Todorova, H. (1978) *The Eneolithic period in Bulgaria in the Fifth Millennium B.C.* International Series 49. Oxford, BAR.

Todorova, H. (1980) Klassifikatsija chislovoi kod plastiki neolita, eneolita i rannei bronzovoi epohi Bolgarii. *Studia Praehistorica* 3, 38–67.

Todorova, H. (1981) Die kupferzeitlichen Äxte und Beile in Bulgarien.

*Prähistorische Bronzefunde, 9/14.* München.

Todorova, H. (1982) Kupferzeitliche Siedlungen in Nordostbulgarien. MAVA13. München.

Todorova, H. (1989) *Kamenno-mednata epoha*. Sofia, Bulgarskata Akademia na Naukite.

Todorova, H. (1995) Bemerkungen zum frühen Handelsverkehr während des Neolithikums und des Chalkolithikums im westlichen Schwartzmeerraum. In Hänsel, B. (ed.) *Handel, Tausch und Verkehr im bronze- und früheisenzeitlichen Südosteuropas*. Prähistorische Archäologie Südosteuropas Band 11, 53–66. München-Berlin, Südosteuropa Gesellschaft.

Todorova, H. (1997) Tellsiedlung von Durankulak. *Fritz Thiessen Stiftung Jahresbericht* 1995/96, 81–84.

Todorova, H. (ed.) (2002) *Durankulak Band II. Die prähistorischen Gräberfelder*. DAI, Berlin – Sofia, Anubis.

Todorova, H. (2002a) Die geographische Lage der Gräberfelder (mt drei Karten). Paläoklima, Strandverschiebungen und Umwelt der Dobrudscha im 6–4. Jahrtausend v. Chr. In Todorova, H. (ed.) *Durankulak Band II. Die prähistorischen Gräberfelder*, 17–24. DAI, Berlin – Sofia, Anubis.

Todorova, H. (2002b) Chronologie, horizontale Stratigraphie und Befunde. In Todorova, H. (ed.) *Durankulak Band II. Die prähistorischen Gräberfelder*, 35–52. DAI, Berlin – Sofia, Anubis.

Todorova, H. (2002c) Die Sepulkeramik aus den Gräbern von Durankulak. In Todorova, H. (ed.) *Durankulak Band II. Die prähistorischen Gräberfelder*, 81–116. DAI, Berlin – Sofia, Anubis.

Todorova, H. (2002d) Die Mollusken in den Gräberfeldern von Durankulak. In Todorova, H. (ed.) *Durankulak Band II. Die prähistorischen Gräberfelder*, 177–186. DAI, Berlin – Sofia, Anubis.

Todorova, H. and Dimov, T. (1989) Ausgrabungen in Durankulak 1974–1987. In Neolithic of Southeastern Europe and its Near Eastern connections. *Varia Archaeologica Hungarica* II, 291–310. Budapest.

Todorova H., Dimov, T., Bojadžiev, J., Vajsov, I., Dimitrov, K. & Avramova, M. 2002. Katalog der prähistorischen Gräber von Durankulak. In Todorova, H. (ed.) *Durankulak Band II. Die prähistorischen Gräberfelder. Teil II*. DAI, Berlin – Sofia, Anubis.

Todorova, H., Ivanov, S., Vasilev, V., Hopf, M., Quitta, H. and Kohl, G. (1975) Selishtanata mogila pri Goliamo Delchevo. *Razkopki i Prouchvania* V. Sofia, Izdatelstvo na BAN.

Todorova, H. and Vajsov, I. (1993) *Novo-kamennata epoha v Bulgaria*. Sofia, Nauka i Izkustvo.

Todorova, H., Vasilev, V., Yanushevich, Z., Kovacheva, M. and Valev, P. (1983) Ovcharovo. *Razkopki i Prouchvania* IX. Sofia, Izdatelstvo na BAN.

Torrence, R. (1982) The obsidian quarries and their use. In Renfrew, C and Wagstaff, J. M. (eds.) *An island polity. The archaeology of exploration in Melos*, 193–221. Cambridge.

Toufexis, G. and Skafida, E. (1998) Neolithic house models from Thessaly, Greece. *Proceedings of the XIII congress of the International Union of Prehistoric and Protohistoric Sciences, Vol. 3*, 339–346. Forli.

Tringham, R. and Krstić, D. (1990) Selevac in the wider context of European Prehistory. In Tringham, R. & Krstić, D. (eds.) *Selevac. A Neolithic village in Serbia. Monographs in Archaeology Vol. 15*, 567–616. Los Angeles, University of California Press.

Tringham, R. (1991) Households with faces: the challenge of gender in prehistoric architectural remains. In Gero, J. M. and Conkey, M. (eds.) *Engendering archaeology*, 93–131. Oxford, Blackwell.

Tringham, R. (1994) Engendered places in prehistory. *Gender, Place and Culture*, I/2, 169–203.

Trogmayer, O. (1990) Der Gott mit Axt. In Raczky, P. & Maier-Arendt, W. (eds.) *Altag und Religion. Jungsteinzeit in Ost-Ungarn*. Frankfurt-am-Main.

Trubitt, M. B. D. (2003) The production and exchange of marine shell prestige goods. *Journal of Archaeological Research* 11/3, 243–277.

Tsirtoni, Z. (2000) Les poteries du début du Néolithique Récent en Macédoine. I. Les types de récipients. *Bulletin de Correspondance Hellénique* 124, 1–55.

Tsonev, Ts. (2004) Long blades in the context of East Balkan and Anatolian early complex sedentary societies. In Nikolov, V., Băčvarov, K. and Kalchev, P. (eds.) *Prehistoric Thrace*, 259–263. Sofia, Institute of Archaeology.

Tsountas, C. (1908) *Ai Proïstorikai Akropoleis Diminiou kai Sesklou*. Athens, Archaeologiki Etaireia.

Tsuneki, A. (1987) A reconsideration of *Spondylus* shell rings from Agia Sofia Magoula, Greece. *Bulletin of the Ancient Orient Museum* IX, 1–15.

Tsuneki, A. (1989) The manufacture of *Spondylus* shell objects at Neolithic Dimini, Greece. *Orient* XXV, 1–21.

Turk, P. (1997) Das Depot eines Bronzegiessers aus Slowenien – Opfer oder Materiallager? In Hänsel, A. and B. (eds.) *Gaben an die Götter. Schätze der Bronzezeit Europas*, 49–52. Staatliche Museen zu Berlin, Berlin.

Turner, J. H. (1984) *Societal stratification. A theoretical analysis*. Columbia University Press, New York.

Vajsov, I. (1992) Antropomorfnata plastika na kultura Hamangia. *Dobrudza* 9, 35–70.

Vajsov, I. (2002) Die Idole aus den Gräberfeldern von Durankulak In Todorova, H. (ed.) *Durankulak Band II. Die prähistorischen Gräberfelder*, 257–268. DAI, Berlin – Sofia, Anubis.

Vandiver, P., Soffer, O., Klima, B. and Svoboda, J. (1989) The origins of ceramic technology at Dolní Věstonice, Czechoslovakia. *Science* 246, 1002–1008.

Verhart, L. B. M. (1990) Refitting and the problems of simultaneous habitation: the Hekelingen example. In Cziesla, E., Eickhoff, S., Arts, N. and Winter, D. (eds.) *The big puzzle. International symposium on refitting stone artefacts*, 569–582. Bonn, Holos.

Videiko, M. (1996) Grossiedlungen der Tripoly'e-Kultur in die Ukraine. *Eurasia Antiqua* I, 45–80.

Videiko, M. (2004) Tripil's'ka kul'tura. In Klochko (ed.) Platar. Kolekcia predmetiv starovini rodin Platonovih i Tarut, 8–75. Kiev

Villa, P. (1982) Conjoinable pieces and site formation processes. *American Antiquity* 47, 276–290.

Villa, P. and Courtin, J. (1983) The interpretation of stratified sites: a view from underground. *Journal of Archaeological Science* 10, 267–281.

Vitelli, K.D. (1995) Pots, potters and the shaping of Greek Neolithic society. In Barnett, W. and Hoopes, J. (eds) *The Emergence of Pottery*, 55–63. Washington DC, Smithsonian Institution.

Von Gernet, A. (1982) Interpreting intrasite spatial distribution of artifacts: the Draper Site pipe fragments. *Man in the Northeast* 23, 49–60.

Vons, P. and Bosman, A. V. A. J. (1988) Inheemse boeren bezochten de verlaten Romeinse versterkingen Velsen I and II. *Westerheem* 37, 1–17.

Vulpe, A. (1970) Die Äxte und Beile in Rumänien I. *Prähistorische Bronzefunde*, IX/2. München.

Vulpe, A. (1975) Die Äxte und Beile in Rumänien II. *Prähistorische Bronzefunde*, IX/5. München.

Waddington, C. (1998) Cup and ring marks in context. *Cambridge Archaeological Journal* 8/1, 29–54.

Wagner, R. (1975) *The invention of culture*. Englewood Cliffs, NJ, Pretenice-Hall Inc.

Washburn, D. and Crowe, D. (2004) (eds.) *Symmetry Comes of Age*. Seattle, University of Washington Press.

Weigand, P. C. (1969) *Modern Huichol ceramics*. University Museum Mesoamerican Studies, Southern Illinois University at Carbondale.

Weiner, A. (1992) *Inalienable possessions: the paradox of keeping-while-giving*. Berkeley, University of California Press.

Weiner, J. (1990) Intra-site analysis by refitting lithic artefacts from a flint-workshop on the Neolithic flint-mine "Lousberg" in Aachen (Nordrhein-Westphalia, FRG). In Cziesla, E., Eickhoff, S., Arts, N. and Winter, D. (eds.) *The big puzzle. International symposium on refitting stone artefacts*, 177–210. Bonn, Holos.

Welbourn, A.(1982) Endo ceramics and power strategies. In Hodder, I. (ed.) *Structural and symbolic archaeology*, 17–24. Cambridge, Cambridge University Press.

Whitelaw, T. (1994) Order without architecture: functional, social and symbolic dimensions in hunter-gatherer settlement organization. In Parker Pearson, M. and Richards, C. (eds.) *Architecture and order: approaches to social space*, 217–243. London, Routledge.

Whittle, A. (1997) Fish, faces and fingers: presences and symbolic identities in the Mesolithic-Neolithic transition in the Carpathian basin. *Documenta Praehistorica* XXV, 133–150.

Whittle, A. (2000) 'Very much like a whale': menhirs, motifs and myths in the Mesolithic – Neolithic transition of Northwest Europe. *Cambridge Archaeological Journal* 10/2, 243–259.

Whittle, A. (2003) *The archaeology of people. Dimensions of Neolithic life*. London, Routledge.

Whittle, A., Pollard, J. and Grigson, C. (1999) (eds.) *The harmony of symbols. The Windmill Hill causeway enclosure*. Oxford, Oxbow.

Williams, M. (2001) *Shamanic interpretations: reconstructing a cosmology for the later prehistoric period of north-western Europe*. Unpublished PhD thesis, University of Reading.

Willms, C. (1985) Neolitischer *Spondylus* Schmuck: hundert Jahre Forschung. *Germania* 63/2, 331–343.

Wilson, P. (1988) The domestication of the human species. Cambridge, Cambridge University Press.

Wood, I. (2004) *Fragmentation in action? A case study at Tremough*. Unpublished undergraduate dissertation. University of Durham.

Woodward, A. (2000) The prehistoric pottery. In Hughes, G. (ed.) *The Lockington gold hoard. An Early Bronze Age barrow cemetery at Lockington, Leicestershire*, 48–61. Oxford, Oxbow Books.

Woodward, A. (2002) Beads and Beakers: heirlooms and relics in the British Early Bronze Age. *Antiquity* 76, 1040–1047.

Wright, R. P. (1993) Technological styles: transforming a natural world into a cultural object. In Lubar, S. & Kingery, W. D. (eds.) *History from things. Essays on material culture*, 242–269. Washington, D.C., Smithsonian Institution Press.

Yates, T. (1993) Frameworks for an archaeology of the body. In Tilley, C. (ed.) *Interpretative Archaeology*, 31–72. Oxford, Berg.

Yates, T. and Nordbladh, J. (1990) This perfect body, this virgin text. In Bapty, I. and Yates, T. (eds.) *Archaeology after Structuralism*, 222–237. London, Routledge.

Yoon, H. (1989) Kinship, gender and personhood in a Korean village. PhD dissertation. Michigan State Unversity. Ann Arbor, MI, University Microfilms.

Zangger, E. (1991) Prehistoric coastal environments in Greece: the vanished landscapes of Dimini Bay and Lake Lerna. *Journal of Field Archaeology* 18, 1–15.

# Indexes

## Author Index

Allison, P., 71
Andreou, S., 20
Anthony, D., 77
Arnold, B. & Murray, M., 99
Arnold, D., 179
Astuti, R., 54, 56

Bačvarov, K., 10, 170
Bailey, D., 7–8, 12–13, 57–58, 71, 176, 187–188, 194, 203
Bánffy, E., 70
Barfield, L. & Bagolini, B., 92
Barley, N., 20
Barrett, J., 106
Battaglia, D., 56
Bausch, I., 92–93
Beausang, E., 70
Bem, S., 57
Berciu, D., 65
Biehl, P., 53, 137–138, 141, 188
Binford, L. R., 71
Blake, E., 55
Bleie, T., 56–57
Boast, R., 18
Bodu, P., 86
Bogaers, J. E., 110
Bohm, D., 173
Bollong, C. A., 82
Bon, S. E., 72
Bosman, A., 110
Boyadzhiev, Ya., 193
Bradley, R., 107, 111, 173, 188, 192
Bradley, R. & Ford, D., 108–109
Brandt, R., 109–110
Broch-Due, V. & Rudie, I., 53
Brück, J., 96, 101
Burgh, R. F., 83
Busby, S., 55–56

Calado, M., 106
Cameron, C. M., 74
Childe, V. G., 71, 200
Clark, J., 56, 143–144

Claassen, C., 143
Classen, E., 83
Cooper, R.,21
Cressey, P., 88
Csordas, T., 56
Czikszentmihaly, M. & Rochberg-Halton, E., 21
Cziesla, E., 2, 82, 84–86

Dalla Riva, M., 92–93, 189
Deal, M., 73–75
DeBoer, W, 19, 72
DeBoer, W. & Lathrap, D., 75
De Grooth, M., 87
DeMarrais, E., 19
Derrida, J., 21
Domboróczky, L., 91
Douglas, M., 20, 55, 78

Ellen, R., 20
Ellis, L., 19
Ellison, A., 96
Eogan, G., 107

Fontana, V., 82, 91–92
Fowler, C., 6–7, 54, 69, 78, 182

Gale, N., 198
Gallis, K., 10, 170
Gamble, C., 5–6, 49
Garfinkel, Y., 3
Garrow, D., 101, 104–105.
Gatsov, I., 185
Gell, A., 198
Gheorghiu, D., 7–8
Giddens, A., 55
Gilchrist, R., 53
Gimbutas, M., 53
Głowacki, M., 143
Godelier, M., 199
Gould, R., 78
Greenfield, H. & Drașovean, F., 83
Grinsell, L., 1–2

Gurova, M., 185

Haită, C., 13
Hall, E. A., 87
Hally, D., 73, 88
Halpin, C. 20
Halstead, P., 20, 153, 160–161
Hamilakis, Y., 3
Harrison, S., 197
Hartz, S., 108
Hașotti, P., 57, 66
Hatt, G., 87.
Hayden, B. & Cannon, A., 72–75, 77
Helms, M., 145, 147, 198–199
Herdt, G., 56
Hetherington, K., 78–79
Hiller, S. & Nikolov, V., 188
Hillman, D. & Mazzio, C., 2
Hodder, I., 2, 19, 21, 69, 77, 187, 192
Hofman, J., 82
Holden, E., 96
Holten, L., 21, 98
Hornsey, R., 107
Horváth, F., 188
Hoskins, J., 8, 57
Hourmouziades, G., 160, 188
Houston, S. & Stuart, D., 136
Hurcombe, L., 5

Ivanov, I., 45

Jackson, M. & Karp, I., 128
Jallot, L., 88
Jażdżewski, K., 87
Jones, A., 5–7, 10, 20, 98 100, 130, 187
Jovanović, B., 198

Kaismer, T., 30
Kalicz, N., 185
Keightley, D., 21–22, 37, 49, 184, 190
Kent, S., 72–73
Klepikov, M., 98
Kobayashi, T., 93–94

Kobyliński, Z. & Moszczyński, W., 84–85
Kokkinidou, D. & Nikolaidou, M., 57
Koleva, B., 113–117
Kostov, R., 67, 199
Kotsakis, K., 13, 187, 189
Kramer, C., 83
Kunchev, K. & Kuncheva, T., 30
Kurz, S., 99
Kurz, S, & Schiek, S., 99

Laqueur, T., 53
Larson, M. & Ingbar, E., 83
Lemonnier, P., 20
Leroi-Gourhan, A., 84
Le Roux, C-T., 107
L'Helgouach, J. & Le Roux, C-T., 106
Lindauer, O., 84, 89
LiPuma, E., 9, 54

McPherron, A. & Srejović, D., 190
Macfarlane, C., 84
Machnik, J., 83
Makkay, J., 89–91
Marangou, C., 6
Margos, A., 45
Marinescu-Bîlcu, S., 22–23
Mauss, M., 8, 53
Megerssa, G. & Kassam, A., 128
Milisauskas, S. 6, 109
Miller, D., 15–16, 21, 23
Miller, M., 144
Millett, M., 81
Mills, B., 106
Monah, D., 57
Moore, H., 56
Morris, B., 21, 143–144
Mosko, M., 56
Müller, J., 144
Munn, N., 199
Munro, R., 79, 174

Nanda, S., 56
Nandris, J., 22
Nanoglou, S., 21
Needham, S., 101
Nikolaidou, M., 170

Nikolov, V., 22, 29, 49
Noble, G., 204

Olivier, L., 192
Orton, C., 81
Ottaway, B., 185

Papa, M., 13, 196
Parker Pearson, M., 99, 192
Parker Pearson, M. & Richards, C., 72
Pernicka, E., 198
Petrequin, P., 91
Petrie, F., 81
Price, T. D., 73

Raczky, P., 188, 190
Raduntcheva, A., 113–117, 188, 191, 195
Reay, M., 156
Renfrew, C., 144
Richards, C., 5, 107

Sahlins, M., 55, 196
Saunders, N., 143
Scarre, C., 106
Schaller-Åhrberg, E., 108
Scheer, A., 107–108
Schiffer, M. B., 17, 71–74, 81, 84, 87–88, 100, 174
Schneider, S., 99
Schwarz, M., 56
Séfériades, M., 144
Seymour, D. & Schiffer, M. B., 74, 100
Shackleton, J. & Elderfield, H., 144
Shackleton, N., 145
Shackleton, N. & Renfrew, C., 144
Shennan, S., 175
Singer, J., 57
Skafida, E., 20, 165
Skeates, R., 130
Skibo, J., 81 – 82, 88
Skourtopoulou, K., 5–6, 141, 165
Smith, W., 83
Sofaer Derevenski, J., 96, 145
Sørensen, M. L. S., 53, 101
South, S., 83
Souvatzi, S., 20, 161, 165

Souvatzi, S. & Skafida, E., 161
Spassov, N. & Iliev, N., 69
Stallybrass, P., 2
Stanislawski, M., 75, 77, 83
Stevenson, M., 73–75
Strathern, A. & Stewart, P., 56
Strathern, M., 55–56, 69
Sullivan, A., 72–73, 82, 89

Thomas, J., 2, 20, 78
Thompson, M., 79
Todorova, H., 57, 64, 68. 95–96, 144, 174, 190
Todorova, H. & Vajsov, I., 184
Toufexis, G. & Skafida, E., 188
Tringham, R., 187
Trogmayer, O., 57
Tsonev, Ts., 185
Trubitt, M., 143
Tsirtoni, Z., 82
Tsuneki, A., 144, 149, 153, 160, 170
Turk, P., 98

Vajsov, I., 58, 62, 64, 66, 70
Van Gernet, A., 84
Verhart, L., 87
Videiko, M., 188, 190
Villa, P., 83–84
Villa, P. & Courtin, P., 83
Vitelli, K., 48
Vons, P. & Bosman, A., 109–110

Washburn, D. & Crowe, D., 20
Weber, M-J., 108
Weigand, P. C., 75–77
Weiner, J., 82, 86–87
Whitelaw, T., 16, 71
Whittle, A., 57. 106, 144
Williams, M., 109
Wilson, P., 189
Wood, I., 100–101
Woodward, A., 98–99
Wright, R., 22

Yates, T. & Nordbladh, J., 53
Yoon, H., 196, 199

Zangger, E., 160

# Site Index

'Abka, 83
Achtal, 107, 176
Agia Sofia Magoula, 169–170
Ai Bunar, 198
Alexandria, 88, 94
Alvastra, 73
Awatovi, 83
AZ:I:1 (Kayenta Anasazi), 89, 94–95
Azmashka mogila, 26, 35–45, 48, 50, 52, 187

Baia-Goloviţa, 65, 70, 175
Balchik, 60–61, 64, 70, 176
Barnhouse, 100
Belen Tash, 117
Blewbury, 20
Borduşani, 13
Boussargues, 88, 94
Branč, 175
Brillenhöhle, 107
Broken K Pueblo, 82, 88, 94, 100

Çatal Höyük, 15, 77
Cernavoda, 58, 60–61, 70
Chalain IIC, 95
Chavdarova Cheshma, 26–35, 48–49, 52, 191

Devnja, 200
Dikili Tash, 81, 144–145
Dimini, 12, 18, 20, 144, 153, 160–171, 175–
    176, 180–181, 188–189
Dimitra, 145
Djadovo, 12
Dolní Věstonice, 5
Dolnoslav, 15, 17–18, 26, 40–48, 50–52, 113–
    142, 176, 179, 181, 183–184, 188, 192–196
Dragomelj, 98
Draguşeni, 23
Drama, 137
Durankulak, 11, 16, 18, 57, 62, 64–70, 78, 95–
    96, 146–161, 165, 168–171, 175, 180–181,
    188, 192–194, 199

Endrőd 119, 89–91, 94
Er-Grah, 106–107

Foeni, 83
Fontbrégoua, 83
Franchthi cave, 48
Frimmersdorf, 122, 83
Füzesabony-Gubakút, 91, 94

Gălăbnik, 199
Gavrinis, 106–107
Gdánsk, 87
Geissenklösterle, 107
Goljamo Delchevo, 92, 200
Gombe Point, 83

Gorzsa, 188
Grivac, 190
Grotte de Hortus, 83

Hamangia sites, 183–184
Hârşova, 13
Hasewisch, 108
Hekelingen, 87
Heuneburg, 99
Hlebozavoda (Nova Zagora), 26, 29–40, 48–
    50, 52
Hochdorf, 192
Hódmezővásárhely, *see* Kökénydomb
Hohmichele, 99
Hopi sites, 74

Itford Hill, 96

Jomon sites, 93–94

Karanovo, 12, 188
Kayenta Anasazi, *see* AZ:I:1
Kilverstone, 101–105, 179
Knowth Site 1, 107
Kökénydomb, 30
Kolomiischina, 190

Lake Gyrinos, 108, 176
Langweiler 9, 87
La Table des Marchand, 106–107
Le Grand Menhir Brisé, 106–107, 177
Lemba, 57
Lepenski Vir, 188, 196, 199
Little Egypt, 88, 94
Lockington, 99
Lousberg, 81, 86–87

Maastricht-Belvédère, 87
Makriyalos, 5, 13, 141, 196
Medgidia, 16, 57, 65–66, 70, 194
Meer II, 83
Molino Casarotto, 91–92
Mušja Jama, 98
Myrtos, 73

Newgrange Large, 107
Nissehøj, 98
Nørre Fjand, 87
Nova Zagora, *see* Hlebozavoda

Obre I, 12
Omurtag, 174, 190, 199
Ovcharovo, 92, 174, 190
Ovcharovo–Gorata, 92, 95

Parţa, 92
Phylakopi, 83–85

Pincevent, 86
Platia Magoula Zarkou, 10, 170
Podgoritsa, 174, 190
Poggenwisch, 108
Polgár-Csőszhalom, 75, 174, 188, 190
Polgár-Kenderföld, 75
Poljanitsa, 174, 188, 190
Pompeii, 72
Radingrad, 188, 190
Rakitovo, 12, 26–35, 48–49, 52, 191
Rio Grande valley, 106
Rocca di Rivoli, 92–93, 95, 179
Rudna Glava, 198
Runnymede Bridge, 73, 100, 102–104, 179

Schela Cladovei, 48
Sedlare, 12, 92, 94
Shakadô, 92–93, 95
Shlyakovsky, 98
Shoofly Village, 89
Sitagroi, 145, 169–170
Skara Brae, 72
Snaketown, 74, 100
Sonoran Desert Site 205, 89, 94–95, 106, 179
Sotira Argolies, 57
Soufli Magoula, 10, 12, 170
Speckhau, 99

Talljanky, 190
Targovishte, 188, 190
Teltwisch I, 108
Terra Amata, 83
Tîrgşoru-Urs, 64–5
Tîrgşoru Veche, 57
Tiszapolgár–Basatanya, 96–98
Topolnitsa, 185
Tremough, 100–101, 104, 179
Trentham, 109, 177
Tripolye sites, 78
Turdaş, 196
Tzeltal Maya, 73–76

Upton Lovell, 99

Vădastra, 7–8
Varna, 12, 18, 24, 26, 45–48, 51–52, 137, 147–
    161, 165, 168–171, 175, 180–181, 185, 187,
    192, 197, 199–201
Velsen I and II, 109–110, 177
Vinitsa, 92, 199, 201
Vinča, 15, 141, 190, 196
Vrokastro, 87

Windmill Hill, 100, 104, 177
Wyszogród, 84–86

Yukon sites, 74

# Subject Index

Accumulation, 4–5, 7, 9, 14, 20, 135, 142, 188–
    189, 196, 201
Activity areas, 71–73, 77–78
Agave-roasting sites, 89
Agency (see also structure–agency), 2, 19–20,
    53–55, 71, 182
Altars (lamps), 92, 116
Androgyny (see also hermaphrodites), 56–70,
    183–184, 186–187
Animal bones, 14

Biographies, 15
    Object biographies, 2, 8, 15, 19–20, 77, 99,
        104, 181, 203
    Place biographies, 8, 192–193
    Shell biographies, 145–146, 149–153, 157–
        163, 165–171
Bronzes, 98, 108–109

Categorisation principles, 9, 15–16, 21–52, 55,
    78–79, 142
Cemeteries, 10–12, 147–160
*Châines Opératoires*, 8, 17, 78, 81, 85, 95, 104,
    107–108, 144–145, 204
Children's play, 74–75, 89, 94
'Clarke Effect', 73
Classification, 23
Co-evolution of consciousness and objects,
    174
Colour, 23, 29, 32, 34, 39–47, 113–116, 143–
    144, 169, 186, 191, 198–199
    Figurine colour, 130–135, 141
    Shell colour, 143–144, 169
Compartmentalisation, 22, 35, 45, 47, 49, 52,
    184–188, 190
Completeness Index, 81, 84–85, 88, 91–92,
    94, 153–157, 161, 169–170
'Concentration Principle', 5, 174
Conduits of disposal, 79
Consumption, 7, 9
Containers, 5
Contexts, 48–49, 62–70, 73–77, 83–84, 113–
    129, 135, 141–142, 161–163, 167–171,
    175–176
Cooking, 48–49
Copper, 14, 185, 196
Craft specialization, 160–161
Cremation, 10, 12
Cultural memory, 9, 14, 135, 192–193, 200
Curation, 91, 99, 101, 111–112, 193–194, 203

Daily practices (see also 'habitus'), 5–7, 15, 21,
    71, 141
*De facto* refuse, 72, 74–75
*Dentalium* shells, 15, 67–68, 118
Deposition (see also disposal), 3–5, 71–79,

83–85, 94, 113–129, 135, 141–142
    Depositional assemblages, 73–78
Differentiation, 21–52
Disposal, 78–79, 174
Dividuals, 6, 9, 54–57, 142, 182, 200
Domestication, 5
Dumping, 73
Dynamic nominalism, 16, 182, 195

Enchainment, 1, 4–7, 9, 69, 91–92, 95, 97–98,
    100, 106–112, 137–147, 170–171, 179,
    188–189, 192–201, 203
Enclosure, 12–13
Exchange and enchainment, 1–2, 5, 9, 14, 106,
    141–142, 171, 199
Exotica, 14, 67–68, 143, 145, 171, 197–201
Experimental fragmentation, 7–8, 204

Feasting, 13
Figurines, 6, 8, 14, 16–18, 53, 57–70, 84–85,
    87, 92, 116–142, 179–180
    Hamangia figurines, 58–70, 183, 186–187
    Late Copper Age figurines, 116–142, 183
    Figurine biographies, 130–135, 141–142
    Figurine burning, 130–135, 141
    Figurine colour, 130–135, 141
    Figurine decoration, 130–135, 141
    Figurine wear, 130–135, 141
Flat sites, 12–13
Fractality, 1–2, 6, 9
Fragmentation Index, 81, 91
Fragmentation premise, 2, 8–10, 18
Fragmentation as universal, 173

Gender, 6, 53–70, 118–123, 136, 183–184,
    186–187, 193–195
    Gender and fragmentation, 63–67, 118–
        123
*Glycymeris* shells, 144–145
Gold, 14, 185
Graphite decoration, 36–38, 40–47

Habitus, 2, 5–7, 174
Hallucinogens, 143
Heirlooms, 85, 96, 99–101, 110, 112, 143
Hermaphrodites (see also androgyny), 56–70
Hexis, 22
Hierogamy, 57
Hoards, 14, 98
Houses, 12–13, 28, 91–2, 100, 113–116, 160–
    163, 187–189
    House repairs, 89
    House burning, 189

Identity, 12, 53–54, 79, 111, 173, 187, 189, 191,
    203

Ideology, 19
Individuals, 6, 54–57, 142, 182, 200
Inhabitation, 106
Inhumation, 10–12
Integration, 22–52, 195–196

'Killing' of objects, 1, 3
Kinship residence patterns, 88

Labour of division, 21, 173–174
Landscapes, 106–112, 196–197
Lithics, 14, 81, 83, 86–87, 101–102, 104, 107,
    116, 177, 184–185, 198

Material citation, 19–20
Material culture, 2–3, 19, 21, 173
Megaliths, 98, 106–107
Metaphorical relationships, 5–6, 49, 116, 143–
    144, 173–174
'Mickey Mouse laws', 71
Middening, 13, 85, 104, 116, 121–123, 176,
    179, 193–194, 203
Middle Range theory, 8, 16, 71–72
Mortuary practices, 10–12, 95–99, 192–193,
    199–200

Neolithic origins, 5
Nucleation, 191

'Old Europe', 53
Operational chains, *see* Châines Opératoires
Orphan sherds, 17, 81, 83, 88–89, 91–92, 95–
    98, 100, 111, 179–181, 193, 197

Patron-client relations, 200–201
Personhood, 12, 14–16, 23, 51–70, 136, 141–
    143, 145–147, 170–171, 182–201, 203
    Melanesian personhood, 55–57, 69–70
    Polynesian personhood, 55
    South Indian personhood, 55–57, 62
Pits, 13, 65–66, 92, 101–102, 104, 176, 203
Place-value, 1, 7, 12, 192–193
'Pompeii Premise', 72–73
potlatching, 160–161
Pottery, 14, 16, 19, 22–52, 81, 83–85, 87–89,
    94–102, 106, 109–110, 116, 179, 184–185,
    187, 191–192
Precision, 22, 35, 45, 47, 49, 52, 147, 184–188,
    190
Presencing, 111
Primary refuse, 72

Re-fitting studies, 17, 20, 81–112, 121–123,
    137–140, 153–157, 163–165, 176–181,
    188, 193, 203–204
    Criteria, 82

Horizontal re-fitting, 83–89, 91–92, 95–102

Vertical re-fitting, 84, 89, 91–92, 98–102

Reinforcement, 24–52

Reflectionism, 20–21, 71–73

Re-use processes, 72–73, 75–79, 88, 106

Rubbish, 2, 13, 17, 71, 78–79

Samian pottery, 109–110

Secondary refuse, 72

Selfhood (see also personhood), 12, 14–16

Settlements, 87, 160–166, 176, 189, 197

Sex, 53–70

Sherd mobility (sherd pathways), 101, 104, 203

Sidedness, 123–128, 137–140, 142, 146, 149, 188, 194–195

Site formation processes, 17, 71–79, 81, 87

Soil micromorphology, 72, 77

Special attention markers, 111

*Spondylus gaederopus* shells, 14–15, 17–18, 67–68, 137, 143–171, 179–181, 188, 199

Shell aesthetics, 143–147

Shell biographies, 145–146, 149–153, 157–163, 165–171

Shell biographical pathways, 150–153, 165–168

Shell burning, 147, 163, 170

Shell micro-stratigraphies, 165–168, 181

Standardisation, , 22, 35, 45, 47, 49, 52, 184–188, 190

Steppe ass (*Equus asinus hydruntinus*), 68–70

Stone–moving, 107

Storage, 48–49

Swords, 108–109

Symbols of power, 143, 145, 174

Symmetry, 20, 22, 35, 45, 47, 49, 52, 147, 184–188, 190

Taphonomy, 8, 82–83, 85, 100, 111, 175

Tells, 12–13, 113–117, 174, 184, 189–196

Time-level, 83

Timemarks, 111

Trees, 204

Trinkets, 110

Typology, 20–21

Up-down relations, 128–129, 140–141, 195

Use-wear analysis, 89, 100

Warfare, 197

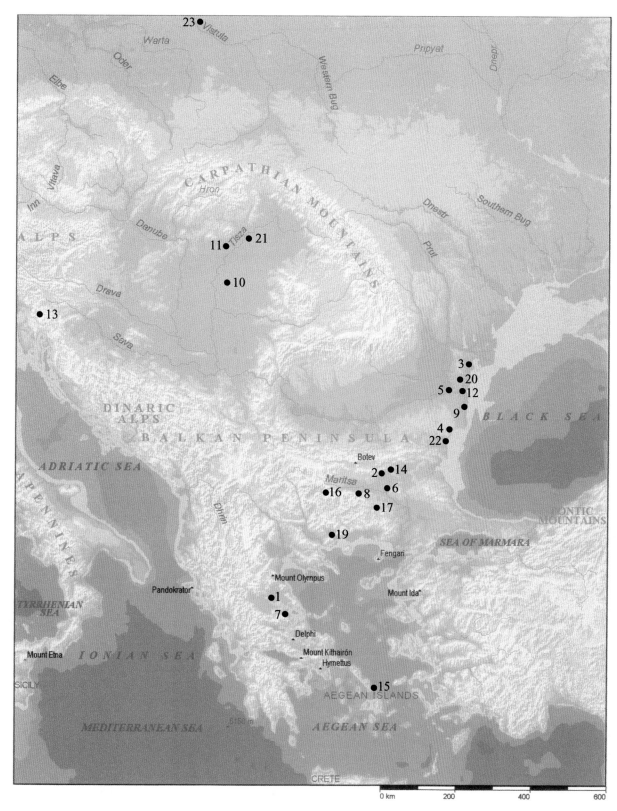

*Plate 1 Map of sites mentioned in the text: South East and Central Europe*

1. Ayia Sofia magoula; 2. Azmashka mogila; 3. Baia – Goloviţa; 4. Balchik; 5. Cernavoda; 6. Chavdarova Cheshma; 7. Dimini;
8. Dolnoslav; 9. Durankulak; 10. Endrőd 119; 11. Füzesabony – Gubakut; 12. Medgidia; 13. Mušja Jama; 14. Nova Zagora –
Hlebozavoda; 15. Phylakopi; 16. Rakitovo; 17. Sedlare; 18. Shlyakovsky (near Volgograd: off map to East); 19. Sitagroi;
20. Tirşoru-Urs; 21. Tiszapolgár – Basatanya; 22. Varna; 23. Wyszogród (near Płock)

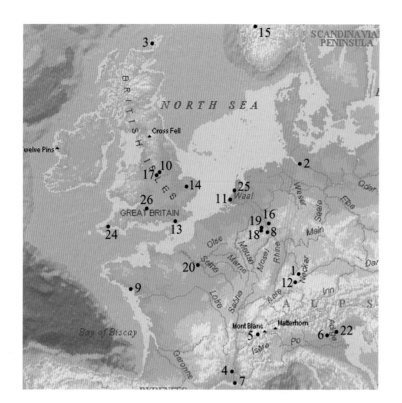

*Plate 2 Map of sites mentioned in the text: Western Europe*

1. Achtal; 2. Ahrensburg tunnel; 3. Barnhouse (Orkney); 4. Boussargues; 5. Chalain lake site; 6. Fimon lake site; 7. Fontbrégoua cave; 8. Frimmersdorf 122; 9. Gavrinis – La Table des Marchand; 10. Hanford – Trentham; 11. Hekelingen; 12. Heuneburg; 13. Itford Hill; 14. Kilverstone; 15. Lake Gyrinos; 16. Langweiler 8; 17. Lockington; 18. Lousberg; 19. Maastricht – Belvédère; 20. Pincevent; 21. Pompeii (near Napoli: off map to South); 22. Rocca di Rivoli; 23. Runnymede Bridge; 24. Tremough; 25. Velsen; 26. Windmill Hill

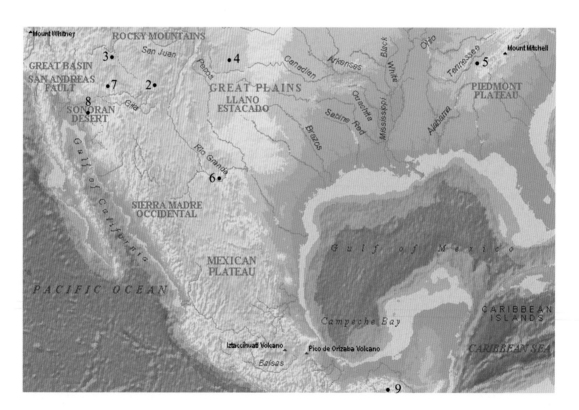

*Plate 3 Map of sites mentioned in the text: North and Meso-America*

1. Alexandria, Virginia (off map to North East); 2. Awatowi (Arizona); 3. AZ I : 1 : 17 (Arizona); 4. Broken K pueblo (New Mexico); 5. Little Egypt (Georgia); 6. Rio Grande survey (Texas); 7. Shoofly Village (Arizona); 8. Sonoran Desert (Arizona); 9. Tzeltal Maya (Mexico)

*Plate 4 Grave 643 from the Durankulak cemetery*

*Plate 5 A rich set of grave goods, Varna cemetery, grave no. 43*

*Plate 6 Tell Karanovo, general view*

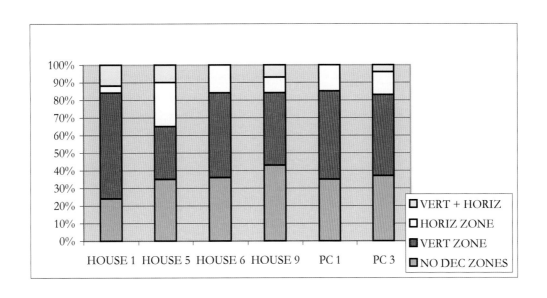

*Plate 7 Decorational reinforcement by context from Rakitovo*

*Plate 8  Black Burnished Ware vessel, late Neolithic, tell Kaloyanovets (source: Kalchev 2005, 21, top left)*

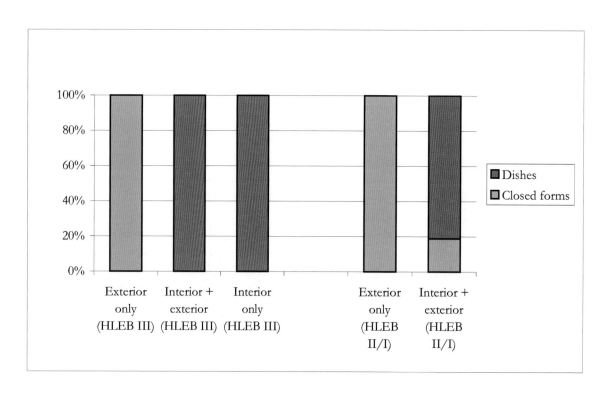

*Plate 9 Place of decoration vs. vessel form by phase, Hlebozavoda*

*Plate 10 Vessels with incised and white incrusted decoration*

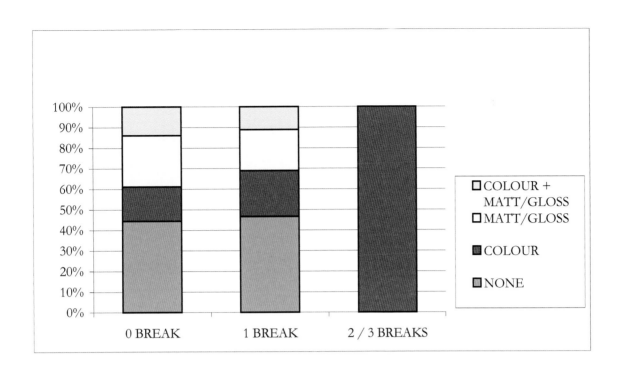

*Plate 11 Type of reinforcement by profile differentiation from Azmak*

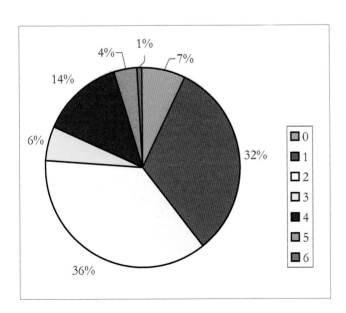

*Plate 12 Distribution of number of vessel profile breaks, Varna cemetery*

*Plate 13 Horned stand, Varna cemetery*

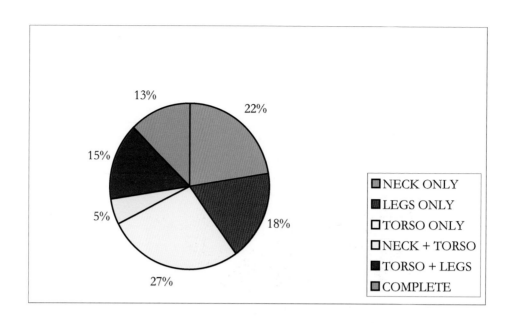

*Plate 14 Distribution of figurine parts in Hamangia settlements*

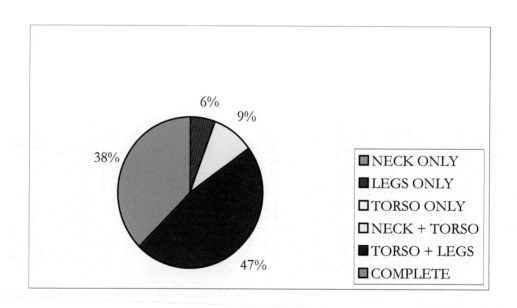

*Plate 15 Distribution of figurine parts in Hamangia graves*

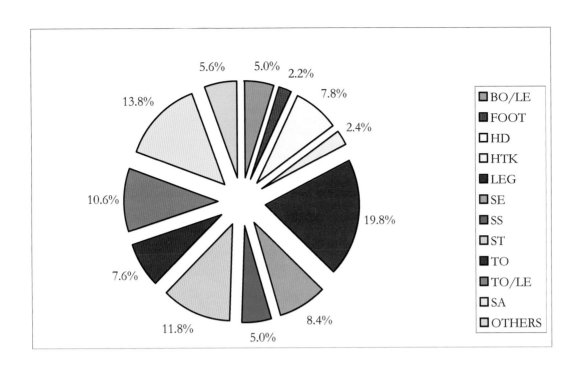

*Plate 16 Distribution of simplified types of figurines in Dolnoslav*

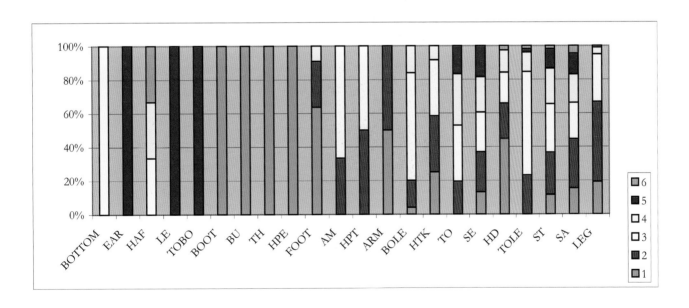

*Plate 17 Figurine types by number of breaks*

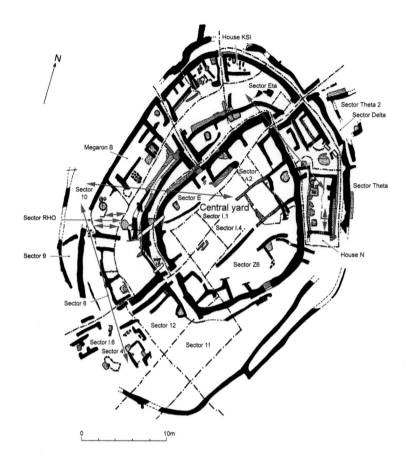

*Plate 18 Site plan with refits between contexts, Dimini*

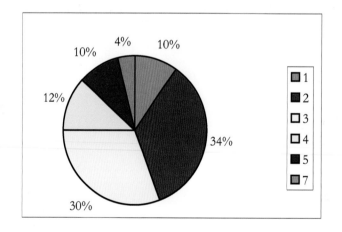

*Plate 19 Number of breaks, re-fitted fragments*

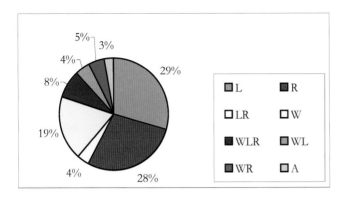

*Plate 20 Categories of sidedness and wholeness*

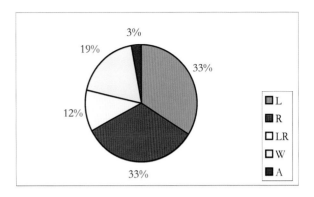

*Plate 21 Unified categories of sidedness and wholeness*

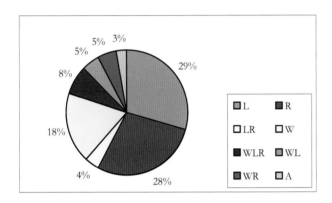

*Plate 22 Categories of sidedness and wholeness, phase C*

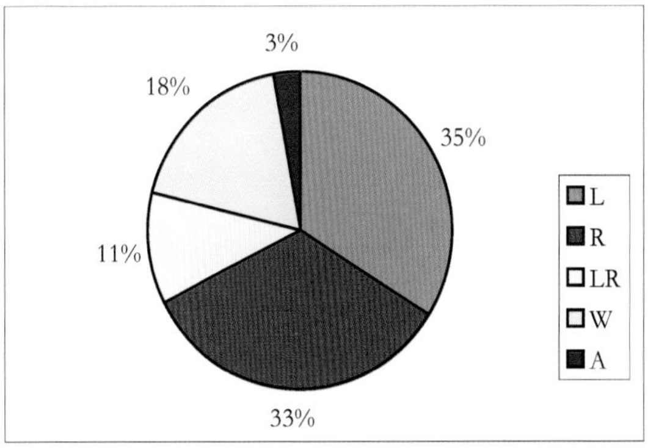

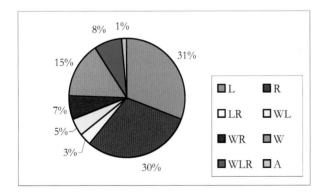

*Plate 23 Unified categories of sidedness and wholeness, phase C*

*Plate 24 Categories of sidedness and wholeness, middens*

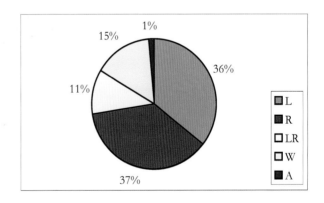

*Plate 25 Unified categories of sidedness and wholeness, middens*

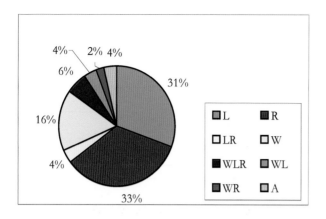

*Plate 26 Categories of sidedness and wholeness, open areas*

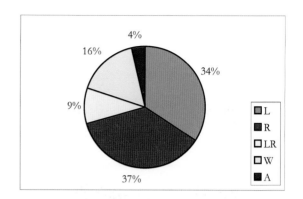

*Plate 27 Unified categories of sidedness and wholeness, open areas*

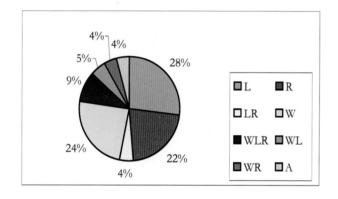

*Plate 28 Categories of sidedness and wholeness, buildings*

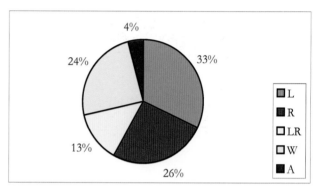

*Plate 29 Unified categories of sidedness and wholeness, buildings*

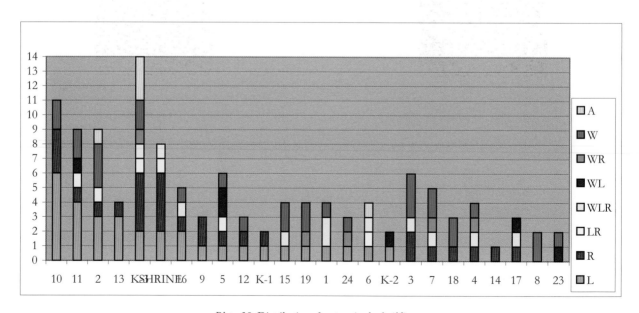

*Plate 30 Distribution of categories by building*

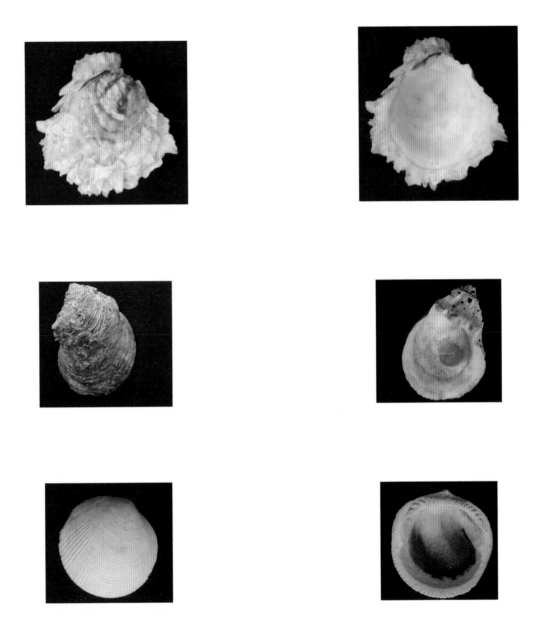

*Plate 31 Unmodified bivalves: upper and middle rows* – Spondylus gaederopus; *lower* – Glycymeris glycymeris

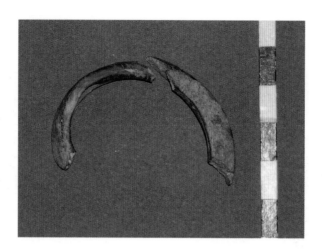

*Plate 32 Pair of re-fitted shell ring fragments, with lines and pitting, breaks, burning and light polish on 312 and lines, breaks, burning and light polish on 315 (Volos Museum Inv. Nos. 312 and 315)*

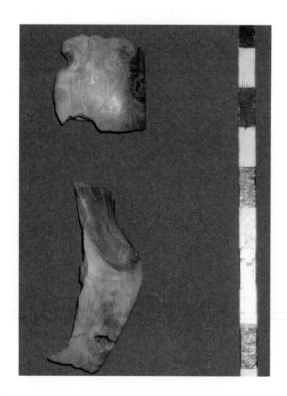

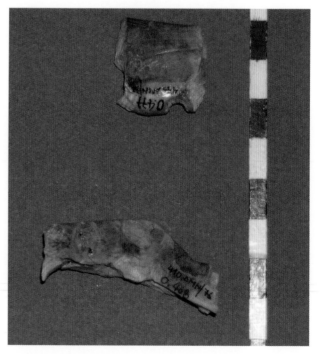

*Plate 33 Pair of re-fitted shell ring fragments, with garlands and notches, breaks, burnish and polish on 468 and sculpting an lines, a possible notch, breaks, burning and polish on 477 (Volos Museum Inv. Nos. 468 and 477)*

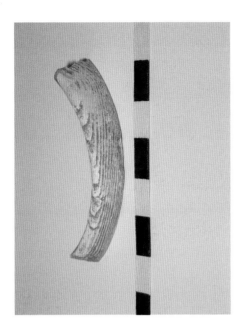

*Plate 34 Shell ring with complex linear pattern and chevrons, light polish, breaks and wear (Volos Museum Inv. No. 306)*

*Plate 35 Shell ring with lines and sculpting, one break, burning, polish and another break and flakes (Volos Museum Inv. No. 307)*

*Plate 36 Shell ring with notch, sculpting and lines, burning, polish, breraks, flakes, wear and stress marks (Volos Museum Inv. No. 318)*

*Plate 37 The only complete ring in the Dimini shell ring assemblage (Volos Museum Inv. No. 532)*

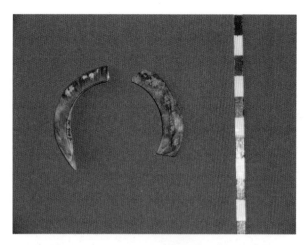

*Plate 38 Re-fitted pair of shell ring fragments, with lines and a notch, breaks, burning over part and all-over polish on 444 and lines and a groove, polish and breaks on 446.1 (Volos Museum Inv. Nos. 444 and 446.1)*

*Plate 39 Shell ring with sculpting, pitting and lines, breaks, heavy wear, flaking and stress marks (Volos Museum Inv. No. 561.002)*

*Plate 40 Shell ring with red lines, polish, one break, deposit and a second break (Volos Museum Inv. No. 488.2)*

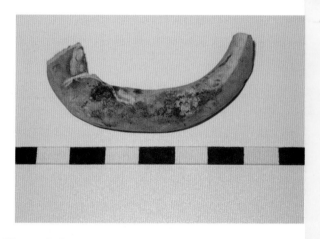

*Plate 41 Shell ring with notches, sculpting, pitting and lines, polish, breaks and wear (Volos Museum Inv. No. 334)*

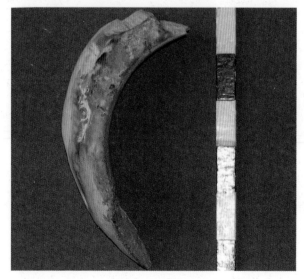

*Plate 42 Shell ring with sculpting and red lines, polish, breaks, deposit and flaking (Volos Museum Inv. No. 509.1)*

*Plate 43 Shell ring with sculpting and lines enhanced by burning, polish, breaks and flakes (Volos Museum Inv. No. 322)*